"Subject People" and Colonial Discourses

SUNY Series
in
Society and Culture in Latin America

Jane L. Collins, Editor

"Subject People" and Colonial Discourses

Economic Transformation and Social Disorder in Puerto Rico, 1898–1947

Kelvin A. Santiago-Valles

STATE UNIVERSITY OF NEW YORK PRESS

Main cover photograph taken from: *Harpers Weekly*, XLIII:2211 (May 6, 1899):462. It is supposed to depict Raphael Ortiz, convicted in 1899 for murdering a U.S. soldier who "won the attentions" of Ortiz's sweetheart when the 47th U.S. Volunteers occupied the Puerto Rican town of Càguas.

Production by Ruth Fisher
Marketing by Theresa A. Swierzowski

Published by
State University of New York Press, Albany

For information, address the State University of New York Press,
State University Plaza, Albany, NY 12246

Library of Congress Cataloging-in-Publication Data

Santiago-Valles, Kelvin A. 1951–
"Subject people" and colonial discourses : economic transformation and social disorder in Puerto Rico, 1898–1947 / Kelvin A. Santiago -Valles.
p. cm. — (SUNY series in society and culture in Latin America)
Includes index.
ISBN 0–7914–1589–9 (alk. paper). — ISBN 0–7914–1590–2 (pbk. : alk. paper)
1. Crime—Puerto Rico—History—20th century. 2. Puerto Rico—Social conditions. 3. Puerto Rico—Economic conditions. 4. Social conflict—Puerto Rico—History—20th century. I. Title. II. Series.
HV6872.S26 1994
364.97295'09'04—dc20 92–30542
CIP

10 9 8 7 6 5 4 3 2 1

. . . in dealing with Indians or Egyptians, or Shilluks, or Zulus, the first question is to consider what these people, who are all, nationally speaking, more or less *in statu pupillari,* themselves think is best in their own interests, although this is a point which deserves serious consideration. But it is essential that each special issue should be decided mainly in reference to what by the light of Western knowledge and experience tempered by local considerations, we conscientiously think is best for the subject race, . . .

—Lord Evelyn Baring Cromer, *Political and Literary Essays 1908–1913* (1913)

Of course there have been many instances of brutality, cupidity and stupidity by the conquerors, but by and large, the subject nations have benefitted. To begin with, in all logic, as a rule, the conquering nation has been the more civilized, certainly the more virile. During the period of its domination it has brought the subject people into contact with knowledge they did not possess, schooled them or vitalized them.

—Theodore Roosevelt, Jr., *Colonial Policies of the United States* (1937)

There are two meanings of the word *subject*: subject to someone else by control and dependence, and tied to his own identity by a conscience or self-knowledge. Both meanings suggest a form of power which subjugates and makes subject to.

—Michel Foucault, *"The Subject and Power"* (1983)

Para Gladys y para mis padres

CONTENTS

List of Tables ix

Preface and Acknowledgments xi

Introduction

1 Post-Coloniality, Corrective Studies, and the (Re)making of History 3

Part I 1898–1921

2 A Contest of Structures 19
3 The Contradictory Mechanisms of Preservation and Transformation 49
4 The Rise of the "Evil-Disposed" Classes, 1898–1909 77
5 "Waging Battle Against Numerous Evils," 1910–1921 111

Part II 1922–1947

6 "Creating a Discontented Working Class," 1922–1929 135
7 "The Age of Criminal Saturation," 1930–1939 165
8 "Rage Concentrated Twice Over," 1940–1947 195

Conclusion

9 The Subjects in Question 229

Notes 243

Index 297

LIST OF TABLES

No. 1 Employment by Occupational Sector in Puerto Rico, Selected Years, Both Sexes, 10 Years of Age or Older 34

No .2 Employment by Economic Sector in Puerto Rico, Selected Years, Both Sexes, 10 Years or Older 36

No. 3 Number and Rates of Arrests in Puerto Rico, Selected Years, Both Sexes 72

No. 4 Number and Rates for Murder and Attempted Murder, and Number and Rates for Suicide Cases in Puerto Rico, Selected Years, Both Sexes 92

No. 5 Principal Specific Causes of Police Arrests in Order of Number of Arrests Carried Out, Selected Years, Both Sexes 100

No. 6 Distribution of Labor Force in Selected Non-Agricultural Economic Sectors, Selected Years, Both Sexes, 10 Years of Age or Older 140

PREFACE AND ACKNOWLEDGMENTS

This study began by relating economic change in Puerto Rico to the forms of social unrest carried out by the Island's working classes from 1898 to 1985. However, I found it increasingly difficult to simply "apply" the (universal) lessons of the new criminology, of the revisionist histories of social control, and of Marxist political economy to something called "the Puerto Rican case." Simultaneously and like many other postwar "native" intellectuals who travelled from the colonized "backwater" to the metropolis/"mother country," I came upon a world—this time, the universe of high academia—that only turned to me "as to the childhood of the world," as Fanon once sarcastically said of Sartre.

Art began to mirror life when I could no longer avoid raising questions in my research about the racialized, gendered, sexualized, and class-based linkages between (a) the history of a colonial process and (b) the social subjects and power relations that otherwise embodied, structured, and signified it. The shift in focus tended to highlight the poststructuralist and postcolonial aspects of the study. For the sake of theoretical depth and of a more nuanced analysis, I also reduced the chronological scope of the original research project (from 1898–1985 to 1898–1947).

Such a redefinition admits a number of problems, including the current—and hotly debated—issue regarding the validity or allegedly extraneous character of discourse analysis within historical and social research. There is also the even greater risk of discussing crime and colonized peoples within the same [con]text, given the role that most Puerto Ricans continue to play (in the continental United States and in Puerto Rico) as the signifiers of social strife. Such turmoil is still understood in highly raced, sexed, and class-specific terms: social disintegration, endangered living standards, moral decay, crisis of national identity, lost or polluted family values, conflicts over cultural perspectives, etc. This study, then, pursues not only the effort of linking history, textuality, and social inquiry. It could also add to a counter-hegemonic explanation of the mentioned social strife by placing the latter in an-other (non Euro/Americo-centric) historical context.

Whatever contributions this study may offer are first indebted to the support I received from my *compañera* and close collaborator Gladys Jiménez-Muñoz and from my parents. During the most critical moments, my parents made this research feasible—financially, technologically, and emotionally. Their confidence in my ability to carry out this project at times surpassed my own faith. Gladys, on the other hand, provided persistent advice and intellectual feedback, suggesting a number of key concepts that found their way into this book. She too gave me reassurance at crucial times, in addition to performing some of the necessary bibliographical footwork and proofreading.

My irreplaceable friend and associate Deborah Britzman read several versions of this study and made definitive recommendations, both theoretical and stylistic. Debbie's expertise and solidarity allowed me to carry out this project in less time than it would have otherwise taken and to render the final outcome more intelligible. I am also obligated to my comrade Laura Lamash for reading earlier drafts of this manuscript and for playing an important part in helping me internalize the basics of tidying up prose in a language not my own. Both Debbie and Laura "learned me their language" and "taught me how to curse" without me having to lose my voice—no small feat in a country and in a social arena whose colonialism (external and internal) continues to parade unmarked. But neither of them should be held accountable for the occasional verbal excesses of this text.

My mother, Toñita Valles de Santiago, in particular, and my dear colleague Israel Silva-Merced, selflessly rendered vital bibliographical assistance in tracking down (and mailing) some of the more obscure documents, without which this entire research would not have been completed. I am also grateful to Pedro Vales and Leonardo Santana, among others, for providing me with copies of their investigations and of documents intended for the first version of this study.

This work has benefited directly from the intellectual stimulus, critical advice, and learned encouragement (oral or written) of additional friends and acquaintances, including: Stuart Hall, Juan Flores, Anibal Quijano, Aide Esu, Etienne Balibar, Ernesto Laclau, Saskia Sassen, Edna Acosta-Belén, Agustín Laó, Anna Davin, Daniel F. Greenberg, Anthony King, John Tagg, Carole Boyce-Davies, César

Rey, and Arturo Torrecillas. Of course, none of them are responsible for whatever shortcomings may be found in this book in its final form. I specifically appreciate the criticisms, comments, and questions that the twenty graduate students in my "Race, Gender, and Nationality" seminar at SUNY-Binghamton shared with me in the spring of 1991. Collectively and individually, they helped me clarify the concepts that oriented the last version of this study.

The Nuala McGann Drescher Affirmative Action Award Leave Grant of the New York State/United University Professions contributed both time and money, which allowed me to conduct part of this research during the spring of 1987. The Dean of Arts and Sciences Semester Research Award for the spring of 1988 sponsored another portion of this study. Then Dean Sidoney Smith played a pivotal role in facilitating this second award, as well as in extending the technical and mechanical support of her office during the determining fall 1988 period, thus making it possible for me to write the initial rendition of the manuscript. In this last capacity, Lisa Fegley-Schmidt guided me through the complexities of computer-assisted manuscript preparation and continued to aid me in this respect until the final version was produced.

Finally, I wish to thank Lois Patton and Rosalie Robertson of State University of New York Press, as well as Jane Collins and Jeffner Allen, whose labor and counsel further expedited the publishing of this book.

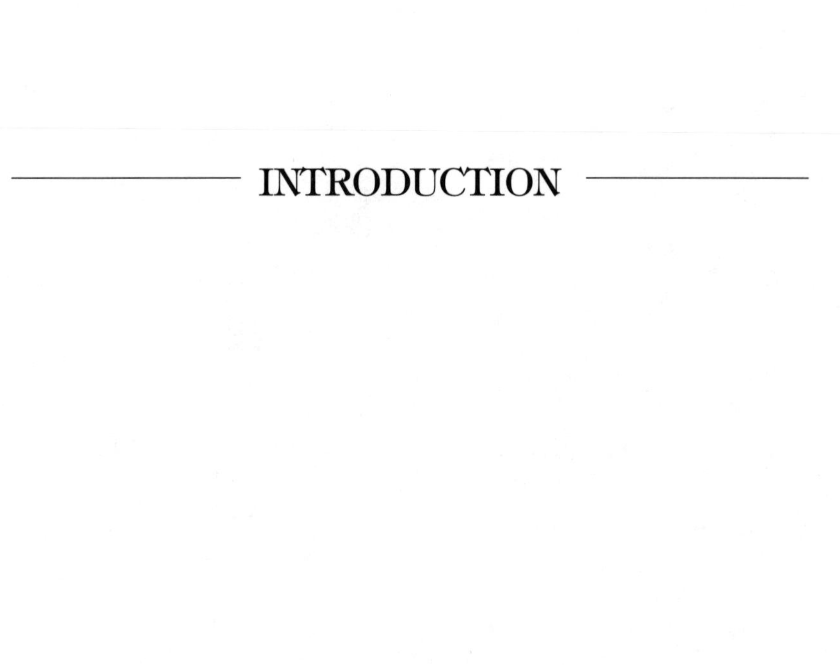

INTRODUCTION

1

Post-Coloniality, Corrective Studies, and the (Re)making of History

> If the economic take-off of the West began with the techniques that made possible the accumulation of capital, it might perhaps be said that the methods for administering the accumulation of men [*sic*] made possible a political take-off in relation to the traditional, ritual, costly, violent forms of power, which soon fell into disuse and were superseded by a subtle, calculated technology of subjection.
>
> **—Michel Foucault, *Discipline and Punish* (1977)**

> But at the outset one can say that so far as the West was concerned during the nineteenth and twentieth centuries, an assumption had been made that the Orient and everything in it was, if not patently inferior to, then in need of corrective study by the West. The Orient was viewed as if framed by the classroom, the criminal court, the prison, the illustrated manual. Orientalism, then, is the knowledge of the Orient that places things Oriental in class, court, prison, or manual for scrutiny, study, judgment, discipline, or governing.
>
> **—Edward Said, *Orientalism* (1979)**

As the rise of the social sciences and the humanities in the West shows, the coupling of social/power relations with representations and meanings is one of the quandaries of scholarly inquiry. Can or should the subjects of historical processes be jointly examined with the subjects of social identity? Among critical currents of social research (e.g., Marxism, feminism, postcolonial studies), this difficulty has contributed to the rift between various objects of analytical intervention. On the one hand, there are those who examine the unfolding of socioeconomic conditions. At best, this would include the political and ideological epiphenomenons of these socioeconomic conditions, though most studies only optionally consider such "cultural effects." On the other hand, there are those who examine the varieties of cultural and representational forms. The latter are generally understood in the absence of any but the most cursory or pro forma socioeconomic contextualizations. Stuart Hall has already described the results of this schism in his critical appraisal of Althusser's essay "Ideology and Ideological State Apparatuses."

> The two sides of the difficult problem of ideology were fractured in that essay and, ever since, have been assigned different poles. The question of reproduction has been assigned to the marxist (male) pole, and the question of subjectivity has been assigned to the psychoanalytic (feminist) pole. Since then never have the twin met. The latter is constituted as a question about the "insides" of people, about psychoanalysis, subjectivity and sexuality, and is understood to be "about" that. It is in this way and on this site that the link to feminism has been increasingly theorized. The former is "about" social relations, production and the "hard edge" of productive systems, and that is what marxism and the reductive discourses of class are "about." This bifurcation of the theoretical project has had the most disastrous consequences for the unevenness of the subsequent development of the problematic of ideology, not to speak of its damaging political effects.[1]

A primary purpose of this book is to contribute to the bridging between the study of, what Stuart Hall terms, "the 'insides' of people, . . . subjectivity and sexuality" and the study of "social relations, production and the 'hard edge' of productive systems." This marks a shift from referencing the subject matter of history to rethinking the manner in which social subjects are historically produced and referenced; from assuming the content of identity categories to examining the assumptions/truths which conflictively constitute subjects as bound to specific identities; and from exploring the intersecting topics of historical reality and identity formation to mapping the genealogy of historicized identities, that is, to the study of the ways in which subjects live their history.

Such efforts may perhaps suggest a reversion to psychologism, that is, to reducing social-historical processes to the realm of the individual. The goals of this book are different because here I only examine individuals as social artifacts of historically specific power-knowledge axes: it is political technologies and disciplines that constitute individuals—through complex and disputed processes—as social subjects.[2] Paraphrasing Foucault,[3] my work explores: how historically concrete and conflictive power relations codify individuals; how their own individuality is created by, within, and against these same power relations; how individuals are oppositionally affixed to their own identities; and how these power relations impose on such individuals "the law of truth" that they must acknowledge, re-member, and whose visage they must replicate in order to be re-cognized by other individuals.

Simultaneously, my research critically distances itself from this Foucaultian perspective in that I consider the subaltern subjects of Western colonialism and not a seemingly decentered Western subject. The latter inevitably becomes recentered precisely because it is abstractly theorized within a Crusoe-like universe that only contains the West (and no "natives").[4] My concern here is with how colonized subjects are historically constituted: as presumably unitary but shot through with endless contradictions; as the apparently homogenous target of useful domination fragmented into multiple embodiments; as totally driven to the margins yet as producing the proliferation of the margins and of myriad resistances. I dismiss the perspective that posits certain national-cultural/racial groups as social subjects that are *born* colonized. Drawing critically from the work of Fanon, Memmi, and Mannoni, my interests lie instead in how these groups *become* colonized,[5] in how people manufactured as a subject race are simultaneously understood as *in need of subjection*:[6] therein the principal title of this book.

I will do more than examine the way in which U.S. capital (as a social condition and a relation of power) created the subaltern subjects of the implantation and development of capitalism in Puerto Rico. My analysis will mainly look into how the once-again colonized laboring poor of this island became constructed as the wayward or criminal subjects of the new colonialist law and order through the deployment of socioeconomic, political, and signification systems.

In this sense, I now have concerns similar to Gayatri Chakravorty Spivak when she distinguishes between the traditional/Marxist political economies of colonialism in India and the research of the Subaltern Studies group. In her essay "Subaltern Studies:

Deconstructing Historiography," Spivak characterizes the traditional approach as defining

> [t]he insertion of India into colonialism . . . as a change from semi-feudalism into capitalism. Such a definition theorizes the change within the great narrative of the modes of production and, by uneasy implication, within the narrative of the transition from feudalism to capitalism.[7]

To this paradigm she counterposes the work of the Subaltern Studies group that, instead, focuses on

> revising this general definition and its theorization by proposing at least two things: first, that the moment(s) of change be pluralized and plotted as confrontations rather than as transition . . . and, secondly, that such changes are signalled or marked by a functional change in sign systems.

One prominent example of such transformations is the discursive and politico-practical shift "from crime to insurgency," because "[a] functional change in a sign system is a violent event. Even when it is perceived as 'gradual,' or 'failed,' or yet 'reversing itself,' the change itself can only be operated by the force of a crisis."[8] These are the concepts that have directed my current research, which, in turn, explains the remainder of this book's title.

My focus is on the linkages among colonialism, economic transformation, punitive structures, and discourse production, and how these processes violently constituted and refashioned Puerto Rican society and most of its members during the first half of the twentieth century. Such a direction requires attention to a complementary set of conceptual lenses: those of the ideological representations of material practices and those of the subjectivities that constitute them. This type of study demands a rethinking of the gendered, raced, and class-based "connection between past history and current historical practice"[9] by examining the process through which subjects are recognized as not just subordinate but also in need of policing and, synchronously, in need of policing precisely because they are subordinate subjects. This is why I have recuperated within my work the conceptual frameworks provided by the critique of Orientalism and by other postcolonial perspectives. However, my use of the critique of Orientalism and of postcolonial perspectives compels a few taxonomical and conceptual clarifications.

What does it mean to critically rethink the subaltern subject of Eurocentric/colonialist paradigms? At first glance, Orientalism references a very different geographical area. However, the concept, as Said has shown, is not just a question of geography, but of colonialist discourse. At issue are the cultural practices and representations that necessarily accompanied and helped make possible a particular collection of colonialist and neocolonialist enterprises that, not accidentally, coincided with the creation of a world capitalist market: the phenomenon otherwise known as the "rise of the West."[10]

The element of the critique of Orientalism re-aligned within this book is, expressly, how the politico-economic structures and dominant knowledges inherent to what Octave Mannoni broadly defined as "colonial situations" (pp. 17–18) constitute a social-geographic space and its subordinate inhabitants. Referenced is any encounter marked by national-cultural/racial hierarchy and inequality. This conceptual point of departure allows for a critique of the era of colonialism (including neocolonialism) that aspires to question the nexus of power and knowledge that made and still makes such colonial situations possible. The intention is to anticipate and further a noncolonialist age by identifying and critiquing, not just the socioeconomic and political roots of colonialism, but also the systems of meaning and ideological representation that ground colonialism—broadly understood. Such is the context in which postcolonial outlooks are pertinent: from Césaire, Fanon, Memmi, and Fernández Retamar to Said, Visvanathan, Spivak, Guha, Nandy, Hall, Bhabha, Trinh, Mudimbe, et al.

Given the sadly pervasive reality of neocolonialism, my use of the term "postcolonial" is very different from a simple allusion to the period after a former colonized people have gained political (though not economic) independence. Given also the widespread tangibility of what Ashis Nandy has called anti-Western oppositions that remain firmly positioned within Western paradigms and structures (formally anticapitalist or not),[11] my use of the term "postcolonial" is equally distinct from what Bill Ashcroft, et al. have defined as "all the culture affected by the imperial process from the moment of colonization to the present day."[12] In my mind, the economic and political effects of neocolonialism are still colonial. A *post*colonial perspective, on the other hand, designates the political, economic, and cultural efforts to uproot and dismantle colonialism altogether—particularly its Western underpinnings.

Likewise, I use the term "colonized" in this study only to denote all those populations and spaces that became the object of national-cultural/racial oppression by the West as part of the historically concurrent and overlapping emergence of capitalism, colonialism, and chattel slavery on a world scale five hundred years ago. The colonized subjects were thus produced as part and parcel of the transformation of "Christendom" into "Europe" and of Christian universalism into Eurocentric universalism.[13] It is no accident that the rise of the colonialist culture of capitalism also brought into "common"—that is, Western—usage the term "ethnic": signalling the shift from the Greek *éthnos,* meaning "nation" and "people," to the Catholic-Latin *ethnicus,* referring to "heathen," "pagan," and "savage": hence, the intertwined genesis of modern racism and nationalism. As Trinh Minh-ha has pointed out in *Woman, Native, Other,*

> The perception of the outsider as the one who needs help has taken on the successive forms of the barbarian, the pagan, the infidel, the wild man, the "native," and the underdeveloped. Needless to say, these forms whose meanings helplessly keep on decomposing can only exist in relation to their opposites. . . . Thus the invention of "needs" and of the mission to "help" the needy always blossom together. The Full Man, the Church, the Humanist, the Civilized-Colonist, and the Professional-Anthropologist all have a human face and are close male agnates descending from the same key ancestor.[14]

This study classifies the opposite of the colonized as the "colonizer," meaning: Europeans, their recognized descendants,[15] and the social space thus constituted as dominant within national-cultural/racial hierarchies. Colonialism has constructed *both* these subordinate and hegemonic spaces and their corresponding populations as *colonial* realities:[16] the various "mother countries" (or metropoli) and their respective colonies—overseas and internal, direct and indirect (neocolonies)—Japan being the only exception that confirms this originally Western taxonomical rule. This colonial reality engendered the world that Sartre described in the 1950s as numbering "two thousand million inhabitants: five hundred million men [*sic*], and one thousand five hundred million natives."[17]

Representing History

A theoretical touchstone of many new postcolonial outlooks is the representational character of history. Does a historical process exist outside of the social subjects and power relations that otherwise embody, structure, and signify it? Can such a process ever have a material reality that is universal, transcendent, and above dispute? These are controversial questions within materialist conceptual parameters since one tenet of the latter is the empirical veracity of history. I agree with Stuart Hall's explanation, in "Signification, Representation, Ideology," that the reality of events unfolds historically: that is, as social conditions and power relations that, across time, perpetually constitute the individual/group subjects who continually transform these conditions and relations (p. 105). The focus on the representational and narrative character of history does not contend the human capacity to understand events that have already transpired. But, in the very similar way in which concrete reality in the present is conceptually volatilized through meaning—that is, textualized—in order to be understood, this no less concrete past is brought to the present through meaning; it is textualized. To be acknowledged, the past must be made to appear again in the present assuming the form of an imagined reasonable facsimile, a narration, which then replaces this past. Knowledge of the past, then, is doubly representational: the past appears again (re-presents itself) in the present, and this re-apparition can only materialize in the shape of an approximation-in-thought that substitutes the original past (re-presents it). Such is the textuality of history.[18]

This construction/reconstruction of the past is a necessarily disputed process. The past is the material manifestation in memory (written, sensorial, and/or artifactual) of previous or persistent social conditions and power relations. These conditions and relations originally unfolded as subject positions (individual and collective) that were/are inherently conflictive and hierarchical in terms of race, gender, class, sexuality, nationality, and so on. This explains why struggles arise around the ways in which this past is re-membered. The various ways in which this past is re-presented (literally: made to appear again) in varying degrees have to reflect the analogous or continuing social conflicts and hierarchies that such a past expresses.

This study, then, examines material reality—including history—as an antagonistic and unstable construct mediated by no-less-material and no-less-contested sign systems. Such an approach allows for a different kind of understanding, one that can acknowledge the instability of subject positions and the social forces that cause their constructions. Unlike materialist theoretical frameworks that posit historical reality as any other set of facts that are always already there, waiting for its discovery,[19] this inquiry begins with a different set of assumptions. My purpose is not to assert the true story of criminality, U.S. colonization, and economic change in Puerto Rico, nor to provide readers with a privileged access to a stable reality. Rather, this study has more suspicious intentions: scrutinizing the ways in which capitalism, colonialism, and the law—as power relations—are embedded in, as well as work through, such categories as universal truths, privileged accesses, and knowledge. In this sense, I agree with Foucault's suggestion:

> "Truth" is linked in a circular relation with systems of power which produce and sustain it, and to effects of power which it induces and which extend it. A "regime of truth."

He immediately adds that "[t]his regime is not merely ideological or superstructural; it was a condition of the formation and development of capitalism," finally stating: "[t]he problem is not changing people's consciousness—or what's in their heads—but the political, economic, institutional regime of the production of truth."[20]

To examine ideological representations requires a renewed consideration of language, how it works to simultaneously point out and inscribe. As Carroll Smith-Rosenberg has pointed out

> . . . [I]f we accept the post-structuralist argument that it is language that endows the social with meaning, we must also insist that language, itself, acquires meaning and authority only within specific social and historical settings. While linguistic differences structure society, social differences structure language.[21]

One of the fundamental ways in which social conditions and power relations fashion people as subjects (for example, as laborers, Europeans, men, criminals, etc.) is by way of the individuational effects and functions that these sign systems (language in the broad sense) assign people. As Louis Althusser has observed in "Ideology and Ideological State Apparatuses," the myth is that people appear as the sole authors of these discourses.[22] Thus, the meanings through which people are seemingly only defining, acknowledging, and recognizing the history they are making, the social conditions under which they are making it, and the power relations within which they are making it, are, coincidentally and in actuality, the meanings through which these people are defined, acknowledged, and re-cognized as individuals (by themselves and by others). The ideological representations of, for instance, propertied and educated social sectors, women, Caribbean people, homosexuals, etc., summon the very people who believe themselves as the initiators of these identities.

Yet the sign systems and textual practices through which individual and collective subjects live this history, these social conditions, and these power relations are necessarily inverted, deflected, and displaced. These discourses allude to history, relations, and conditions that are perceived, for example, as the Law, Reason, Human Nature, Historical Destiny, and so on. The history, relations, and conditions thus conceived are different from the history and relations and conditions that actually constitute these individual/collective subjects in the first place—such as capitalism, gender oppression, racism, heterosexism, colonialism, etc. Such textual displacements do not make social conditions and power relations any less material or any less terrible. As Ashis Nandy has noted in the case of History and Christianity as metonymically Western, "None of them is true but all of them are realities" (p. xiv). The formation of social subjects is, then, doubly imagined. On the one hand, the primary dimensions in/through which this takes place are the realm of the mind (thought, language, discourses, meanings, signs, and the like). On the other hand, the social conditions and power relations being referenced are not the ones that are indeed fashioning these individual and collective identities. The very people that make history are circumscribed and unstably fixed by textual forms of representation, as ideological representations become an integral element of the conditions and relations with (and within) which people make history.

Yet this study attempts to break with positivist and metahistorical traditions in general, particularly with the "false consciousness" paradigm: I do not pretend to have uncovered the hidden truth of the colonial mind, of its representations, nor of social unrest in Puerto Rico as revealed to me in the signs left behind by its protagonists. As Diane Mcdonnel has argued, "Without a set of universal truths or a privileged access to reality, nothing can be proven beyond dispute"[23]—and I neither claim such a truth nor have such an access. This study is one other interpretation, an-other account, of events and processes that transpired between 1898 and 1947 in Puerto Rico: in this sense, it is closer to the subtle ambiguity suggested by the Spanish word for "history" (*historia*), alluding not only to the past and its analysis, but also to narrative practices in general (as in "story" or "tale"). As Janet Abu-Lughod has remarked, "[I]n historical reconstruction there is no archimedan point *outside* the system from which to view historical 'reality.'"[24]

My research stems from an effort to triangulate previously unexamined axes/elements in the case of the social-history/historical-sociology of Puerto Rico. This is the way I have tried to read these events and the—mostly displaced and furtive—voices of their subaltern participants. However, I know full well that these voices were not "speaking to me" and that my reconstruction of their meanings is not to be confused with whatever meanings these subaltern social practices may have had for their participants and for their detractors—all of those meanings being inaccessible to me (and to any other historical analyst). Gayatri Chakravorty Spivak is correct when, in "Can the Subaltern Speak?", she states:

> When we come to the concomitant question of the consciousness of the subaltern, the notion of what the work *cannot* say becomes important. . . . The sender—"the peasant"—is marked only as a pointer to an irretrievable consciousness. As for the receiver, we must ask who is "the real receiver" of an "insurgency"? The historian, transforming "insurgency" into "text of knowledge," is only one "receiver" of any collectively intended social act. With no possibility of nostalgia for that lost origin, the historian must suspend (as far as possible) the clamor of his or her own consciousness (or consciousness-effect, as operated by disciplinary training), so that the elaboration of the insurgency, packaged with an insurgent-consciousness, does not freeze into an "object of investigation," or, worse yet, a model of imitation. "The subject" implied by the texts of insurgency can only serve as a counterpossibility for the narrative sanctions granted to the colonial subject in the dominant groups. The postcolonial intellectuals learn that their privilege is their loss. In this they are a paradigm of the intellectuals. (p. 287, emphasis in the original)

These are odd contradictions: that ideological representations author the subject as the subject struggles to claim ownership and that the history of narratives cannot elude the narrative character of history. Entering such apparent incongruities requires highlighting, in social research, the formation of social subjects, history, socioeconomic conditions, and discourses.

The Moments of Transgression

What it might mean to address the above distinctions was partially suggested more than a decade ago, when Steven Spitzer observed:[25]

> The relationship between patterns of economic organization and punishment is always indirect at best. It is mediated by a number of different structures, processes, and contradictions that make it impossible to precisely deduce the anatomy of the economic order from a study of punishment or vice versa.[26]

How are the subaltern subjects of the popular illegalities[27] in Puerto Rico positioned with respect to the subaltern subjects of colonialist forms of punishment and the subaltern subjects of the colonial economic order? To what extent are these subaltern subjects one and the same? In this book I do not intend to deduce the forms of punishment by re-examining the types of social change that took place in Puerto Rico. Instead, I am interested in how that important part of the everyday existence of the laboring-poor majorities in the Island—namely, the subjectivity of the popular illegalities—was structured and lived as a mediation between these "patterns of economic organization and punishment."

Because the survival practices of the laboring classes have, historically, cut through the ways that the accumulation of capital is implanted, these survival practices have been frequently constructed as transgressive. Given the forms of social disruption that emerge in each particular historical situation, it becomes necessary to demonstrate why the unique forms adopted by the dispossession process structurally required and specifically included what Foucault in *Discipline and Punish* called the "methods for administering the accumulation of men" (p. 220).

I examine this problem by delineating the contours of such punitive methods in Puerto Rico. Yet the concrete details of colonial criminal justice and of the penal system's development will not be examined in this book. Rather, my analysis concentrates on: (1) the implantation and disruption of the accumulation of capital and (2) the ideological representations that radiated from and were determined by these punitive methods. The persistent autonomy of these survival practices set limits to advancing capitalism's ability to effectively summon and fashion the impoverished majorities in Puerto Rico as a docile potential labor force. In turn, these contrary survival practices were supposed to have been identified, explained, controlled, penetrated, and redirected by the new and changing forms of punishment, particularly by the discourses on criminal justice.[28]

Given the necessarily opaque, displaced, and elusive textual traces left by these popular illegalities, one of the other objectives of this study is to identify the physiognomy of such prohibited subaltern practices by examining the normative direction and substance of both the colonial-capitalist narratives and the law-and-order discourses at this time. Much of this study involved inspecting a large number of the official documents, scholarly essays, and newspaper articles of the day that recorded both the practices and the voices of these disorderly subaltern subjects. My own research into these chronicles and sociographies was carried out with attention to the conflictive way that they structured and logged the subaltern voices. Although coming from another context, Deborah Britzman's advice is, in this sense, still quite pertinent:

> Re-presenting the voices of others means more than recording their words. An interpretive effort is necessary because words always express relationships, span contexts larger than the immediate situation from which they arise, and hold tensions between what is intended and what is signified. . . . The retelling of another's story is always a partial telling, bound not only by one's perspective but also by the exigencies of what can and cannot be told.[29]

Therefore, at this level too, my research is similar to the work of the Subaltern Studies group. In the case of the official record of rural disorder in nineteenth century India, Ranajit Guha has remarked:

> It is of course true that the reports, dispatches, minutes, judgements, laws, letters, etc., in which policemen, soldiers, bureaucrats, landlords, usurers, and others hostile to insurgency register their sentiments, amount to a representation of their will. But these documents do not get their content from that will alone, for the latter is predicated on another will—that of the insurgent.[30]

In "The Prose of Counter-Insurgency," Guha suggests that "a closer look at the [official] text can detect chinks which have allowed 'comment' to worm its way through the plate armour of 'fact.'"[31] Such reports, dispatches, etc. regarding disorder among the colonized do not make much sense except in terms of the disciplinary codes of colonial-capitalist pacification. My own research also reads the imprint of analogous subordinate resistance/survival practices within their, oftentimes, only written record. This is why, according to Gayatri Chakravorty Spivak in "Subaltern Studies: Deconstructing Historiography," you "can only read against the grain if misfits in the text signal the way. (These are sometimes called 'moments of transgression' or 'critical moments')" (p. 211).

In no way, however, am I advancing a romantic notion of what these often criminalized survival practices were or have been. As Martha Knisely Huggins has advised, "Spitzer's dictum [re: the construction of problem populations] need not imply that criminals are motivated by revolutionary objectives, only that people are labeled deviant when their behavior or personal qualities represent a significant impediment to the maintenance and growth of a system."[32]

In this study, then, I am not denying the very real violence and pain resulting from some of the illegalized subsistence practices and turbulent reactions to the colonialist dispossession process. The perspective adopted in this book, though, is twofold. First, even in these particular cases such intrinsic violence, as well as the very palpable suffering that may and many times does follow in its wake, is nevertheless devoid of any moral or immoral essence. Moral culpability is a socially variable, historically determined, and extremely contested ideological representation. The harshness and the anguish may all be there. What is neither inherently nor ontologically there, however, is the criminal/delinquent identification: this is a changing, socially constructed interpretation of real and contradictory practices, power relations, and social conditions. It is a form of discourse.

Second, because crime and delinquency are historically variable ideological representations of such practices, relations, and conditions, then the conflation of *social* violence[33]—that is, illegal or illegalized violence—with violence *sans phrase* amounts to a major oversight. This maneuver omits or excuses the very real violence and brutality inherently present in many of the legal, systemic, and/or exonerated practices of hegemonic elements: the State, capital, and the propertied and educated classes and individuals in general. Such officially condoned violence is mostly relocated outside of the epistemological and administrative terrain of the criminal justice system altogether. Collapsing the signifiers of violence by reducing all violence primarily to the violent practices of the dispossessed merely reinforces the reconstitution and continuation of the existing codes of legal/punitive regulation. Another element this book examines is precisely the ways that the economic and colonialist dispossession process was furthered by such fusion of violence markers.

These are the principal questions addressed in this study. The order of exposition began in this chapter with a detailed description of the general concepts and theoretical concerns that have directed my recent research: knowledge-power relations; the historicity of textuality and the textuality of history; colonialism and punitive discourses; and the links between socioeconomic structures and subjectivity. The second and third chapters are an explanation of the imposed colonial-capitalist structures, their signifying practices, and the sociocultural repercussions of this process in Puerto Rico, from the U.S. invasion of 1898 running through the end of its foundation-building period after the European War of 1914–1919.

Chapters Four and Five examine the contradictory response and resistances of the "native" majorities in the Island to the machineries of dispossession during that first pivotal period; the colonialist institutions and discursive operations that contained and represented the disorders of the colonized are also explored. The remaining primary chapters (six, seven, and eight) deal with the ways that this process of containment and transgression, the text of the popular illegalities versus its official representations, were coupled and at the same time unraveled in the 1920s, 1930s, and 1940s. The closing chapter summarizes the main themes of this book.

Edward Said remarked in *Orientalism* that the corrective study of colonized majorities turned most "native" populations into " . . . something one judges (as in court of law), . . . something one disciplines (as in school or prison), something one illustrates (as in a zoological manual). [Something that] . . . is *contained* and *represented* by dominating frameworks" (p. 40). Whereupon Said asked: "Where do these come from?" In the case of Puerto Rico, this is the question to which we will now turn, regarding the crucial 1898–1921 period.

PART ONE

1898–1921

2

A Contest of Structures

> There is little to encourage a belief that the native people will be disposed to make a radical change in their nature and habits, and transform themselves from a lazy, easy-going, and, in the main, idle people, into active and energetic workers.
>
> Of mechanical industry there is now little or nothing. . . . Raw materials for almost any business would have to be imported, and the education of a race to persistent day in and day out labor would be no simple matter. Most of the industry with which the native people have been at all acquainted, has been of a nature which permitted them to consult their personal inclinations to a considerable extent.
>
> **—Albert G. Robinson, *The Porto Rico of Today* (1899)**

> This is the way that the West carries the burden of the Other. Naming is part of the human rituals of incorporation, and the unnamed remains less human than the inhuman or subhuman. The threatening Otherness must, therefore, be transformed into figures that belong to a definite image-repertoire.
>
> **—Trinh Minh-ha, *Woman, Native, Other* (1989)**

As a pivotal juncture in Puerto Rico, the 1898–1921 period expressed, among other things, the uneven materialization of colonialist capitalism in the Island. Such a transformation rode on the coattails of the War of 1898, an event that became a watershed in the lives of North Americans and Puerto Ricans with respect to the social relations that structured them/us from then on: socioeconomically, juridico-politically, and discursively. Old signifying vessels in the United States set new bearings with respect to the "lesser races," and time-honored cultural maps were restructured as well as reinforced by new geopolitical and economic forces. The U.S. economy needed new markets, new sources of inexpensive raw materials, and a larger supply of cheap labor, and the U.S. Navy needed new coal-refueling stations. However, the order embodied by the North American republic also demanded a new chaos in need of reorganization.

This introductory period also launched the large-scale social disorganization and dispossession of these Caribbean-island majorities. This process recast the existing conflicts and relations between the laboring and the propertied classes (Creole and North American). It additionally transformed the contradictions and linkages that existed within the colonized laboring classes themselves, generating new social and cultural disparities. Widespread "native" practices embodied an important number of these disparities that, in turn, became inscribed as unlawful. The social fabric of Puerto Rico would never be the same again.

The period from 1898 to 1921 became the hearth that, in a new way and with a new direction, originally forged most of the Island's inhabitants—and, ultimately, the entire colonized space—as wayward and unruly. This chapter addresses some of the socioeconomic, political, cultural, and textual changes that unfolded during the first two decades of the U.S. occupation of Puerto Rico: the period that initially and simultaneously fashioned the Island and most of its population into a major source of cheap labor, an important source of industrial raw materials, and a chaos in need of order.

The United States and the 1898 Juncture

If, as Carroll Smith-Rosenberg has noted, "language, itself, acquires meaning and authority only within specific social and historical settings" even as "linguistic differences structure society,"[1] which social and historical setting authorized the language of U.S. colonialism in 1898? What geopolitical context gave rise to and legitimized the hegemonic subject of North American capitalism at this time? Where was Puerto Rico located within this political, socioeconomic, and semiotic cartography?

After the Spanish-Cuban–North American War,[2] external forces shifted Puerto Rico into a different position within the political and economic gridwork of the world. Between 1898 and 1947, the Island became an increasingly wage-based site of cheap colonized labor for the purpose of generating sugar, tobacco, and needle-works products for export.[3] Several forces made the results of the Spanish-Cuban–North American War with respect to Puerto Rico less than surprising, one of them being the way that Puerto Rican society had been constituted beforehand, particularly in regard to the linkages established between the Island and the U.S. market as of the 1830s. Spain was unable to consume large segments of Puerto Rico's cheap raw materials (in the form of agricultural output) partially because the configuration of the Spanish economy structured such consumption as a superfluous practice from the perspective of the predominant social forces. This situation cleared the road for the uneven incorporation of the Island into the production circuits of the U.S. economy, then in a stage of burgeoning expansion.[4]

In part, this absorption incapacity on the part of the Spanish economy became entwined with the other factor that contributed to the results of the Spanish-Cuban–North American War: the absence of a local monopoly capital in Spain before 1898. The absence of such a transformation is one of the main reasons why Spain did not significantly reorient its Caribbean, African, and Philippine colonial enterprises toward the exportation of capitalist production, even during the last quarter of the nineteenth century.[5]

During the latter decades of the nineteenth century, a handful of Western European, North American, and Asian interests started expanding and transforming their colonial and neocolonial systems by way of the exportation of capitalist production. Countries including Germany, France, Holland, Belgium, Japan, and the United States moved in this direction because, among other reasons, of the industrial growth and the rise of monopoly capital taking place on their own soil. As is otherwise well known, the ensuing rapid industrialization (under the aegis of monopoly capital) took shape due to the increasing need for new sources of cheap labor, new markets, and new sources of cheap raw materials. This last development resulted from the need to forestall the general tendency of capitalist economies to generate a declining rate of profit—a tendency now made more severe by the dramatic rise in production capacity. Because of Hilferding and Bukharin, we know that when the market of origin became rapidly saturated with the growing industrial output and as the rates of profit fell due to the increasing use of machinery and other nonlive labor, the trusts and cartels began to channel greater portions of their productive capital into the noncapitalist and/or nonindustrialized regions of the world.[6]

Which language, which dominant narrative, endowed this social situation with meaning, thus constituting the hegemonic subject of North American capitalism in the Caribbean? Some budding U.S. political leaders read this juncture explicitly as historical destiny. In September of 1898, for instance, Albert J. Beveridge proclaimed to a cheering audience at the Republican Party's National Convention in Cincinnati that "[w]e are raising more than we can consume . . . making more than we can use. Today our industrial society is congested."[7] Since "there [was] more capital than there [was] investment," Beveridge encouraged his avid listeners to "[t]hink of the thousands of Americans who [would] pour into Hawaii and Porto Rico [*sic*] when republican laws cover[ed] these islands with justice and safety!" (ibid.) For Beveridge, then, these far-off tropics were a dark space lying in waiting: an attendant/site where a materially and geographically confined, overabundant, and tense American industrial society could go and—in more ways than one—relieve itself.

In economic terms, the new colonial relationship thus constituted evolved in a manner qualitatively unlike the one over which Spain had presided. This difference partially allowed dominant structures in the United States to carry out—with very relative success—a radical reorientation of the preexistent colonial venture in the Island. The existence of U.S. monopoly capital was the original structural premise of this great transformation. Without this modality of capitalism, State structures in the North American republic would probably not have been so enthralled with ingesting and transforming Puerto Rico. And without monopoly capital, the outcome of such an unlikely seizure would have turned out similar to the Spanish variant of colonialism. Monopoly capital played a decisive role in laying the material foundations of Puerto Rico's structural metamorphosis by determining the breathtaking speed in which this change, however partially, took root.[8]

But such economic forces were concurrently coupled with equally important political and military directives. The uneven economic absorption of Puerto Rico by the U.S. economy initially entailed two concurrent and complementary processes. First, the juridico-political edifice of the United States would integrate the Island within its structures, transforming the State in Puerto Rico into an extension of the State in the North American republic. This became one of the partial outcomes of the Spanish-Cuban–North

American War. Second, continental forces would convert Puerto Rico into a U.S. military and naval stronghold. Both of these goals were achieved very rapidly. There were several—literally—global reasons that made this necessary for the ruling interests in the United States.

For one thing, this *peaceful* occupation of one of the noncapitalist and/or nonindustrialized countries or regions by the monopoly-capital investments of Western Europe, North America, and/or Japan usually found itself coupled with the *military* occupation of these noncapitalist/nonindustrialized countries by one of the industrialized capitalist States. With respect to the United States, the first major expression of this new type of expansionism was the Spanish-Cuban–North American War.[9]

Once again, mainstream intellectuals tended to frame such conflicts in racist and Euro/Americo-centric terms. For instance, Professor Harry H. Powers in 1898 used the Caribbean outcome of this war as an illustration of what awaited the rest of the globe during the coming generation, when " . . . the entire world [would be] within the 'sphere of influence' of half a dozen powers . . . [thereby proceeding with] the struggle for race supremacy with increasing definiteness and determination."[10] Beveridge obviously concurred, when in a September 21, 1898 letter to an industrialist friend he warned: "Never forget that we are Anglo-Saxon at heart. . . . We are of the blood which furnishes the world with its Daniel Boones, its Francis Drakes, its Cecil Rhodes . . ." (*Beveridge*, 77). And what could a Daniel Boone possibly mean without "Indians," a Francis Drake without Caribbean "natives," and Cecil Rhodes without African "natives"? In this sense, both the hegemonic subject of the new North American expansionism and the subaltern subjects of U.S. colonial capitalism in Puerto Rico could only emerge simultaneously, each one conflictively determining the existence of the other. As Albert Memmi has pointed out, for the colonialist "to [completely] eliminate the colonized from the roll of the living . . . would be impossible . . . to do . . . without eliminating himself."[11]

The War of 1898 was partly the result of the social forces within North America interested in having the United States displace Great Britain and keeping Germany at bay in the Americas, a maneuver closely related to the U.S. drive to gain control over the interoceanic canal whose construction would take place in Central America. But the array of social forces behind this war became just as interested, if not more interested, in obtaining a safe route for the invasion of Asia by U.S. monopoly capital, which was suffering at the time from considerable Western European competition in the Pacific Rim.[12]

The military occupation of Cuba and Puerto Rico by North American troops, being part of a much larger constellation of operations, took place without major difficulties for the U.S. government.[13] With the signing of the Treaty of Paris on December 10, 1898, an island designated as "Porto Rico" was ceded to the United States as part of the spoils of the war.[14]

Such imperial fiats and feats were signified, among other things, by the creation of a formerly nonexistent place now to be known generally as "Porto Rico." Henceforth and until 1932, colonial personnel in the United States and North American public opinion would tend to refer to this place by that name—the "natives," of course, continued to refer to "their" country as Puerto Rico.[15] Recalling Said's critique of Orientalism,[16] then, knowledge of "Porto Rico," because it was generated out of the strength of U.S. colonialism, created a cluster of subjects and a social space—namely, "Porto Ricans" and "Porto Rico"—which, "while appearing to exist objectively, . . . only [had] a fictional reality": these being the very same dominant knowledges and power relations that now supplied "Porto Ricans" with a mentality, a genealogy, and an atmosphere.

These exploits of the imagination and of power confirms the currency of what V. Y. Mudimbe has recently noted about the origins of the term *to colonize.* Mudimbe has reminded us that to colonize stemmed from the same Roman/Latin words as *to design, to cultivate, to develop, to define.*[17] This etymology further corroborates the intrinsic linkage between (a) the socioeconomic and military invention of a geographic space (the colony) over which the outsiders (the colonizers) have mastery in order to reap political and economic benefits and (b) the textual invention of human space (the colonized) over which another people (the colonizers) exercise mastery in order to obtain ideological advantages—a linkage that emerges textually as always already white, male, propertied, and of the West.

Obtaining control of this former Spanish colony became one of the vital objectives of this war. As the U.S. naval strategist and expansionist ideologue, Alfred Thayer Mahan, explained several years later,

> [The] estimate of the military importance of Porto Rico [*sic*] should never be lost sight by us as long as we have any responsibility direct or indirect, for the safety or independence of Cuba. Porto Rico [*sic*], considered militarily, is to Cuba, to the future Isthmian Canal, and to our Pacific Coast what Malta is,

> or may be, to Egypt and the beyond; and there is for us the like necessity to hold and strengthen the one, in its entirety and its immediate surroundings that there is for Great Britain to hold the other for the security of her position in Egypt, for her use of the Suez Canal, and for her control of the route to India.[18]

The geopolitical positioning of the Island by North American economic, political, and military interests illustrates just how interchangeable the noncapitalist and nonindustrial regions could become for the industrialized States. A chain of comparisons thus emerged—Puerto Rico to Malta, the Central American Isthmus to Suez, the Caribbean to the Mediterranean, and the Pacific Ocean to the Indian Ocean—*precisely because* the United States could only be compared to Great Britain. The British allegory was, of course, not accidental because Britain still hegemonized the world market and many of its oceanic routes through an impressive navy and a vast colonial and neocolonial system. Beveridge openly proposed that the United States emulate just such a politico-military, capitalist, and racist vocation. "If England can govern foreign lands, so can America. If it can supervise protectorates, so can America," he declared. "Will you affirm . . . that we are of the ruling race of the world; that ours is the blood of government; ours the hearts of dominion; ours the brain and genius of administration?" (*Beveridge*, 74).

The field of battle emerged as the preferred domain for testing such comparisons. Mahan was quite aware of this. "What means less violent than war," he asked with blunt candor, "would in half a year have solved the Caribbean problem, shattered national ideas deep-rooted in the prepossessions of a century, and planted the United States in Asia?"[19] Beveridge, too, was keenly aware of the necessity of war to achieve these aims. In an April 27, 1898 tribute to Ulysses Grant, he asserted: "[Grant] never forgot that we are a conquering race, and that we must obey our blood and occupy new markets, and if necessary new lands" (*Beveridge*, 68).

This political-economic, military, and cultural-national/racial discursive cluster fashioned entire regions of the world (including Puerto Rico) as problems to be solved and as stretches of (empty) land to be seeded by the "advanced races" who embodied the highest stage of cultural, economic, technological, and social evolution. Reverend Josiah Strong had saluted this vision in a paean to U.S. overseas expansionism:

> Only those races which have produced machinery seem capable of using it with the best results. It is the most advanced races

> which are its masters. Those races which, like the African and the Malay, are many centuries behind the Anglo-Saxon in development seem as incapable of operating complicated machinery as they are of adopting and successfully administering representative government.[20]

Former Senator W. A. Peffer had anticipated this genre of arrogance, affirming a year before that "God must have intended that savage life and customs should yield to higher standards of living or he would have made the earth many times larger."[21] This was the geopolitical equivalent of the argument that had been current in paleontology, embryology, and comparative anatomy—then codified in the axiom: "ontogeny recapitulates phylogeny."[22] Social gospel champion Lyman Abbott then made similar linkages, but this time comparing a Spain undeserving of Western heritage and ignorant of divine science to a United States of America that, under God's guidance, had proved its technological and cultural mettle. According to Abbott, the "real reason why the American navy beats the Spanish navy" stemmed from the fact that "we have learned to use 'God's projectiles' and they have not learned [that] in Spain."[23] Abbott understood that the United States had been "taught how to lay hold of the muscles of the Almighty, and this knowledge [was] the fulcrum by which man and God work[ed] together to elevate the human race" (ibid.).

In 1900 Columbia sociologist Franklin H. Giddings could observe casually and with implicit ambiguity: "We read to-day of the superiority of the Anglo-Saxon, and of the decadence of the Latin race."[24] Regardless of whether the comparison was with Latin America and the Caribbean or with decadent Spain, this was the cultural mapping that informed Theodore Roosevelt's comments in a 1906 letter, after a brief visit to the Canal construction project: "There the greatest engineering feat of the ages is being attempted. It is the kind of work our people are peculiarly fitted to do . . . "[25] It was the same cultural map that then Senator Beveridge publicly summarized in January of 1900. "[God] had made us the master organizers of the world to establish system where chaos reigns," he declared before a fully assembled Senate. "He has made us adept in government that we may administer government among savages and senile peoples" (*Beveridge*, 121).

Such magnificent signs proclaimed the United States as the legitimate heir to Western Civilization's mantle and as the mightiest embodiment of Science and Progress itself. Given the results of the War of 1898, this sociotextual universe centered the North

American republic as having a greater command of science and of modern technology, all of which allowed this country to supplant the oldest of Europe's empires. The teleology of modernity and the liturgy of science positioned the United States as the culmination of the West. This entailed a monumental obligation, as Shiv Visvanathan has asserted in another context,

> The increasing accumulation of science is seen as a sign of "grace." The West is seen as paradigmatic of scientific and technological culture.
>
> The West as modernity obtains the mandate of power and responsibility over this world left behind by history. It is science as the modern man's "gaze" that brings the primitive and the archaic back into contemporaneity. It is science, once again, that must aid in their march to modernity.[26]

The "White Man's Burden," after all, had a scientific foundation.

Achieving mastery, first over "senile" Spain and then over the "savages" in the Philippines, took considerably longer (four years) due to the tenacity of the local nationalist guerrillas.[27] But with the subsequent consolidation of the U.S. troop presence in the Philippines, the definite annexation of Guam, Samoa, and the Hawaiian archipelago was also sealed. This created the geopolitical conditions for launching the U.S. canal project in Panama and for the multiplication of U.S. investments in the lucrative Asian Market.[28]

These gains for U.S. interests laid the groundwork for two additional but related processes. For one thing, it now became possible to easily transform the new colonies and neocolonies into armed strongholds and coal-refueling stations for U.S. military and economic operations. Mahan summarized the historical importance of such activities, stating that three elements, namely production ("with the necessity of exchanging products"), shipping ("whereby the exchange is carried on"), and colonies ("which facilitates and enlarges the operations of shipping and tend to protect it by multiplying points of safety"), comprised "the key to much of history, as well as the policy of nations bordering upon the sea."[29]

In turn, such gains secured and augmented the preexistent investments of U.S. monopoly capital in some of these islands—for instance, Hawaii and Cuba—while initiating the massive economic saturation of some of the other islands, such as the Philippines and Puerto Rico. In Hawaii, as well as in the two Antilles, one of the major considerations for U.S. monopoly capital was securing a larger source of sugarcane raw material.[30]

The general direction of these military and economic operations led to several corollary developments during the first three decades of this century. Among them were: the centralization of the State apparatus in the United States, particularly its military components; the restructuring of the Caribbean and Central American governments being promoted by the U.S. State Department; and, in case of extreme instability, the execution of U.S. military interventions in the region. In each case, the results were an increase in the economic invasion of these countries by U.S. capital in the wake of its restructuring efforts, with or without military occupations.[31]

Building on the foundations of this laboriously secured Caribbean and Central American arc, U.S. monopoly capital rapidly extended its holdings throughout the more southern portions of Latin America, without the need for prolonged military expeditions.[32] With the defeat of its German rival and with Great Britain and France considerably weakened in the Great War in Europe, the United States emerged as the principal financing agent of Latin America: New York replaced London as the banking capital of the world. Unlike most of the other countries intervened at this time,[33] Puerto Rico became a direct colony of the United States. Nevertheless, the Island constituted a significant link in the geopolitical and economic chain of North American expansionism and overseas investments.

The March of Capital in Puerto Rico Between 1898 and 1921

In order to examine the existing mediations between the new colonialist patterns of punishment and the changing patterns of economic organization after 1898, the general trends of the latter need to be graphed. Likewise, any joint analysis of (a) the subaltern subjects of emergent capitalism in Puerto Rico and (b) the subaltern subjects of colonized labor and criminology requires an overview of how the implantation of capitalism unfolded—particularly in terms of the initial transformations that occurred regarding land use, production forms, consumption systems, and the labor process.

One of the major alterations that took place in the new Caribbean possession of the United States was the recomposition of the principal uses given to farmland. For example, between 1899 and 1919 the total area planted in sugarcane more than tripled. The available data also indicates that this particular farmland, as a proportion of all cropland, more than doubled. Tobacco cropland experienced an extremely dramatic growth during these first twenty years. There was a more than sixfold jump in absolute area and an almost fourfold increase in proportional area. This situation contrasted sharply with the conditions of coffee production: the farmland planted in coffee virtually remained the same in absolute terms, as its position in terms of the percentage of total cropland was almost cut in half. The restructuring of agricultural production is significant because sugar and tobacco—as had not been the case for coffee—were precisely two of the economic sectors undergoing major levels of concentration and centralization directed by U.S. corporations. These changes in the places occupied by different sectors of agrarian output were reflected in the concurrent shift within the hierarchy of the major agricultural export items produced in Puerto Rico. The displacement of some products by others, in turn, evidently expressed the changes that were taking place within the leading economic sectors.[34]

This transformation of agricultural production—together with the emergent controlling interests in the banking, commercial, manufacturing, and utility sectors in Puerto Rico—was orchestrated by a tight network of monopoly corporations headed by the National City Bank and the Morgan Guaranty Trust. Some of the largest sugar mills in the world were set up in the Island during the first five years of the U.S. occupation, together with their plantation satellites and all of the corresponding financial, trade, and transportation infrastructure. Simultaneously, these processes rewove the entire social tapestry of the Island in order to partially turn Puerto Rico into a prominent agricultural site and manufacturing workshop for U.S. tobacco-products interests.[35]

During most of the first fifty years of U.S. colonialism in Puerto Rico, there was a close correlation between two processes. First, there was the shift in the Island's position within the world economy, regarding which Puerto Rican production items were primarily being exported. And second, there were the changes in the organization of the labor process within colonial agriculture, unevenly going from overwhelmingly noncapitalist social relations of production to mostly wage-based patterns. Ultimately, this meant depopulating the landscape of "native" direct producers, repopulating parts of the land with U.S. capital, and relocating as many of these direct producers within a cheap, wage-labor market.

The writings of a whole succession of businessmen-voyagers and economic journalists had textually anticipated this process of depopulation/relocation during 1898–1899. Their visionary gaze scoured the face of a remote Island that loomed so alien and exotic, searching among the markers of such strangeness for potential sources of raw materials and cheap colonized labor. As with the case of Cuba, the Philippines, and Hawaii, the travels of people such as William Pettit, Murat Halstead, Frederick Ober, O. R. Austin, A. D. Hall, and Alfred G. Robinson generated an entire cottage industry of writings with extremely evocative titles: *Pictorial History of Our New Possessions; Porto Rico: Its History, Products, and Possibilities; Porto Rico and Its Resources; Our Islands and Their People; Our West Indian Neighbors*; "Our New Possessions and the Interest They Are Exciting"; "Porto Rico and Its People"; "The Value of Porto Rico"; and so on.

Robert T. Hill, for example, described the Island by suggesting the divine design that had "so suddenly and unexpectedly" dropped the "microcosm . . . [of 'Porto Rico'] into the responsibility of our jurisdiction," complete with "its people, habits, customs, language, and products so entirely different from anything hitherto possessed by us."[36] Hill saw such a responsibility as "challeng[ing] every aspect of our so-called Yankee civilization," a task that dared "the application of every art, science, industry, and administrative method by which we have made our own land great" (ibid.).

The distribution of responsibilities for defacing this tropical Eden (during the tenure of the previous colonial regime) was, in turn, complemented by the endless possibilities suggested by this prose poem to economic colonialism. For Hill, these anthropomorphic "impoverished soils and deforested mountains of Porto Rico [*sic*]" literally "cr[ied] aloud for agricultural experiments to apply the magic wand of chemistry, drainage, and irrigation," so that they could be "rescue[d] . . . from the waste and ruin of four centuries," thereby "rehabilitat[ing] and transform[ing] the island into an agricultural and scenic paradise" (ibid.).

Here again are the familiar signs of Josiah Strong's "advanced races" vs. "incapable [races]," for only the former "have produced machinery [and therefore] seem capable of using it with the best results," and only they can wield "the magic wand" of technology and knowledge. Here again are the power-knowledge effects of what Mary Louise Pratt critically designated as the intersection between the "physical description of the globe" and the "physical appropriation of the globe" by Western men. And here again is the anticipation of the depopulation of "native" land and the relocation of "native" people, whereby

> indigenous peoples are relocated in separate manners-and-customs chapters as if in textual homelands or reservations,

> where they are pulled out of time to be preserved, contained, studied, admired, detested, pitied, mourned. Meanwhile, the now-empty landscape is personified as the metaphorical "face of the country"—a more tractable face that returns the European's gaze, echoes his words, and accepts his caress.[37]

However, the depopulation/relocation process that linked the changes in Puerto Rico's place within the global market, on the one hand, and the changes in the organization of the agricultural labor process, on the other, was extremely varied and contradictory—much more so than Hill, Ober, Halstead, Robinson, and others had anticipated. For one thing, the subaltern subjects of colonized labor were variously resistant to being fashioned as compliant, docile, and cheap sources of profit. Moreover, the structures of capitalist production historically prevalent during the first half of the twentieth century in Puerto Rico were mainly constituted along the lines of simple cooperation and the putting-out system.[38]

The persistence of simple cooperation and the putting-out system meant that the full dispossession embodied in the large-scale organization of a collective work force, characteristic of industrial production, was mostly absent for the majority of the "native" laboring classes. Both simple cooperation and the putting-out system left fairly intact the former and/or coexisting noncapitalist forms of technical development, thus facilitating the slippage from capitalist to noncapitalist forms of production. This is one of the primary reasons why the corresponding work skills of the local agricultural labor force were characterized as being at very low levels when compared to many of the other regions where North American capital was operating under U.S. jurisdiction. Moreover, throughout much of the 1898–1947 period, the several types of land-rent and/or wage-labor arrangements unevenly combined with the usurious practices of the rural stores—the latter acts being, in turn, linked to the large land owners.[39]

From the purely statistical point of view, several things become evident between 1899 and 1949. The number of workers lost to the Island's agricultural sector was proportionate to those gained by manufacturing, mining, construction, transportation, and public utilities, and, to a lesser degree, by commerce, trade, finance, etc. (see table 1). Something very similar occurred in the related occupational distribution of the colonized work force during this period (see table 2). Although it is true that most of these former agricultural laborers became operatives, they did not necessarily become operators of machine tools. The existing reports previously indicated that the majority of the nonagricultural/nonservice sectors that increased their percentage within the corresponding portions of the labor force at this time used very little or no machinery. Here we must consider the exigencies of industrial factory discipline and of the proto-Taylorist organization of the labor process in general. During the first half of the twentieth century, Taylorism was only embryonically emerging in a few sectors of the economic sphere in Puerto Rico.[40] Extremely small, artisan-based shops tended to predominate within the manufacturing sector throughout the first half of the century. In 1910, 66.3 percent of all manufacturing establishments employed less than six workers.[41] And as late as 1946, " . . . the Bureau of Labor Statistics of the Puerto Rico Department of Labor revealed that over half the enterprises employ[ed] less than six workers . . . "[42]

As a counterpoint to the socioeconomic changes just described, certain mainland firms made a concerted effort to transform the Island into an important market for U.S. goods. Significant inroads were made in the mass consumption of items such as codfish and rice. This transpired when U.S. firms absorbed and/or gained control of the financial resources, sectorial markets, physical facilities, and import/export mechanisms of the principal merchant houses that existed in the Island before 1898.[43] Such a process of centralization and concentration of commercial property was further advanced when the direct-sales subsidiaries of U.S. corporations were transplanted to this Caribbean colony during the first decades of the twentieth century. The specific weight of their operations in Puerto Rico was roughly equivalent to their economic importance within the continent.[44]

"The Education of a Race to Persistent Day In and Day Out Labor Would Be No Simple Matter"

The creation and expansion of the new production forms demanded the promotion of certain conditions; so did bringing such transformations to their greatest possible fruition. One of the main corollary requirements in this regard was the constitution of large aggregates of relatively cheap, compliant, dispossessed, and accessible "native" labor. This labor had to be made potentially available to the corresponding corporations and firms. The centralization and concentration of property itself took care of part of this structural need. Most of the measures taken during the first decades of this century by the State (local and federal) had similar effects, both in terms of economic force and political coercion.[45] But, once again, this dispossession mechanism was not completely successful.

Melossi's dictum was empirically verified in Puerto Rico during the first half of this century: "Capitalism had to destroy completely the subsistence economy in the countryside before having former peasants, vagrants, 'idle rogues' completely in its hands."[46] The centralization and concentration of property, as well as the economically coercive governmental activities, only accounted for part of the historical tasks objectively assumed by monopoly capital and by the leadership of the new colonial administration between 1898 and 1947. Yet as mechanisms partially responsible for the constitution and regulation of the colonized laboring classes, this process of concentration/centralization of property and these State measures were by no means enough.

The type and level of capitalist production beginning to unfold in the Island emerged at odds with a potential work force that, during this period, became more and more difficult to reproduce as cheap and compliant labor. As we shall see in subsequent chapters, this was partially due, first, to the organizing efforts and protests spearheaded by the budding labor movement. Second, it was also due to the rising costs and increasing complexities associated with the social pacification of the impoverished majorities of the colonized population. Third, not only did directly wage-related resistances emerge, but there was also an entire spectrum of forms of social disorder (criminally inscribed or not) that flourished at this time, many of them linked to independent income-gaining activities. These three axes traced the outline of the subaltern subjects in Puerto Rico. The subjects' social practices mediated the new punitive forms of U.S. colonialism and the emergent patterns of economic organization of North American capitalism in the Island: the extraeconomic police vigilance intersected the gaze of the overseer and the foreman, and the social discipline of moral hygiene and the law intersected the labor discipline of the sugar plantation, the cigar factory, and the needle-products putting-out system.

Colonial dispossession could never completely occur until the alternate forms of making a living had vanished and until the social responses of the "native" laborers became normalized. Insofar as colonialist capital failed to carry out this destruction and normativization in any definitive and all-encompassing way, it was endlessly limited to having only partial access to the growing mass of potential wage-labor being unevenly generated. A colonized labor force, constituted in such a random and wayward manner, would yield only in the most erratic way.

Table 1 Employment by Occupational Sector in Puerto Rico, Selected Years, Both Sexes, 10 Years of Age or Older

		FARMERS AND FARM ADMINISTRATORS	AGRICULTURAL LABORERS	PROFESSIONALS, TECHNICIANS, AND RELATED SALARIED PERSONNEL; MANAGERS AND NONFARM ADMINISTRATORS	SALESPERSONS; OFFICE WORKERS AND RELATED SALARIED PERSONNEL	CRAFTSMEN, FOREMEN AND RELATED WORKERS	OPERATORS AND RELATED WORKERS	NONFARM LABORERS	DOMESTIC SERVANTS	OTHER SERVICE WORKERS	TOTAL
1899	number	33,163	165,202	11,180	10,660	15,950	11,778	19,061	44,453	4,278	315,725
	percentage	10.5%	52.6%	3.5%	3.4%	5.1%	3.7%	6.0%	14.1%	1.4%	100.0%
1920	number	39,189	205,465	19,755	20,110	19,112	47,761	15,675	35,924	5,937	408,928
	percentage	9.6%	50.3%	4.8%	4.9%	4.7%	11.7%	3.8%	8.8%	1.5%	100.0%
change	number	6,026	40,263	8,575	9,450	3,162	35,983	-3,386	-8,529	1,659	
1899–1920	percentage	18.2%	24.4%	75.9%	88.5%	19.8%	305.8%	-17.8%	-19.2%	38.8%	
1930	number	51,657	210,172	31,997	31,971	22,430	87,204	17,011	39,754	11,715	503,910
	percentage	10.3%	41.7%	6.4%	6.3%	4.5%	17.3%	3.4%	7.9%	2.3%	100.0%
change	number	12,468	4,707	12,242	11,861	3,318	39,443	1,336	3,830	5,778	
1920–1930	percentage	31.8%	2.3%	62.0%	59.0%	17.4%	82.6%	8.5%	10.7%	97.3%	

1940*	number	47,761	178,304	39,677	41,539	27,550	91,651	26,274	39,335	18,507	510,598
	percentage	9.4%	35.0%	7.8%	8.1%	5.4%	18.0%	5.1%	7.7%	3.6%	100.0%
change	number	-3,896	-31,868	7,680	9,568	5,120	4,447	9,263	-419	6,792	
1930–1940	percentage	-7.5%	-15.2%	24.0%	29.9%	22.8%	5.1%	54.5%	-1.1%	58.1%	
1950*	number	36,230	173,219	60,079	56,664	42,187	92,644	31,160	32,649	29,859	554,691
	percentage	6.5%	31.3%	10.8%	10.2%	7.6%	16.7%	5.6%	5.9%	5.4%	100.0%
change	number	-11,531	-5,085	20,402	15,125	14,637	993	4,886	-6,686	11,352	
1940–1950	percentage	-24.2%	-2.9%	51.4%	36.4%	53.1%	1.1%	18.6%	-17.0%	61.3%	
change	number	3,067	8,017	48,899	46,004	26,237	80,866	12,099	-11,804	25,581	
1899–1950	percentage	9.3%	4.9%	437.4%	431.6%	164.5%	686.8%	63.5%	-26.6%	598.1%	

*Refers to laboring population 14 years of age or older

SOURCE: José Vázquez Calzada, *La población de Puerto Rico* (Río Piedras: Centro Multidisciplinario de Estudios Poblacionales, 1978), 374–375.

Table 2 Employment by Economic Sector in Puerto Rico, Selected Years, Both Sexes, 10 Years of Age or Older

		AGRICULTURE	MANUFACTURE, MINING; CONSTRUCTION AND OTHER PUBLIC UTILITIES	PROFESSIONAL SERVICES; COMMERCE AND TRADE	DOMESTIC AND PERSONAL SERVICES; OTHER SERVICES	PUBLIC ADMINISTRATION	TOTAL
1899	number	198,791	32,643	20,129	62,289	2,513	316,365
	percentage	62.9%	10.3%	6.2%	19.2%	0.8%	100.0%
1910	number	240,845	62,280	29,854	57,584	3,585	384,148
	percentage	62.5%	15.9%	7.6%	13.9%	0.9%	100.0%
change	number	42,054	29,637	9,725	-4,705	1,072	
1899–1910	percentage	21.2%	90.9%	48.3%	-7.6%	42.7%	
1920	number	245,284	81,781	32,526	44,894	4,443	408,928
	percentage	60.0%	20.0%	8.0%	9.7%	1.1%	100.0%
change	number	4,439	19,501	2,672	-12,690	858	
1910–1920	percentage	1.8%	31.3%	9.0%	-22.0%	23.9%	
1930	number	263,577	128,820	52,657	51,699	7,052	503,805
	percentage	52.6%	25.6%	10.5%	9.6%	1.4%	100.0%
change	number	18,293	47,039	20,131	6,805	2,609	
1920–1930	percentage	7.5%	57.5%	61.9%	15.2%	58.8%	

1940*	number	229,926	138,009	69,858	58,251	8,824	504,868
	percentage	45.5%	27.3%	13.8%	11.5%	1.7%	100.0%
change 1930–1940	number	-33,651	9,189	17,201	6,552	1,772	
	percentage	-12.8%	7.1%	32.7%	12.7%	25.1%	
1950*	number	215,998	152,142	102,261	57,750	24,642	552,793
	percentage	39.1%	27.5%	18.5%	10.4%	4.5%	100.0%
change 1940–1950	number	-13,928	14,133	32,403	-501	15,818	
	percentage	-6.1%	10.2%	46.4%	-0.9%	179.2%	
change 1899–1950	number	17,207	119,499	82,132	-4,539	22,129	
	percentage	8.7%	366.3%	408.2%	-7.3%	880.6%	

* Refers to laboring population 14 years of age or older.

SOURCE: José Vázquez Calzada, *La población de Puerto Rico* (Río Piedras: Centro Multidisciplinario de Estudios Poblacionales, 1978), 376–377.

Despite the relatively rapid incorporation of Puerto Rico into the internal circuits of U.S. metropolitan production and circulation at this time, a large part of the more autonomous features of the preexisting social structure and its corresponding cultural linkages were, to a great extent, left intact. This in part had to do with one of the compensatory and secondary tendencies akin to monopoly capitalist expansion on a world scale during this period: the objective inclination to append and/or reconstitute as subordinate articulations some of these noncapitalist forms, both socioeconomic and cultural.[47] But it also had to do with the multiple and contradictory resistances that many of these forms—or, rather, their corresponding human social bearers—have historically displayed towards being destroyed or even encroached upon or restrained by advancing capitalist production and its necessary conditions of existence, notably the wage-labor market. In other parts of the world, this took shape among those forms and bearers of "plebeian" origin.[48]

In Puerto Rico, the preexistent sociocultural patterns had an extremely long history. The structural matrix that forged most of the "native" population during most of the past four centuries was that of a free and independent peasantry. Between the sixteenth and eighteenth centuries, these direct producers had practiced mainly subsistence agriculture and smuggling. As in other peasant- and/or artisan-based, noncapitalist societies throughout history, such survival practices were inscribed within deeply ingrained family/patriarchical hierarchies that were also intertwined, in contradictory yet complementary ways, with loosely communal and cooperative neighborhood networks. Before 1898, the various nationalities that occupied the Island (originally, by subsequent arrival, and/or in captivity) had originated in both sides of the Atlantic, in this last case immediately to the North and South of the Mediterranean and of the Sahara. These nationalities, subjected to the several colonial forms of exploitation prevalent in nineteenth-century Puerto Rico, were peoples that primarily emerged from different modalities of a basically similar socioeconomic bedrock: isolated and dispersed communities of small subsistence farmers and artisans. The noncapitalist servitudes that developed in Puerto Rico during the nineteenth century conflictively built upon these free-peasant, free-artisan, and smuggler foundations as much as was then possible, evidently wreaking more havoc in the case of chattel bondage. But the original socioeconomic and cultural armatures of the population, unevenly emerging as "native," were strong enough to outlive the once relatively dominant noncapitalist land-tenure systems based on servile labor and slave-holding relations. While undergoing transformations, these sociocultural forms were also strong enough to last into the mid-twentieth century.[49]

Between 1898 and 1947, the materialization of these socioeconomic and cultural forms involved the contradictory persistence of several outstanding components. Probably the most important configurations in this regard were the imbricated structures of (a) the family, (b) ritual kinship (*compadrazgo*), and (c) neighborhood mutual-aid and labor-exchange customs. These structures greatly mediated the way that subjects (individual or group-family) performed a number of vital functions: securing their livelihood and distributing use values; locating themselves within or outside of housework; arranging for health care and the upbringing of children; exchanging affection; practicing biological reproduction; taking part in recreation; positioning themselves within a community-based social-control network; instituting religious/supernatural practices; and generating other meanings that made sense of all of these practices. Most of these functions tended to result in imbricated combinations of firmly entrenched patriarchical modes of subjectification with nonclass or anticlass communal solidarities and identity formation mechanisms on an everyday basis.[50] Such functions irregularly cut through the different mechanisms deployed by the emergent and preexistent, great-propertied classes to subordinate the laboring-poor majorities in Puerto Rico. Despite their widespread currency throughout the Island, these patterns tended to materialize within communities that were extremely isolated from each other.[51]

As historically occurred during the transition to capitalism in Europe and the rest of Latin America, the accumulation of capital in Puerto Rico necessarily and simultaneously partially involved establishing a separation between the "native" direct producers and their conditions of subsistence. As far as the majority of the local population was concerned, however, this economic rupture did not materialize in a definitive and comprehensive manner. Such were the conditions under which this sociocultural framework persisted. Throughout much of the 1898–1947 period, the relations of production that predominated within agriculture—which is where most of the Island's laboring population was located—consisted of a rather complex, asymmetric, and incredibly diverse combination of noncapitalist sharecropping, transitional wages-in-kind, and some *strictu sensu* capitalist wage-work.[52] Consequently, the majority of the colonized population during this period were unevenly stratified as poor peasants. Within such a context, these destitute rural laborers found themselves caught up in various forms of direct and/or indirect labor contracts and rents with the large landowners (in this case, mostly Creole). Since several different labor stipulations could entangle the same peasants,[53] the socioeconomic boundaries of these working arrangements became considerably blurred.

Taken as a whole, then, these "native" direct producers increasingly became separated from legal ownership over the land they worked on. Nevertheless, they often still had effective possession and/or use of relatively small tracts of land, mainly for subsistence purposes. These tracts of land were generally too diminutive in size and poor in quality to allow for an adequate—much less buoyant—standard of living. Therefore, this limitation, along with the seasonal character of rural labor, led growing numbers of these poor peasants to pursue several complementary subsistence strategies. A number of these survival practices were located within the legal wage market: temporary work in the docks, carrying out needle-products manufacture/wage-labor at home, and/or migrating internally from one crop's cultivation period (such as tobacco and coffee) to another crop's cultivation period (for example, sugarcane). All of this attests to the ever spreading socioeconomic precariousness and mobility of much of the Island's population at this time.[54]

But these forms of economic survival have historically had contradictory results within the transition to capitalism, the micro land plots being a case in point. As studies of other localities have shown, the existence of diminutive plots of land (for subsistence purposes) has tended to serve one of two functions—from the perspective of the large property owners. It has either contributed towards the reproduction of a very cheap source of labor,[55] or it has permitted property owners who lack sufficient liquid capital to subordinate the semiproletarianized labor force.[56] In the large sugar plantations in Puerto Rico at this time, for instance, the situation was more akin to the former case than to the latter. A major conceptual problem immediately arises, however, when one reduces the effects of having such land plots to the manner that this phenomena influenced the large property owners. This reductionism disregards completely the uses (socioeconomic and cultural) that the impoverished peasantry themselves may have made of these land plots. Much of the literature on Puerto Rico regarding the existence of micro land plots, vis-à-vis the existing means of peasant subsistence/survival, has addressed the issue unilaterally: from only the perspective of great-propertied class interests (Creole and North American).[57] Yet a much more enigmatic and contradictory phenomenon requires explanation: namely, the uses—both socioeconomic and cultural—that the impoverished peasantry may have made of this land.

In Puerto Rico, these economically sustaining practices had several repercussions, the latter being counterproductive from the point of view of capital and the State (on both local and federal levels). The very existence of these land plots, for instance, was one of the factors that tended to continually block all but the most formal, intermittent, and haphazard connections between this peasant mass and the wage-labor market. This ultimate barrier was inseparable from the—legal, extralegal, and illegal—corollary subsistence practices that this unevenly dispossessed "native" mass had created.

Rift and Continuity Between the Laboring Classes of Town and Country

During the 1898–1947 period, most of the Puerto Rican population had been *legally* separated from the land. But agriculture continued as the chief condition of social existence at this time because the land became *effectively* alienated only from a reduced number of the Island's population, most of which ended up as the laboring poor in the shanty towns. Their indigent living quarters surfaced in the small urban centers of rural municipalities and in the outskirts of the few large cities. A modest but growing portion of the coastal workforce (living near or within the sugarcane plantations) was also actively separated from the land. This condition among the sugarcane labor force merged in varying degrees with the situation of the rural direct producers. Numerically speaking, these coastal laborers constituted a noteworthy segment of the colonized wage workers involved in manufacturing, mining, construction, transportation, as well as in other public utilities. During the first half of this century, the laborers belonging to these sectors increased their proportions by 366.3 percent (see table 1). A glance at the occupational distribution of the colonized labor force will reveal a noticeable accretion in the corresponding niches that, as a rule, were then being filled by the urban laboring poor (see table 2).

The original socioeconomic nucleus in this respect was made up of the artisan pockets left over from the nineteenth century. From very early on, popular national culture in the towns and cities bore the mark of these craft workers. This was especially true of those former slaves and/or members of the "free people of color" living at the turn of the century in the coast, urbanized or not. For example, U.S. Special Commissioner Henry K. Carroll noted in his 1899 report that among the artisans of San Juan he interviewed, "[n]ine of the eleven were colored men, who seem to monopolize the trades, at least in the capital."[58] These "native" artisans became increasingly dispossessed with the advent of capitalist manufacture in the urban areas located in the mountainous interior and in the coastal zones. There, such artisans constituted an alternate core of everyday meanings and ways of living, in many ways counterpoised to the predominant cultural configuration of the Creole propertied classes and more educated strata. These black and mulatto artisans became a parallel ingredient of the burgeoning, urban "native" culture as a whole.[59]

According to the U.S. Bureau of the Census, the demographic group that many of these artisans and urban/coastal laborers belonged to shrunk in size as a distinct sector, particularly during the Great Depression and the Second World War.[60] It appears that this sector fused together with the incoming colonized population of peasant background, the latter being of both white and mulatto "native" background. In part, this seems due to the further decay of coffee production, the long-term decline of tobacco prices, and the eventual reduction and mechanization of the sugar plantations.

Admittedly, the urban-laboring poor in Puerto Rico were much more dependent on the wage system than their rural counterparts. The everyday lives of these urban workers were also considerably more intersected by goods originating within the capitalist market. Such a convergence resulted from the severed ties between these laborers and the land, a forced process for the most part. Nonetheless, as a group they did not constitute a relatively stable bloc of wage-earners within the manufacturing sector. Far from it: broad sectors of the urban-laboring poor were generally marked by widespread unemployment and underemployment, specifically by a growing involvement in underground economic activities.[61]

Despite their separation from the land, the material reality of the urban nucleus of the dispossessed "natives" indeed resembled the sociocultural conditions of the rural poor at several levels. For one thing, a number of the originally peasant-based, blood-related, and ritual-kin linkages and cultural patterns were still present among the urban-laboring poor. This is one of the reasons why, in diverse and contradictory ways, migration to the urban centers was not a complete and irreversible break with the peasant background of most of the Island's population. In most cases, many features of these rural sociocultural structures were conflictively transposed, adapted, or reconstituted within a qualitatively different spatial setting: one in which access to a tract of land did not represent the focus of everyday life. As Eric Wolf has observed in "San José: Subculture of a 'Traditional' Coffee Municipality," new ritual and neighborhood connections were redrawn or reborn (both, kin and immediate), while ties with the old rural ones were maintained—within certain limits and to varying degrees (p. 232).

Together with the existing patriarchical and family hierarchies, these reconstituted/transformed networks were instrumental in mediating and structuring the meanings regarding the various components of social life. These included the ways in which each person and family group: procured earnings; disseminated use values; positioned themselves with respect to housework; attended to matters of health; raised children; participated in recreation; circulated affection; accomplished biological reproduction; performed religious/supernatural practices; and located themselves within an informal web of community-based social regulation.[62]True, to a larger extent than in the countryside, these patterns bore the imprint of the capitalist-market and class polarization.[63] The social subjects fashioned in this manner were also more affected by the tendency towards greater spatial and social mobility that characterized urban areas. Yet the intersection between these sociocultural patterns and the earmarks of the town/city environment only conditioned the measure in which this adaptation took place. These new conditions did not in any way wipe clean the slate on which the originally noncapitalist/rural patterns were indited.[64]

The Contradictory Structuring of Race and Class within the "Native" Impoverished Majorities

This racial, class, and geographic heterogeneity was enacted in different ways and fashioned through different distancing mechanisms as the laboring classes intersected each other at a mass level. As we will see in the forthcoming chapters, these elements were present in the way the subaltern subjects of colonialism, capitalism, and the criminal justice system were structured in Puerto Rico during the 1898–1947 period. Race, class, and geography also intersected the construction of the subjects of social identity and of historical change at this time in the Island, determining the ways in which these subjectivities were lived, represented, and contested.

Two major sign systems emerged, positioning the coastal/town laborers against the rural laborers and vice versa. The contradictions that arose as a result of this confrontation, in turn, set limits on the degree to which the peasant majority and the urban-laboring poor established sociocultural linkages between each other. The complications involved appear to respond, among other things, to the contradictory and layered amalgamation occurring within the colonized dispossessed sectors as a whole. This diachronic process was significantly affected and informed by three factors: (1) the incipient but growing demographic displacements that were taking place as a result of the mentioned socioeconomic changes; (2) the respective and nineteenth-century class lineages of the various sectors of the laboring classes; and (3) the narratives of social subordination related to "the [disreputable] primitive" (the "savage" whose nature these discourses encoded as an instance of class debasement or of racial degradation). These ideologies emanated from the different fractions of the Creole propertied and educated classes.

A number of the nineteenth-century cultural mappings, together with their respective socioeconomic foundations (particularly the incidence of slavery), still weighed heavily on the "native" laboring classes during the first half of the twentieth century. Although found even in the coffee- and tobacco-producing interior, the bastion of slave relations of exploitation in Puerto Rico was the sugarcane-producing coast.[65] The sociocultural impact of slavery was considerable because it tended to solidify the growing demarcation between the laboring population of the coast and most of the people that worked and resided in the mountainous interior. This textual universe made the coastal laborers understandable primarily as slaves and/or kindred to slaves (including large numbers of urban artisans), while the rural laborers became discursively constituted as peasants (free or bound) and/or as their relatives and descendants.[66]

Two additional factors reinforced the boundaries of culture and nationality that defined the laboring classes in the Island between 1788 and 1898. One was the fact that, even as late as the 1830s, the majority of the captives had been born in Africa.[67] The other was that knowledge of the Island's lingua franca (Spanish) was also not common among the Afro-Caribbean sugarcane cutters from the British West Indies that migrated to work in the Eastern and Southern coasts of Puerto Rico, later settling there during the second half of the nineteenth century.[68] The racialization of these topographic and class boundaries was not as coherent nor as tidy as the post–1940s Puerto Rican historiography has legendarily assumed. The latter tended to imagine a "white" peasantry majority nostalgically representative of Puerto Rican national-culture vs. a handful of "dark" coastal laborers who were *in* but *not of* the Island.[69] On the contrary, important segments of this mountainous peasantry were of mixed African and Iberian heritage, harking back to the period between the sixteenth and late-eighteenth centuries when runaway slaves (of both sexes) settled and intermingled with fugitive galley prisoners and former soldiers of various backgrounds and with the remnants of the indigenous population.

Nevertheless, the original cultural-national differences that signified the existent class divisions within the laboring population in Puerto Rico became the formal axis of a number of clashes among the Island's "natives." For example, the less-educated and landless peasants who migrated to the urban areas and coastal zones in search of sources of income would immediately confront these same artisans of color, just falling prey to a process of uneven dispossession. Within the parameters of this conflict over jobs, income, housing, and sociocultural space, the black and mulatto artisans could appeal to their still limited but nevertheless higher levels of education; the white and lighter-skinned mulatto peasants could only appeal to not being black. These initial cultural and national divergences also contributed decisively to the disputed, episodic, and discontinuous sedimentation of a common national base among the Island's population during the twentieth century: it too was a " . . . product of the historical process to date which has deposited . . . [within the laboring classes] an infinity of traces without leaving an inventory."[70]

U.S. personnel had varying understandings about the racial configuration of the "native" population, particularly the mountainous peasantry. Leo S. Rowe's report, for example, tends to characterize this peasantry as overwhelmingly white. Rowe found it an "interesting fact" that "the racial composition of the Porto Rican [*sic*] colored population" registered a "surprisingly small percentage of persons of pure negro blood . . . "[71] According to Rowe, a "casual visitor"—presumably a U.S. colonizer—would find that "the colored element in Porto Rico [*sic*] seems to be a far more important factor in the ethnic composition of the population than is actually the case." The explanation behind this illusion lies in "the tendency of the negroes to congregate in coast towns," a mistaken impression that dissapears when "one penetrates into the interior" where "the preponderance of whites becomes evident" (ibid.).

However, Brigadier General George W. Davis, one of the colonial Governors of Puerto Rico, stated that "[b]etween the negro and the peon there is no visible difference."[72] Davis found it difficult to "believe that the pale, sallow, and often emaciated beings" were indeed "the descendants of the conquistadores who carried the flag of Spain to nearly all of South America, and to one-third of North America" (ibid.). As was often the case, propertied and educated classes (Creole and North American) usually attributed such degeneration to the extensive racial mixing within the "native" population as a whole.[73]

After the U.S. invasion and however contradictorily, the mostly white and mulatto peasantry tended to continue appropriating the anti-artisan, anti-urban, and anti-coastal narratives of the large landowners. These ideological representations were partially based on the subordinate *racial* identification of the laboring poor of the towns, the cities, and/or the coast. This last sector of the laboring classes actually was, or appeared to be, descendant from a preexistent laboring class whose members were sold as chattel: the African slaves. In this manner, the boundaries that specified the everyday meanings of "family," "community," and "nationality" for much of the peasant population in part relied on—and were therefore limited by—a distinct textual mechanism. Such sign systems contributed decisively to socially inscribing the Island's nonwhites as being the ones that had a "race," leaving Creole whites to represent the (non-raced) universal standard within generic national culture in Puerto Rico.

This way of racializing the perceived (degenerate) class ancestry of the laboring-poor "strangers" situated these urban/coastal dwellers outside of the peasant-defined frontiers of kin, neighborhood/vicinity, and country–nation. For example, during the 1898–1947 period, sharecroppers, poor farmers, and landless peasants closed ranks on a micro-cultural scope with hacienda owners against the alleged "insensibility" and "lack of hospitality" of townspeople as a whole, a signifying practice that blended right in with the witchcraft and alien customs many in the countryside claimed were prevalent among the darker-skinned people of the coastal regions.[74]

On the other hand, the laboring-poor population of the towns, the cities, and/or the coast were also inclined to appropriate the anti-peasant narratives of the urban[e] professionals, merchants, bankers, manufacturers, bureaucrats, etc. This textual bridge was usually based on the subaltern *class* identification of the laboring poor of the mountains and fields. This country population actually was, or seemed to be, the offspring of allegedly witless peasants. In this case, the etiology of the term historically synonymous with "peasant" (*jíbaro*) becomes suggestive. As Stan Steiner has observed, the expression harks back to the popular resistances against the "civilizing mission" of the Spanish colonization:

> In adopting the name of *jíbaro*, the Spaniards used it to describe the Indians, and later the mestizos and the Blacks

> who escaped to the mountains, fleeing servitude, Don Pedro said. Later, it came to identify the *criollos* [Creoles] or Puertorriqueños in the rural zones "who kept the rustic way of life and who were free of assimilation."[75]

The very term itself and, consequently, the laboring population so defined, became signifiers for "savagery" and "primitivism." Creole and Spanish philologists, historians, and social philosophers could not agree on the exact origins of a term that, in any case, had no "civilized" (therefore, no reputable) genesis. This merely served to further enshroud the sociocultural and class terrain thus inscribed in an enigmatic veil: from the perspective of the population in the towns, cities, and coast, the *jíbaro* was, accordingly, strangeness and unruly conduct itself. According to Steiner,

> In the *Nuevo Diccionario Velázquez* the word "jíbaro" is said to be of Cuban Indian origin, meaning to "run wild." The historian Coll y Toste, in his *Prehistoria de Puerto Rico,* doubts this: "Our provincial word jíbaro [derived] from the root *jiba* [native bush]," he writes, and was "indigenous"; although he notes that in Cuba it was used to "designate a wild dog." And the historian Salvador Brau, in his *Historia de Puerto Rico,* writes that the Spaniards used the word fearfully to describe "the country folk of Puerto Rico," because of "their rough and wild habits." He too insists the word was of Indian origin. There is no Spanish equivalent for *jíbaro.* (pp. 93–94)

These urban ideological mechanisms often informed the way that the better-educated[76] laboring population of the towns, cities, and/or coastal areas fashioned the meanings associated with being included within or excluded from a family, a community, and a nationality. In Wolf's ethnology, for example, one finds that urban laborers and/or residents of the coastal districts at times ridiculed all rural people, particularly country laborers, collectively perceiving them as ignorant hicks (pp. 232, 258). Such discourses were in part grounded on the class inscription of those that were perceived within the towns and cities as being the epitome of ignorance, bizarre behavior, and ingratitude: the thus debased peasantry.[77]

The impoverished "native" majorities were not only the authors of these contradictory cultural mappings; most of the Island's population was simultaneously being constituted through this cartography of signs. As we have seen, however, the process that inscribed the colonized laboring classes was materializing on a much larger socioeconomic and political canvas: the colonial-capitalist dispossession process. How did such a dispossession process become the blind author of its own conditions of existence on an Island-wide scale? How did the mechanisms of dispossession get a grip on such an elusive laboring population? Finally, what was the laboring population's answer to this process and how did the colonialist enterprise respond to, as well as anticipate, this "native" reply? These are the broader socioeconomic relations and forms of subjectivity to which I will now turn.

3

The Contradictory Mechanisms of Preservation and Transformation

We have not come to make war upon the people of a country that for centuries have been oppressed, but on the contrary, to bring protection, not only to yourselves, but to your property, to promote prosperity and bestow upon you the immunities and blessings of the liberal institutions of our government.

—Major General Nelson Miles,
"The War with Spain" (1899)

Those were bleak and unhappy times. Times of desperation and of uncertainty. I remember—and I still feel the sadness—the time in which my mother made a "malanga" [a tuber] stew, because there wasn't anything else to eat that day. This happened during the earthquake of 1918. I was only six years old . . .

—Andino Acevedo González,
***¡Qué tiempos aquellos!* (1989)**[1]

. . . Ethnology has introduced law and order into what seemed chaotic and freakish. It has transformed for us the sensational, wild and unaccountable world of "savages" into a number of well ordered communities, governed by law, behaving and thinking according to consistent principles.

—Bronislaw Malinowski,
***Argonauts of the Western Pacific* (1950)**

The economic changes originated by the U.S. invasion did not automatically generate their own structural foundations—either socially or textually. Seizing the Island was one thing; establishing the capitalist exploitation of cheap raw materials and low-wage colonized labor was an entirely different story. Capturing Puerto Rico did not equal capturing its laboring population. Juridically constituting the subaltern subjects of U.S. colonialism did not automatically create the subaltern subjects of U.S. capitalism in the Island because capital and colonialism are not things but social relations that require the construction of two pairs of opposed social subjects that embody these relations.[2] Peasants, artisans, and other direct producers and consumers all had to be trained "to renounce their desultory habits of work"[3] and to discover the virtues of working for somebody else in exchange for a wage. In Puerto Rico, these common men, women, and children had to be willing to do this under circumstances structurally worse than anything their North American counterparts experienced in that same period. Emerging conditions required the creation or realignment of signifying practices in order to explain as natural and legitimate the socioeconomic and national-cultural/racial inferiority of these "natives."

As Dario Melossi has argued in a more general way, "To train a horse you must first capture it. Perhaps, if it cannot find food anywhere else it will finally settle down to the training. However, it is a long and painful process."[4] This chapter explores just such "a long and painful process," together with its conflictive semiotic configurations: the textuality of the economy and of disorder versus the economy and disorder of textualities; social relations and antagonistic subjectivities. The process of capture expressed the complementary, brutal, yet indispensable mechanisms that made possible the rise of colonialist capitalism in Puerto Rico by fashioning a "native" population into beasts (of burden), workhorses: yet horses that in various ways could never be entirely broken.

The Economic Logic of "A Long and Painful Process"

In Puerto Rico, capital and the new colonial extension of the U.S. State deployed a particular set of methods to further its economic hold and to obtain control over the organizational foundations of its own production during the first half of this century, particularly between 1898 and 1921. Once again, I have carried out the analysis of the capitalist projects of exploitation encountered by the laboring poor of town and country according to what Stuart

Hall termed the coupling of "social relations, production, and the 'hard edge' of production systems" with "the 'insides' of people, . . . subjectivity and sexuality."[5] Such an effort requires that we first examine the structural logic of these social relations.

The "native" laboring classes experienced these socioeconomic methods as inordinately brutal and excruciating insofar as this working population suffered the notably exorbitant corresponding social costs. Chiefly field-based, such projects soon became grounded in the putting-out system, and/or became incipiently situated within factories. In this undertaking, the constitution of an adequate labor force towered as a problem from the very beginning. This difficulty partially surfaced because the capital that arrived in Puerto Rico did not find as a given the organizational foundations of its reproduction and regulation; neither did it initially control the available organizational foundations. In a different context, Jean-Paul de Gaudemar explains that the first capitalists who introduced the wage-based collective production of surplus value " . . . reproduced within the factory a discipline inspired by the existing social models: with all probability, the family and the army. These two models sometimes coexisted within the same enterprise. These were built upon a direct, even physical, relation of domination."[6]

This type of predicament, faced by the initiators of capitalism on an Island-wide scale, became directly related to a demarcation described by Steven Spitzer in broader terms: the difference between extractive and extensive forms of labor-force exploitation and regulation and those that were intensive. According to Spitzer, the extractive economies " . . . were socially extractive in the sense that the economic value of the masses was defined almost completely in terms of the level of surplus-product that could be pumped out of the working class under the existing conditions of social and economic organization."

The quality of life and the basic working conditions of these laborers were irrelevant: capital assumed that the productive output of the laboring population was limited by the low-skill levels and demeaned bodies of the workers inserted within this labor process. Spitzer has suggested that the ways that these populations became regulated and productively utilized, however, were extensive mainly because the material wealth created and the available labor power treated both as fixed measures, capable of being augmented only by increasing the extent of labor, land, raw materials, and other resources available to the ruling classes. On the other hand, Spitzer characterized intensive production as

> . . . economic rationalization, which came to depend in turn on both the regularization of the social context which surrounds and conditions all economic activity on the one hand, and the cultivation and investments in *human capital* on the other. These developments created enormous pressure on traditional institutions and policies of social regulation. And despite its claims to be based on principles of *laissez-faire*, as capitalism sought to free itself from the fetters and limitations of feudal society it was forced to tighten rather than loosen its grip on the everyday lives of domestic populations.[7]

To some extent, Puerto Rico between 1898 and 1947 (particularly during the 1898–1921 period) comprises an amalgam of both the extractive-extensive and intensive methods, albeit the first tended to predominate over the second.

None of this requires necessarily interpreting such a process as the product of a conscious and deliberate imperialist plan.[8] It thus becomes possible to locate many of the related compensatory measures within this context, specifically in the case of the accomplishments of the colonialist regime (Island-based and federal) or the deeds carried out under private North American auspices to cushion the more devastating consequences of the dispossession methods and social discipline that unfolded during the first forty-nine years of U.S. domination. Such compensatory measures did not just surface as the effects of colonialist paternalism, refined condescension, Progressive Era reformism, and/or missionary philanthropy. These measures were also inscribed within the general, structural logic of the methods of dispossession themselves.

By counterbalancing the blind yet organized ruthlessness that socioeconomically re-positioned the colonized laborers as having to work for somebody else in exchange for a wage, these compensatory measures textually repositioned the structural brutality as a natural misfortune, a fact of life, something in need of personal conquest through individual hard work and sacrifice, etc. This, in turn, had two related discursive effects: it verified the colonizers themselves as the protective agents of such enlightened benevolence, at the same time collectively constructing the "native" majorities as needy children and dependent females. Such measures offset some of the worst excesses of the dispossession process itself without necessarily altering its general course. In light of Spitzer's general observations these compensatory measures become part of what he apparently meant by the "regularization of the social context that surrounds and conditions all economic activity" insofar as they too "created enormous pressure on traditional institutions and policies of social regulation."

One of the fundamental manifestations of the dispossession process' structural brutality and one of its principal technologies of power was the generalized malnutrition and the bouts of starvation that prevailed at this time. The separation of the direct producers from their conditions of existence and the construction of the subaltern subjects of capitalist labor were two processes that unfolded in extremely irregular and haphazard ways. But in the end such inconsistency and randomness hardly blocked the starvation and malnutrition that, with increasing frequency, materialized as everyday features among the colonized laboring classes in general and among the poor peasant majority in particular. Both hunger and undernourishment persistently visited most of the Puerto Rican population during this first half-century: as an imminent threat, as an irregularly prolonged borderline situation, and/or as a sudden calamity.

The descriptions that follow, detailing the devastating results of one of the dispossession process' principal mechanisms, are not meant to evoke a social-realist—and retroactive—sympathy for wretched individuals: the conceptual framework of this study does not hark back to the work of Charles Dickens, Emile Zola, or Benito Pérez Galdós. To paraphrase Foucault once again, while going beyond the latter's Eurocentrism, the colonized individuals described here (whom an Enlightenment-Age rationalism invites us to set free as metahistorical Subjects of History), are in themselves the effect of a subjection much more profound than themselves. A social identity inhabits them and brings them into existence as colonized subjects, "which is itself a factor in the mastery that power exercises over the body":[9] the colonial-capitalist power that produces the scarred body of the subaltern subjects. These are the telltale signs of a text—both the written (though misrecognized) record and the lived text of the dispossession process—that was read on the emaciated bodies of the colonized majorities. In this sense, the following descriptions intend to contribute to the inventory of an infinity of traces left behind by the hunger (structurally derived from colonial-capitalism) that marked the bodies of the subaltern subjects during this period. Yet this is a critical inventory, not only aimed at rethinking the socioeconomic and political changes that both structured and were enabled by this widespread hunger. This inventory also intends to critically re-examine the dominant knowledges of the day, the colonialist regimes of truth that ultimately inscribed as natural such social devastation.

Granted, malnutrition and particularly starvation as social conditions also existed in the nineteenth century, but they were not commonplace features—at least not common enough to compel people to perform this type of surplus labor on a regular basis.[10] For instance, upon visiting the Island during the U.S. invasion, Alfred G. Robinson, one of a whole series of North American travellers and/or entrepreneurs who visited the new Caribbean possession in 1898–1899 to survey the Island's economic potential, observed that the "tones of the mandate which implies man's starvation if he will not work were but feebly heard in Porto Rico [*sic*]," this being a place where "nature weakens the force of even so much of it as may be heard, by a lavish bounty which reduces the necessity for work to its minimum."[11] Another of these colonialist agents of economic tourism, Robert T. Hill, simultaneously reached very similar conclusions.[12]

Robert E. Pattison explained on his 1900 trip to Puerto Rico why he thought that generalized starvation did not seem (as several federal authorities thought) related to the colossal hurricane that flogged the Island in 1899. In a *New York Journal* article significantly titled "Robert E. Pattison Describes How Imperialism Has Made of Porto Rico a Land of Horror," the ex-Governor of Pennsylvania declared that the hurricane "occurred a year and a two months ago" and that this was "a period long enough in a country of such fertility to have entirely eradicated the traces of disaster."[13] Pattison understood that "[t]hey had cyclones in Porto Rico [*sic*] before American occupation was dreamed of" and in spite of this, "even during the halting, laggard, lazy government of Spain, the country rose from its ruins in less time and prospered again" (ibid.).

For Pattison, the difference marked by the 1898 juncture was not atmospheric but political: the "land is as fertile as ever, the elements of recuperation are unchanged." Now "the only difference [was] that American misrule ha[d] been substituted for Spanish despotism, and yet the people are dying of hunger by the hundreds . . ." (ibid.).

All of this appears to indicate that the mentioned hardships became much more acute immediately afterwards. For the most part, this seemed due to the direct and indirect effects of the massive socioeconomic disruption created by the U.S. invasion, as well as to the inroads made by the advancing capitalist dispossession process. And this ensued despite the good intentions and wishful thinking of liberal colonizer-reformers (as illustrated by the case of Azel Ames). The U.S. invasion literally ushered in the age of having to perform labor for somebody else in Puerto Rico for structural reasons of economic need. During the first decades of the U.S. colonization, these conditions only appeared unevenly and haphazardly. Nevertheless, the crushing conditions that promoted this social requirement among the laboring-poor "natives" indicated a qualitative difference with respect to the nineteenth century.

"The Swarming Armies of the Starving" During 1898–1921

Increasingly, death from hunger was just a crop failure away. And the already precarious situation of a peasant family or of an urban/coastal-laborer household could—now, with greater frequency—instantly appear as threatening: with the coming of a strong hurricane, with a change of heart on the part of the large landowner, with sudden mounting debts in the company store or in the hacienda's "tienda de raya," with a jump in the price of imported rice or codfish, with an unexpected contraction in the official labor market, and so on. Undernourishment and, to some degree, famine, were very much present in the daily lives of most of the Island's population throughout the first half of this century.

At the turn of the century many reports circulated in some of the newspapers, making note of how hunger affected certain sectors of the "native" population in the Island.[14] For instance, in March of 1900 the Puerto Rican daily *La Democracia,* indicated that in the central-northern municipality of Morovis, "misery has reached such proportions that many peasants use the seed of the 'cadillo' [a local prickly bur-weed], toasting it and drinking it as if it were coffee."[15] According to Silvestrini, the newspaper had reports that a few days before, "at dawn, five hapless individuals were found starved to death" in Ponce, the Island's second largest city, located on the central-southern coast. She quotes this journal as stating: "We are not surprised. Throughout the streets and plazas one can find the swarming armies of the starving . . . " (ibid.).

The same newspaper, cited by Silvestrini, reported that by late April of the same year, "the existing misery [was] so great that all across the fields of Barros, Ciales, and Juana Díaz" adjacent municipalities located in the central mountain region and in the central-southern coast, respectively, "many families die[d] of hunger due to lack of work" (ibid.).

At the time, a number of U.S. journalists covered the same ground. In the same 1900 *New York Journal* article cited above, the authors found that "[i]t was a ghastly journey ex-Governor Pattison took through the famine districts of Porto Rico [*sic*] in his effort to learn the truth of our colonial experiment . . . " (p. 49). Pattison "saw the famished people crowding to the charity at Ponce and fainting before their hands could clutch the bits of food that meant another day's life to them" (ibid.).

These dismayed and reluctant colonizers journeyed throughout the mountainous interior (where most of the Island's population lived), confirming their worst fears concerning the U.S. invasion's social toll. According to Pattison and Michelson, these were "not alarmist figures" insofar as the numbers had been provided "by the United States military surgeon in Adjuntas, in the coffee district" of the central-western mountains, and because such figures "were borne out by the statistics of mortality for the district" (p. 52). More than two hundred "natives" were dying on a monthly basis, out of a municipal population of eighteen thousand—"the births [were] not one-tenth as many"—and "[n]early every death [was] directly or indirectly due to starvation" (ibid.).

Some of the North American personnel that went into the field in order to inspect the new Caribbean outpost, admitted that the local population went through serious hardships in the area of nutrition. According to Edward Berbusse, Brigadier General George W. Davis, in a February 26, 1900 letter to the Secretary of War, acknowledged that the pathetic physical condition of the "native" children being herded into the Island's public schools proved that " . . . the attendance would be meager and the result unsatisfactory. The anemic, half-starved and often naked children would not or could not attend. . . . their parents indifferent or unable to satisfy the natural cravings of hunger that the children had learned would but make them unhappy and discontented . . . " (p. 106). And one of the civilian observers who ventured into this remote portion of the newly expanded North American realm, U.S. Department of Labor researcher Azel Ames, admitted to being "painfully impressed, whether in the streets of city or town, or in the hill country," with a Caribbean version of Kurtz and Marlowe's "The horror! The horror!" Here were the countless "number of human wrecks, the many beggars, and the sunken-eyed, pallid, anemic men, women, and children," among which "[e]xtreme poverty, inanition, and decrepitude" abounded.[16]

Although this general situation seems to have relatively improved by the end of the first decade of U.S. colonization, living and everyday-life conditions worsened considerably during the second decade. News items, social-science reports, and memoirs depicting this all-too-familiar and grim reality persisted through the years spanning the European conflict as well as its immediate aftermath.

Before the First World War, for example, then Dean of the "University of Porto Rico" and U.S. rural sociologist, Fred K. Fleagle, after ten years of residence in the Island, felt authorized to issue the following explanation:

> There is also a close relationship between sickness and poverty, the average countryman in Porto Rico [*sic*] being only partly as efficient a worker as he should be, due to physical weakness caused by anemia or malaria. Poverty is closely related to degeneration and crime, especially when it descends into pauperism and absolute dependence upon charity.[17]

His avowed affection for the Island and its inhabitants (p. iv), of course, did not preclude the middle-class, North-American, reformist moralism and colonialist paternalism of his observations. Yet the fact that his research formed an integral part of the dominant knowledges creating and regulating "Porto Rican" reality did not prevent Fleagle from recording with pity the dismal food and health conditions of the "natives": "Malnutrition among children is frequent and leads to such diseases as rickets, which we find has an exceptionally high death rate" (p. 82). Such statements did not amount to "a criticism of Porto Rico or of the Porto Ricans" (p. iii). On the contrary, such observations verified the fact-based character—but not the factitiousness—of these social conditions: once again, he read these as natural misfortunes, facts of life, etc. The studies that discovered this natural reality, in turn, simply amounted to "an exposition of the social situation as it exists, and do not differ greatly, either in quality or character, from similar facts which could be gathered relating to any country" (pp. iii–iv).

The textual effects of such ideological constructions and the physical consequences of this aspect of the predominant structural brutality have subsisted in the recollections of countless members of the colonized labor force and their families. In a memoir written in his old age, former peasant Andino Acevedo González included this item: "There was a lot of hunger at the time. I remember with sorrow that my two sisters and my parents went through a really black [i.e., somber and dismal] period. And I say this because I too went through similar times; and if this happened to me, they had it even worse."[18]

The European War and its aftermath hardly improved matters in the Island. The colonial Governor at the time, Arthur Yager,[19] acknowledged in one of his annual reports to the federal government that the number of ships bringing food into the Island during 1918–1919 had been the lowest in a decade. Within this context, the inroads made by the dispossession process and its conditions of existence produced clearly disastrous results for the impoverished "native" majorities. According to Silvestrini, one local newspaper, *El Mundo*, reported in April of 1919 that "Beggars continue appealing ceaselessly to public charity in the streets of Ponce. A cloud of hungry people blankets the city despite the stipulations found in the Municipal Code" (p. 59). As had happened after the U.S. invasion, this situation worsened due to capricious atmospheric developments. For instance, another U.S. researcher and social reformist, Helen V. Bary, commented at this time that: "A storm in the western end of the island in 1921 brought thousands to the verge of starvation."[20]

"[North] American Prices" vs. "the Superabundance of His Numbers"

As some of these last quotes conclusively indicate, widespread hunger and malnutrition very much involved questions of chronically constrained income-gaining opportunities and the longitudinal rise in the cost of living.[21] Between 1898 and 1900, the U.S. military government initially froze all local credit and suddenly devalued the local currency, thus touching off a wave of speculative commercial/financial activities.[22] This translated into a sharp escalation in the prices of basic consumption items. Pattison—despite some rather quaint notions about monetary policy—said as much in his visit to the Island. First, he described the situation preceding the U.S. invasion by saying that the "rural population in the Island buys its supplies in small quantities," meaning that "a man in the Spanish time was accustomed to go to market with a 5-cent piece with which to make a day's purchases" (p. 52). This same man "would buy the leg of a foul, a spoonful of lard, one onion, etc.," his most useful coin being "the centavo, about equal in value to half a cent in our money" (ibid.).

Pattison then goes on to describe the consequences of the financial changes that took place under the new colonial administration. "We took his half cent and gave him nothing in return," for now there were "innumerable commodities he require[d], the price of which is always the smallest coin in circulation," hence by "doubling this unit of value we have practically cut the poor Porto Rican's [*sic*] money supply in two." "Native" merchants "have advanced their prices to fit the American standard but there has been no corresponding advance in wages," therefore a person who previously "got fifty cents Porto Rican [*sic*]—the average wages for a laborer in the interior— . . . now gets thirty to forty cents" (ibid.).

Soon afterward, the colonial Secretary of the Treasury, G.H. Hollander, introduced a fiscal reform bill in the local legislature that upon being ratified resulted in an increase in commercial and territorial property taxes.[23] This burden was passed on to the "native" masses as a further increase in the prices of basic goods. However, the income of these working classes did not rise commensurably. The data presented by Azel Ames corroborates this situation for 1901: eighty-three percent of the laboring occupations surveyed in rural areas and sixty-nine percent of the laboring occupations surveyed in the urban areas reported their after-income savings as "small" or "none" (pp. 400–407).

The rising land prices brought about by the Hollander Bill, the incorporation of the Island within the production circuits of the United States, and other measures affected the laboring classes in another way. A number of the large and medium-sized landowners decided to take advantage of this increase in land prices and sell their land. This resulted in the expulsion of the sharecroppers, tenant farmers, and other poor peasants living on the lands now being sold. Forty years later, the North American sociologist Raymond Crist in "Sugar Cane and Coffee in Puerto Rico: The Pauperization of the Jíbaro, Land Monopoly, and Monoculture," compared this eviction to the effects of the English Enclosure Acts:

> And the results in both cases were the same: the returns benefitted only a few, while the many, now landless and displaced, formed a great reservoir of cheap labor. In England, however, some of the landless proletariat gradually emigrated, some were slowly absorbed in the industrial revolution, but in Puerto Rico the process of uprooting the peasantry has been so rapid that chaotic conditions have inevitably resulted, and in consequence adjustments have been painful.[24]

The following decade saw some gains, particularly among the wage workers in the coastal zones and in the urban areas. Partially due to the advances made by the labor movement at this time, this relative improvement was far from permanent. With the coming of the European War, the income levels for laborers in town and country had deteriorated further to a considerable extent, even as the cost of living soared once more. According to the local Labor Bureau (*Negociado del Trabajo*), the Island's working conditions had deteriorated since 1913, "wage levels of almost all the occupations" dropping over the past year, "while the wages of the field workers"—"especially of those that work in the sugar plantations"—had been "reduced from ten to thirty percent."[25] "At the same time, the cost of living [was] just as high, if not higher, than it was last year. The prices of basic goods have increased in many of the regions in the Island" (ibid.).

The remaining years spanning the First World War further generalized this situation. The cost-of-living problem became compounded by several factors. This included: (a) a shrinkage of the official labor market; (b) the proliferation of speculative activities and usurious practices; and (c) the overall scarcity brought about by the limits that the War placed on a budding internal market increasingly dependent on the importation of basic goods.[26] At that time an editorial in a local mainstream daily acknowledged that the dramatic rise in prices had despairing effects on the laboring population.[27] Such conditions partially contextualize the exceptionally widespread and militant labor struggles that took place during World War I, as well as the numerous expressions of illegalized survival activities and other corollary social practices during these years.

These factors, in turn, overlapped with the large number of colonized laborers periodically seeking employment. The official labor market surfaced as only one of the several—but relatively limited—sources of income available between 1898 and 1921. I have not been able to determine with any degree of certainty the extent of this limitation when considering the Island as a whole given the extremely irregular character of the labor market itself. But the limited absorption capacity of the wage market additionally seemed due to the uneven nature of the process of capitalist accumulation that partially structured the sale of labor power. As other historical studies of Puerto Rico have found, general unemployment statistics for this period are imprecise.[28] Nonetheless, enough descriptions and scattered official records exist to allow for some reconstruction and approximation.[29]

One example of the unemployment situation at this time comes from the research of Berbusse who, in the third quarter of 1900, found that a "dramatic expression of public need occurred in August 14 when more than a hundred laboring men with their wives and children marched from San Lorenzo to the capital," a distance of about twenty to twenty-five miles, "with the purpose of seeking work" (p. 186). "They marched with the United States flag at their head directly to the executive mansion and asked for an audience with the acting governor" (ibid.).

Azel Ames confirmed this problem the following year when he reported that it was "beyond question that the condition of the laboring classes of Porto Rico [*sic*] in general, and of the peon class in particular," was then "and ha[d] long been, very deplorable—largely due, doubtless, to insufficient employment" (p. 385). His entire report is full of such observations. For example: "A potent, depressing, disturbing, unyielding component in the untoward conditions to which the wage worker is subjected is the superabundance of his numbers for the work" (p. 410).

Again, although the availability of jobs seems to have improved, relatively speaking, between 1906 and 1910, by 1913 various craft trades registered rising levels of unemployment, notably the dock workers, carpenters, and cigar makers (62 percent, 56 percent, and 23 percent, respectively), while unemployment levels among agricultural laborers—taken as a whole and on the average—reached 47 percent that same year. The reports issued by Fleagle (p. 66) and Mixer[30]said as much. Taking the male laboring population as a whole during the entire 1899–1920 period, the levels of official unemployment increased from 17 percent to 20 percent.[31]

The Narratives of Preservation and Transformation

At first glance, this structural brutality of the dispossession process would seem odd given the lofty aims that framed many of the colonialist discourses of the day. For example, the officer in charge of the original contingent of U.S. troops that landed in Puerto Rico, Major General Nelson A. Miles, issued a proclamation in July of 1898 (partly cited in the first epigraph of this chapter). The sentence immediately following the previously cited quotation reads: "This is not a war of devastation, but one to give you all, within the control of its military and naval forces, the advantages and blessings of enlightened civilization."[32]

I am not suggesting that, in light of the socioeconomic consequences of the U.S. invasion, these words were deceitful.[33] Rather, my goal here is to explore the relationship between, on the one hand, these and other official declarations and, on the other hand, the unplanned yet no less methodical ruthlessness then laying the groundwork for the capitalist dispossession of the "native" laboring classes that embodied the subaltern subjects of colonial capitalism in Puerto Rico. Having already examined part of the historical process that produced the majority social subjects in the Island, let us now probe in greater detail the new regime of truth that conflictively constituted these subjects as being bound to specific identities: racialized, feminized, infantilized. This analysis further contextualizes and empirically documents the bridge between the colonized subjects of the capitalist labor process in Puerto Rico (what Stuart Hall designated as "the 'hard edge' of productive systems") and the subordinate subjects of colonialist corrective studies ("the 'insides' of people"). Such an analysis lays the groundwork for the examination, in the next two chapters, of the popular illegalities of the colonized majorities and the punitive strategies—social and textual—deployed to contain this "native" disorder between 1898 and 1921.

So far we have seen that, in effect, "a war of devastation" was waged on the dispossessed majorities of the Island: an economic war of attrition whose effects spanned the first half of this century, in particular during the 1898–1921 "take-off" years. It materialized as a war primarily directed against the majority of the local population, then practically devoid of any property titles—in need of protection or otherwise. The few propertied Creoles that existed did not exactly receive protection, many of their profit-based possessions being engulfed by the advancing North American trusts or driven to ruin by these same forces and/or by the colonialist regime (local and federal). Such contradictory narratives of preservation and transformation served to corroborate the allegedly natural and historical need for other genres of colonialist paternalism. Azel Ames expressed such sentiments, being so "painfully impressed, . . . by the number of human wrecks" (p. 385), even as the colonizers' dominant knowledges, as in the case of Fred K. Fleagle, became faithful "exposition[s] of the social situation as it exists" (p. iii). Fleagle explained the conditions of the "Porto Rican" laborers, unfortunate as they may have been, as objective facts of life that "[did] not differ greatly . . . from similar facts which could be gathered relating to any country" (p. iv).

Accordingly, the preservation of the newly acquired colonial subjects then being re-constructed not only became understood as protecting them from what the new colonizers considered as outside enemies; the preservation concerned protecting the colonized from themselves. Through such normalizing discourses, preservation also became the elucidation and codification of the "native's" difference: what Mary Louise Pratt called the "fix[ing of] the Other in a timeless present where all 'his' actions and reactions are repetitions of 'his' normalizing habits."[34] In this manner, "native" poverty became "closely related to degeneration and crime, especially when it descend[ed] into pauperism and absolute dependence upon charity," as Fleagle had indicated (p. 74). However benevolent the intentions, this racial/national-cultural lineage nevertheless became [con]fused with social decay, moral decomposition being both the result and the verification of an ancestry found lacking.

The North American republic's "Porto Ricans," like the British Empire's "Oriental" critically examined by Said, had to be "*contained* and *represented* by dominating frameworks."[35] The substance of this colonialist capitalism and its dominant knowleges produced "Porto Rico" and "Porto Ricans." Such a place and its people emerged as the effects of these other socioeconomic, political, and discursive forces: "Porto Rico" and "Porto Ricans" had no meaning or existence outside this geography, this political economy, and this ethnology. Containment meant establishing the limits of the permissible within the colonized space (socioeconomically and juridico-politically), as well as encircling this space with the necessary technologies of power so as to ensure the reproduction of the colonized as social subjects—both as capable of the initiatives defined by these strictures and as subordinated to this encirclement. Representation meant manufacturing the colonized as a property-appendage and a property-characteristic of the dominant socioeconomic, juridical, and textual structures; it meant appearing in place of the geographic and social space that these dominating frameworks had defined as vacant, uninhabited, and wanting; and it meant defining and preserving the interests of "subject peoples"—who were, as such, incapable of representing themselves.

The colonizers embodied and commanded the means of such containment and representation because they could fashion the "Porto Rican" majorities as needy children and women in distress. One of the principal effects of this narrative was to socially construct the colonizers as the manly protectors and the teachers/masters of an "enlightened civilization" that had arrived on Island shores under the auspices of U.S. battleships, soldiers, and generals. For instance, on the eve of the war with Spain, Beveridge had declared that God's plan called for the United States to foster " . . . the disappearance of debased civilizations and decaying races before the higher civilization of the nobler and more virile types of men."[36] And in a speech before the Hamilton Club of Chicago, on April 10, 1899, Theodore Roosevelt described the results of this war by proclaiming that "[i]f we drove out a medieval tyranny only to make room for savage anarchy, we had better not have begun the task at all," for it was "worse than idle to say that we have no duty to perform, and can leave to their fates the islands we have conquered."[37] "Such a course . . . would be followed at once by utter chaos in the wretched islands themselves. Some stronger, manlier power would have to step in and do the work . . . " (ibid.).

The example of the British in "the Orient" is equally emblematic: in Said's words, "The Oriental is irrational, depraved (fallen), childlike, 'different'; thus the European is rational, virtuous, mature, 'normal'" (p. 40). Similar to what colonialist capitalism had done and continued to do with respect to the "Indians," "Negroes," "the Latin race," and "the heathen Chinee" in North America, the new overseas colonies of "Porto Rico," the Philippines, Hawaii, Guam, the Panama Canal zone, together with occupied Cuba, provided an additional socioeconomic and textual space in which to reinscribe this discourse of Western-masculinist and cultural-national/racial superiority within a mythical sense of supraclass homogeneity.[38]

But the discourse of racial childhood and of feminization of the "lesser races" had corollary sources of formation as well. The whole discussion on whether to grant the new Caribbean wards U.S. citizenship—or much less self-government—exemplifies the gendered and age-graded signification practices of the new colonialists.[39] For example, Congressman Sereno E. Payne stated in 1900 that, regarding "Porto Ricans," the U.S. government should "Keep them all in leading strings until you have educated them up to the full stature of American manhood, and then crown them with the glory of American citizenship."[40] That same year, another congressman, George C. Perkins, asserted in a statement regarding Puerto Rico and the Philippines: "If we retain them, a period of pupilage—a time of education—must be theirs . . ."[41]

The famous decisions that the U.S. Supreme Court handed down in 1901 (known in constitutional literature as the "Insular Cases") juridically expressed the cultural-national/racial difference marked by this virile master, on the one hand, and by his childlike and effeminate ward, on the other, thereby definitively engraving the juridico-political relationship between the Island[ers] and the United States. Its most pristine manifestation was the dictum of Downes v. Bidwell. Chief Justice Fuller summarized the Court's majority position in the following manner: "there seems to be concurrence in the view that Porto Rico [*sic*] belongs to the United States, but nevertheless, and notwithstanding the act of Congress, is not a part of the United States."[42] As José A. Cabranes informs us, the purpose of turning Puerto Ricans into citizens, "as Senator Foraker noted as early as 1900, was merely 'to recognize that Porto Rico belongs to the United States of America.'"[43] According to Cabranes, Foraker had reminded his colleagues that "[t]he word 'citizen' . . . meant nothing more than 'allegiance on the one hand and protection on the other'" (ibid.).

"Porto Rico" and "Porto Ricans" comprised the attachments and belongings (literally: possessions and lieges) of the United States; not unlike the ancient Roman notion of *familias*, as in the father's property, including *his* woman and *his* children. But "they" were the juridical and physical appendages of a juridico-political field that, nevertheless, remained always already external to "them." Ultimately, such a subaltern and inferior location could never correspond to the "full stature of American manhood," no matter how much "time of education" had transpired—as the 1915–1917 U.S. Congressional debates on the matter would confirm. In 1917, for example, a third member of Congress, Senator Albert B. Fall of New Mexico, reported to his fellow Congressmen that "he knew the people of Spanish descent very well," such as Puerto Ricans, and was fully aware that "they must be led,"[44] reiterating in this manner the narrative of the incapability of the colonized to represent themselves—both in the formal-political sense and in terms of their social subjectivity.

Most "Porto Ricans" therefore continued to be like the "Oriental." The Island's majorities developed as interchangeable with other Latin American and tropical "incapable races" (inside and outside North America), and, consequently, as similar to the Egyptians and Indians that Lord Evelyn Baring Cromer had ruled. As Said has noted, "One of the convenient things about Orientals for Cromer was that managing them, although circumstances might differ slightly here and there, was almost everywhere the same" (pp. 37–38). Additionally, most of the "Porto Rican" population was, like the "Oriental," critically dissected in *Orientalism* because it too was fashioned as "something one studies and depicts (as in a curriculum), as something one disciplines (as in school or prison) . . ." (p. 40). Theodore Roosevelt provided the explicit logic behind this when, after visiting San Juan in 1906, he wrote to one of his sons, saying: " . . . there is something pathetic and childlike about the people. We are giving them a good government and the island is prospering."[45]

According to the prevailing cultural maps (then and now), only children and women needed protection, guidance, supervision, and instruction. The colonized masses of all ages and of both genders, like the infants and adult females of Western Civilization, represented the lower stages of development that the antediluvian forefathers of civilized (white) men had already gone through. For the new colonizers, going to "Porto Rico" was similar to going back in time to their own cultural-national past and racial childhood.[46]

Like the disorderly children and capricious women of North America and Europe during the second half of the nineteenth century,[47] the "Porto Rican" subaltern subjects also required instruction in self-control by the men of civilized lineage who had mastered such complicated matters. Once again, these were the tropes that populated the North American discussion on the degree of political responsibility allowed to this particular "native" mass.

This discussion illustrates the extent to which the colonized became fashioned as "naturally" inclined to thoughtless and rash behavior insofar as they personified what Shiv Visvanathan has critically termed "the 'contemporary ancestors,' the past the West has already lived out"[48]—the West in this case being white North America. As in most colonial situations, the manufacture of the colonized space as a journey through the colonizer's past enabled the constructed backwardness of the colonized, a past that—without the colonized, without the non-Western spaces and peoples, and without these primitive "contemporary ancestors,"—materialized as a past without a tangible expression in the present: in other words, a past that would be gone forever from the colonialist gaze and grasp. Christopher Miller's recent critique of the pervasiveness of such Euro/Americo-centrism suggests a perspective that seemed completely absent in turn-of-the-century North America—as well as, unfortunately, in the United States of today: "This conflation of space and time is so much a part of our current assumptions about non-European cultures that we may not even recognize its metaphorical basis."[49]

Beveridge popularized and legitimized the colonialism endemic to this "conflation of space and time." In September of 1898, he reminded a Republican audience that "[t]he opposition tells us not to rule a people without their consent," to which he added: "the rule of liberty, that all just government derive their authority from the consent of the governed, applies to those who are capable of self-government . . . " (*Beveridge*, 73–74). Referring to "wolves of conquest" such as Germany, Russia, France, and Japan, Beveridge rhetorically asked, "Shall we save them from these nations to give" the new U.S. possessions "the self-rule of tragedy? It would be like giving a razor to a babe and telling it to shave itself" (ibid., 74).

Within this context, Josiah Strong, in his ever peculiar bricolage of Protestantism and Social Darwinism, drew on the scientific recapitulationist axiom by stating that "modern science has shown that races develop in the course of centuries as individuals do in years."[50] Strong then immediately declared that "an undeveloped race, . . . incapable of self-government," was "no more a reflection of the Almighty than [was] an underdeveloped child who [was] incapable of self-government."

In the case of "Porto Rico," then Secretary of War Elihu Root concluded in his 1899 Annual Report that:

> . . . before the people of Porto Rico [*sic*] can be fully intrusted with self-government they must first learn the lesson of self-control . . . This lesson will necessarily be slowly learned, because it is a matter not of intellectual apprehension, but of character and of acquired habits of thought and feeling. It would be of no use to present to the people of Porto Rico [*sic*] now a written constitution or frame of laws, however perfect, and tell them to live under it. They would inevitably fail without a course of tuition under a strong and guiding hand.[51]

The weakening effects and dark forces of a tropical nature, both [sub]human and environmental, became the underlying reason behind the "acquired habits of thought and feeling" of the "Porto Rican" "babes" and "underdeveloped child[ren]."[52] Alfred G. Robinson had described this tropical nature as "a lavish bounty which reduces the necessity for work to its minimum" (p. 161). It was the nature that Brigadier General Davis had depicted in his 1899 report as having retrogressed "the descendants of the conquistadores" into "pale, sallow, and often emaciated beings," thus erasing the difference "[b]etween the negro and the peon" (p. 18). The nature that, according to Robert T. Hill, "dare[d] the application of every art, science, industry, and administrative method . . . [that had] made . . . [the United States] great" in order to rescue the mountains of the Island "from the waste and ruin of four centuries" (pp. 418–419). And the nature that Milton G. Fowles, in his visit to the Island, had described as "the excitable nature and uncompromising temperament of Latin Americans."[53]

Defying the Twin Pincers of Exploitation and Starvation

Since an "excitable nature and uncompromising temperament" became such a fundamental element in the structuring and textualization of the "Porto Rican" subaltern subjects, this reading of the "native" body also became an essential—and essentialist—component in the policing of the many "native" survival strategies and reactions that ran counter to the colonial-capitalist social order. This was one of the fundamental reasons why the subaltern subjects of the popular illegalities emerged as the principal intersection between colonialist forms of punishment (institutional and textual) and the new patterns of economic organization.

On the one hand, the dispossession process that unfolded during the first half of this century, especially during the initial twenty-three years that constituted its take-off period, compelled the deployment of extremely brutal technologies by capital and the State. On the other hand, the structural ruthlessness of this process in part explains why the colonized laboring classes opted to intermittently, but persistently, pursue alternative sources of income vis-à-vis the formal labor market (capitalist and transitional). In this context, it also becomes clear why many of these "native" reactions to the dispossession process were officially textualized as social violence.

For the Island population positioned within the rural/land-rent economy of the haciendas, as well as for emerging laboring-poor in the urban centers and/or coastal areas, these illegalized subsistence practices and reactions did not just imply a question of resisting the encroachment of capitalist expansion. Nor was it just a matter of not being engulfed by the production/circulation linkages of the declining local version of a Jünker economy, including merchant capital. For significant portions of the laboring classes, these unlawful survival strategies and this social violence also involved trying to make ends meet within very specific and increasingly asphyxiating constraints: the crushing gears of a socioeconomic engine ultimately bent on smashing the growth of an independent subsistence sector while the engine itself did not produce sufficient sources of social—and, oftentimes, even physical—survival. Everyday living, therefore, became more and more transformed into multiple forms of social transgression (individual and collective), breaching the structural barriers erected by the propertied classes in general (Creole and North American) and by capital in particular.

The struggle taking place in the terrain of the prohibited economic activities did not always materialize as a metaphorical battle. The informal economy and the popular illegalities in general, including social violence, all partially upset the orderly formation and reproduction of capital in Puerto Rico. Insofar as emergent capital and the waning noncapitalist systems could not completely eliminate the popular illegalities among the laboring classes, to some degree these modes of social *contention* tended to define the boundaries of both modes of colonial *exploitation*. As the oppressed majorities tortuously and painfully crossed the boundaries delineated by the propertied classes (Island-wide and U.S.-based), these majorities in turn redefined the very limits of the socioeconomic field of operation corresponding to private property as a whole. Meanwhile, both the implantation and expansion of capitalism, on the one hand, and the persistence of the hacienda system, on the other, also transpired under conditions sharply contested from within the camp of property itself—internally and externally.[54] As in the nineteenth century,[55] the breadth of the popular illegalities surfaced as the outer limit of political and economic technologies trying to inscribe the laboring populations in the Island as subaltern subjects with a compulsion to work for someone else. Likewise, it became the social measure—and the limit—of just how disciplined, proper, and peaceful the processes of economic exploitation were or were not going to be, including their large-scale reproduction. An understanding of this period cannot or should not ignore these unruly social practices, however contradictory or disagreeable they may seem. Such an analysis requires referencing the efforts intended to regulate the survival practices that went beyond and against the legal market and the workplace. This sort of analysis calls for a re-examination of exploitative production as a whole—related to agriculture or not, both industrial and manufacturing, capitalist and noncapitalist.

The relationship between (1) the nature of these Island-based forms of exploitation in general and of capitalist enterprises in particular and (2) the instability of the dispossessed sectors, did not become a simple matter of the latter being the effect of the former. Rather, it appeared as a dynamic and conflictive feedback "loop." To a certain extent, the re-structuring of colonial exploitation created a social climate that, in turn, generated the overall opposition of significant portions of the colonized laboring classes towards working for somebody else. The popular resistances towards the initial phases of large-scale, capitalist accumulation in the Island are a case in point. Yet the dangers posed by this social restlessness also had bearing on the transformations experienced by the principal exploiters in the Island during the entire first half of this century. Both capitalist and noncapitalist, North American and Creole—the great-propertied classes—very rapidly became aware of the risks involved in structuring exploitation on such unstable ground. This awareness and the social threats that induced it, in turn, catalyzed some of the changes that took place in colonial capitalism and the hacienda system—as we shall see in the second half of this book.

The great majority of the urban working classes and their rural counterparts, of course, opted to work for somebody else rather than to starve, the latter being a distinct possibility. But it was also overwhelmingly true that they seem to have preferred self-employment to working for someone else. And for good reason: "Thus it will be seen that when the individual workman [*sic*] is at the mercy of the employer, he [*sic*] has no independent status such as he [*sic*] would have were he [*sic*] the owner of even a very modest piece of property, and it is inevitable that he [*sic*] will find employment only part of the year."[56]

Willingly or not, the colonized majorities were in most cases inclined to shift constantly between sources of income that were occasionally at odds with each other. In varying degrees, these dispossessed sectors managed to alternate whatever wage income might have been forthcoming and/or advantageous with a multiplicity of independent gainful activities, legal and illegal. Also translated into and inscribed as social violence, this precariousness emerged as a phenomenon whose complex and irregular vectors become intermittently visible during the entire 1898–1947 period.

Several conditions unfolded at this time, unwittingly widening the scope of the popular resistances and reactions as well as diversifying the forms they adopted. The formal and mainly urban institutions of the propertied and educated classes directly intervened only to a relatively limited extent in the subjectification of the colonized majorities. In addition to the budding public educational system, the local party system also became one of the points at which the mostly urban, regulatory forms of discourse cut across class and settlement lines. The concrete ideological representations embodied by most political organizations became translated within popular discourses as socially foreign, Creole-propertied artifacts: outside the concrete, everyday experience of the "native" laboring masses—perhaps the only major exception to this trend being the "Partido Socialista" (primarily during its first decade of existence). As a rule, most of the population tended to frame these institutions as sources of periodic patronage and piecemeal favoritism. Consequently, the impoverished majorities perceived most political parties as one of the spaces where poor people negotiated with, as well as resisted, their social betters/aliens in exchange for money, food, and so on.[57]

Often the image of the local political parties (the ones that alternately controlled the colonial legislature) became [con]fused with the neighborhood-party boss or representative. The latter, usually members of the propertied and more educated strata and/or of their managerial agents,[58] tended to reinforce the relative social externality of the corresponding political formations. This made them not unlike the creditor-merchant and the State-regulated marketing agencies in the case of the poor farmers or the labor contractor in the case of the rural and urban underemployed—as Wolf has already observed (pp. 211, 212, 241). In other words, they became organic agents/bodies contradictorily mediating and interceding between the direct producers and the different social spheres: e.g., the capitalist market or the decision-making process within the Island's government. These spheres were constituted structurally as being beyond the reach and understanding of the overwhelming majority of the Puerto Rican population. In this way, institutions like the political party system contributed considerably toward reproducing the socioeconomic and cultural subordination of the laboring poor in town and country. Yet their mostly exotic and politically "imported" nature, socioculturally speaking, structurally limited the extent to which they could carry out this regulatory function.

These are some of the reasons why the socially disruptive practices of the colonized laboring classes did not surface as completely contained or transformed during this first half-century, in particular between the formative years of 1898–1921—social violence being one of these disruptive practices. These practices overlapped with a sizeable portion of the underground economy. In part, this seemed due to substantial aspects of the parallel subsistence activities being registered as felonious and actively interdicted by the police. But it was also related to the preference of the "native" majorities for informal social control mechanisms. The latter frequently materialized as the direct, illicit, and at times lethal use of physical coercion by members of the laboring classes: against themselves, against the propertied and educated classes, and against property—individually and collectively. As recent mainstream criminological research has noted, the official record is not as organized and consistent in this respect as its counterpart for the 1948–1985 period.[59] However, I have found sufficient information to reconstruct the way the colonial regime (local and federal) represented social violence in particular and the popular illegalities in general.

A statistic, such as the number of arrests carried out in a given period, includes some inherent imprecisions.[60] However, this is one of the few accessible indicators for Puerto Rico during the first half of this century. As shown in table 3, the rate of arrests (per 100,000 inhabitants) more than quadrupled between 1899 and 1905. Then this figure flattens out for the following thirty years, only to double again during the late thirties and early forties. On the whole, the available government information would appear to indicate a steady longitudinal expansion in the social practices

Table 3 Number and Rates of Arrests in Puerto Rico, Selected Years, Both Sexes

YEAR	NUMBER OF ARRESTS MADE	TOTAL POPULATION OF PUERTO RICO	RATE PER 100,000 INHABITANTS
1899	4,252	953,243	446.1
1902	19,553	998,180*	1,958.9
1903	22,078	1,013,159*	2,178.6
1905	61,867	1,043,117*	5,931.2
1906	56,561	1,058,096*	5,344.7
1910	54,662	1,118,012	4,490.0
1911	50,895	1,134,983	4,484.3
1912	52,967	1,152,214	4,597.7
1913	41,759	1,169,705	3,570.2
1916	53,006	1,223,789	4,329.0
1924	57,983	1,392,442	4,166.7
1927	69,638	1,466,223	4,750.6
1929	68,945	1,517,569	4,543.4
1931	62,968	1,573,720	4,001.6
1933	66,007	1,635,070	4,037.1
1935	74,700	1,698,813	4,397.5
1938	177,983	1,799,117	9,901.0
1940	166,667	1,869,255	8,912.6
1941	154,707	1,903,400	8,130.1
1942	180,227	1,948,664	9,259.3
1943	113,387	1,971,689	5,750.4
1946	155,452	2,093,461	7,427.2

*My estimate

SOURCES: George W. Davis, *Annual Report of the War Department for the Fiscal Year Ended June 30, 1900—Part 13: Report of the Military Government of Porto Rico on Civil Affairs* (Washington, D.C.: Government Printing Office, 1902), 100–101, 228; William H. Hunt, *Second Annual Report of the Governor of Porto Rico* (Washington, D.C.: Government Printing Office, 1902), 327; William H. Hunt, *Third Annual Report of the Governor of Porto Rico* (Washington, D.C.: Senate Document no. 26, 58th Congress, 1st session, Government Printing Office, 1903), 308; Beekman Winthrop, *Fifth Annual Report of the Governor of Porto Rico* (Washington, D.C.: Government Printing Office, 1905), 144–145; Beekman Winthrop, *Sixth Annual Report of the Governor of Porto Rico* (Washington, D.C.: Government Printing Office, 1906), 200; George R. Colton, *Tenth Annual Report of the Governor of Porto Rico* (Washington, D.C.: Government Printing Office, 1910), 57; George R. Colton, *Eleventh Annual Report of the Governor of Porto Rico* (Washington, D.C.: Government Printing Office, 1911), 68-69; George R.

Colton, *Twelfth Annual Report of the Governor of Porto Rico* (Washington, D.C.: Government Printing Office, 1912), 62–63; A. Hyatt Verrill, *Porto Rico, Past and Present and San Domingo of Today* (New York: Dodd, Mead, and Company, 1919), 152–153; Fred K. Fleagle, *Social Problems in Porto Rico* (Boston: D.C. Heath and Co., 1917), 84–86; Horace M. Towner, *Twenty-fourth Annual Report of the Governor of Porto Rico* (Washington, D.C.: Government Printing Office, 1925), 705; Horace M. Towner, *Twenty-Seventh Annual Report of the Governor of Porto Rico* (Washington, D.C.: Government Printing Office, 1928), 61; Horace M. Towner, *Twenty-Ninth Annual Report of the Government of Porto Rico* (Washington, D.C.: Government Printing Office, 1929), 79; Theodore Roosevelt, Jr., *Thirty-First Annual Report of the Governor of Porto Rico* (Washington, D.C.: Government Printing Office, 1932), 56; José C. Rosario, *El problema de la criminalidad en Puerto Rico* (Río Piedras: Colegio de Pedagogía, Universidad de Puerto Rico, 1952), 78; Teobaldo Casanova, *Estudios estadísticos del crimen* (San Juan: Casanova, Inc., 1967), 22, 390.

being intersected by the police at this time. Accordingly, it seems to reflect a proportional escalation in the "native" activities then constituted as unlawful.

For the colonialist personnel (local and federal), these "native" transgressions exemplified the dark, primeval, and chaotic nature of a people always already known and always already strange. Granted, this "Porto Rican" unruliness paled—literally—in comparison to the large-scale Filipino insurrection of 1898–1904. Thus, the new colonialist narratives and dominating frameworks of the United States tended to locate "Porto Ricans" toward the top of the "[Tropical] Chain of Being,"[61] imagining the new Caribbean possession and its inhabitants as not as dark, strange, and disorderly as the Filipinos positioned at the lower levels of this scale. Beveridge in 1898–1899 had contrasted the "blazing fires of joy and the ringing of bells of gladness in Porto Rico [*sic*] . . . [that] welcome[d] . . . our flag" to the "savage," "unscrupulous," and "incapable" Filipinos (*Beveridge*, 74, 120, 121). Representative Thomas Spight in the Congressional debates of 1900 went to the extreme of distinguishing the Caribbean colony, whose "people are, in the main, of Caucasian blood, knowing and appreciating the benefits of civilization," from the Philippine Islands, whose "inhabitants are of wholly different races of people from ours—Asiatics, Malays, negros, and mixed blood. They have nothing in common with us and centuries cannot assimilate them."[62]

On the other hand, the relative compliance of the "Porto Ricans"—in comparison to the Filipinos—tended to feminize the entire Caribbean Island and its inhabitants. As Congressman Jacob H. Bromwell had argued in 1900, "Puerto Rico came to us voluntarily and without bloodshed. She welcomed us with open arms."[63] Such feminization ultimately became the mark of unreliability, capriciousness, and instability within the predominant cultural mappings in the West at this time. This established the limits locating the "Porto Rican" national-culture/race within the colonialist narrative of the "lesser races." Paraphrasing Edward Said, the "good 'native'" is ultimately an oxymoron: in the end, all "natives" become suspect of disrupting the colonial social order precisely because only colonizers remain above such suspicion (pp. 33, 38–39).

The "tendency to lawlessness"[64]—that, in varying degrees and according to the dominant knowledges, continued to prevail among the majority of these Caribbean "natives"—emerged as one of the very things that made them so much in need of what Elihu Root had called "a strong and guiding hand." This, again, marked the need for the containment and representation of the "Porto Rican." Of course, only an "enlightened civilization" could provide this supervision, illumination, and lesson in self-control. Whatever protection arrived would supposedly assume the shape of Beveridge's "ruling race of the world"; the one who, according to Lyman Abbott, had "learned to use 'God's projectiles'"[65] so as to solve Alfred Mahan's "Caribbean problem" by establishing order. Through this means, Major General Miles' vow to "the people of a country that for centuries have been oppressed" would be kept as these people savored the benefits of moral and social uplift and enjoyed "the advantages and blessings of enlightened civilization": darkness would give way to illumination. This was the brilliant North American knowledge and power that Josiah Strong, several years before the Spanish-Cuban–North American War, had prophesied would spread " . . . like a ring of Saturn—a girdle of light—around the globe."[66]

Otherwise, if such nature and people continued under the sway of what Secretary of War Root had characterized as their own "acquired habits of thought and feeling"—so "closely related to degeneration and crime," according to Fleagle—Theodore Roosevelt's "pathetic and childlike . . . people" were destined to fulfill Root's prediction: they "would inevitably fail." Ultimately, were not "Porto Ricans" so very like what Josiah Strong had said about other dark, primitive, and tropical races such as "the African and the Malay"? Were not these new Caribbean subjects also " . . . many centuries behind the Anglo-Saxon in development . . . as incapable of operating complicated machinery as they are of adopting and successfully administering representative government"?

Mahan remarked that this part of the "Caribbean problem" also required rectification as the War of 1898 began—the same event that Theodore Roosevelt characterized as " . . . bringing order out of chaos in the great, fair tropic islands from which the valor of our soldiers and sailors has driven the Spanish flag."[67] But what visage did this "chaos" specifically have in "Porto Rico"? The remaining chapters address this very question.

4

The Rise of the "Evil-Disposed Classes," 1898–1909

The evil-disposed classes rose against the Spaniards, and murders, robberies, and arson were common. . . . This lawlessness was not stopped until the American troops had taken control and established garrisons in the most disturbed districts.

—Brigadier General George W. Davis,
***Report of Brigadier General George W. Davis, U.S.V. On the Civil Affairs of Puerto Rico* (1900)**

Modernity was a vision of conquest. Every structure of conquest needs a calendar as a liturgy of power. It has therefore to capture or to rewrite time, since time till the emergence of modernity was cyclical and hence open to reversal.

—Shiv Visvanathan,
"From the Annals of the Laboratory State" (1987)

To wait in heavy harness
On fluttered folk and wild—
Your new-caught, sullen peoples,
Half devil and half child.

—Rudyard Kipling, "The White Man's Burden" (1899)

I have subdivided the popular illegalities that emerged in Puerto Rico between 1898 and 1921 into two moments, particularly in the case of the manifestations of social violence. The War of 1898 and the European War of 1914–1919, together with their subsequent aftermaths, mark the chronological frontiers of these transgressions. The interval between these two wars also became the years in which the contours of the colonial capitalist enterprise assumed its definitive shape, a basic pattern maintained throughout the first half of this century.

The 1898 juncture and the years from 1914 to 1919 indicate the crests of two waves that swept the Island. This chapter examines the earliest peak of this period, when the frontal assault of colonialist capitalism—what Stuart Hall called the "social relations of production and the 'hard-edge' of productive systems"[1]—for the first time met the myriad of microdisorders that, in response, spread out across the newly re-colonized space. Here we will survey the all-too-often overlooked features of that first contentious exchange: a bloody dialogue whose various social authors were not completely aware of each other, of their own capacities, nor of the terms of their engagement; a confrontation where old forms of identity—Hall: "the 'insides' of people . . . subjectivity and sexuality" (p. 102)—were exhumed and paraded as newborn creatures while new forms of identity still wore older uniforms.

"The Tendency to Lawlessness," 1898–1899

The interregnum of direct military rule (1898–1900) that preceded the creation of a civilian colonial government brought about an immediate increase in the registered levels of social violence and clandestine economic activities. In part, this arose as a direct consequence of the sudden collapse of the laboring classes' conditions of existence. In this sense, the U.S. invasion swiftly catalyzed the unevenly developed crisis in the living standards of the "native" masses, qualitatively transforming the content of the peasantry's socioeconomic deterioration in particular.

As a result of the gradually worsening conditions during the turning point of the late 1890s and the several months immediately preceding the U.S. invasion, isolated outbreaks of attacks transpired, carried out by extremely impoverished peasants. These took the form of isolated and random thefts and the killing of cattle. However, the neutralization of the Spanish garrisons in the Island by the U.S. troops temporarily threw the local police forces into disarray (particularly the rural patrol units). This resulted in an exponential growth in these acts of—primarily peasant—class vengeance. Burned haciendas and warehouses fell to the ground;

large landowners and their families became the objects of vilification, expulsion, or murder, while the raiders distributed among themselves the hacienda's stolen properties. On some occasions, these insurgent bands mobilized as many as one hundred fifty to two hundred peasants at a time.[2]

During 1898–1899 U.S. colonial officials, North American reporters, and local journalists chronicled these activities extensively. Examination of such records offers a vivid picture of the contending socially hegemonic subjects (Spanish, Creole, and North American). Gayatri Chakravorty Spivak has indicated the usefulness of studying such manuscripts: "it is only the texts of counterinsurgency and elite documentation that gives us news of the consciousness of the subaltern."[3] In this sense, the misfits in the texts of the propertied and educated classes (local and U.S.-based) readily materialized the unintentional registers of the subaltern subjects' will to resist.

For instance, on October 28, 1899 the mayor of the municipality of Quebradillas, Manuel Reyes Ruiz, informed U.S. Commissioner Henry K. Carroll of "about fourteen burnings in my district of houses belonging to Canary Islanders" because "these gentlemen during the Spanish rule tortured the people there and imprisoned about thirty-five of them" (p. 600). Although perhaps an act of hacendado bravado on his part, Reyes Ruiz gauged the number of peasant rebels in one group, he claims to have fought off, at much more than the 150–200 average for such armed gatherings: "Recently a party of 700 natives organized to burn some property in my district, and I personally was able to restrain them" (p. 602).

Other members of the propertied and educated classes made similar denunciations before the envoys of the new colonial regime. Dr. Manuel F. Rossy issued parallel declarations to Carroll on November 9, 1898, which I will quote at length. Rossy began by providing insight into the composition of one cluster of large properties being razed, the lines of demarcation being more social than national-cultural. There were municipalities in which "as many as twenty-two estates [had] been destroyed, and in many cases the coffee crop ha[d] been ruined. . . . In four days there have been seven murders," three of the casualties were Spaniards, "one a Frenchman, and the rest wealthy Porto Ricans [*sic*]" (p. 603).

From there, Rossy—a lawyer, prestigious local political leader, and editor of the local newspaper *El País*—went on to furnish ample though unintended indications of the character of informal social-control mechanisms among the peasantry: here the force of the Creole landowners' authorial voice, mediated by the translation of the new colonizer (as exemplified by Carroll), must re-cite the voiceless force of the subaltern subjects. In the prominent coffee-growing municipality of Yauco, in the southern coast, "a mob visited a coffee estate owned by a Spaniard from the Balearic Islands," finding the man in the parlor, killing him "in the presence of his wife and daughters to whom, however, they offered no insult or injury. Later they met his major-domo and cut off his ear and nailed it to a tree" (ibid.).

Rossy also provided evidence of the motley configuration of those participating in the scattered uprising. Once more, the primary boundaries between the assailants and the assailed did not spring up along national-cultural lines. Again, social disorder transformed the writings of the hegemonic subjects of property (Creole and North American) into the unwilling witness of an unwritten program against the existing social relations.

In the central-northern coast, near Arecibo, a "band of marauders . . . led by a Spanish captain of the Alfonso regiment" was captured and the ringleader described as "a deserter from the Spanish army." Carroll quotes Rossy as indicating that these bands, "which in some cases number almost a hundred," pursued "loot and revenge." Usually "armed with revolvers, machetes, and clubs," these rural guerrillas were not known for "offer[ing] any indignity to women" (ibid.).

The "native" peasant's armed critique of property relations was immediately made to extend to the *juridico-political* compulsion that defined the subaltern subjects of Spanish colonialism as having to work for somebody else. In both cases and in retrospect, this larger but shorter-lived rebellion seemed to prefigure the more microlevel rebellions against the *economic* compulsion that inscribed the subaltern subjects of U.S. colonialism as having to work for somebody else. Near the municipality of Barceloneta, adjacent to Arecibo, a "mob took from one estate . . . over 100 head of cattle," the owner retrieving the majority of the animals "because the bandits could not make away with them. They killed two or three of them for immediate use and had to abandon the rest." "[T]hose who do not want to work" were typically identified as the sort of individual who "joined these bands. One of those who surrendered had been a member of the guardia civil [i.e., the previous colonial constabulary]" (ibid.).

The armed peasant bands became known popularly as "the soot-faced ones" (*los tizna[d]os*) because they tended to camouflage their features in this manner. Not easily suppressed, the fractured and faint expressions of this somewhat erratic *jacquerie* persisted until 1902–1903. In any case, the waves of arrests and captures during late 1898 and early 1899 seriously crippled the movement.[4]

Military Governor, Brigadier General George W. Davis, first characterized the 1898–1899 peasant insurgency in his 1899 report by evoking visions of the U.S. cavalry moving into hostile and uncharted Indian territory,[5] a "Porto Rican" Heart of Darkness: "The difficulties encountered by the United States Army in stopping these outrages were very great. All was strange to the officers and men—the country, the people, the laws, and the language."[6] Such earlier colonialist visions were no doubt still fresh in the minds of many of these U.S. soldiers and officers since a good number of them had battled what they understood as another "native"/"savage" obstacle to the spread of Euro-American civilization. On that occasion, the struggle had unfolded in the Western Plains of North America and in the mountains of the Dakotas and Colorado, as in the case of Nelson A. Miles. As Colonel, Miles fought alongside George Armstrong Custer against the Sioux, as well as having participated in the capture of Chief Joseph of the Nez Perces in 1878 and in the capture of the Apache guerrilla chief Geronimo in 1886, while as a Major General he led the first expeditionary force that invaded Puerto Rico on July 25, 1898.[7]

Brigadier General Davis, showed partially gifted insight into the immediate, underlying conditions regarding the peasant insurgency of 1898–1899. His 1902 report expressed understanding for the "native" complaints "against the local authorities and against those who had been in sympathy with the beneficiaries of Spanish rule," who would be the ones to "suffer from the vengeance of the unchained masses," the latter usually being joined by "the criminal classes . . . in the raids" (p. 97). This led to

> . . . a Saturnalia of crime—forced contributions, out-and-out robbery, burning, assassinations, violence to women, etc. With such mob turned loose on society, it is not strange that friend and foe suffered alike. It has been claimed that property to the value of several million dollars was stolen and destroyed during the weeks of a reign of terror. (ibid.)

The remainder of Davis' second report, though mostly accurate, seems politically self-serving. Additionally, his narrative illustrates the extent to which the emergent colonialist discourses inscribed this "native" violence as one of the few unfortunate consequences that followed in the wake of the otherwise emancipatory military occupation.

> Let it be supposed that under conditions such as are recited a government of oppression should be suddenly relaxed and for

> it another substituted which is the predominating characteristic; would it not be strange if, when released from restraint, the tendency to lawlessness should greatly increase and a reign of terror take the place of a reign of oppression?[8]

Despite recognizing some of the social contradictions involved, this prominent example of the new colonial regime's signifying practices tended to recast the uprising as a mere epiphenomenon, devoid of any historical antecedents or ulterior material foundations. Within this textual universe, the "Porto Rican" peasant majorities and their resistances, taken as a whole, had no history or historical substance in and of themselves: they were a mere blank, an absence before the historically meaningful presence of what Beveridge called "the higher civilization of the nobler and more virile types of men."[9] The thus feminized and racialized "native"/peasant insurgency only seemed to confirm the manly superiority of the new invaders insofar as this rural insurgency became translated, paraphrasing Visvanathan,[10] as the "contemporary ancestry" that the no-longer barbaric Europeans and their North American descendants had already lived out.

The plethora of aporias populating the colonialist fashioning of the subaltern subjects—for example, the violence of the rebellion vs. the racialized feminization of the rebels—as inconsistencies, did not seem to bother the authors of these narratives. As Memmi has suggested, these aporias merely provided "additional proof that it is useless to seek this inconsistency anywhere except in the colonizer himself."[11] Consequently, the transgressions of the subaltern masses further confirmed what the emergent colonizers already knew: that most of this population thus emerged as a meaningless and bewildering vacuum in need of both "contain[ment] and represent[ation] by dominating frameworks."[12] For Brigadier General Davis and his kind, the peasant insurgency validated the need to re-fasten these "unchained masses" to the course of [a new] history—the history of "enlightened civilization"—and the need to reshackle them with the (North American) bonds of self-control and virtue. Only such a civilization could bring to an end future "Saturnalia[s] of crime," hence avoiding added violations of the "ordinary standards of public morality."

Additionally, such dominant containment and colonialist representation authenticated again the supremacy and agency of the new colonizers. To paraphrase Said's comments about the British and French dealings with "Orientals": since the "Porto Rican" peasant majorities were members of a subject race, they had to be subjected—it was that simple.[13] By stopping "[t]his lawlessness . . . [through taking] control . . . in the most disturbed districts," Davis' troops continued the noble mission later characterized by President Theodore Roosevelt as "bringing order out of chaos" in this particular "fair tropic island from which the valor of our soldiers and sailors has driven the Spanish flag."[14] The chaotic darkness, effeminate past, and savage strangeness of Puerto Rico would give way to an orderly, potentially manly (or at least adolescent), illuminated, and normalized "Porto Rico."

In this new Caribbean U.S. possession, only the preceding colonial regime had a history. And, in turn, the emergent masters understood this history as contemptible due to the cruel despotism it had inflicted on the "natives." The Spaniards had not taken adequate care of their Caribbean wards. To represent this situation in such a way, therefore, was to confirm the contemporary North American discourses regarding the decadence of most of contemporary Europe in general. In particular, it authenticated what Beveridge saw as the "senility" of a "debased civilization" such as Spain, and legitimized the role of the United States as the hegemonic subject in "the mission of our race, trustees under God, of the civilization of the world," the mission of "his chosen people," for which "God had . . . been preparing the English-speaking and teutonic peoples for a thousand years" (*Beveridge*, 68, 119, 121).

Accordingly, the new colonial order would usher into history an entire people (including the Creole propertied and educated classes), all of whom were perceived as inheriting varying degrees of primitivism, medievalism, and national-cultural infancy: the racial antiquity that "English-speaking and teutonic peoples" had long surpassed. Although understandable to a certain extent, those "weeks of a reign of terror" clearly demonstrated that reasonable, civilized, and respectable social subjects—with inherently adult identities—did not inhabit "Porto Rico." U.S. colonialism would accomplish this tutelage, this "civilizing mission," in the very process of erasing the abominable and uncultivated history of Spanish colonialism. As Visvanathan has more generally indicated, "The West as modernity obtains the mandate of power and responsibility over this world left behind by history. It is science as the modern man's 'gaze' that brings the primitive and the archaic back into contemporaneity" (p. 41).

In particular, the burden of such "enlightenment" compelled the United States to police—morally and literally—the new dispossessed "natives" who, according to this colonialist narrative, had sprung up in such an unseemly manner: therein the imported, imposed, and caricaturesque vision of the French Revolution—the Terror. Such a vision explains the displaced desire for a Jacobinist upheaval without a massive and bloody retribution. The new hegemonic subject required the invocation of a phantasm, but one that would impossibly incarnate the completely methodical yet absolutely unrestricted disruption of the previous socioeconomic and political system.

"We Are Not in the Heart of Africa, Gentlemen!"

Mainstream newspapers in the Island at this time expressed their surprise and indignation at the spreading rural-class violence, designating it as the product of "seditious bands" (*partidas sediciosas*). Consciously or not, the local newspapers tended to elide the manifestations of similar incidents during the preceding ninety-some years. Through these means, the voices of the educated and propertied classes in the Island (Creole and/or European-born) sought to re-member a legendary idyll where pastoral harmony reigned supreme: ostensibly, a desire to recapture an ideal innocence that never had existed yet nevertheless persisted in memory. Such ideological maneuvers surfaced as heavily laden with the multiple contradictions of a colonial reality they tried desperately, yet unsuccessfully, to grasp and re-imagine.

For example, *La Democracia,* in early November of 1898, echoed Brigadier General Davis' representation of the poor-peasant-turned-brigand as a foolhardy brute. This description includes the suggestion of peasant social suicide and individual self-destruction as causal factors, even as the journal capriciously reconstructs the social history of the Island while ingratiating itself to the new colonizers.

> General Brooke should be made to know that we never had any bandits in Puerto Rico and that no common sense man shoulders with such people if they exist. He must take in consideration that what happens today is due to our former administration. Our poor country people have many grievances to avange [*sic*]; they are malducated [*sic*], they believe their time has come to redress and go at it [the] best way they can[,] knowing that they will have to suffer from it.[15]

This text establishes a clear demarcation between the "common sense man," on the one hand, and "bandits," "such people," "our poor country people," "vengeful," "uneducated," etc., on the other hand. To a certain extent, the newspaper editors recognized the end of their cultural monopoly as members of the propertied and better educated classes in the Island in relation to the new colonialist power. Ironically enough, this transpired at the very juncture in which the Creole segments of these classes attempted to hegemonically reconstitute themselves: as the authentic representatives and legitimate territorial heirs of all things true to the Island's birthright (as compared with the majority of the Puerto Rican population). These social sectors also fashioned the "native" majorities as ignorant and even as self-destructively inclined—when left to follow their own base instincts. Such an ideological representation merely validated the need to politically mobilize the propertied and educated Creole and/or European-born sectors. At the same time, this discourse justified their leadership within Puerto Rico's political arena.

These Creole and/or resident-European textual practices coupled two discursive clusters, the first one being the Otherness that framed the local laboring classes during much of the nineteenth century. And, secondly, there were the narratives through which the new and contradictory bloc of propertied and educated classes in the Island (Creole and North American) henceforth constructed and represented the "native" majorities. The late nineteenth-century texts are quite eloquent, despite their inconsistencies. But, as with the inconsistencies of the "Porto Rican" masses that haunted the imagination of the new colonizers, the fact that "the traits ascribed to the colonized are incompatible with one another . . . does not bother his prosecutor" (Memmi, p. 83)—in this case "his" Creole or European-born prosecutor. The vision of the peaceful, primitive, idle, apathetic peasant counterposed to "humanity" and civilization exemplifies one of these discrepancies. For instance, a late nineteenth-century journalist described the peasantry as thinking "very little of revolts," being "docile, indifferent," and having "little malice," but possessing an "ignorance . . . as crude as one could expect from men who spend their lives in the forests and almost beyond all human contact . . . "[16]

But the "native" peasant also personifies the self-centered brute, prone to numerous depravities: the very incarnation of a dangerous nature and evil notions. Another educated writer of the same period stated that the Puerto Rican peasant goes on with "his" life with "[the emptiness of the] night in his brain, driven by miserly egotism, lacking any kind of great ideal," a situation followed by "the natural human inclinations, unmodified by education and morals, accompanied by vices and harmful instincts," all of which allegedly gave rise later to "the most wicked ideas, mostly as a result of backwardness and of error" (ibid.).

Hence, the continuing re-codification of the majority of the Puerto Rican populace as Caliban by the previously dominant sectors in the Island (socioeconomically and/or politically). The laboring poor still materialized within these texts as logically suspect of unlawful activities in general and of violent disruption of the social order in particular. An early twentieth-century Creole historian recalled the paradoxical character of peasant inscription in the following manner: If the peasant was found in the caves, "as a believer in the spirit cults might," the neighborhood deputy (*comisario*) would immediately record the peasant's activities "for acting *suspiciously* and for being an enemy of the Government."[17] If the peasant "squatted by the seashore, to contemplate the movement of the waves," the local constabulary (*Guardia Civil*) would demand to see a personal-identification pass, searching "him" because "he" was believed to be "watching furtively, awaiting a filibuster expedition" (ibid.).

In one form or another, the formerly hegemonic classes persisted in this cultural mapping for most of the 1898–1947 period. Most of the time these discourses dovetailed nicely with the looming colonialist narratives. In this manner, the Creole—and Creolized (European-born)—propertied and educated classes re-constituted their own agency as new political subjects and as [colonized] citizens. These nineteenth-century narratives concerning the need to establish order in one's own house substantially informed the urgency these social elements felt for recapturing the lost Eden of the Great Puerto Rican Family[18] or for reaching the New Jerusalem of full rights as U.S. citizens. History and Destiny had called upon these classes to pacify and contain a social space ("one's own house") simultaneously *theirs*—as the rightful Heirs of the Land—and *not-theirs,* being unevenly contested from above and outside (by the U.S.-based propertied interests and their juridico-political agents) and from below and inside (by the "native" laboring classes). At best, some colonized variant of liberal paternalism, propertied nationalism, and/or "brotherly" intentions of moral uplift attenuated the Creole and Creolized textual construction of the peasant majorities.

Besides the social insurgency in the countryside, other corollary popular practices erupted during the first two years of the U.S. occupation. Inflationary levels jumped considerably and, together with a whole chain of additional factors, this had a negative impact on the more impoverished urban contingents of the laboring population. The response to this social dislocation took the form of an increase in urban violence and in alternate economic practices—all, in turn, heavily criminalized.[19] Intertwined with all of the above were the brawls, clashes, and even full-scale riots that broke out between U.S. soldiers and Puerto Rican civilians, mostly poor laborers. For the most part, these and other conflicts that erupted during 1898–1899 did not connote an organized and massive nationalistic resistance to the U.S. invasion.[20]

However, the proliferation of conflicts (small and large) between U.S. troops and "native" civilians underlined several social and national-cultural/racial contradictions that had until then remained submerged: contradictions between North Americans and "Porto Ricans," as well as contradictions between the different segments of Island society. In particular, this is illustrated by the clashes that involved the propertied and educated local population. One minor incident implicated two "respectable [Creole] ladies" who, while strolling down the streets of Ponce, became the unwary targets of unnecessary manhandling at the hands of U.S. soldiers on patrol. According to Picó in *1898,* on October 4, 1898, an editorial in a local newspaper asserted:

> If General Henry, . . . does not try to stop such scenes from taking place, scenes which the town of Ponce is not accustomed to witnessing, we will be forced to send a strong message to the government of Washington signed by all the inhabitants of this city. We are not in the heart of Africa, gentlemen! (p. 178)

This complaint reflects the racist and Euro/Americo-centric fantasies of choice members of "Porto Rican" society. Ironically, this editorial also illustrates the extent to which the upper stratum of the Island refused being interpellated by the element of the new dominant U.S. knowledges that positioned these privileged "natives" as *mere "natives."* Since most of the propertied and educated inhabitants of the Island saw themselves as the fellow progeny of European descendants (vis-à-vis North Americans), they therefore saw themselves as deserving treatment very different from the one meted out to "the races which like the African and the Malay," as Rev. Josiah Strong said, "were many centuries behind the Anglo Saxon in development."[21]

The fact that such a differential treatment did not always occur began confirming a reality that materialized throughout the entire 1898–1947 period: in Memmi's words, "the bourgeois colonized, . . . the most favored colonized will never be anything but colonized people . . . [meaning] that words, that certain rights will forever be refused them, and that certain advantages are reserved strictly for [the colonizer]" (p. 9). For the propertied and educated "Porto Ricans," this colonial situation also contextualized the limits of what Homi Bhabha has called colonial mimicry: namely, the persistence of the colonizer's " . . . desire for a reformed recognizable Other, as *a subject of difference that is almost the same but not quite*. Which is to say that the discourse of mimicry is constructed around an *ambivalence*; in order to be effective mimicry must continually produce its slippage, its excess, its difference."[22]

The racialization of intrapopular discrepancies also surfaced within this setting of colonial mimicry, gesturing toward both the previous and the coming colonizers: for instance, the case of the light-skinned laborer José Maldonado (a.k.a., "Aguila Blanca"), whose outlaw peasant band became the target of unrelenting pursuit by U.S. troops across the southern part of the Island during the second half of 1898. Subsequently a legendary figure among the anticolonialist educated Creoles (from the 1930s to the present), José Maldonado also became known in his day for having repeated and vehement disputes with black and mulatto laborers.[23]

"A Strong Central Power Should Exist . . . to Cope with these Masses of Ignorant, Half-Starved Inhabitants"

Dismantled by 1899, the old Spanish police units gave way to the new colonial police force created to address the more widespread incidents of social violence and theft. Between 1899 and 1902, two corps existed within this institution (the Insular Police and the Municipal Police), then organized by a U.S. civilian ultimately under the direct control of the colonial Governor. In the course of the following six years both of these police bodies fused, having jurisdiction over the entire Island. As of the 1902–1908 period, this consolidated corps had one police precinct per municipality, each under the general command of the central police headquarters in San Juan. The new laws placed the colonial Police Chief under the immediate orders of a three-member Police Commission appointed by the Island's Governor.[24] Although the high command recruited the rank and file members of the police force from the masses of "native" landless peasants and unemployed urban laborers, the medium level and top officers tended to come from the lower stratum of the Creole propertied and educated classes. Until the late 1930s, this institution had a North American officer as its head.

A number of corollary institutions also surfaced at this time. The administrative authority of the new colonial Justice Department, organized in 1899, encompassed the judges, courts, and prisons. With the abolition of the Spanish court system that same year, its U.S. counterpart divided the Island into five judicial districts. In 1900 the federal Congress passed a law (the Foraker Act) constitutionally legitimizing the Island's colonial condition, establishing a local civilian-led government, creating a Supreme Court in Puerto Rico, and giving official recognition to the judicial reforms introduced under the U.S. military regime of 1898–1900. The latter changes included the founding of a "U.S. District Court for Porto Rico" (known locally as the Federal Court) that attended to the claims and litigations of U.S. citizens in the Island. ("Native" residents became U.S. citizens only after the U.S. Congress passed the Jones Act in 1917.) Between 1902 and 1904, the federal government laid the final groundwork for the Island's new judicial system when Congress acknowledged the "Porto Rican" legislative assembly's authority over the local courts and partially over the Island's Justice Department. The local legislature approved new Penal and Civil Codes, federal strictures compelling the latter body to borrow heavily from the corresponding codes of Montana, California, and Louisiana.[25]

Most judicial districts had a jail, San Juan being the site of the colonial penitentiary. Semi-autonomously administered between 1901 and 1909, the Island-wide carceral archipelago first fell under the management of a Director of Prisons and later under a Director of Health, Charities, and Corrections. Local jails remained under the supervision of the municipal governments. This penal system did not suffer any important modifications until the late 1940s.[26]

The police register of "native" transgressive behavior clearly indicates a rise in a whole spectrum of popular practices then officially represented as very high levels of social violence and illegal economic activity. For example, the rate in the number of people arrested for murder seemed higher than the proportion that prevailed until the Great Depression and subsequent War years (see table 4). This occurred despite the differences between the previous categories in the preexistent penal code and the forthcoming code and despite the confusion that reigned in the local court system during 1898–1899. The latter events emerged in the midst of an exceptionally low rate of arrests for all crimes. Even so, this also occurred at a time in which, as reported by Brigadier General Davis in 1902, property crimes such as theft, burglary, and horse stealing were located higher on the list of principal specific causes of arrest than in the following forty or so years (pp. 100–101, 228).

One of Brigadier General Davis' recommendations in his 1902 report becomes, in this sense, particularly significant as well as prescient. Even within the racist terms of its delivery this passage encapsulated, to a large extent, a fundamental task of the new regime in terms of restructuring the profit-oriented organization of the economic sphere. Such eloquence and transparency were rare within the dominant knowledges and frameworks instituted by the U.S. occupation. Although Davis appreciated the prophylactic measures adopted by Spain to "control the criminal class" as "summary and probably effective," "[n]o such rigorous and arbitrary means [could] again be employed" because "[i]n all enlightened countries possessing representative institutions the public will determine[d] the repression and restraining measures and their execution" (p. 105). In his best estimation, "[t]hree-fourths of the people living in Porto Rico [*sic*]" were "of the very lowest class of those who [were] rated civilized," their "moral senses" described as "blunted." Since the "process by which their moral consciences may be developed" was understood to be "one of slow application and development," a "strong central power should exist," not only "equipped to cope with these masses of ignorant, half-starved inhabitants," but to also "protect the persons and property of the well-disposed, whether poor or rich" (ibid.).

This official statement provides another opportunity to carry out what Ranajit Guha calls "detect[ing] the chinks which have allowed [subaltern] 'comment' to worm its way through the plate armour of fact."[27] Davis' text not only registers the "native" resistance to the *prevailing* social order and property relations. His report extrapolates from this revolt (the peasant uprising) by anticipating the "native" resistances to the *projected* social order and property relations. In doing so, he identifies the existence—in the practices of these "evil-disposed classes"—of an alternate way of ordering society and organizing relations of property: an alternative whose expansion and triumph required prevention at all cost—the "containment and representation" of the subaltern subjects "by dominating frameworks"[28]figuring prominently in this respect.

Given the structural objectives inherent to the successful and rapid implantation of colonialist capitalism in "Porto Rico," the reader should remember Foucault's admonition:

> If the economic take-off of the West began with the techniques that made possible the accumulation of capital, it might perhaps be said that the methods for administering the accumu-

> lation of men [*sic*] made possible a political take-off in relation to the traditional, ritual, costly, violent forms of power, which soon fell into disuse and were superseded by a subtle, calculated technology of subjection.[29]

For Davis, then, in order to guarantee "the persons and property of the well-disposed," that is in order to establish the conditions under which such property could exist and flourish (Foucault: "the economic take-off") against the resistance of those whose "moral senses are blunted," certain corollary circumstances needed to be created: "a strong central power should exist" (Foucault: "the techniques that made possible the accumulation of capital"). The need to develop the "moral consciences" of "the very lowest class of those who are rated civilized" concurrently merged with a process that eventually would do without "summary and probably effective . . . rigorous and arbitrary means" (Foucault: "the traditional, ritual, costly, violent forms of power, which . . . [would fall] into disuse"). In order to have the "public determine the repression and restraining measures and their execution" (Foucault: "a political take-off"), once more it became imperative that "a strong central power should exist" (Foucault: "the methods for administering the accumulation of men") so as to cope with the opposition of "these masses of ignorant, half-starved inhabitants."

Once again, a series of linkages come to the fore, among: an effective colonialist capitalism and the State/discursive containment and representation of the subaltern subjects of the popular illegalities; the politization of the economy and of the dispossession process' structural brutality as an economic force; the laws of value ruling by means of the rule of law; the containment and representation of the "Porto Rican" majorities; and the colonial territorialization of the new power-knowledge nexus. By analogy some of Trotman's observations are equally apropos.

> But this concern with property was intensified because of the nature of the society. In a society where the majority was propertyless and where the continued wealth of the elite depended on their continuing in that state, there was obvious cause for concern . . . The incidence of crimes against property clearly reflected the level of distress and inequalities in the society and the actions that individuals took as they sought to relieve this distress or to redress the perceived inequalities. It also revealed the actions the elite initiated in defense of their interests and property.[30]

Table 4 Number and Rates of Arrests for Murder/Attempted Murder and Number and Rates for Suicide Cases in Puerto Rico, Selected Years, Both Sexes

YEAR	TOTAL MURDERS	TOTAL POPULATION	RATE PER 100,000 INHABITANTS	TOTAL ATTEMPTED MURDERS	RATE PER 100,000 INHABITANTS	TOTAL SUICIDES	RATE PER 100,000 INHABITANTS
1899	130	953,243	13.6	N/A	—	N/A	—
1902	41	998,180*	4.1	52	5.2	N/A	—
1903	52	1,013,159*	5.1	37	3.7	N/A	—
1905	81	1,043,117*	7.8	35	3.4	N/A	—
1906	34	1,058,096*	3.2	16	1.5	N/A	—
1910	61	1,118,012	5.5	34	3.0	N/A	—
1911	46	1,134,983	4.1	42	3.7	N/A	—
1912	63	1,152,214	5.5	38	3.3	N/A	—
1913	42	1,169,705	3.4	27	2.3	153	13.1
1915	35	1,208,911	2.9	N/A	—	83	6.9
1916	41	1,223,789	3.4	30	2.3	75	6.1
1919	N/A	1,281,629	—	N/A	—	79	6.2
1924	34	1,392,442	2.4	N/A	—	106	7.6
1926	101	1,446,271	7.0	N/A	—	117	8.1
1927	74	1,466,223	5.0	N/A	—	123	8.4
1929	76	1,517,569	5.0	N/A	—	102	6.7
1931	N/A	1,573,720	—	N/A	—	313	19.9
1934	246**	1,674,050	14.7	N/A	—	370	22.1
1936	338**	1,739,118	19.4	N/A	—	536	30.8
1937	294**	1,771,652	16.6	N/A	—	551	31.1
1938	258**	1,804,187	14.3	N/A	—	512	28.4

1940	223**	1,869,255	11.9	N/A	—	476	25.5
1943	254**	1,971,689	12.9	N/A	—	407	20.6
1946	309**	2,093,461	14.8	N/A	—	528	25.2
1948	N/A	2,142,413	—	N/A	—	463	21.6

*My estimate

**Includes voluntary manslaughter

SOURCES:In addition to sources already cited in table 3, see: Nilda Rivera de Morales, *Mortalidad en Puerto Rico, 1888–1967* (Escuela de Salud Pública, Recinto de Ciencias Médicas, Universidad de Puerto Rico, 1970), pp. 34, 43, 51, 55, 58, 61, 64, 67, 70, 76, 79, 82.

"The Wave of Blood," 1900–1906

The first six years of this century constituted a very difficult period for the oppressed sectors in the Island. The recorded levels of farm-animal theft at this time partially reflected this social distress. Between 1902 and 1906 the number of arrests for this kind of stealing oscillated between 204 (in 1902) and forty-nine (in 1906), as compared to between seventeen (in 1912 and in 1913) and twenty-three (in 1915) for the 1910–1916 period.[31]

The Silvestrini study indicates that for the first years of this century, in the monthly reports issued by the municipal police of San Juan, there were "countless cases of violations to the theft laws, especially of animals and food," a situation that possibly indicated "an increase in criminal activity that was being provoked by the prevailing economic crisis" (p. 38). This activity had increased to such an extent that "the residents of the Barrio Magueyes protested," stating that "they could no longer tolerate the brazen acts that the bandits had been carrying out there. Stealing was going on every day, every night, at all hours" (ibid.).

Although as a social practice the pilfering of farm and hacienda belongings tended to affect the small property owner more than it did capital, it nevertheless unsettled the sanctity of property itself—regardless of its quantity or character. Furthermore, it tended to undermine the savage iron laws of large-scale dispossession, hunger, inflation, and unemployment in the Island. Paraphrasing Trotman, one could say that, through such activity, these "native" laborers maintained their economic autonomy, not being forced into the colonial labor market (p. 115). Predial thieves would be even less persuaded to perform wage labor insofar as they supplemented what they could obtain from working the small land-plots available to them (but, mostly, not owned by them) with whatever income they could gain from this illegalized survival practice.

As was the case at other critical junctures during this first half century (such as 1915–1921 and 1930–1947), the literary production of local journalists and essayists tended to portray the illegal economic activities, together with social violence as a menacing wave. Such images materialized as a fundamental component in the inventory of meanings structuring the contradictory subject positions of the propertied and educated Creole classes, feeding into this social bloc's discourses regarding the laboring-class majority.

The racialized gender codes, the gendered racial scripts, and the sexualization of both of these textual practices materialized in very contradictory and complex ways, because, among other things, the dominating frameworks thus deployed by the privileged "natives" frequently found a homologous expression in the U.S. colonialist discourses structuring *all* of the "native" population—the educated and propertied Creoles included. More often, however, the colonialist knowledge-power nexus cemented the colonial pact along gendered, racialized, sexualized, and class-based lines. This tacit contract brought together all of the propertied and educated males ("native" and continental, colonized and colonialist) against all of the (colonized) dependent populations: females of all classes and the impoverished majorities of both genders. On this plane, the respectable, self-controlled, heterosexual, and enlightened masculinity/adulthood of the propertied and educated men (Creole and North American) now fashioned all of the laboring poor in the colony, together with all colonized women in general, as unruly (children) and willful (females).

Inasmuch as they ran counter to Reason and Order, disorder itself and particularly the trespasses of the colonized majorities became feminized and infantilized, all "native" women being re-presented as children, by both colonized male professionals, intellectuals, bureaucrats, bank administrators, hacendados, et al., as well as by colonialist male functionaries, plantation personnel, and bankers. At this second level, only the colonized impoverished masses of "Porto Rico" and the "native" women were Caliban to the manly Creole Ariels and U.S. Prosperos. Yet, the instability and uncertainty of such joint dominating frameworks and of the privileged "native" men's colonial mimicry persisted insofar as, ultimately, "the bourgeois colonized, . . . the most favored colonized [would] never be anything but colonized people" (Memmi, 9)—a tension that catalyzed this colonial mimicry even further.

For example, while commenting on his experiences as a district attorney in Mayagüez, one of the most prominent members of the Creole intelligentsia, José de Diego, quoted from an article (apparently written by himself) in *The San Juan News* circa 1900 in favor of the death penalty. According to de Diego, in Puerto Rico "the wave of blood [was] rising, rising so high that it [would] soon reach its ceiling," being "only limited by the law that Garofalo calls the [law of] criminal saturation."[32] De Diego was "not referring precisely to the previous years," when he understood there could have "existed special and very powerful causes in the development of delinquency," namely "the war [of 1898] and the [subsequent] political transformations" as well as "the terrible atmospheric influences and the state of misery that has blanketed the country as if in clouds of tears and fire." For him, these were "well known causes that always determine the growth of crimes against [individual] persons and against property" (ibid.).

After signalling—as historical context—the peasant insurgency that ensued during the period of direct military rule, the eminent pro-hacendado politician, anticolonialist orator, business lawyer, and literary figure, asks with alarm:

> But who has not observed the wave of blood, an evident sign of a great moral flood, and of the dreadful path created by the advent of the *detritus* deposited on the soul of our very noble people? Twenty-five years ago our mothers would make the sign of the cross whenever they heard or passed on the news of a homicide, as if the act was as rare as the presence of Lucifer; and now scarcely a day goes by without the press reporting the horrendous crimes that were taking place in all the towns of the Island. (ibid.)

In a text so abundant in Christian symbology, the signifier for "the soul of our very noble people" necessarily towered as "native"-white, masculine, and sexually honorable—as well as propertied and educated. Therefore, its opposite and relational dependent (the "evident sign of a great moral flood") would have been textualized as womanly, non-white, and/or libidinously perverse. On the other hand, local women (as "our mothers")—and, by implication, all those who have suffered (including former slaves and their descendants)—also stood for the bearers/makers of another sign: "the sign of the cross." In a way similar to that of the laboring poor, ex-captives, and children in general, Puerto Rican females exemplified both purity and danger, innocence and peril, the tenderly familiar and the absolutely strange and alien. This explained how the signifying practices of the Creole propertied and educated classes could metonymically link women, ex-captives and their descendants, children, and the laboring poor. The otherwise cleansing qualities of the new Great Flood and the spread of this, if not senseless, bloodshed contradictorily sutured together the various subject positions invoked by these tropes.

Yet, for de Diego, how could "our mothers" and "our" bloodline include former slaves, their descendants, and/or the laboring poor? After all, this was the same José de Diego who, together with other propertied and educated "natives," had in these same years protested the designation of Dr. José Celso Barbosa (a Jacobinist politician, leader of the "Partido Republicano," the political organ of many urban professionals and of the large sugar landowners) to the colonial Governor's cabinet because "Barbosa was black and Puerto Rican society regards such an appointment as [an] insensitive affront."[33] The answer seems to lie in the fracturing effects of the garbage that washed up on the shores of the Island's life force. By engulfing only the more ignorant and dispossessed sectors, paradoxically this waste had helped to cleanse and define what de Diego and his ilk understood by "Puerto Rican society": this flood had separated the former slaves, their descendants, and the laboring poor from "the soul of our very noble people." This virile, respectable, and sexually honorable "soul" now had to rise as a bulwark—moral, political, and civic—against the foreign bodies that threatened it from above (the U.S. colonizers) and from below (the colonized masses and all womanly influences), because, among other things, even this propertied and educated "soul" unfolded as the feminized, infantilized, and sexually depraved (colonized) "soul" fashioned by U.S. colonialist discourses.

Such exclusions trace what Gayatri Chakravorty Spivak in "Subaltern Studies: Deconstructing Historiography" has called the "moments of transgression" (p. 211) within the official text—even in the case of this official "native" text. In the final analysis, the "wave of blood" signalled by de Diego ontologically demarcated a "Puerto Rican society" menaced by subaltern subjects that ultimately could not be imagined—much less addressed—as constitutive elements of "his" society. The (informal) law of the ruled, the personification of the "[law of] criminal saturation"—a "law" whose embodiment he saw as external to "our very noble people"—raised questions, in practice, about de Diego's call for the rule of (institutional) law. For de Diego, the spread and institutionalization of the new dispossession process' large-scale economic violence could not possibly legitimize, much less explain, such bloodshed now that the "War . . . , [its] political transformations . . . [including] the state of misery" had allegedly passed.

His invocation of the State's right over the lives of its subjects and of the legitimate monopoly it had over the use of physical coercion stood as a desperate response to the "horrendous" right then practiced by the isolated but growing number of colonized masses: namely, "the dreadful path created by the advent of" putative rights over the lives of all subjects, rights by which criminal authors empirically negated the authority of the State. The fact that these misfits surfaced within a "native" text (even more so: in the text of an eminent anticolonialist politician) only indicated the non-subaltern character of the propertied and educated colonized subjects. Such misfits also exemplified the extent to which de Diego's colonial mimicry reproduced what Homi Bhabha calls "its slippage, its excess, its difference" (p. 126).

De Diego ends by adjudicating political responsibilities for what he understood as an otherwise unexplainable surge of social violence.

> It is not necessary to talk about the number and the nature of the scandalous acts perpetrated in the year 1898: since the time in which in the midst of the [Island] House of Representatives robbery was declared a political crime, it is best not to mention those politics and those crimes; but two long years have elapsed, we are under the tutelage of a perfectly organized civil government and the murders and the homicides have reached, with the end of the century, a terrifying number. (p. 34)

This same year, one of the local hacendado dailies corroborated de Diego's fears and condemnations by reporting that it was "evident, unfortunately, that criminal activity [was] on the rise" and "specifically around this southern portion of the Island, where apparently the sense of morality has reached its most extreme level of perversion . . . "[34] "Could it be," this same newspaper piece asked, "that the absence of work has stimulated this propensity towards crime?" Or could it have been the case that "a certain political propaganda ha[d] started exerting its effects?" It seemed that "this type of unlawful activity [was] increasing with each passing day, and that the authorities contemplate[d] such a serious social evil with indifference" (ibid.).

Once again, the absence of morals and idleness emerged as some of the perceived driving forces behind all of this violent criminal activity among the "evil-disposed classes." From this perspective, the random violence of the colonized masses appeared to stem from an amorphous alien subject that menaced the ancestral essence of Puerto Rican society. The official apathy, the political opportunism, and/or the obstacles placed in the path of Educated Aims loomed as the reasons behind this surge of social evil. De Diego seemed to understand such goals as embodied by the more responsible elements from within the propertied and educated classes taken as a whole (Creole and/or North American). This outlook supported the underlying premise that the "native" laboring classes, being of sound mind and given the opportunity, would *always* rather work for somebody else than pursue independent survival practices fraught with multiple risks. Only pernicious influences—stemming from a deficient lineage or from external factors that prey on the ignorant—could steer the dispossessed majorities away from the path of Law and Virtue. This too emerged as an integral part of the corresponding official discourses between 1898 and 1947.

Some of the mass responses, fashioned at this time as social violence, did not just destabilize the large-scale relocation and reproduction of colonial-capitalist relations. During the early years of the twentieth century, capital and the State also partially rearticulated and recuperated a number of these violent reactions to the even more violent dispossession process. The general context of such violence for 1900–1906 indicates the higher levels in this type of phenomenon: the arrests for disorderly conduct (fighting included) and for assault (all types) serve as two cases in point (see table 5). Additionally, there was a sharp rise in the frequency of riots, a practice that directly related to the incidence of both disorderly conduct and assault. These events took two principal forms.

First, the report just quoted from *La Democracia* shows that mob attacks ensued against the person and property of the political-party organs of the Creole hacendado bloc hegemonized by the large coffee landowners—namely, the "Partido Federal Americano" that, after 1904 and until 1924 was known as the "Partido Unión de Puerto Rico" or "Unionistas." Landless peasants and the urban poor that settled in the fringes of towns and cities figured prominently among those participating in these assaults and vandalism.[35] Although I have not found sufficient empirical data in this respect, these outbreaks appeared as a rather confused and transplanted echo of the rural/class violence and peasant settling-of-accounts of 1898–1899.[36] Whatever the direct association, the similarities between both events were not lost on some of the members of the hacendado's political leadership. Another editorial in the previously mentioned newspaper explicitly designated the attacks by urban multitudes with precisely the same term used in 1898–1899 to identify the peasant bands. It was "no longer a matter of isolated abuses, of attacks on property, of unbridled mobs careening through the streets harassing defenseless citizens, but of something more serious," this being a case of "perfectly organized *seditious bands* [*partidas sediciosas*] that march on peaceful populations."[37]

This linkage metamorphosized into a direct accusation when the political rivals of the Creole hacendado bloc—then in control of the lower house of the colonial legislature—passed a resolution in late 1900 proposing amnesty for the jailed peasant rebels.[38] These events have gone down in local historiography and in the Island's political memory as the "Republican Mobs" (*"turbas republicanas"*)

Table 5 Principal Specific Causes of Police Arrest in Order of Number of Arrests Carried Out, Selected Years, Both Sexes

1899	1902	1903	1905
1. Theft (all types)	1. Disorderly conduct (incl. fighting)	1. Disorderly conduct (incl. fighting)	1. Disorderly conduct
2. Burglary	2. Theft (all types)	2. Gambling	2. Violation of sanitary laws
3. Gambling	3. Assault (all types)	3. Assault (all types)	3. Gambling
4. Horse stealing	4. Gambling	4. Theft (all types)	4. Assault (all types)
5. Murder	5. Drunkenness	5. Violation of sanitary laws	5. Theft (all types)
6. Escaped prisoners	6. Abduction	6. Drunkenness	6. Arms violations
7. Robbery	7. Violation of sanitary laws	7. Abduction	7. Drunkenness
8. Assault (all types)	8. Resisting arrest	8. Smuggling and revenue fraud	8. Abuse of confidence
9. Arson	9. Burglary	9. Arms violation	9. Resisting arrest
10. Rape	10. Arms violations	10. Fugitives of justice	10. Smuggling and revenue fraud
	11. Cattle theft	11. Swindling	11. Seduction
	12. Vagrancy	12. Seduction	

1906	1910	1911	1912
1. Disorderly conduct	1. Disorderly conduct	1. Disorderly conduct	1. Disorderly conduct
2. Violation of sanitary laws	2. Gambling	2. Gambling	2. Gambling
3. Gambling	3. Violation of sanitary laws	3. Arms violations	3. Violation of sanitary laws
4. Assault (all types)	4. Violation of road laws	4. Assault (all types)	4. Arms violations

5. Arms violations	5. Assault (all types)	5. Violation of sanitary laws	5. Assault (all types)
6. Theft (all types)	6. Arms violations	6. Violation of road laws	6. Violation of road laws
7. Seduction	7. Theft (all types)	7. Theft (all types)	7. Theft (all types)
8. Drunkenness	8. Abuse of confidence	8. Abuse of confidence	8. Requisitioned
9. Resisting arrest	9. Corruption of minors	9. Malicious injury	9. False representation
10. Smuggling and/or revenue fraud	10. False representation	10. Sunday closing	10. Corruption of minors
11. Burglary	11. Burglary	11. False representation	11. Abuse of confidence
12. Requisitioned	12. Requisitioned	12. Requisitioned	12. Crimes against public justice

1913	1916	1929	1931
1. Disorderly conduct	1. Gambling	1. Disorderly conduct	1. Disorderly conduct
2. Gambling	2. Disorderly conduct	2. Assault (all types)	2. Assault (all types)
3. Violation of sanitary laws	3. Violation of sanitary laws	3. Violation of sanitary laws	3. Violation of road laws
4. Assault (all types)	4. Theft (all types)	4. Arms violations	4. Violation of sanitary laws
5. Arms violations	5. Arms violations	5. Theft (all types)	5. Theft (all types)
6. Theft (all types)	6. Assault (all types)	6. Liquor law violations	6. Gambling
7. Abuse of confidence		7. Gambling	7. Sunday closing
8. Sunday closing		8. False representation	8. False representation
9. Robbery		9. Malicious injury	9. Embezzlement
10. False representation		10. Child neglect	10. Malicious injury
11. Crimes against public justice		11. False weights & measures	11. False weights & measures
12. Burglary			12. Child neglect

Table 5 *(Continued)*

1934	1938	1940	1943
1. Disorderly conduct	1. Traffic violations	1. Traffic violations	1. Disorderly conduct
2. Traffic violations	2. Disorderly conduct	2. Disorderly conduct	2. Traffic violations
3. Assault (all types)	3. Assault (all types)	3. Assault (all types)	3. Assault (all types)
4. Theft (all types)	4. Gambling	4. Gambling	4. Gambling
5. Arms violations	5. Arms violations	5. Liquor law violations	5. Theft (all types)
6. Gambling	6. Theft (all types)	6. Arms violations	6. Arms violations
7. Liquor law violations	7. Liquor law violations	7. Theft (all types)	7. Burglary
8. Violation of road laws	8. Violation of road laws	8. Burglary	8. Liquor law violations
9. Burglary	9. Burglary	9. Abuse of confidence	9. Abuse of confidence
10. Abuse of confidence	10. Abuse of confidence	10. Violation of road laws	10. Violation of road laws
11. Murder/manslaughter	11. Murder/manslaughter	11. Murder/manslaughter	11. Murder/manslaughter
12. Sexual crimes	12. Sexual crimes	12. Buying/Selling stolen property	12. Sexual crimes

1946
1. Disorderly Conduct
2. Traffic Violations
3. Gambling
4. Theft/Robbery
5. Arms violations
6. Burglary
7. Rape/Prostitution/Sexual Crimes
8. Assault (all types)
9. Murder/manslaughter

SOURCES: (See table 3)

because of the political recuperation and reorientation coming from the political party led by the emergent sugar interests and by the Jacobinist liberal-professionals, namely, the "Partido Republicano."

Particularly during the second half of 1900, these incidents of urban mob attacks began taking place almost on a daily basis—and were not just limited to the larger cities such as San Juan and Ponce. In the mountainous town of Cayey, for example, laboring-class multitudes stormed the jails to free other previously arrested members of these unruly crowds. U.S. troops rescued the local constabulary stationed at this jail but not before armed members of the crowd fired upon both these soldiers and the policemen. Unknown assailants stoned the mayors of several towns, while these officials also became the target of random shootings and of anonymous threatening letters.[39]

These mob attacks exemplified in particularly explicit ways the class hatred between the hacendados and the urban multitudes, as illustrated by this same newspaper editorial, a month later. In this piece, *La Democracia* represented the landless peasants and urban laborers as "the thieves, the murderers, the burglars, the vagrants, and all that rabble of dagger and cudgel," they being the ones who lived "in these [urban] centers, the only places where one can perceive the environment necessary for their existence."[40]

As would happen throughout the 1898–1947 period, various other forms of social antagonism were often read through the prevailing gender and sexual codes. Since the victims of this wickedness appeared as the noble, manly, yet increasingly former Fathers of Tenant Property (*Padres del Agrego*), the victimizers—the social opposites—signified the gendered antithesis of these Lords of the Land: hence, the feminization and sexually depraved inscription of disorder. The loathing that this dispossessed "rabble" felt toward their previous historical masters surfaced in no less expressive ways, their signifying practices being no less gendered and sexualized. This time the masculinism of the dispossessed, re-inscribed the hacendado (male) politicians and ideologues as useless and faint-hearted women. Occasionally, this particular sign system was sexualized further by fashioning these great-propertied politicians as cross-dressing men, that is, as less-than-men and not-quite-women. In this manner, the urban multitude recast itself as intrepid, daring, and irrefutably masculine/heterosexual. This textualization of "native" conflicts further complicated the existing contradictions and coincidences in the practices of feminization and sexualization within the propertied/educated classes—Creole and North American—thus destabilizing the very meanings and lived experiences of "race," "gender," "class," "nationality," and "sexuality" in the Island at this time.

One particular incident persuasively illustrates this very point. According to Negrón Portillo in *Las turbas republicanas,*

> One of the more "picturesque" activities took place in February of 1901, when Mauleón [one of the principal leaders of these rowdy urban gatherings] ran through the streets of San Juan dressed as a "loca" [transvestite; literally: a mad woman] and the "loca" that was being impersonated was none other than Muñoz Rivera [the principal leader of the hacendado party]. . . . He was followed by "several ill-featured elements" with signs that read "The Mobs of San Juan." A loud multitude in an oxcart led on the latter. . . . The shouts of the paraders were typical: "Long live the peoples rights!" "Down with the despots!" And, obviously, considering the purpose of this activity, they also screamed, "Death to the 'loca'!" (pp. 97–98)

In this way, the contested space of local representation became textualized. Repeatedly, these conflicts played themselves out through the authorial functions of social definition and the authority to appear in place of the Other in the political arena. The so-called "Republican Mobs" loomed as one of the few instances in which, however contradictorily, the laboring poor erupted within the official terrain of conventionally defined Island politics.

The racialization of such social antagonisms also took shape at this time. For instance, *La Democracia* thundered against one of the leaders of the Republican Mobs in Ponce, the black laborer Antonio Guilbe (a.k.a., "El Negro"), calling him "the worst species of vulgar individual," one of the members of "Mayor Guzmán's black guard."[41] The fact that the largest contingents of these disorderly urban gatherings inhabited the coastal cities of Ponce and in San Juan, which were populated by large concentrations of laborers of African descent, further contextualizes the racial specificity of "all that rabble of dagger and cudgel" from the standpoint of the Creole hacendados and intelligentsia. In turn, Guilbe signified "race" because only nonwhites possessed such markers of difference within the Island's racial codifications. This particular aspect of the fashioning of race in Puerto Rico coincided with some of the U.S. racial scripts, despite the broader divergence with respect to other racial lines of demarcation in the North American republic as opposed to most of the Caribbean area.

Consequently and as a paradoxical counterpoint to the colonialist feminization and sexualization of all the "natives" (including the privileged ones), disorder not only unfolded as always already feminized and sexualized within many of the textual practices of the Creole propertied and educated classes: it also materialized as metonymically racialized in terms of being hidden, shadowy, dark. Once again, like children, all females, and the impoverished majorities in general, the black and mulatto laborers of the coast and urban areas would accordingly incarnate similar tropes. "They" became cast as naive, innocent, and dependent including corollary attributes such as ignorance and vulgarity. Yet "they" loomed dangerously, as in: "the thieves, the murderers, the burglars, the vagrants." "They" were tenderly familiar, as in the usage of the term "negro" or "negra" as an expression of endearment among all social sectors. But "they" also exemplified the absolutely strange and alien, as in the witchcraft and bizarre customs many in the Island's countryside attributed to the darker-skinned people of the coastal regions and urban centers. These metonymical associations among all women, children, the laboring poor in general, and black and mulatto laborers in particular, especially within the context of disorder and unruly behavior, would once more couple the signifying practices of the Creole propertied and educated classes with those of their North American counterparts. And this transpired, both despite and because the latter, nevertheless persisted in racializing, feminizing, and sexualizing as social inferiors *all* of the colonized population, a category that ultimately encompassed the upper stratum of "native" society.

The police and the propertied classes at this time also mobilized members of this same pauperized mass of urban laborers and recently migrated landless peasants against the incipient trade-union activity of the "Federación Libre de Trabajadores" (FLT). The latter organization was one of the other forms of social resistance adopted by a different sector of the laboring classes: the impoverished artisans. Nonetheless, the sociopolitical rationales behind the mob attacks against the FLT representatives are much more complex. For one thing, these desperately impoverished urban elements needed income and carrying out such acts garnered them money and other material benefits. Yet, within this context, additional factors require consideration, such as the de facto political alliance that briefly existed during 1902–1904 between the political party of the hacendados and the leadership of the budding labor movement. Within the multiply displaced meanings of these freshly uprooted rural laborers, the physical symbols that identified their recent class enemies readily blurred—in the terrain of political representation—with the emblems of the organized destitute craftsmen. Additionally, let us not forget that in the towns and cities these artisans competed with the landless peasants for sources of income (legal and illegal).[42]

"The Mob Became Turbulent and Ungovernable," 1900–1909

This type of rioting, and social violence in general, also emerged as the trademark of many labor conflicts and became one of the salient features of most of the electoral activity between 1898 and 1947. This explains the custom of reinforcing the police with provisional recruits during electoral years. Throughout this first half century, electoral contests rapidly developed into moments when social violence could legitimately surface and be openly expressed, as long as it remained identifiable within the parameters of the election process. Of course, this practice developed as valid in mostly de facto terms: by no means did it ever become official policy—governmental or party-related. However, all the political parties tacitly recognized the utility of such practices, down to and including the use of extraofficial party-thugs.[43]

Among the laboring classes, electoral violence appeared as another way of settling old accounts and disputes of all sorts: individual, family, community, class, gender, racial, traditional-political, monetary, and so on. Under the cover of a *civil and peaceful* electoral conflict, the oppressed sectors drew and redrew the features of other types of grievances *through the use of a physical force* not at all tolerated in other moments and contexts by the State apparatuses: therein the complexity and socially contradictory character of such a phenomenon. To simply dismiss it as either popular irrationality, or as another case of laboring-class elements being turned into the useful but foolish tools of the ruling classes, is a serious mistake.[44]

As in the case of the rural insurgency of 1898–1899 and in other similar cases of recurrent social violence throughout the first half of this century, the colonialist dominating frameworks would reinscribe "native" electoral violence as yet another instance of what Milton Fowles called "the excitable nature and uncompromising temperament of Latin Americans"[45] and of the fact that "they [were] a pathetic and childlike . . . people."[46] Once again, "Porto Ricans" became defined as in need of both representation-construction and representation-guidance.

The general practice of settling social scores (while resisting the inroads of the colonial-capitalist dispossession process) contextualizes, among other things, the mass violence directed by the laboring classes against the large property owners and against the State during wage-labor conflicts. Much of this labor resistance was basically defensive and trade-union related. The first big wave of strife took place during the ferociously repressed strikes of 1900–1902 that occurred in the construction, dock, and tobacco-manufacturing sectors. The other major strike wave (1905–1907) withstood equally harsh suppression. These strikes not only affected the same sectors implicated during 1900–1902, but they also involved the workers in the sugar and bakery-products sectors.[47]

The strikes in the dockyard trucking company and in the sugar plantations were particularly notorious for the significant degree of militant resistance on the part of the striking laborers during 1905 and 1906. In 1905, "twenty or thirty discontented agitators . . . preaching incendiarism, were ready to sacrifice the sugar crop of the island."[48] As in the recent past, such situations brought about "the appointing of 75 men for temporary duty," in addition to "compelling this department to practically withdraw police protection from other parts of the island to send them to the sugar-cane districts" (ibid.).

The 1906 account of Police Commissioner Hamill explicitly describes the clashes with the trucking company, which this time included the surrounding community. As included in colonial Governor Winthrop's report of that year, Commissioner Hamill declared that the strike had "lasted over a month and on July 31 the conditions assumed a serious aspect" when that afternoon the truckers "attempted to interfere with a private truckman" (p. 199). When the police were called, the "strikers held their ground in defiance of the police" and subsequently a "clash occurred and several were hurt." Finally, the striking truckers "dispersed [and] a number of arrests were made" (ibid.).

Winthrop's report, however localized, portrays the 1906 dockyard strike as an urban insurrection with the colonial police acting as an occupation army. The panorama evokes a riot in one of the British colonies in Asia or Africa, complete with implied praise for the "Porto Rican" Ghurkas.

> August 1 saw the climax of the situation. The mob became turbulent and ungovernable. Throughout the day there were encounters between the lawless crowd and the police. The police used force but the gangs retaliated in the same measure.

> They used stones, bottles, revolvers, and refuse as weapons against the police. (ibid.)

Nightfall brought more than darkness, the strangeness of these "native" hordes in the colonialist gaze being metonymically related to the unlit environment: the white North American officer once again faced the barbarism that his kind had long left behind in the caves of Europe.

> When night fell upon the city it was found that all the electric lights had been destroyed and absolute darkness enveloped all. The unruly element intrenched [*sic*] themselves upon the housetops, from where they kept up a continual attack on the police. It was useless to dislodge them. (ibid.)

To borrow again the words of Ranajit Guha in "The Prose of Counter-Insurgency," "these documents make no sense except in terms of a code of pacification" (p. 59). Such official accounts surfaced as additional sites where the "turbulent and ungovernable mobs" and "lawless crowds" proposed another form of social governance and a different law: one where the urban dispossessed would not be caught in the colonial double pincers of a rising cost of living and starvation wages.

The dockyard strike of 1906 ended with the triumph of (colonial-capitalist) law and order thanks to the wiles of the constabulary's North American leadership. According to Winthrop, the police "were withdrawn, and, as all the fury was against the police only, they became pacified by their retirement" (p. 199). Early the following morning, the police were "stationed on the roofs to prevent a repetition of the scenes of the night before," a maneuver that "brought matters to a standstill, and several days after, the strikers abandoned their cause. The strike cost the loss of one life and a number of wounded" (ibid.).

The strikes of 1906 in the sugar sector provoked a similar response on the part of the workers and the police. This time confined to the Arecibo district, the strike began relatively peacefully. However, "when the sugar planters comprehended the situation which confronted them and began to bring in raw hands who had never earned such a high salary," strikers "changed their tactics" (p. 200). "Several attacks were made upon these men, and attempts were made to disable the machinery and set fire to canefields on several plantations" (ibid.).

This movement ended as did the dockyard strike of that year, again—allegedly—for the same reasons. Governor Winthrop's 1906 report proudly informed the U.S. War Department that the police "were ever on the alert and frustrated many attempts to ruin property," attacking the striking dock workers by "putting the guilty parties promptly in jail." In all the affected areas, "police officers were put in command as an evidence of the determination to prevent violence by the strikers" (ibid.).

In 1906, police collaborating with close to 1,500 strikebreakers (recruited in the nearby municipalities to suppress the Arecibo strike) clashed with strikers, leaving one worker dead, several injured, and 113 strikers arrested. Within this context, an all-time high ensued in the absolute number of arrests for disorderly conduct, mayhem, riot, and fighting registered by the police,[49] a figure only surpassed by the social turbulence of the thirties. The remaining four years of this decade seemed to have revealed the final restoration of social order and peace in the new U.S. colony. Although at least twenty-three important strikes took place at this time (twenty-two of them involving cigar makers), these strikes did not achieve their goals, nor did they become as well known for the presence of social violence.[50] The relative calm undoubtedly contributed to the auspicious and favorable investment activity that characterized these years.[51] However, this evasive respite did not last very long; this, in and of itself, portended the more troubling times of the following decade.

5

"Waging Battle Against Numerous Evils," 1910–1921

> We spend our lives constructing schools to eradicate ignorance; dictating more and more health laws to eradicate diseases; building and maintaining prisons and courts and paying an extremely expensive army of functionaries —judges, district attorneys, policemen, jail wardens, executioner—to eradicate crimes. . . .
>
> And, nevertheless, everyday the evils we are waging battle against appear to be more numerous, more fierce; and the brutality, and the disease, and the crime invincibly divide among themselves the world's domain.
>
> **—Nemesio Canales, *Paliques* (1915)**

> Take up the White Man's Burden
> In patience to abide,
> To veil the threat of terror
> And check the show of pride;
>
> **—Rudyard Kipling, "The White Man's Burden" (1899)**

The period from 1910 to 1921 contained the second wave of social disorder spanning the War of 1898 and the European War. This chapter also addresses the social combat that ensued during the formative years of colonialist capitalism in Puerto Rico. Once again, the effects of the unfolding socioeconomic relations were belligerently coupled with emergent subjectivities: a conflict that unfolded in multiple fronts and through numerous proxies; a battle whose text was staged by force and by wiles, and where the shrill prose of North American officialdom and the staid gaze of the privileged "natives" met the elusive and allusive sign systems of subaltern illegality.

The War at Home During the Years Spanning the European War

On the eve of the War in Europe there was a marked erosion in the social conditions of the Island's laboring classes. Coincidentally, some of the official indicators of the popular illegalities began experiencing an appreciable growth. Although the murder rates at this time do not give signs of ascent, the suicide rates do (see table 4). As this last phenomenon indicates, part of the popular violence in question was socially centripetal and implosive.

Public order was also being disrupted with increasing frequency. Rates of disorderly conduct are not the best indicator in this regard: these proportions for the most part remained at the same levels as during the first years of this century. Such disruptions were expressed in the rising violation of laws enacted in exercise of police powers. When added to the corresponding number of convictions for crimes against persons, the combined figure amounted to fifty-three percent of all convictions in 1914 and sixty-eight percent of all convictions in 1915—as can be gleaned from the information provided by Fleagle.[1] Part of the social violence thus constituted was officially registered within the terrain of the workplace. According to Verrill, "[d]uring the strikes of the cigar makers an unusual number of assaults and murders occurred, and usually the number of such crimes is much less."[2]

The 1910–1913 strikes reopened the period of conspicuous outbreaks of violent labor disputes. Meyer Bloomfield, Director of the Vocational Bureau of Boston and Massachusetts businessman, was commissioned at this time to survey the labor situation in some of the Island's factories. His 1912 report confirmed the deteriorating working conditions that contributed to these disturbances in the case of the tobacco-manufacturing workers. Bloomfield found that there were "certain complaints of breach of good faith on the part of certain tobacco manufacturers."[3] Workers in Caguas (a prominent tobacco-products center), "where strikes [had] culminated in a murder" in 1910, told him that "four years ago they consented to a voluntary reduction of wages on the representation of a leading manufacturer that tobacco market was in poor condition . . . " According to Bloomfield, "[a]n unsanitary workplace was not something particular to the cigar shops insofar as workers in other sectors were being afflicted in similar ways," a situation that contributed to the "threatening mood" of these laborers (ibid.).

Bloomfield registered the complaints of tobacco workers "forced in some places to drink out of an unclean common drinking cup," working with "an insufficient number of spittoons"—this being a basic need for cigar makers. Poor "washing facilities" and unsanitary conditions led many of them to catch tuberculosis (p. 25). "Bakers made the same complaints," while the painters "complained that a very poor quality of paint increased their risk from lead poisoning" (ibid.).

Social violence at this time took on additional forms. This type of contention often included attacks on the "constant" embodiments of capital (such as work tools, raw materials, the workplace, etc.), as well as against other forms of property. This was partially reflected in the rise of arrests for malicious injury and arson during these years, despite the fact that property crimes as a whole did not increase.[4]

The hallmarks of this sort of confrontation were the strikes in the sugar plantations. These conflicts, among other things, involved setting the cane fields on fire. The years roughly encompassing the European War were exceptionally emblematic of this type of violence and sabotage. "During the period of the Foraker Act [1900–1917], the most widespread strikes and violent clashes between strikers and police were during the administration of Governor Yager [1913–1921]."[5]

The first strike wave of these war years occurred during 1915–1916, affecting mostly the sugar plantations. Eighteen thousand laborers paralyzed twenty-four of the thirty-nine most important plantations for three months in 1915 and the following year forty thousand laborers did the same for approximately six months. This is roughly equivalent to ten percent of the officially active labor force, there being approximately 400,000 persons gainfully occupied in the whole Island at this time. During these two years, large numbers of laborers in the tobacco factories and in the docks also went on strike, among others.[6]

Although the 1915–1916 strikes in the sugar plantations resulted in noticeable pay raises for the laborers of the entire sugar sector (as the Victor Clark report of 1930 remarked[7]), they were obtained at a very high social cost. The ensuing physical confrontations between the strikers and the police were exceptionally bloody. In his 1915 report, Governor Yager called the strike of that year " . . . the most important in Porto Rico [*sic*] since the American occupation," (p. 424). It was so ruthlessly repressed that a federal commission had to intervene to investigate the corresponding activities of the colonial police and court system. The local Labor Bureau—the "Negociado del Trabajo"—issued similar condemnations. This agency declared that "[w]hatever the actions of the strikers may have been, there cannot be any justifiable cause for the actions of the police and of the municipal authorities," the latter having "violated the individual rights of the strikers, oftentimes treating them with unforgivable brutality" that in turn resulted "in the deaths of several people . . . "[8] Other strikers "were being held in jail under excessive fines," in this manner "denying them access to the due process of the courts and forcing upon them extreme and unjustified punishments." The report concludes that the "blame for such conditions appears to rest primarily on the shoulders of the rural police and of the local magistrates" (ibid.).

Despite the reformist character of the report's denunciations, it ultimately recuperates the legitimacy of the colonial-capitalist regime and the relations of property it was supposed to safeguard. If the strikers were treated with "unforgivable brutality," then that means there legitimately existed a degree of brutality that was indeed "forgivable." If these were "excessive fines," then that means that allegedly there were fines that were considered "acceptable" in spite of the reported ten percent to thirty percent drop in the wages of sugarcane cutters two years before conditions had deteriorated and led to a strike—as indicated in the 1914 summary of labor conditions issued by the Negociado del Trabajo.[9] If the police and the local magistrates were responsible for "forcing upon . . . [the strikers] extreme and unjustified punishments," then that means that supposedly these workers could and should have been inflicted with punishments that would have been considered "normal" and "justified." Why were such punishments—both the "unjustified" and the "justified"—primarily reserved for the workers? Why were the police, the local magistrates, and particularly the plantation owners exempt from both of these punishments?

At the same time, though, the federal investigation and the denunciations made by the Negociado del Trabajo marked the explicit—and necessarily unstable—incorporation of the desires and grievances of this portion of the laboring classes within the colonial regime as a whole (in the Island and in the United States). The colonial extension of the metropolitan State in Puerto Rico was thus placed in the position of having to register, however relatively, the legalization and legitimization of these subordinate social concerns. The very intervention of local and federal amelioration mechanisms demonstrated the degree to which the colonial-capitalist enterprise was being menaced by the labor insurgency. In this sense, not only the widespread brutality of police repression, but also the official calls for civility in the maintenance of law and order both tacitly recognized the magnitude of the subaltern threat and the force of the "native" will. This recognition unfolded even as part of the interests of the colonized laboring masses was being embodied in explicitly illegal and disorderly acts. Consequently, the acknowledgement of these grievances additionally illustrates the condensation and materialization of important social contradictions with (and within) the various State apparatuses (local and federal).

The juridical repositioning of "native" wage laborers was one of the effects brought about by the State's internalization of such grievances: these workers would now be located within the social-colonial category of civil membership (citizenship) in a still more conflictive fashion than in the past. This contested positioning added to the already complex patterns through which the oppressed majorities in the Island had been socially constructed between 1898 and 1910. The State's internalization of some of the laboring poor's grievances expressed the advent of the wage laborer, in particular, as an individuated subject within the legitimate juridico-political scene: this meant a shift in the mechanisms through which such subjects were represented (juridico-politically and textually). Regardless of its instability, such a novel subjectification elevated the rights of these laborers—or, rather, the formal and contradictory representation of their rights—to the realm of acceptable and legal political discourse.

The incorporation of the colonized workers' grievances within the terrain of the State, however, had additional effects. In a new way, it juridically inscribed these fractions of the dispossessed, even as it further generalized the misrecognition of the juridical ideologies' class orientation among the "Porto Rican" majorities. This misrecognition would soon be translated into an interpellation of the leadership of the labor movement to refrain from overstepping the boundaries of colonial-capitalist civility. Granted, the State's acknowledgment of these rights was to some extent perfunctory, while remaining extremely contradictory and immediately much eroded. Yet such acknowledgment, and at such a high level, was nevertheless a relative social victory for the oppressed majorities in the Island.

These partial shifts in the juridico-political and textual representation of the laborer-subjects within the terrain of juridico-political rights were, therefore, coupled with corollary representational phenomena within the Island's political scene. One such phenomenon was the FLT's decision to organize in 1915 a permanent political instrument—the "Partido Socialista"—for the elections conducted that year. The new forms of subjectification and legitimation embodied in this sequence of events initially generated other differences within the administrative agents of the ruling classes at this time—these being translated into a second relative achievement for the "native" laboring classes. The contradictions that emerged within the colonial regime can be appreciated in the angry letter that Governor Yager sent to President Wilson in 1916. According to Truman Clark, in this letter Yager had indicated that "the so-called labor leaders and agitators of the strike in Arecibo," the third most important municipality in terms of sugar production, were "in reality political leaders of a recently organized socialist party and [were] playing a game for political control of the municipality" (p. 17).

The 1915 local elections and the clashes between the strikers and the police were, in turn, directly reflected in the arrest patterns of that year. The Fleagle report indicated that from 1914 to 1915, " . . . we had about 17,000 laborers engaged in strikes throughout the Island, and . . . in addition to this there was a general Insular election." He found "that the number of crimes against property dropped by 17 per cent," although the number of crimes "in violation of laws enacted in exercise of police powers rose from 23 per cent to 45 per cent" (p. 87). For Fleagle, this corroborated the fact that "the average law-breaker in Porto Rico [*sic*]" was "easily influenced by economic circumstances and by social surroundings," thus confirming that during strikes or elections "criminal tendencies [took] the direction of breach of the peace and violation of municipal ordinances," instead of such crimes as "arson, burglary, embezzlement, or forgery" (ibid.).

Fleagle's text, though, at best reduces the subaltern subjects of this law-and-order narrative to an epiphenomenon of widespread poverty: "Poverty is closely related to degeneration and crime" (p. 14). And let us remember that he understood such poverty as natural facts of life (pp. iii–iv), in no way related to the structural logic of colonial-capitalism. At worst, these subaltern subjects were the effect of mindless social mimicry: "the average law-breaker in Porto Rico [*sic*] *is easily influenced* by economic circumstances and by social surroundings" (my emphasis). In both cases, the "average law-breaker" is reduced to an ethnological trope, the blind product of a statistical moment, with no will or social direction. Yet Fleagle is forced to recognize that these "criminal tendencies" have an overall aim—namely, the "violation of laws enacted in exercise of police powers"—and that this target was being consistently and repeatedly attacked under concrete though unnamed circumstances (the "economic circumstances and . . . social surroundings").

This is why David Trotman's observations about late-nineteenth-century Trinidad are helpful in terms of understanding the underlying significance of "native" unlawful practices. Perceiving in this sense "the public peace" and the laws enacted in exercise of police powers as symbols of the existing social order, it could very well be said that such practices—as registered by the police record—have even broader social implications in the case of early twentieth-century Puerto Rico because such crimes "are useful indicators not only of the effect of economic conditions but also of the extent of social discontent and disorder."[10] For Trotman, "[d]iscontented citizens may vent their feelings against property as the only tangible symbol of the source of their discontent" (ibid.).

The strikes of 1916 were not as bloody as those of 1915. In spite of this, the Negociado del Trabajo's report that year stated that these conflicts involved their fair share of intense confrontations between strikers and the police with the expected results in terms of laborers and the resident-poor turning out dead and wounded. In several instances the violent sweeps of the police were so indiscriminate that the, once again, military-like operations extended to the townships near the plantations amidst much massive outcry (pp. 12–13, 16).

The second strike wave spanned the 1917–1918 period. Approximately forty-five thousand laborers participated in eighty-eight stoppages across the entire Island, again mostly involving the sugar sector, the tobacco-manufacturing shops, the dockyards, as well as an indeterminate number of generic agricultural laborers. Although not as harshly contested as the strikes during the preceding two years, the 1917–1918 strikes also involved a number of incidents of both social violence and State violence. The 1917 strike in the dockyards of San Juan produced a clash between strikers, strikebreakers, and the police that resulted in one death and several wounded. As in the 1906 dockyard-trucking strike, the result was another small-scale urban uprising. The angry residents of the nearby laboring community stoned the police and the ensuing melee was quelled when the police finally stormed the workers' district, capturing it at gunpoint. Later that same year, sugarcane strikers in Guayama—one of the top two sugar producing municipalities at this time—confronted the police with an equally high cost for the laborers: two of them dead and four policemen wounded.[11]

The more than one hundred strikes of 1919–1921 mobilized about 32,000 laborers, once again paralyzing an indeterminate amount of agriculturally-based enterprises, dockyards, and tobacco factories, as well as bringing the railroad system to a halt. The situation continued the pattern of the previous five years. There was another riot during the San Juan dockyard strike of 1919 in which several people were reported wounded. Once more there were armed battles between strikers, strikebreakers, and the police, as well as cane fields set on fire—the sugarcane strike of 1920 in the north-central coastal municipality of Bayamón serves as a case in point.[12]

Then colonial Governor E. Mont T. Reily bluntly summarized the strangely familiar situation: what probably seemed to him as restless natives defying the civilized order whose racial childhood they so naturally represented. "When I arrived in Porto Rico [*sic*]," declared Reily, "I found labor and capital crosswise, unable to agree, and I made it my first important work to try to settle differences without further bloodshed or strife" (p. 35). For example, he detected "five strikes running in fullblast, . . . the outlook was discouraging," some of these strikes having been "'on' for over nine years," while "[e]ight thousand cigar makers were walking the streets idle." According to Reily, a "great railroad strike was on, and trains were running intermittently," with disastrous results: "[s]everal serious wrecks occurred, and five or six men were killed." The laborers "in the canefields were 'out' in many places, and a number had been killed and wounded" (ibid.).

Beneath the colonizers' dread and uneasiness chronicled here ("the outlook was discouraging"; "several serious wrecks occurred"; "a number had been killed and wounded"), lay the righteous will and justifiable cause of the colonial-capitalist social order. It would appear that this upheaval—serious as it was—was ultimately a mere episode within the continuing saga of "the advantages and blessings of enlightened civilization," announced by Major General Nelson Miles when his troops invaded the Island in 1898. All these "strikes running in fullblast," even the "strikes [that] had been 'on' for over nine years," were but fleeting instants, social ephemera, against the backdrop of a much grander and more stable historical force: that of U.S. colonialism.

This type of report only centered those who performed the "important work of try[ing] to settle differences without further bloodshed or strife." After all, this was the task of civilization: in Theodore Roosevelt's words twenty years before, to "bring order out of chaos" and, as indicated in one of Kipling's famous verses "To veil the threat of terror." Once again, the subaltern subjects are represented as having no agency and as located outside of history, even outside the history of this very same labor militancy. Reily's reports on this strike wave in "Porto Rico," like the British chronologies of peasant unrest in colonial India analyzed by Guha, "serve admirably to register the event as a datum in the life-story of the Empire"; however, they "do nothing to illuminate the consciousness which is called insurgency."[13] In "Porto Rico," too, "[t]he rebel has no place in this history as the subject of rebellion" (ibid.).

The colonial Governor's metonymy between labor, on the one hand, and violence and disorder, on the other, surfaced repeatedly in the press of the period—as summarized by Silvestrini (pp. 61–64). One newspaper went so far as to exhume the terminology used during the rural violence of 1898–1899, directly designating the sugarcane workers on strike in the Bayamón plantations as a "seditious movement" (ibid.). Evidently, within some "respectable circles" (Creole and North American), the ideological representation of the laboring classes as part of the citizenry was current as long as they demonstrated their adherence to the prevalent social order and its rules.

Many of the strikes of 1915–1921 resulted in wage gains for organized labor in the Island. This was particularly the case of the workers in the sugar sector, who obtained the highest average income levels they had obtained in the previous twenty years and in the following twenty.[14] Yet, once again, capital and the State, local and federal, exacted a heavy toll in "native" lives and other injuries. During the 1920s capital would perform adjustments and countermeasures in order to compensate for the gains made by this sector of the colonized labor force.

The Coming of "Beastly Crimes"

The gendered character of social violence at this time was often very evident. Despite an official record that registered violence against women as not rising, such violence was quite common and widespread.[15]

A newspaper story of the day, retold and interpreted by a local lawyer and celebrated "native" intellectual, is not untypical of this type of event. It also exemplified the ideological representations of gender, race, class, and illegality inscribing such events within popular literature and within Creole academic discourses at this time. Both of these textual forms were considerably intersected by the official gaze of the colonial police. In this sense, it is an emblematic narrative.

Juan B. Soto, a University of Puerto Rico law professor and Island politician, begins by establishing the event's setting. A newspaper in Ponce published an article on "an act by all accounts painful," committed in this same city. The report identified the perpetrator as a man who "was reputed to be an excellent citizen, honest, kind, and loved by all who had dealings with him." The purpose of Soto's account was to decipher how and why even someone with such a reputation—"apparently moved by jealousy"—turned into "a horribly ferocious assassin."[16]

From there Soto literally transcribes the details of the incident as it was rendered by a local newspaper reporter. Here the description becomes more specific, as the class, racial, and gender markers come to the fore. In March of 1919, a twenty-two-year old "dark-skinned" woman named Otilia Rivera from the largest city in the western coast (Mayagüez) abandoned her thirty-one-year old lover, Artemio Martínez, "dark-skinned" and born and living in Ponce, "she a *bonchera* and he a cigar maker in the 'La Sultana' factory, that is operating here" (p. 73).

The reporter, as recorded by Soto, then establishes the circumstances of the crime by pointing out that on repeated occasions, Artemio Martínez had demanded that Otilia Rivera "return to his side," something she invariably refused to do. "Yesterday afternoon, surely burning with jealousy," the cigar maker allegedly headed towards the house of Luisa Lugo on Protestante Street, where Otilia Rivera was known to stop and drink coffee every afternoon (ibid.).

Soto then proceeds to quote the grisly details of the event's first moments. Although Artemio repeatedly attempted to reconcile himself with Otilia, she refused his advances. Then, he "drew a blade and attacked her, causing nine wounds, most of them serious," and distributed in the following manner: "[o]ne in her skull, another in the right side of the neck, another on the upper lip, two over the left eye, two in her left arm, and one in her right hand" (ibid.).

The recalcitrant "native" female laborer is forced to give way to the "native" artisan's knife: failing to possess the body and will of "his" woman, the colonized male worker proceeds to reduce both to a bloody pulp. The initial fray is complicated by the intrusion of the neighbor, Luisa Lugo, who is also ruthlessly cut down by the temporarily distracted aggressor. Immediately afterwards, Artemio Martínez turns the blade on himself, resulting in serious self-inflicted wounds. His mutilated first victim takes advantage of the situation and attempts to escape: "[Martínez] abandoned Luisa to run after Otilia, leading to a struggle between the latter and her aggressor Martínez, which ended when she broke loose of Artemio, for he, weakened by the hemorrhage he was suffering from, could not stop her nor follow her, falling lifeless to the ground" (pp. 73–74). The reporter ends the gruesome tale by noting the admirable background of the otherwise trustworthy artisan: "Artemio was an excellent laborer, hard-working, and honest; [he was] fun to be with, all who had contact with him appreciated him for the thoughtfulness of his character" (p. 74).

Here Soto's authorial voice returns, immediately providing his own explanation for this seemingly inexplicable event. Soto described "the perpetrator of this beastly crime" as "[u]ndoubtedly, . . . a sick man, a psychopath perhaps, driven to break the law by causes strange to those of a healthy determination." Reminding the reader that "the psychological mechanism is not constituted by the intellect alone," Soto proceeds to explain that "[f]eelings and determination," that "figure among the states of consciousness constituting the human spirit," can also become diseased and that such pathologies "are not something new, nor ignored, by those initiated in the study of abnormal psychology" (ibid.).

Such narratives mediated the identification and regulation of "natives" constructed as criminals, thereby fashioning the signifiers of disorder. In turn, both the event and its [re]constructions expressed contentious positions, [re]producing and regulating the subordinate sectors in the Island. The violence against Puerto Rican women and the corresponding discourses carried out several concurrent and conflictive operations that tended to merge into each other.

This form of social violence, these discourses, and the colonial mimicry they embodied, policed the local gender order by brutally maintaining its matching categories at a time in which the Island's social fabric was being torn by rampant scarcities and class strife, aggravated and heightened by the effects of the European War and the prevailing colonial-capitalist situation. Such events laid bare the fissures within the subaltern subjects, revealing the imagined character of their sociocultural wholeness: by metaphorically and literally cutting down the will and bodies of "their" women, "native" male laborers revealed the rents in the supposedly unitary "native" social body. The violent maintenance of gender categories tended to verify Homi Bhabha's observation that colonial mimicry "coheres the dominant strategic function of colonial power, intensify[ing] surveillance" (p. 126).

Yet, paradoxically, this type of transgression also contributed to the destabilization of the legitimate/State monopoly over violence because these subordinate social sectors were the ones enacting this violence. This self-appropriation was also gendered: it was primarily the men from the laboring classes who practiced such social violence. And it occurred at a time in which this monopoly was not only questioned from within (by the mentioned strike waves) but also from without (by Germany). At this level, colonial mimicry as analyzed by Bhabha "pose[d] an immanent threat to both 'normalized' knowledges and disciplinary powers," once again confirming the ambivalent character of such practices: "mimicry is at once resemblance and menace" (pp. 126, 127).

Several additional things come to mind regarding the journalistic/police account, quoted at length by Juan B. Soto. The author signals the nonwhite inscription of the victimizer and of the victim. This continued to be characteristic of the popular narratives of the period. Such a designation was usually made when the social subjects involved were not positioned toward the "white" end of the Creole and/or North American phenotypical spectrum, the obvious implication being that only nonwhites are raced. Such "darkness" always already anticipated the obscure and concealed nature (latent or active) of the culprit.

There is also the initially paradoxical location of the "native"/familiar yet alien, artisan and assassin, inside and outside. Coincidentally, Artemio Martínez appears both as a "model citizen" and as the "dark" author of a "beastly crime" against women. It displays an impasse in the formal logic that links the representations emanating from newspapers, neighbors, witnesses, and the police pertaining to the guilty party. Piercing the veil of apparent kindness, honesty, and amiability, it is the university professor who restores order and understanding by uncovering the true, pathological features of the seemingly "native"/familiar but actually strange and dark monster, calling him by his real name and recognizing his hidden/shrouded nature: "a sick man," "a psychopath, perhaps," the personification of "abnormal psychology," and so on.

Through their own colonial mimicry, the "native" intelligentsia would verify (for themselves, for the laboring classes, and for the colonizers) the intellectuals' command of dominant knowledges, seemingly vindicating the Creole propertied and educated classes as astute pupils of the "advantages and blessings of enlightened civilization." And by means of such proficiency in containing and representing the transgressions of the impoverished majorities, the Creole propertied and educated classes erected themselves as foreign to such unruly behavior—the latter being instead signified by the no-longer "native"/familiar subaltern subjects, now appropriately positioned on the outside of the social boundaries.

Such gendered, racially inscribed, and class-identified violence and their received meanings reinforced many of the representations assumed by both Creole and U.S.-based propertied and educated sectors regarding the indigent masses of the colonized. For these bureaucrats, intellectuals, entrepreneurs, etc., events such as the ones involving Artemio Martínez tended to confirm the alleged savagery, alien-ness, instability, and lack of control perceived to be generally intrinsic to the colonized laboring poor, particularly to the dispossessed nonwhite males. It must be borne in mind that such events transpired during a strike-wave period in which many of the local fractions of these asymmetrically hegemonic sectors desperately sought to criminalize all forms of proletarian and semiproletarian disorder.

In this manner, "native" crime was individuated while the boundaries between it and the social classes and racial sectors thus implicated became appropriately blurred by the doubt that was objectively cast upon this nonwhite laborer. The perpetrator of such subhuman/inhuman acts against defenseless women could only have been a (common) man of *this* type, class, and race and no other. Implicitly, though, the also gendered victims did not escape unscathed within this expert narrative either. Had *this* type, class, and race of (common) woman not been consorting with *this* man, then her fate would have been otherwise. Clearly, respectable "native" women were not found in such dubious company, preferring to remain under the protection of respectable Creole men (such as Juan B. Soto). Order was now possible because the enemy had been named, the victims had been socially located, the intangible had been grasped and controlled, and the disease had been diagnosed.

"Children Who Are Entirely without the Influence of Parental Control"

During the years of the European War, there was also recorded evidence of infant nomadism and of children being involved in breaches to the social order. The social transformations of the day left their mark on the ways in which the households of the colonized poor were making ends meet—particularly those in urban areas. Occasionally, many of these social responses and survival schemes were carried out at the expense of the "native" children. This situation prompted a number of these minors to abandon their homes and join the ranks of those independently involved in the popular illegalities. As Fernando Picó explains in *Los gallos peleados,* it was "not unusual, then, that during the period being studied," not only in the inland coffee-growing municipality of Utuado, but in other urban areas of the Island, "there was an abundance of the wandering, thieving, aggressive child, the habitual delinquent" (p. 33). According to Picó, this was a child "that came to be the victim, also habitually, of that world that was turning inhospitable, as the traditional frameworks were being torn asunder by the agrarian crises" (ibid.).

Fleagle quotes the Insular Chief of Police who, in the moralizing tone that characterized colonial social reformers of this period, reported in 1910 that

> It is estimated that the city of San Juan alone has 500 homeless children and that there were at least 10,000 children in the Island who have absolutely no home and who are entirely without the influence of parental control. . . . In very few cases do they attend the public schools, and they must remain in this homeless condition, living as best they can, stealing or begging, when honest means of obtaining food do not avail. (pp. 101–102)

This was another variant of the colonialist circular logic already inaugurated in the Island by Brigadier General Davis and the federal Labor Department researcher Azel Ames: "native" poverty bred "native" crime which, in turn, only flourished within "native" poverty. The principal difference was that this time such degeneration involved "native" children. Fleagle further cites this colonial officer as concluding that errant infants grew up "learning the vice that [could] be found among the most poverty-stricken and criminal classes with whom they associate"; in this manner such children constituted "a group of people with criminal tendencies," thereby bringing about "another generation of children who will be handicapped by the environment and the training which their fathers have received" (p. 102). The underlying determinant suggested by these reports, of course, is again ill-fated breeding, both in terms of ancestry and in terms of upbringing. Knowlton Mixer quotes the U.S. Chief of Police for "Porto Rico" as saying in 1910 that such children "lived largely by begging, stealing, or charity," the majority of them having "no permanent lodging and [sleeping] as they might, in boxes or on doorsteps."[17] According to Mixer, this same functionary understood these minors to be primarily "abandoned children of illegitimate parentage or orphans. Surely a fertile soil for crime and an acute danger for the community" (ibid.). As Silvestrini (p. 64) and Picó (p. 45) have shown, wayward children and adolescents, nevertheless, were hardly spared the force of police or civilian violence.

Special judicial and punitive institutions were created at this time to identify, contain, and represent the growing transgressive activities of "native" minors. In 1915, Juvenile Courts were established in each Island district and the judges already assigned to these areas were now authorized to serve in the Juvenile Courts. (Until then, young lawbreakers had been processed and detained within the criminal justice system.) A handful of reform schools were also organized to house youngsters under sixteen years of age who had broken the law. The immediate forerunner of these institutions was the Industrial School set up in Mayagüez in 1905. These were the judicial and custodial parameters that would define and regulate juvenile delinquency until the 1950s.[18]

The Creole intellectuals of the day and the mainstream local press in particular authored numerous accounts of the illegal activities of these minors. In a talk delivered in early 1915 at the Insular Library of San Juan, the "native" lawyer Luis Samalea Iglesias began by reminding the audience that several weeks before the local press had run stories on the larcenies carried out by "several gangs of youths, between the ages of 12 and 17." According to Samalea Iglesias, the police had caught them in the act; when apprehended, the youths confessed to having previously executed similar crimes.[19]

As with the account retold by university law professor Juan B. Soto, Samalea Iglesias underlined the treacherous and forbidding nature that hid behind the apparent innocence of these youths. The lawyer jogged the listeners' memories by advising them not to forget that such thefts were "being carried out under the cover of night, a fact that reveals to us the preconceived premeditation [*sic*] of very awake minds." According to the declarations of one youngster, whom the police assumed to be the ringleader, "[o]ne of these gangs . . . had the coldness of heart and the insolence to protest that their attempt at carrying out an armed robbery had been frustrated" (ibid.).

To this incident, Samalea Iglesias added three anecdotes from his own personal experience. The first recalls the familiar tropes of the *Lazarillo de Tormes* and *La Charca* or, for English-language readers, of *Oliver Twist*. In one instance, occurring in the Plaza

Colón of San Juan, "when we gave the coin to the little boy, the latter fled towards the east wall of the Teatro Municipal. We followed him." Samalea Iglesias came upon "a game of 'heads or tails' . . . taking place," explaining that in a such game of chance "the daring tramp robs the small tramp the coin he laid down for the wager, assuring him that he did not really bet on the 'face' but on the 'symbol,' or vice versa." The results of the bet were "made right by a pair of bronzed fists [and] does not allow for any discussion. And the poor little tramp goes on to continue panhandling, panhandling *for being hungry* . . . " (p. 4, emphasis in the original).

The second account covers similar territory, this time referencing the criminal anthropology of late-nineteenth-century Europe. Upon hearing "the weak voice of an eight year old boy begging" in the Plaza de Baldorioty, presumably "to be able to buy food," Samalea Iglesias and his companion "gave him a 'dime' [in English in the original]," but stalked him to the corner of Luna and San José streets in San Juan. "[T]here was a young man" on that spot, "robust, with features that would have interested Lombroso, to whom the little boy gave my coin," both minors then leaving "toward a warehouse-and-grocery store: To eat, I said to myself. And, gentlemen, I saw the young man pouring liquor and the boy drinking it very fast!" (ibid.).

Violations of the colonial-capitalist normative codes were framed repeatedly in terms of threatening and bizarre phenomena. Everyday calm was transformed into menacing disruption: the innocence of childhood appeared as cunning and dangerous, and the familiarity of infant conformity became a foreign expression of discord and defiance. All of this was reiterated in Samalea Iglesias's third anecdote.

> Once, when I took it upon myself to defend, before the Municipal Court of Río Grande, a little one accused of stealing, he invited me, with unparalleled impudence, to "instruct him"—such was his graphic phrase—in the penal precepts of our Code regarding larceny, assault, and swindling. Lack of proof forced the court to absolve him. Five days later he visited my office to offer me, "in gratitude and friendship" a tie pin made of gold that—gentlemen, I transmit to you his own expression—he "had stolen especially for me"! This boy appeared to straighten up later on, thanks to an incident I must not mention, obtaining a job in a commercial house; but subsequently he was responsible for a fraud. (pp. 5–6)

Semiotically, this resonates all too readily with the other inscrutable threats to the existing order that were materializing at that time, such as the seemingly endless labor strife, the mysterious growth of social misery, and the unsettling consequences and apocalyptic logic of the European War. In this manner, the expansion of juvenile delinquency meshed right in with the other forms of strangeness and turmoil that unequivocally marked these years. Among "respectable" Creole circles the genre of analysis, illustrated here by Soto and Samalea Iglesias, was very popular because it was perceived as fulfilling a genuine need: namely, as being the beacon that—under the protective gaze of the overlords on high—would show the way out of the storm.

Again, this type of account illustrates the perception of the propertied and educated classes ("native" and North American) pertaining to the incomprehensible inclination of the dispossessed "natives" to refuse, on the one hand, to perform labor for someone else if other means of income were readily available and, on the other hand, to refuse to bear their poverty with solemnity. The temerity of such children was an insult added to the disciplinary codes being injured. The incivility of these minors (as social inferiors) became all the more serious within a civil society desperately being cast by the Creole intelligentsia as orderly. Yet, at the same time, this was a civil society being brutally pounded into a new shape by the sledgehammer of colonialist capitalism. Nonetheless, the gendered and colonized identity of the narrator and of the subjects discussed reached a certain common ground within the masculinist practices of both. The only things that established the limits of this seeming (male) harmony were the ways in which these "native" children continued to upset the class-based and age-mediated categories of Samalea Iglesias and of the readers of his day.

Local journalists also contributed explanations of this phenomenon. One such case was presented as seasoned delinquency by the reporter Dalmau Canet. The latter, in a 1915 article titled "Daring Thieves Are Arrested," informed the reading public of an Island newspaper that plainclothes and uniformed policemen had arrested three audacious delinquents who confessed to having "used procedures that they had seen in various movies."[20]

Here is the recurring theme of the "true/hidden nature" of these minors: they concealed through artifice and guile their prey upon the trusting public. In other words, innocence masked evil, distress cloaked predatory behavior, and so on. According to the news reporter, the first delinquent—Juan Serrano—would enter homes in the guise of a disabled person, asking for alms. If and when exposed, Serrano "would pretend he was having an epileptic seizure, throwing himself on the ground, under the grip of great convulsions." By Serrano's own account, the unknowing families would then "take pity on him and would load him up with donations and help" (ibid.).

The second juvenile, Juan Pagán, (a.k.a., "Monteverde"), was depicted in similar terms. Bragging "about being scholarly," he said he had "learned stealing in the 'Red Hand' ('La Mano Roja') books" for which he had paid twenty cents. Although he was Serrano's accomplice, Pagán treated Serrano "very badly," holding Serrano "solely responsible for the larcenies committed." Pagán, from Ponce, "was interned in the Correctional School at the age of 11 years" where he spent six years learning the tailor trade. As he was "a very bad apprentice, they threw him out of all the 'bad luck' establishments where he worked" (p. 11).

The last "young ruffian," however, seemed more deserving of the journalist's pity. The newspaper story identifies him as nineteen-year old Celestino Ruiz, "a poor young man," the "most pathetic" one of the three, and with a previous six-month jail record for larceny. "Thinking back on it, he says: 'yes, I stole, but it was because I was starving to death, I was not strong enough to kill myself.'" With Serrano, he admits to having stolen a watch from a woman in the city of Bayamón. (p. 11)

The first two young offenders were said to have been exceptionally adept at breaking the law. Serrano was perhaps the more notorious of the two. Already twenty years old, with eighteen preceding jail terms (the most serious, a four-and-a-half year sentence for first degree burglary), Serrano acknowledged having stolen a nickel-plated watch in Bayamón, but "was complaining that for such a worthless item he was going to end up in jail." He also confessed to having stolen "a doorbell, from a house in front of the Hotel Miramar" in the tourist district in Santurce (adjacent to San Juan). "Serrano gives evidence of an invincible cynicism" (p. 10).

Meanwhile, the "scholarly" Pagán, faithful student of the "Red Hand" Books, had also been arrested in Bayamón. His ruse of being "a bargain-goods salesman" had not fooled the detectives who "confirmed that everything he sold had been stolen." Police headquarters stated that Pagán, too, had a previous record (p. 11).

Inasmuch as they were mostly the product of misbegotten births, these juveniles were subsequently fashioned as abandoned and as lacking parental supervision. This deprivation was, in turn, supposed to have led them to proscribed activities within the realm of property due to their abandonment of traditional social mores.

Illegitimate breeding was perceived as conducive to illegitimate social behavior. Serrano, for example, "does not have any known parents," all of his features being "those of a bandit." Mr. Lewis, the Chief of Police, reminded Serrano that morning "that he had served a jail term for attacking a policeman." When "the Head of the Detective Unit, Mr. Quiñones" informed him that "he had barely escaped then because Serrano had seriously attacked that policeman," Serrano exclaimed, "I wish I would have died; that way, I would have been the one who won." To which he added: "I like the penitentiary life; you should tell the judge to give me a thirty-year term; . . . " Serrano was recorded as saying that "his parents brought him into the world to annoy other people" (p. 10).

Ruiz, though not depicted as a hardened delinquent, was equally inscribed within the parameters of a family guidance found wanting. When asked for the whereabouts of his parents, Ruiz was reported to have answered, "Do you think that if I had any parents I would be a thief? I steal only to eat. And I sleep where I can, on the porches, in the marketplaces, where the night may find me" (p. 11).

This is clearly the narrative of de-generation and illbirth so common at the time to explain the social practices of wayward children in particular and the dispossessed classes in general. Such respectable and manly signifying practices existed openly among both the members of the Creole propertied and educated classes (like Samalea Iglesias, Soto, and Dalmau Canet), as well as among the North American colonizers.[21]

The proper identification (police, journalistic, and scientific) of wayward youths became a component of the juridical discourses of U.S. capital and colonial law—local and federal. Increasingly, the task was carried out not just directly (through North American personnel), but by means of the normative practices of Creole experts. As in the Orient critically examined by Edward Said, the transgressions of the laboring poor in the Island, "and everything in it was, if not patently inferior to, then in need of corrective study by the West" (p. 41). Yet the disciplinary/colonialist narratives that fashioned the inferiority of the impoverished, unlawful, "Porto Rican" majorities were discourses interceded by the modernist aspirations and Westernized diligence of the Creole propertied and educated classes. Borrowing here from Foucault, it could very well be said that the author-functions of these North American colonialist discourses of instruction/correction "simultaneously . . . [gave] rise to a variety of egos and to a series of subjective positions that individuals of any class"—or any race/nationality—"[could] come to occupy."[22] These "subjective positions" were increasingly being occupied by the "native" intelligentsia. Therein lay the contradictions of these ideologies of criminalization: the colonized/laborer/criminal subject they fashioned was increasingly being authored by a sector of the colonized themselves. As Abdul JanMohamed has pointed out, "since this [author] 'function' in the imperialist context confers on the author all the moral and psychological pleasures of manichean superiority," it is then possible for a "native" writer to be "inducted, under the right circumstances, to fulfill the author-function of the colonialist writer."[23]

Reappropriating police narratives, the petit-Creole and middle-class intellectuals such as Dalmau Canet attempted to undermine these heinous practices by calling into question the intellectual capacities of the young thieves and by ridiculing their sources of inspiration (movies, cheap crime novels, prison life). At worst, these juveniles come across as abhorrent fiends, such as Serrano and Pagán; at best, they were seen as poor devils (e.g., Ruiz). Either way, they were textualized as subterranean, netherworldly: the incarnations of sinister perils. Their shadowy origins and obscure operations signaled the Creole racialization of the disorder for which these young dispossessed "natives" were responsible. Inferior descent led to a descent into immorality.

Since the social order that these juveniles were violating was inscribed as masterfully male, the disorder thus embodied was cast as its gendered antithesis: therein the need to refashion the delinquents' sources of inspiration (Serrano and Pagán) or their social conditions (Ruiz) as pathetic, worthless, impotent, unmanly. Yet the phenomenon of wayward children left additional questions unanswered with regards to the structuring of gender relations in the Island. One of these references the documentation practices of the day: why did most of these reports mainly identify boys—rather than girls—as the ones who wandered the streets? Were there not just as many girls "entirely without the influence of parental control" or were they simply not registered by the corresponding custodial institutions and by the literary gaze?

If, in fact, boys outnumbered girls in terms of runaway children, how did this practice compare with the existing levels of child abuse and domestic violence? If (as the scarce information suggests) such battering remained about equal for both genders, then several preliminary conclusions become inevitable. However precarious and even dangerous the situation both inside and outside the home, the world of colonized children seemed sharply divided regarding the ways in which these youths survived. It appears that "native" adolescent women, and particularly younger girls, not only bore the brunt of their elders' physical rage and desperate fury, but also found it more difficult to establish survival networks in the streets of Island towns and cities. Although I have not come upon sufficient material in this area, the following chapters will continue to examine some of the gendered aspects of these practices and their corollary effects.

In summary, made more acute by the War in Europe, the various forms of social contention enacted by the "native" majorities accordingly informed many of the dominant frameworks of colonial containment and representation: both Creole-propertied and U.S.-capitalist, both State-oriented and quotidian-discursive, both official and informal. By breaching the established social-colonial boundaries, popular illegalities of all stripes interfered with the orderly flow of the principal forms of social control during the critical juncture of 1910–1921. In this manner, child nomadism and delinquency joined other manifestations that sutured together many of the signs of disorder, uncertainty, and impending doom.

PART TWO

1922–1947

6

"Creating a Discontented Working Class," 1922–1929

"We divide the people of Porto Rico [*sic*] into four categories for purposes of [criminal] identification," said the [North] American chief of Insular Police, "according to the shape of their feet. The minority, mostly townspeople, wear shoes. Of the great mass of countrymen [*sic*], those with broad flat feet, live in the cane lands around the coast. The coffee men [*sic*] have over-developed big toes, because they use them in climbing steep hills from bush to bush. In the tobacco districts, where the planting is done with the feet, they are short and stubby. It beats the Bertillon [police identification] system all hollow."

—Harry A. Franck,
***Roaming Through the West Indies* (1920)**

And when your goal is nearest
The end for others sought,
Watch Sloth and heathen Folly
Bring all your hope to nought.

—Rudyard Kipling, "The White Man's Burden" (1899)

In retrospect, the 1920s may be seen as the first moment of the economic crisis confronted by the colonial-capitalist project. This decade also marked the beginning of the end for the Island's hacienda system. In this chapter we will examine the ways in which U.S. corporate interests counterattacked, substantially rolling back the wave of popular resistances and breaches of the social order that multiplied during the peak years of the previous two decades.

Several new features emerged at this time. These include the socioeconomic, political, and discursive shifts adopted by capital and the colonial State, at both federal and local levels, and the repositioning of the privileged Creole identities within the colonialist normative practices that defined and regulated most of the "Porto Rican" population. These two features, along with the concomitant reactions of the "native" masses, are the principal characteristics of the period to be covered in this chapter.

Given the lines of inquiry inaugurated in the first half of this book, it is important to keep several questions in mind throughout the remainder of this study, starting with the present chapter. As always, the central issue is the seemingly unitary but actually fragmented subaltern subjects: their practices and contradictions vis-à-vis the ways in which they were constructed, contained, and represented by dominating frameworks. To what extent do (a) the subaltern subjects of U.S. capitalism in Puerto Rico and (b) the subaltern subjects of colonial labor and of law and order, both, have to be examined under new empirical boundaries? Which aspects of these concrete conditions remained the same as during the 1898–1921 period? What shifted in the making of the subaltern subjects of the popular illegalities? How did these subjects continue to materialize as an array of points on the colonial-capitalist grid, where the lines of punishment (particularly their textual dimension) intersected the plane of economic organization? How did these points shift on the grid's political anatomy? Did these points delineate new patterns of capitalist formation, punitive discipline, and social resistance? If so, what were they? How did they change the manner in which social identities were lived and historical processes were produced, imagined, and disputed? As before, I will start by graphing "social relations of production and the 'hard edge' of productive systems" (Stuart Hall, 102).

The Empire Strikes Back

During the decade of the twenties, the principal agricultural exports went through a decline as a proportion of all Island exports. Sugar fell from 64.5 percent to 55.3 percent, tobacco went from 19.3 percent to 17.5 percent, and coffee dropped from 4.8 percent to 0.5 percent.[1] Only molasses rose: from 1.2 percent to 1.4 percent (ibid.). According to the 1950 study *Puerto Rico's Economic Future,* for the entire first three decades of this century, " . . . the area planted in sugar increased by over 400 percent from 1899 to the early 1930s and the production of sugar increased fifteen fold . . ." (p. 71). Nevertheless, in the same study the statistics generated by U.S. economist Harvey Perloff allowed me to conclude that between 1920 and 1930 this same area increased only slightly in absolute terms, actually experiencing a percentage change of -5.0 percent in terms of its place as a proportion of all cropland. (pp. 83–84) In this sense, the twenties already indicated the relative structural limits of the new productive forms.

Granted, these symptoms of stagnation cannot be ascribed simply to the social resistances and alternate subsistence economies of the dispossessed "natives." The world-market price fluctuations of goods such as sugar and tobacco products are a case in point. The decade of the twenties signaled a shift in the marketability of tobacco products as one of the leading monopolized portions of the colonized economic sphere. The figures produced by Perloff suggest that between 1920–1932, for instance, the percentage change in the world price of tobacco (in cents per pound) was -76.9 percent (p. 91). At this time, tobacco products from Puerto Rico gave evidence of being in crisis, after their initial rise before the European War.

Although not under the direct influence of U.S. corporate investment, coffee production also experienced similar difficulties during this period. Some of these complications had been accumulating since 1898. Coffee prices in the world market began showing signs of deterioration by the turn of the century.[2] Additional factors contributed to the eventual collapse of this sector during the twenties. According to Quintero Rivera,[3] these factors included: the shifts and changes in U.S. tariff laws; the credit freeze imposed by the Foraker Act of 1900 and the subsequent problems in terms of securing loans; the devastation caused by the 1899 hurricane; the competition of Brazilian coffee within the U.S. market; the taxes dictated by the "Hollander Law" and the arbitrary manner in which property was evaluated subsequently; the rapid rise in cost of living levels in the Island; and the initial measures that unevenly integrated Puerto Rico within the U.S. economy.

By the late 1920s and early 1930s, most agriculturally-based sectors of the local economy were in dire straits. Even sugar production and the corresponding price levels in the New York and world markets started running into trouble.[4]

There were other factors related to this crisis and to the readjustments made by large property-owners at this time, starting with the 1920s and extending onwards to the early 1940s. In one way or another, all of these mechanisms can be seen as a response by the principal propertied classes (Creole and North American) to the "restlessness" and disorder unevenly enacted by the colonized laboring classes. This social unrest materialized during the previous two decades, particularly during the War years, and extended unevenly and to a lesser degree through the decade of the twenties.

Despite this decline in sugar exports and in the percentage of cropland that was being cultivated in sugarcane, there was a 54.9 percent increase in the tonnage of sugar produced between 1920 and 1928.[5] This was accompanied by a moderate rise in the number of laborers employed in the sugarcane sector in general—a percentage change of 6.1 percent—and in sugar mill manufacturing in particular—a percentage change of 31.3 percent (see tables 3 and 6). Relatively speaking, it would seem that there was an intensification of the cultivation process and an expansion/intensification of the refining process.[6] Compared to the notable rise in the tons of sugar produced, there was not a proportionately significant increase in the amount of labor employed. However, the Victor Clark study surmised that the length of the working day in agriculture in general and in sugarcane in particular remained just as long as it had been during the previous two decades: about ten to twelve hours during the active season (pp. 119–120, 559). The same study showed that this was also true for the manufacturing phase of sugar production (p. 85). In other words, the extraction of absolute surplus value within the sugar sector had by no means disappeared with the relative rise in the intensification of the labor process.

What tends to be overlooked,[7] though, is the degree to which this intensification in the production of sugar was also a partial attempt on the part of capital to carry out two vital goals. The first was the recuperation of monetary losses due to the wage gains made by labor during the strike wave of 1915–1921, while the second was the need to compensate for the rising instability within the Island's socioeconomic sphere. This instability was generated by the outbreaks of broader "native" social violence and illegal economic activity during the European War and the second half of the twenties. Such insecurity eroded the solidity and predictability of the Island's market. This situation was analogous to what Karl Polanyi has argued in the case of the nineteenth-century European economies.

> The market system was more allergic to rioting than any other system we know. . . . breaches of the peace, if committed by armed crowds, deemed an incipient rebellion and an acute

danger to the state; . . . A shooting affray in the streets of the metropolis might destroy a substantial part of the national capital.[8]

The price fluctuations during the decade of the twenties can be better understood within this context, the problem of social disorder thus becoming more than just a passing aggravation. To some extent, the sugar interests were successful in counteracting the advances made by labor in terms of wages, insofar as Gayer, et al. found that by the mid to late 1920s the wage levels returned to what they had been in 1919.[9] It also appears that capital was (a) attempting to reestablish order by intensifying its control over this sector of the employed labor force, even as (b) it tried to beat into submission the corresponding labor periphery by limiting their access to employment.[10]

The long-term decline of the hacienda system also began at this time. This deterioration very much accelerated the uneven collapse of coffee and tobacco agriculture as a whole. Large coffee planters, unable to obtain sufficient credit for their operations and unable to count on a sufficiently pliable and economically reliable labor force, began exploring other options: reducing the intensity of cultivation, abandoning their land in increasing numbers, and moving to the urban centers. In one of the principal coffee-growing municipalities of the Island during the mid-twenties the Commissioner of Agriculture and Labor reported (as quoted in the Victor Clark study): these hacendados "have ceased long ago to live on the farms. In the municipality of Yauco, a representative coffee section, 28 of the most important coffee growers live[d] in the town" (p. 521). In the case of Yauco, these planters owned "4,959 acres of coffee, which represent[ed] 86.1 per cent of the total coffee acreage for the municipality" (ibid.).

According to Victor Clark, the Commissioner of Agriculture had added that the "partial abandonment of many of the coffee farms ha[d] brought about the poorest cultivation and farming practices known in the Island," the result being that "today coffee cultivation [was] a 'myth'"(p. 522). The colonial official then concluded: "Under these circumstances of almost complete abandonment of the farms, it is easy to understand the alarming decrease in [coffee] production" (ibid.).

This marked rise in the migration of large rural-property owners to the cities and towns laid the material basis for the proliferation of the modernist narratives of the "respectable city" during the 1930s and 1940s.[11] Part of this Creole desire for urban order was

Table 6 Distribution of Labor Force in Selected Nonagricultural Economic Sectors, Selected Years, Both Sexes, 10 Years of Age or Older

		MINING	CON-STRUCTION	SUGAR MILL MANUF.	OTHER FOOD PROD.**	TOBACCO PRODUCTS	NEEDLE-WORK AT HOME	OTHER TEXTILE PRODUCTS	OTHER MANUF.***	TRANSPOR-TATION AND COMMUNI-CATION	TOTAL
1910	no.	116	7,797	6,155	3,270	11,315	11,200	2,000	11,338	9,090	62,271
	%	0.2%	12.5%	9.9%	5.3%	18.2%	18.0%	3.2%	18.2%	14.6%	100.0%
1920	no.	202	9,317	8,723	3,622	16,811	14,382	3,693	14,968	10,063	81,781
	%	0.2%	11.4%	10.7%	4.4%	20.6%	17.6%	4.5%	18.8%	12.3%	100.0%
change	no.	86	1,520	2,568	352	5,496	3,182	1,693	3,630	983	
1910–1920	%	74.1%	19.5%	41.7%	10.8%	48.6%	28.4%	84.7%	32.0%	10.8%	
1930	no.	364	12,766	11,446	4,160	15,508	42,122	13,197	11,717	17,137	128,417
	%	0.3%	9.9%	8.9%	3.2%	12.1%	32.8%	10.3%	9.1%	13.4%	100.0%
change	no.	162	3,449	2,723	538	-1,303	27,740	9,504	-3,251	7,074	
1920–1930	%	80.2%	37.0%	31.3%	14.9%	-7.8%	192.9%	257.4%	-21.7%	70.3%	
1940*	no.	1,181	16,037	19,731	5,631	6,121	44,731	16,780	7,699	20,238	138,149
	%	0.9%	11.6%	14.3%	4.1%	4.4%	32.4%	12.2%	5.6%	14.6%	100.0%
change	no.	817	3,271	8,285	1,471	-9,387	2,609	3,583	-4,018	3,101	
1930–1940	%	224.5%	25.6%	72.5%	35.4%	-60.6%	6.2%	27.2%	-34.3%	18.1%	

1947*	no.	972	32,083	14,258	9,682	4,378	57,245	21,714	13,234	30,317	183,883
	%	0.5%	17.5%	7.8%	5.3%	2.4%	31.2%	11.8%	7.2%	16.5%	100.0%
change	no.	-209	16,046	-5,473	4,051	-1,743	12,514	4,934	5,535	10,079	
1940–1947	%	-17.7%	100.1%	-27.8%	71.9%	-28.5%	29.4%	71.9%	50.0%		
change	no.	856	24,286	8,103	6,412	-6,937	46,045	19,714	1,896	21,237	
1910–1947	%	738.0%	311.5%	131.6%	196.1%	-61.3%	411.2%	985.7%	16.7%	233.9%	

***Includes: wood products and furniture; paper and related products; printing and publishing; chemicals; fertilizers; leather products; stone, clay, and glass products; metal products and machinery; transport equipment.

**Includes: bread and bakery products; canned fruits and vegetables.

*Refers to laboring population 14 years of age or older

SOURCE: Thomas Hibben and Rafael Picó, *Industrial Development of Puerto Rico and the U.S. Virgin Islands* (n.p.: Report of the United States Section, July, 1948), 247–249.

informed by the corollary increase in the migration of the rural laboring population to these very same towns and cities. The forcible eviction of squatters and landless peasants during this period should be kept in mind.

Then, too, there was the selective mechanization of the sectors where machine tools had already obtained a foothold, together with the selective introduction of these types of instruments in capitalist sectors until then characterized by handicraft labor—cigar manufacture being a case in point, as the Victor Clark study indicated (p. 465). This polarized still further the skill levels of the corresponding workforce. The same Brookings Institute report leaves little doubt as to the immediate cause of these changes:

> Another handicap to the development of large-scale enterprise is found in the alleged restlessness of labor and the fear occasionally expressed by large employers that the introduction of big manufacturing enterprises would create a discontented labor class. This attitude is probably the result of a long series of disputes between the Porto Rico Tobacco Company and its operatives, especially the cigar makers, which is said resulted in that corporation's transferring many of its activities to the mainland. (ibid.)

The cigar-makers' strikes of 1915–1921 and of the late twenties are pertinent to the report just cited, as are the rising rates in some of the official indicators of social violence (see table 4). In the case of tobacco manufacture, significant portions of the entire operation were virtually wiped out in the Island while the machine production of this item expanded in the U.S mainland—though not in Puerto Rico.[12]

During this decade and throughout the forties, more than half of the "native" population was located in the mountainous rural areas of the interior. As the Perloff study asserted, this population had traditionally depended on coffee and tobacco for important portions of their income and/or employment (p. 88). Part of the vacuum began being filled by the needle-products sector through a budding network of subcontractors that rapidly consolidated as a putting-out system circuit.

Around the time of the War in Europe, a handful of needlework companies started setting up shop in Puerto Rico.[13] As a sector of the U.S. economy, needlework and textile manufacture underwent monopolization at a later date than tobacco or sugar. The latter two fell under the sway of major trusts and cartels by the late-nineteenth century. At the same time that these interests surfaced in Puerto Rico, the textile sector as a whole and needlework in particular were coming under the direction of initially secondary New York City banks.[14] As early as 1919, U.S. labor economist Joseph Marcus remarked that, within the "native" peasant household in the Island,

> . . . the earnings of the head of the family are insufficient to feed, clothe, and house them properly. For the girl members of the family of the *jibaro* in the mountains there is absolutely nothing else to do to assist the father in maintaining the family. It is for this reason that the girls consent to do needlework so cheaply—-they have no alternative.[15]

Given the retreat regarding investments in the tobacco-products sector during the decade of the twenties, the structural logic of capital as a whole would seem to suggest an adjustment to the increasing instability of the Island's laboring classes by expanding domestic needle-products manufacture. In this way, the colonized labor force could perhaps be unevenly yet profitably reinserted within the circuits of capitalist production and the wage labor market. According to the Descartes study of 1946 (pp. 50, 53–58) and the Perloff report (pp. 136–137), overseas needle-products exports from the Island increased almost seven-fold between 1921 and 1931 at the expense of this extremely impoverished labor.

U.S. corporations continued to extend their control over the Island's market for consumption goods, rice again serving as a case in point. By the early twenties, the "Porto Rican" market had a dramatic impact on rice growers in several Southern provinces in the United States. A 1923 promotional report published in San Juan stated that "free trade between the Island and the continent has not only been advantageous for Puerto Rico," but had also "equally benefitted [*sic*] the United States," because it had "permitted them to absorb almost all" of the Island's "import trade and because as a result of this Louisiana and Texas, for example, raised their rice production, which happened to be insignificant before 1898."[16]

When its preponderant role within the Island's market is taken into account, one can see that by the middle of this decade the influence of the California Rice Growers Association had grown considerably.[17] Between the early twenties and the late forties, edible products still constituted the principal though declining item of importation—despite the marked increase in the importation of machinery and other capital goods.[18]

Yet what were the general social-class features of the subaltern subjects being refashioned during this decade? How did the socioeconomic changes just described affect the morphology of the colonized laboring classes?

The Permanent Transition?

Unlike the traditional rural work force, by 1920 local women and very young girls constituted the absolute majority of the nonagricultural manual occupations and continued to do so until the mid-forties. With all probability one of the principal factors behind the increase in the female portions of this workforce was the expansion of the needle-products at this time.[19]

I have not been able to find much information regarding the specific features of each economic sector within capitalist production as a whole in Puerto Rico nor of the changes that occurred in each sector. Nevertheless, some broad approximations are still possible. Until the mid 1920s, the wage-based production of surplus value by dispossessed laborers was mainly centered around six sectors. In order of importance, they are: (a) the agricultural phase of sugarcane cultivation; (b) the factory manufacture of tobacco products; (c) the mostly home-produced manufacture of needlework items (then, mainly structured as wage labor); (d) the privately-owned utilities and transportation companies; (e) the construction sector; and (f) the (largely industrial) sugarcane processing in the mills. In a sense, the nucleus of this ensemble was the tobacco-products and sugar-refinery workers. Relatively speaking, these two fractions constituted the most concentrated and stable portions of the wage-earning, "native" labor force involved in capitalist production during the first twenty-five years of U.S colonialism. The other four fractions—home needlework, in particular—overlapped to varying degrees with a heterogeneous spectrum of families that worked in agriculture. Taken together, these six sectors grew from approximately a fourth to about two fifths of all employed persons in the Island by the twenties and thirties.[20]

Other sectors of the colonized laboring classes—not linked to the wage-based production of surplus value—merged irregularly with the smaller proletarianized mass. During the first two-and-a-half decades of this century, for instance, there was a gradual decline in the proportional number of small farmers and sharecroppers. The combined number of these last two groups, dropped from between one-half and one-third to approximately one-fourth of all "natives" officially involved in income-gaining activities during these years. There were corresponding reductions in other minor fractions of the laboring poor, the urban day laborers (wage workers and/or independent odd-jobbers) and domestic servants being a case in point. Taken as a group, the proportional number of this second pair of groups also diminished: this time from a little over a sixth to about one-ninth of all those employed. Further in the margins, there was no significant rise in the proportional number of laborers that worked in the commercial and service sectors. Wide fluctuations characterized the social distance between this last segment and the unevenly proletarianized mass. The commercial and service laborers, as a whole, accounted for about five percent of all Island employment at this time.

In sum, all of this appears to indicate that the colonial proletariat (rural and urban) that came into being between 1898 and 1920–1925 was mostly typical of what elsewhere is known as the transition phase of early capitalism: simple cooperation and manufacture. The proportion of sugar mill workers within this spectrum was very reduced. It oscillated between 9.9 percent (1910) and 10.7 percent (1920) of all nonagricultural, nonservice, and noncommercial employment (see table 3). Evidently, this was a mass that, seen as a whole, continued to maintain noncapitalist, agrarian, and/or artisan technical work skills.

The absence of technical dispossession among the colonized laboring classes was reinforced by several factors. The perpetual—though declining—land plots and feudal rents among a significant part of the labor force were included among these factors.[21] But the lack of technical dispossession within this labor force was also replicated and preserved by a considerable imbrication between two additional elements. For one thing, many households were involved in all the myriad manifestations of noncapitalist agriculture. For another, there was the equally seasonal, unstable, and shifting incorporation of many of these households—as a whole or in part—within the sphere of capitalist manufacture. This materialized both in its tobacco-products and primarily factory form[22] and in its domestic needlework and primarily putting-out system form.[23]

In this sense, inasmuch as the "native" peasantry was not a morphologically stable and clearly defined social class at this time, neither was the proletariat that this amorphous peasantry was unevenly and partially becoming. It appears that the uncertain social contours and partial indetermination of one class had a feedback effect on the ambiguous physiognomy of the other.

This has been a reality either much lamented or elided among the recent historiographies of labor in Puerto Rico.[24] Such complaints and oversights seem to be related to a certain evolutionist and teleological paradigm that sees the proletariat (that resulted from the economic effects of the U.S. invasion) as an overwhelmingly positive event—in historical perspective.[25] In addition to acknowledging and documenting the exploitative character of capitalism per se, these historiographies tend to frame the drawbacks of the new colonialism primarily in terms of the North American control over this economic transformation and/or in terms of the U.S. domination over the Puerto Rican political scene—over State affairs, in particular.[26]

This suggests a linear viewpoint (even in the case of dialectical interpretations) akin to perceiving history as ultimately moving ahead and upward. Coincidentally, this perspective is located within the same Enlightenment and modernist parameters shared by many of the artisan and trade-union activists whose writings and lives the new historiography has so admirably begun recovering from oblivion.[27] Most of the new historical inquiry on Puerto Rico has absorbed and built upon these artisan visions.[28]

Such concerns contain the telltale signs of evolutionist perspectives: the only way in which the authentically and legitimately anticapitalist phase of struggle became possible was through the rise of a proletariat that, in turn, could only evolve (literally) through the implantation and/or advancement of capitalism—that is, the highest stage of economic and historical maturation. Capitalism, per se, equals the advent of modernity and progress, while being the necessary (though regrettable) condition for the further advancement of society.[29] Ultimately, this much-sought-after Puerto Rican proletariat is simultaneously an economic and historical epiphenomenon, on the one hand, and the incarnation of History itself (the Historical Subject), on the other.[30]

As the first half of this book has shown and as I will continue to demonstrate in the remaining chapters, I have attempted to heed the admonition directed by Fernando Picó to the new historiographers. In his 1983 study, Picó insists that there is "a certain tendency in all historians to study only those sectors of past societies which are the seed-bearers of future institutions and future struggles."[31] According to Picó, the problem with this practice is that it carries with it the risk of "anachronism, because it easily could lead others to think that only the social and economic sectors being studied carried weight during their time" (pp. 174–175). The end result is that it "leaves without a history of their own those people that eventually did not become hegemonic, nor a powerful antagonist to those in power" (p. 175).

I partially differ with Picó in his evaluation of these subordinate subjects. As my own research shows, these were indeed "powerful antagonist[s] to those in power" despite the fact that such subjects "did not become hegemonic." Their atomization, their youth, and often their oppressed gender should not in any way deny the danger they posed (concrete and imagined) to the existing social order—any more than their preponderant absence from classical proletarian inscription denied them historical subjectivity.

Furthermore, it should also be remembered that, in spite of the preceding statistical description and its corollary perusal of the transition from pre-capitalist to capitalist forms of production, my research is not primarily moved by what Gayatri Chakravorty Spivak has called "the great narrative of the modes of production" and "the narrative of the transition from feudalism to capitalism."[32] My chief objective is still to continue plotting these social transformations as confrontations rather than as simple transitions, as well as to further map the violence of the functional changes in the corresponding sign systems. This effort has not primarily involved adding new data to the political economy and social-history/historical-sociology of Puerto Rico. Rather, this effort involved rethinking the terms of the more conventional paradigms by contributing to an archeology of the subaltern subjects in the Island: the conflicts, signs, and conditions that structured these subjects and the resistances and social practices that these subjects enacted.

"The Food Supplied Is Not Enough"

During the 1922–1929 period and particularly during the second half of the twenties, the colonized laboring classes were still very much threatened by malnutrition, hunger, a high cost of living, and elevated unemployment rates. Begging, for example, was not only still widespread; it even seemed to be growing. As U.S. social reformer Helen V. Bary observed on the situation of "native" children during the early part of this decade, the "northern visitor in Porto Rico [*sic*] is shocked at the institution of begging," because the "mendicants have their stations along the sidewalks of their regular routes through offices, restaurants, and residence districts."[33] Bary stated that Saturday was "Beggars Day," when "[s]hops and individuals put aside small funds and pennies," as "beggars [made] their rounds with businesslike regularity" (ibid.).

At best, Bary could not help but blame this situation on the deficiencies of Iberian culture and lineage: here was the obvious signet of turn-of-the-century discourses. This was the heritage that Columbia professor Franklin H. Giddins had described in the aftermath of the War of 1898 as "A people that idly sips its cognac on the boulevards as it lightly takes a trifling part in the *comedie humaine* . . . "[34] At worst, Bary attributed such complacent or even excessively tolerant attitudes toward begging to a "native" people and tropical society that had not yet learned "the lesson of self-control" that Elihu Root in 1899 had said was necessary for "Porto Ricans"[35]: "they" had not yet understood nor replicated [North American, White, masculinist, middle-class] frugality, respectability, and hard work. In Bary's words: "The Latin spirit tends to personal rather than organized charity, but begging has reached such proportions that its control has been repeatedly discussed—so far with little result, as the prohibition of begging could not be accomplished without fundamental economic and industrial changes" (p. 26). At this level of analysis, all "Porto Ricans" had a basic essence that determined their individual and collective behavior: "their" rudimentary nature impeded "them" from marshalling by themselves the necessary technological and material resources to eradicate the revealing signs of degeneration and dependency: namely, rampant begging.

The economic situation of the laboring classes did not improve towards the end of this decade. The 1931 study by Justine and Bailey Diffie observed that falling wages in the needlework sector (where growing portions of the rural population were seeking employment) led the local Labor Bureau to warn in 1927 that malnutrition and disease were menacing to spread more than in the recent past, reaching disastrous proportions (p. 182). A study carried out by the Island's legislature during the late twenties reached alarming conclusions. The study found that, even in the case of what were then exceptionally small families (two adults and only one child), the average income available to these laborers could not possibly meet the most basic needs of all the family members. The report concluded that considerable portions of the population seemed to be making ends meet at the expense of their own physical existence.[36] At the time, the Brookings Institution report edited by Victor Clark commented dryly: "It is evident . . . that the food supplied is not enough, even granting that it may be of the right kind" (p. 565). The report indicated that such conditions were "especially evident" when one remembered that "during from four months to six months" laborers could only find work "half a day and, therefore, the purchases" had to be "reduced by one half." The result was that "an immense majority of the rural population of Porto Rico [*sic*]" was "living on the verge of starvation" (ibid.).

Within this context, major climatological changes had cataclysmic social and economic consequences. In a significantly titled article in the *New York Herald Tribune Magazine* of December 8, 1929—"The Children of Famine"—then colonial Governor Theodore Roosevelt, Jr. described the social consequences of the 1928 hurricane in the following unequivocal terms:

> I have seen mothers carrying babies who were little skeletons. I have watched in a class-room thin, pallid, little boys and girls trying to spur their brains to action when their little bodies were underfed. I have seen them trying to study on only one scanty meal a day, a meal of a few beans and some rice. I have looked into the kitchens of houses where a handful of beans and a few plantains were the fare for the entire family.[37]

Moreover, the decade of the twenties did not significantly improve the cost of living situation, as may be partially surmised from the information just cited, together with the findings of the 1927 local Labor Bureau report and of the 1930 colonial legislature's report. Other local studies of the period confirm this.[38] The situation was made even worse by the rising tax burdens of 1923 regarding such mass consumption items as soap and matches.[39]

Taking the first three decades as a whole, socially conscious U.S. writers such as the Diffies accused North American colonialism of bringing about a degradation in the buying capacity of "native" peasant income and labor power. The Diffies first describe the corresponding situation before the U.S. invasion.

> . . . the native foods of the Island decreased to half during the 32 years of American occupation and that in the case of the chief foods now consumed rice has been more than half. Since bananas, plantains, mangoes, etc., which formed the bulk of the food consumed in 1897 were obtainable at a small cost, or in most cases at no cost, the food of the *jíbaro* was very cheap. With his small wage in 1897, he could have bought only 16 pounds of rice, as compared with 20 pounds today, but in 1897 he had to purchase only 82 pounds a year of imported rice, whereas he now must buy 125 pounds from abroad. (pp. 174–175)

Then they proceed to contrast this with the purchasing power of local peasant income during the late twenties, drawing logical conclusions in terms of daily labor. "The average family of five today must have 625 pounds of foreign rice a year, as against only 410 in 1897" (p. 175). If the "410 pounds bought in 1897 cost about 12½ pesos, as against $25 for the 625 pounds today," then—converted into a day's labor—"we find that the *jíbaro* today must devote about 33 days to earning his rice as against 25 days in 1897" (ibid.).

The unemployment situation was comparably grim. The 1930 report issued by the Island's legislature found that between 1920 and 1926 unemployment among the male laboring population rose from twenty percent to thirty percent (p. 61). Governor Theodore Roosevelt, Jr. stated in his 1930 annual report that the rate of unemployment for the whole Island (both sexes) that fiscal year had been sixty percent.[40]

"The Work of Hoodlums" and other "Fatal Blows"

The laboring poor in the Island reacted in different ways to the economic violence and structural transformations visited upon them during the twenties. The trade-union struggles and the intensification of the ever less autonomous activity of the Partido Socialista, as well as the attempts to play off and win favors from the traditional parties of the propertied classes,[41] were all intertwined with this social violence and vagabondage. Most of these expressions of popular maneuvering bear the mark of progressively higher levels of disarticulation and social disarray. But the colonized laboring classes also responded by reactivating and extending all kinds of alternate economic strategies, both legal and illegal. In *Desafío y solidaridad* Quintero Rivera and García describe the proliferation of street vendors, hucksters, and legal odd-jobbing, all of which were in many ways complementary to itinerant labor practices (pp. 94–98). The rise of unlawful independent-subsistence activities also overlapped in various degrees with the expansion of petty street-sales, odd-jobbing, social violence, nomadism, and organized labor struggles.

On-the-job labor resistance took many forms. The Victor Clark study acknowledges the considerable irregularity, low discipline, and high absentee rates prevalent among the existing nuclei of industrial workers and of laborers in the manufacturing sectors in general (pp. 461–462). But there was some strike activity as well. Although much less numerous than during the preceding War years, these strikes were also marked by widespread social violence. One example of this was the work stoppages of the early twenties. Truman Clark affirms that "two strikes of farm laborers [occurred] in 1922 and 1923. The strikes involving laborers from sugar plantations were usually more bitter," because they involved "violent clashes between police and workers and with fires set in the cane fields" (p. 125). According to Truman Clark, "[t]he normal response of the insular government was to increase the police force of the island by a hundred men or more" (ibid.).

Another example of this form of opposition was very militant mobilizations and work stoppages on the part of the laborers in the tobacco factories during the final years of this decade. This was partially a response to the changes taking place within the tobacco-products sector at this time. Such was the case of the tenacious defiance displayed by the tobacco-manufacturing workers during their walkout in the central-western mountain municipality of Utuado. Regarding the illegal activities of two strikers, Picó in *Los gallos peleados* quotes the policeman on duty as indicating that on July 28, 1926, at 9:30 A.M., on Barceló Street in the tobacco workshop or factory of the "Porto Rico-American Tobacco Company (Utuado Branch)" (in English in the original), these strikers employed coercion to intimidate the strike breakers (p. 121). Making use of "offensive language such as [']damned be the mother[']" and "[']they're sons of bitches if they do not rise up: people have to have dignity and feel shame and be enraged[']," the two strikers "made threats against the workers or 'torcedores' [i.e., tobacco-leaf twisters], which led to the complete paralysis of the day's operations in said factory" (ibid.).

True to form, the police text reduces all violence (effective or announced) to the violence enacted by the subaltern subjects. "Coercion," "intimidation," "offence," "threats," and so on, are understood as strictly the (illegitimate) domain of the two strikers. Both the police and the Porto Rico-American Tobacco Company are excluded from this semiotic and punitive field. Even economic violence is solely attributed to the strikers: "the complete paralysis of the day's operations in said factory." The "Utuado branch" of the U.S. corporation is once again exempt from any such accusations. This entire textual maneuver positions the actions of the two "native" male laborers as being completely senseless, an incivility marked by the dutifully noted—and gendered—epithets attributed to the strikers: in this manner, the latter (as social subjects) become located outside any regard for convention, tradition, and propriety; outside reason, they were therefore outside the law.

Picó then describes the aggressive anti-scab activities of one of these tobacco workers. On September 12, 1926, at 4 P.M. in the Utuado sector of Cumbre Alta, Manuel Felicié, a "torcedor" on strike, was arrested again and "accused of assaulting Rafael Rodríguez, the cigar maker, with a mortar handle for grinding coffee" (p. 121). According to Picó, Felicié allegedly "inflicted four concussions on Rodríguez because the former believed that the latter was against the strike" (ibid.).

In terms of Puerto Rico as a whole, the colonial Secretary of Agriculture and Labor characterized the 1927 Island-wide strike of the Porto Rico-American Tobacco Company as the "most serious strike of recent years," involving "several thousand cigar makers" who "struck for higher wages and better living conditions."[42] "The department of labor acted with the mediation and conciliation commission to bring about an agreement, but without success, and the strike lasted many months" (ibid.).

Yet social violence took more mundane and everyday forms as well. The empirical evidence for the other types of transgressive activities and survival mechanisms between 1922 and 1929 is not as abundant as for the previous decades. Nevertheless, certain approximations can be made. True, the suicide rate stayed at the same level it had been during the Great European War (see table 4). However, the number of cases solved by the local courts for murder and voluntary homicide reveals a different story. This last manifestation of criminalized social violence more than doubled from the first years of this decade to the mid-twenties, maintaining these higher levels until the late twenties.[43]

As in the 1898–1921 period, this implosive social violence was often expressed through the enactment of manliness by the peasant and urban-laborer men. It was not uncommon to have such violence directed against women and young girls.[44] Yet it often occurred between "native" male laborers themselves. An example of this was the 1926 murder case against Pascual Ramos that took place in the southern coastal municipality of Guayama. According to Córdova Chirino, Ramos, described in the newspapers as "a big mulatto of 23 years of age," was seen by fellow laborers as he fatally struck with one machete blow another worker, Carlos Rossó ("well built despite his 60 years of age . . . [distinguished by his] heavy, dark-skinned shoulders") (pp. 233, 234). The incident was reconstructed later by a local reporter, during 1948–1949, in the characteristic manner of the tabloid crime journalism of the forties. Once again, as in the Dalmau Canet narrative of 1915, the events were initially contextualized by the Creole reporter turned detective's apprentice by observing that the future assassin, Pascual Ramos, until recently had been employed as a day custodian in the same hacienda where his future victim, Carlos Rossó, had just gotten a job as a night watchman. When Rossó noticed that his gas lamp had disappeared from the warehouse, he accused Ramos of having stolen it. This accusation brought about the immediate dismissal of Ramos, as well as "the subsequent animosity between the two men" (p. 235).

Then, with meticulous care, the circumstances leading to the crime were reconstructed and the predatory nature of the offender was morbidly detailed. According to eye witness accounts, on December 23, 1926, Pascual Ramos went to the Hacienda Sabater and "[n]ervously, . . . circled the oxcart where Rossó was working. He stalked his prey for forty minutes, waiting for the proper moment to strike the mortal blow." Those present were unaware of Ramos' "fierce intentions" and, because of this "unfortunate circumstance, Pascual [Ramos] was able to close in repeatedly, machete in hand, where Carlos Rossó was working." Ramos tarried, "waiting for the moment in which Rossó was more exposed so as not to miss and make the blow more effective" (pp. 235–236).

Finally, the bloody climax was retold with a heightened sense for the macabre particulars of the incident. The "lethal instant came" when Rossó kneeled to unscrew the wooden slab usually placed below an oxcart to keep it horizontal, lightening the load for the oxen while the cart was at rest. As Rossó "lowered his head" Ramos, "with the agility of a beast, with the speed of a lightning bolt, lifted the weapon and let it fall with all his strength" in the center of Rossó's neck, "miraculously not completely severing it" (p. 236). "The head was left dangling from a thin muscle and, as Rossó's body fell, lifeless, it resembled a heap of human flesh" (ibid.).

As during the preceding decades, the subaltern body constructed through such events appeared as racialized only if the corresponding social subjects did not fall within the "white" end of the Island's phenotypical spectrum. This immediately contextualizes part of the—not too subtle—feral characterization of the murderous subject: "stalked his prey," "fierce," "with the agility of a beast," and so on. Ramos' acts are hence textualized within the predominant cultural maps. His desires could then be read as logically matching the true (savage) ontology Ramos so naturally embodied, not only as a vulgar laborer (body rather than mind), but also as a dark, ominous brute (primitive flesh rather than enlightened spirit). His victim, on the other hand, met the expected fate inasmuch as he also shared the basic, essentialist, corporeal, class/race features of the victimizer. Would Rossó have met a different fate if he had been a respectable, propertied, and educated citizen (Creole or North American), working in a more refined environment? In this way, the victim is reduced—physically and textually—to a mere piece of meat: simply an-other body. However gruesome, this manner of debasement can be represented as somehow appropriate given the hegemonic sociocultural logic.

Pascual Ramos was sentenced to death. He was the last person in the Island to perish at the gallows, dying on September 15, 1927 (pp. 239–243): his was the last body to hang according to the power of the colonial-capitalist regime over the lives of its subjects. Once again, the guilty met his fate, the social class and racial expectations of the unevenly predominant elements within colonial society ("Porto Rican" and U.S.-based) were confirmed, the discursive expertise and disciplinary efficiency of the Creole intelligentsia and law enforcement agents was verified, and order was reestablished.

It would seem that the changes that were taking place in the primary and legal sources of subsistence were partially responsible for these expressions of unfocused social violence. The brutality of the *police* violence of the War years was apparently now superseded by the brutality of the *economic* violence of the restructuring process, which involved the escalation and intensification of production in the sugar and tobacco-manufacturing sectors; the dismantling of the tobacco factories; the partial abandonment of the coffee haciendas; and so forth. All of these transformations seem to have brought about severe dislocations within the dispossessed "native" majorities. The laboring poor partially responded to this situation with greater implosive violence, illegal economic activities, and nomadism.

"Her Educated People, . . . Primarily Latin in Culture, Blood, and Tradition"

During this decade, some of the previous colonialist narratives underwent some changes of form, a transformation intimately related to the juridico-political struggles and textual practices of the privileged Creoles. The labor disputes of 1915–1921 and of the rest of the twenties, together with the broader forms of social disorder that transpired in both periods, illustrated some of the contradictions inherent to the juridical subject-formation of all "Porto Ricans" in the Island, particularly among the upper strata of this population. In this sense, the multiple efforts made by the Creole propertied and educated classes to culturally and socially distinguish themselves from the unruliness of this "native" laboring majority produced partially successful results.

Toward the end of the European War these relatively privileged "native" sectors expanded their role in the administration of the colony by swelling all the ranks of the colonial[ist] bureaucracy in the Island and through the growth of the local legislative body when, after 1917, upper-house posts became elective (by adult male suffrage).[45] The accretion of high-ranking "Porto Rican" members even in the Federal levels of the colonial civil service was one of the major achievements of these social classes, as was their increasing influence in the affairs of the colonial executive branch. The tracks of this ascent were recorded in a letter that one North American colonialist official sent to the U.S. War Department's Bureau of Insular Affairs in March of 1933:

> When I first came to Puerto Rico in 1915 . . . all the Federal positions except a few of the lower grades were held by Americans, and in the Insular Government the Governor, the Attorney General of Porto Rico [*sic*] and his principal assistants were all Americans and Democrats. Now only a few of the highest Federal positions are held by Americans and in the Insular Government there is not now an American in any position of importance except those who are appointed by the President and confirmed by the U.S. Senate.[46]

What is usually suggested is that the Creole bureaucrats and the local intelligentsia made such headway within the Island's political scene, along with other gains, by grovelling before the resident and absentee colonizers, as well as by playing off and/or by resisting different sectors of the colonial-administrative power in the U.S. mainland. Truman Clark (pp. 76–105) and Mattos Cintrón (pp. 66–91), for example, are two of the scholars who have concluded as much. I am not denying such activity, but rather proposing complementary ways by which official colonialist circles recognized the juridico-political "adolescence" of the privileged Creoles—in light of the fact that juridical "manhood" was still reserved for the colonizers.

This colonialist function was accomplished through the insistent pursuit of what Foucault called "author-functions":[47] specifically, through inscribing, regulating, and fashioning as "childlike" and "feminine" the disorderly practices of the "native" impoverished majorities. Arcadio Díaz Quiñonez, in "Recordando el futuro imaginario," has eloquently described the emergent electoral paternalism of Creole politicians, particularly during the late thirties and early forties (pp. 27, 31). But this was only the tip of an otherwise ludicrous tropical iceberg. It was this often-overlooked "author-function" that greatly contributed to bestowing the Creole intellectuals and bureaucrats with, what JanMohamed has designated as, "the moral and psychological pleasures of manichean superiority."[48] Through such colonial mimicry these privileged "Porto Ricans" were "inducted . . . to fulfill the author-function of the colonialist writer" (ibid). The extent to which they could successfully re-present and produce the "native" majorities as "lamentably alien . . . [and] as problems to be solved or confined"—to once again borrow Said's explanation of the Orientalist version of Western colonialism[49]—was the extent to which the privileged Creoles would be admitted into the kingdom.

Yet despite these gains, these colonized intellectuals and bureaucrats were not admitted into the kingdom *as equals*. In this sense, they would continue to fulfill what Bhabha designated as the colonialist "desire for a reformed, recognizable Other."[50] Propertied and educated "natives"—just as all "Porto Ricans" in the Island—remained under the direct supervision of the North American colonial Governor, the U.S. Congress, and the President (none of which were elected by Island residents).[51] At this level, even privileged "Porto Ricans" could not fully represent themselves.

As in the colonialist narratives that emerged in the first years of the U.S. occupation, "Porto Ricans" as a whole ultimately continued to be inscribed as having a deficient nature. This was the nature that more straightforward colonialists, such as U.S. House Speaker Joseph Cannon, said in 1916 was responsible for "Porto Ricans" not being capable of dealing with self-government due to profuse racial mixing in the Island and to the "enervating effects" of a tropical existence.[52] Although some of the forms of this textual universe did undergo subsequent modification, this tutorial and custodial discourse did not change substantially with the extension of U.S. citizenship to the inhabitants of the Island with the Jones Act of 1917. Let us not forget that one of the avowed purposes of the Jones Act of 1917 was, in the words of Senator Albert E. Fall of New Mexico, not only to "teach them self-government," but also to do so in the context of "rais[ing] them in the scale of civilization."[53]

The narratives that fashioned all of the "natives" as incapable persisted in part because most "Porto Ricans" continued to reside in the tropics and also because "Porto Rico" was still located in the "[North] American Mediterranean."[54] The Jones Act did not transform the subject position of the "native" residents of the Island with respect to their "fellow Americans" in the U.S. mainland because it did not fundamentally alter the juridical conditions of the inhabitants of this Island: "they" still belonged to but were not a part of—that is, equal to—the United States. The recent study by José A. Cabranes of the corresponding legal-constitutional history contends that "the citizenship granted was not complete; it was never intended to confer on the Puerto Ricans 'any rights that the American people [did] not want them to have.'"[55] Terminologically, "citizenship," per se, "suggested equality of rights and privileges and full membership in the American political community," indicated Cabranes, "thereby obscuring the colonial relationship between the great metropolitan state and a poor overseas dependency" (pp. 6–7). Even within the parameters of North American, bourgeois, juridical ideology, the implications of such a decision are nevertheless ironic. "Thus, half a century after the United States proclaimed the inadmissibility of the ownership of persons," concludes Cabranes; "it affirmed its acceptance of the contemporaneous European concept of the ownership of peoples" (p. 96).

Despite the underlying persistence of these narratives (content-wise), changes did take place in the forms assumed by these custodial and tutorial North American discourses and their corollary juridico-political expressions. These changes were oriented towards acknowledging the growing proficiency of the Creole propertied and educated classes in defining and regulating the backwardness of "their own" people, as exemplified among other things by the capacity of "native" intellectuals to carry out social diagnoses among the impoverished majorities of the Island.[56]

Motivated in part by these alleged signs of cultural advancement (on the part of the privileged Creoles) as well as by the changing situation in the rest of Caribbean, the apex of U.S. overseas-colonial administration started shifting its policies toward granting some reforms and moderating the bluntness that had previously characterized such procedures in the Island. The granting of U.S. citizenship for "Porto Ricans" was an example of this, as were some of the other provisions of the Jones Act of 1917. This change may be better illustrated by briefly comparing the two colonial governors that opened and closed the 1921–1929 period.

E. Mont Reily, colonial Governor between 1921 and 1923, was one of the last diehards of colonialist tactlessness. According to Truman Clark, Reily's inaugural speech as the colony's highest official was extensively edited by President Harding: the word "ruler" being substituted for "executive" and the phrase "the territory over which I may rule" was changed for "administer" (p. 52). During the preceding two decades, such curt narratives would have passed on an everyday basis, meeting neither the protest nor the acquiescence of the few Creoles in the top ranks of the colonial administration. But describing the Island's inhabitants as "children . . . [who] change their attitudes almost daily," and even portraying one of his principal Creole aides, Roberto H. Todd, as "a half-blooded negro . . . [who] deserted his wife and is living with a woman of the streets" in letters to President Harding, did not precipitate Reily's demise as the leading colonial official (Truman Clark's research has confirmed this. See pp. 62–63). Neither did his proclivity towards corruption, inertia, nor his tirades against the display of the (unrecognized) national flag of the Island to the detriment of the stars and stripes (pp. 56–61).

What brought about his removal by the President was Reily's propensity to act, not only without consulting the Creole-based colonial legislature, but also without consulting his superiors in the Bureau of Insular Affairs. The last time such a serious confrontation ensued between the colonial legislature and the Governor had been in 1909. President Taft then solidly backed colonial Governor Allen, chastising the "native" legislators for being incapable of exercising self-control and governmental authority.[57]

On the other hand, Theodore Roosevelt, Jr., colonial Governor during 1929–1932, was a dynamic reformer who delivered his inaugural speech partly in Spanish and who liked being referred to as *"el jíbaro de la Fortaleza"* (the *jíbaro* in the Governor's Mansion).[58] He collaborated extensively with the Creole legislature. The young colonial Governor was keenly aware of the new waves of resistance that were emerging in the Caribbean against U.S. interventionism—particularly in Nicaragua, Honduras, Cuba, and the Dominican Republic.[59] He had tried to impress upon President Hoover the importance of using "Porto Rico" as "our connecting link. She might be, so to speak, our show window looking south."[60] Truman Clark illustrates the extent to which, more than any other colonial Governor before him, Theodore Roosevelt, Jr. had extended the usage of the first-person plural when delivering allocutions regarding "Porto Ricans" (pp. 141, 150). Roosevelt, Jr.'s tenure was as atypical as E. Mont Reily's for no other North American colonial Governor (except the last one, Rexford G. Tugwell) would go as far as he had in terms of colonial reform and trying to ingratiate himself with the "natives." It was Roosevelt, Jr., not Reily, who represented the real wave of the future regarding colonialist signifying practices in the Island.

The colonialist imprimatur of Roosevelt, Jr.'s administrative perspective is still evident in the terms in which he defined this "show window looking south." The relevance of these recommendations is not so much that, in retrospect, they seemed to anticipate the putative, post-World-War-Two "home-rule" project of the "Commonwealth of Puerto Rico" (still known —misleadingly—in the Island as the "Estado Libre Asociado," literally: Free Associated State).[61] What I find interesting about Roosevelt, Jr.'s statements is the extent to which they explicitly codified the Euro/Americo-centric parameters of the author-functions being carried out by the privileged "natives" in both the juridico-political and cultural realms. The class limits of the emergent transformation are quite clear: "the university [of Puerto Rico] could be developed with visiting students and professors from both continents," and "young Puerto Ricans trained in the United States" could be utilized "as part of our diplomatic and consular service in South America"—"they would be ideally suited for representatives of American banking or industry in the Latin-American countries" (pp. 119, 194).

In a similar manner, the hierarchical location of each link in this chain is also made evident: "Her educated people, though primarily Latin in culture, blood, and tradition, would speak English and be acquainted with America and America's method of thought" (p. 119). Here, again, are the familiar Eurocentric tropes of the Great Chain of Being. The "natives," even the privileged ones, embodied the past and things ancestral ("blood and tradition"). As Visvanathan phrased it, they were "the past the West has already lived out."[62] On the other hand, the colonizers, per se, were identified with an enlightened tomorrow and the capacity to reason ("method of thought")—Visvanathan: "the West, the modern West, is in turn the future these societies will encounter" (ibid.).

These two colonial administrations—from Reily's to Roosevelt, Jr.'s—demonstrate the displacements that were taking shape within U.S. colonialist discourses in the Island. Such shifts hardly exemplified any substantial transformations insofar as the colonizers still directly (even in the enlightened paternalism of gone-primitive Roosevelt, Jr.) or indirectly (as in the broader overseeing functions of the colonialist bureaucracy and the corporate headquarters in the U.S. mainland) determined what was best for the Island and its inhabitants. Rather, these changes indicated that, as far as public discourse was concerned, the social colonial order could and should be regulated with the increasing and more active participation of the colonized themselves: first and foremost, with the involvement of intellectual and administrative cadre from the Creole propertied and educated classes.

The terms of this emergent colonial pact did not only mean, in some cases, having the colonizers—literally—speak the language of the colonized. They also required that the colonized—in particular, the privileged Creoles—speak the corrective, disciplinary, and paternalist/masculinist language of colonial-capitalist surveillance. It appeared that the growing numbers of educated "native" subjects who performed these colonialist author-functions were indeed invested with (as well as invested in) Euro/Americo-centric knowledge. Recalling Fanon's comments about the educated Martinicans returning from France, the educated "Porto Rican" too "confronted with the most trivial occurrence, . . . becomes the one who knows."[63] If being a "native" was to be always already found wanting, then the only means to distance themselves from this terrible ontology was to participate, however partially, in the colonizer's fullness—if not economically then, at least, intellectually. This was one way of reading Theodore Roosevelt, Jr.'s statement that by learning English and "America's method of thought," these privileged colonized subjects "were enriched not impoverished" (p. 119). Or, in the words of Fanon, "they convey[ed] the impression that they have completed a cycle, that they have added to themselves something that was lacking. They return literally full of themselves" (p. 19).

For these members of the "native" intelligentsia, the parameters of their contradiction were defined, on the one hand, by their desire for the colonialist knowledge/language: as Trinh Minh-ha has pointed out, "[k]nowledge belongs to the one who succeeds in mastering a language, and standing closer to the civilized language is, as a matter of fact, coming nearer to equality."[64] On the other hand, as colonized subjects they tended to be permanently trapped within the boundaries of colonial mimicry: of being, what Bhabha called, "almost the same [as the colonizer], but not quite" (p. 126).

"The Ingeniousness of the Country People"

The literate ideological representations of the transgressions of the "native" poor occasionally experienced some modifications. The colonized laboring classes were still fashioned as ignorant and, in this context, immoral. Yet, as had already started taking place during the previous decade, this semiotic map was being redrawn with some frequency. At times, it would register the impoverished majorities of the Island as possessing a certain instinctive cunning, wily nature, artful methods. For example, according to Picó, the selling of noninspected and/or watered-down milk in the municipality of Utuado was one of the illegalized economic-subsistence practices that at this time was periodically portrayed as being crafty (pp. 51–52). Such depictions sometimes accompanied the accounts of minor theft and the home-production of bootleg rum.

Moral and legal condemnation was still the rule, though now the element of criminal dexterity was increasingly noted. Some of these activities were officially classified as petit larceny. This was particularly common pertaining to the illegal practices of the urban poor. The Knowlton Mixer report of 1926 states that petty thieving was also "very prevalent in San Juan and extremely annoying to automobile owners," insofar as cars left "parked in front of places of amusement in the evenings" were "likely to lose everything that is removable."[65] According to Mixer, everything was sure to go—"[b]ulbs, tools, extra tires, mats, robes." There was also one recorded case of "over eighty grease cups being removed from various parts of the engine during an evenings entertainment," while the coil boxes of Ford automobiles had to be "securely locked" if one did not "wish to walk home." Such exploits were, "of course, the work of hoodlums," but these felonies were "so deftly done that it [was] extremely difficult for the police to catch the offenders" (ibid.).

Once more, petty thieves became just another species of nocturnal pest: they were like the mosquitoes and the rodents that could invariably be counted on to prey upon the unwary North American visitor not yet accustomed to the bothersome behavior so natural to the invisible denizens of the tropical night. Surely the "natives" were no strangers to these "extremely annoying" practices. But, then again, the vast majority of "Porto Ricans" were not "automobile owners"—yet another fact that made these very same "natives" suspect of being evening stalkers themselves. So, just as sundown separated the daytime from the night, law and civilization separated the colonizers and their handful of trustworthy "natives" from those who were located outside of the social order, outside of the light, and—unfortunately—often outside the reach of the colonial police.

As in the previous decade, poor and wandering children were, significantly, included among those identified as petty thieves. And, as before, the narratives of an illegality bred by illegitimacy were frequently present. For example, the federal Children's Bureau researcher Helen V. Bary observed that

> In most cases brought before the juvenile courts the charges have been petty theft, neglect, and abandonment, offenses which are largely traceable to poverty. Many of the children involved were homeless, and about one-third were illegitimate; about half had never attended school. The responsibility of parents for illegitimate children has not been definitely established, decisions on this point being in conflict. (pp. 28–29)

A conference delivered in San Juan before one of the bastions of Creole, propertied, and educated respectability (the "Ateneo Puertorriqueño"), disclosed similar findings. On that occasion, the well-known judge, Pablo Berga y Ponce de León retold the following anecdote. Once more, the drama unfolds in three acts: first the circumstances of the offender are described and the evidence is presented. The Juvenile Court judge tells the story of an eight-year old delinquent, living with his mother, and repeatedly apprehended by the police for theft. His skills are duly noted: "The boy had a great ability in terms of entering stores, opening cash registers, and taking money. He stole the purses of ladies that were going shopping." So was his audacity: "Sometimes he would also search automobiles to steal objects [left inside]. He did this to my own [car] on one occasion."[66]

The second act brings forth the derelict or absent parent, from the dispossessed "native" population, coming into view for public scrutiny.

> This child's welfare was a problem for me because, being a delinquent, he could not be sent to the Boys' Charity School and, on the other hand, his tender age advised [one] that he be kept within the bosom of the home. In this case, it struck me as odd that, every time the boy was detained, the mother would rapidly materialize looking for him, as if she was following his footsteps, and then she would declare that she would strip him naked and tie him up so that he would not leave the house and she would hit him hard whenever he carried out any of those acts he was accustomed to. (pp. 11–12)

Finally, the burden of guilt is deposited on appropriate—that is, destitute—shoulders. This time the corresponding guilt is associated with the ignorance of the laboring poor, the juridico-political and textual effects however remain the same. The members of the impoverished majorities in the Island continue to be inscribed as lacking in virtues, intelligence, or both. Berga y Ponce de León indicates that the last time the young thief was detained, the latter confessed he was only doing his mother's bidding. It was she who "would usually lay her hand on his head and tell him, 'Son, go and bring me money, I need it.' The boy responded to the influence of the mother." The mother, however, was identified as being just as ignorant as her son, equally lacking in morals, equally dependent on the guidance of others more respectable than she: "[w]e do not think that she did this with the intention of introducing the idea of robbery [in his head]" (p. 12).

In all of these accounts we again encounter the narratives of broken childhoods, picaresque Artful Dodgers and "Lazarillos," broken morals, and so on. As had happened during the European War, this ideology of the lack of appropriate parental supervision cum illegitimate/consensual unions was one of the ways through which the de-generation of the dispossessed sectors was codified and the nature of wayward children explained. Certain sectors of the Island's propertied and educated classes clearly perceived an inadequacy within the family structures of the "native" laboring classes regarding the *parental* policing (of their own children). For these privileged Creoles, such inadequacy only verified the need for State intervention in terms of *general* policing in a decade when police violence was being unevenly displaced by economic violence. During the decade of the twenties, however, such an ideological program was only incipient—despite its prescient character. Official normative discourses of this sort, together with the corresponding institutional expressions, actually gained more currency and thrived during the following decades.

The production and marketing of bootleg rum during Prohibition is perhaps the best example of mass-based, illegal economic activity. Although the production of clandestine liquor spanned the entire first half of this century, the Prohibition period greatly increased the number of people pursuing this form of subsistence income—as Picó has shown in the case of Utuado (p. 57). According to Knowlton Mixer (p. 200) and colonial Governor Towner's report of 1928 (p. 61), arrests for violation of liquor laws soared from 1,283 in 1922 to 4,625 in 1927. Despite police harassment, the practice continued to be quite widespread. Among other things, this was due to the low-level of the technical base needed to set up such a microenterprise, making this expertise readily available to the average laborer. Within this context, José Enamorado Cuesta's 1929 sociography insisted:

> The ingeniousness of the country people of the island in the manufacture of their stills is truly marvelous. Any "peón," given an empty kerosene can, a few pieces of copper wire or rubber hose, and enough cheap molasses (the kind commonly used to be fed to horses), will become a rum manufacturer over night.[67]

The proliferation of this illegal survival mechanism was so pervasive that its control became not only virtually impossible, but perhaps even administratively undesirable. "If every 'peón' found on the road carrying a pint or two of rum were to be dealt a jail sentence," Cuesta indicated, "space would soon be lacking to accommodate them, and untold hardship would be caused to their dependents," given that "a large majority of the cases brought in court [was] made up of such as these" (p. 76).

This illegal subsistence practice was widespread not only because the poor laborers implicated were so hard to arrest. As Truman Clark recognized fifty years later, "Prohibition was even less successful in Puerto Rico than in the United States" because every year "the insular government announced the number of homemade stills captured and destroyed," while "each year the figure was approximately that of 1923—-1,067 stills" (pp. 33–34). According to Clark, one of the principal, mainstream politicians of the Island, Unionista leader Antonio R. Barceló, declared in 1921 "that there were 10,000 illegal stills in Puerto Rico, and he may have been correct" (ibid.).

Violations of Prohibition were also widespread because the persistent collaboration between the perpetrator and the surrounding community short-circuited the colonial-capitalist juridical machine designed to convict people for such violations. Cuesta is in this case quite explicit in declaring that it became "harder every day to obtain a conviction by jury in a prohibition case, no matter what the proof produced against the culprit may be" (p. 75). The reason for this difficulty was that the "witnesses for the State [were] very hard to obtain in these cases, at least willing witnesses, while as a rule the defendant [was] able to muster a host of them" (ibid.).

As with the other forms of social transgression that transpired during the 1920s, the making of bootleg rum was the type of survival mechanism and social response that became generalized during the forthcoming Depression years.

7

"The Age of Criminal Saturation," 1930–1939

Manuel was born in a normal peasant home. When his mother died, his father took care of the children, over whom he worried a great deal. One night when the children were asleep he set fire to the house. Manuel, then five years old, was able to run away but his two younger brothers were burnt to death.

—José C. Rosario, *A Study of Illegitimacy and Dependent Children in Puerto Rico* (1933)

. . . Me, X, instead of torching the cane field, I woulda torched his [i.e., the manager's] house with all o' his family inside. This is the sort o' thing we should be a republic for [i.e., an independent country]: so that we could turn t' banditry and get even with all o' the wrongs that the workingman is suffering.

—José C. Rosario and Justina Carrión, "Rebusca sociológica: una comunidad rural en la zona cañera" (1937)

Take up the White Man's burden—
And reap his old reward:
The blame of those ye better,
The hate of those ye guard—
The cry of hosts ye humour
(Ah, slowly!) toward the light:—
"Why brought ye us from bondage,
"Our loved Egyptian night?"

—Rudyard Kipling, "The White Man's Burden" (1899)

During the period between 1930 and 1939, most of the propertied sectors went into a tailspin, bringing about savage restructuring within the Island's economic sphere. This drove growing numbers of the already painfully desperate "native" impoverished majorities to the physical limits of their subsistence capacities. The torrent of mass and individual rage that erupted rose above the previous peaks of social disorder.

This decade also witnessed an even greater expansion of the disciplinary functions of the Creole intellectuals and bureaucrats, concomitant to their looming place within the colonized political scene. Regardless of its seeming insignificance and of the ostentatious manner with which it was announced, changing the official name of the Island in 1932 back to "Puerto Rico" (that is, having the federal government recognize the pre–1898 nomenclature) signified the ascent of the privileged Creoles. The punitive and surveillance mechanisms and discourses embodied in the term "Porto Rico" had seemed to be, to borrow the words of Edward Said, "morally neutral and objectively valid; it seemed to have an epistemological status equal to that of historical chronology or geographical location."[1] Now, with the official disappearance of the term, it might seem that such mechanisms and discourses had exhausted their usefulness.

As we shall see in this chapter, however, this name change did not mean the demise of the disciplinary survey, inscription, and regulation of "native" disorder, particularly of the practices carried out by the colonized majorities in the Island: even more than in earlier decades, the subaltern subjects of the popular illegalities were located on the cross hairs of both official punitive patterns (textually, in particular) and bodies of colonial-capitalist organization. The corrective study of this colonized population, which had formerly crystallized in the terms "Porto Rico" and "Porto Ricans," was now entering a new phase: that of the growing moral and literal policing of most "natives" by an entire army of functionaries and administrative officer-corps composed of other "natives." This meant the further social bifurcation of the colony's "subject people."

The decade of the thirties can be seen as a conflation of the propertied classes' economic violence of the twenties and the State's police violence of 1915–1921, while simultaneously representing a qualitative augmentation of both. In both cases these measures were mainly directed against the Island's laboring classes. Certain aspects of this reality were not completely lost on a few contemporary Creole observers of a phenomenon, whose consequences extended into the following decade. As one of these privileged "native" observers, Miguel Meléndez Muñoz, commented, "Puerto

Rico suffered the effects of the economic crisis that followed immediately after the signing of the Peace Treaty."[2] For Meléndez Muñoz, "one of its principal effects" for Puerto Ricans "was the paralysis of the tobacco industry which employed twelve to fifteen thousand workers in different tasks," as well as "the crisis of the sugar and tobacco crops, resulting in large masses of unemployed people." The sum of these ingredients—"the psychological effects of the war reflected on the social mass, the production and consumption of illegal alcohol, the unemployment situation, the moral dislocation"—constituted "the original elements that promoted that age of *criminal saturation*" (ibid., emphasis in the original).

Once again the colonized laboring classes were ideologically constituted as degenerates under the sway of immorality and vice. The best that liberal intellectuals ("Porto Rican" and U.S.-based) could do was to attribute this fall to the grueling social strife. The underlying expectation was still that the laboring classes would rather carry out surplus labor for somebody else than further their own survival through self-appropriation, individual or communal, legal or illegal.

At this time, the subaltern subjects experienced equal portions of ruthlessness, excruciating transformation, and bold experimentation. The 1930s, therefore, are comparable to the first years after the Spanish-Cuban–North American War in terms of the levels of general social violence. Yet this decade is also comparable to the period of the Great War in Europe, particularly in terms of the levels of labor militancy. To a large extent, this decade echoed the martial and belligerent nomenclature of the two other periods, despite the masked nature of this particular—social—war.

These are the social and textual parameters to be studied in the present chapter. Here we will explore the principal elements of such an economic, social, political, and textual turning point, providing an alternate reading of the most tempestuous period in Island memory—written, oral, or lived.

Crisis and Displacement among the Propertied Classes

One of the major transformations that materialized at this time was the marked decline in U. S. investments in Latin America and the Caribbean. Two other factors had a long term impact on the area (including Puerto Rico). One was the recomposition of the U.S. economy, particularly of its leading sectors. The other was the drastic fluctuations in the world prices of raw materials that were important to the Caribbean economies—such as molasses.[3] Even though Puerto Rico was not affected in exactly the same way by the changes that were altering the face of the Caribbean, the same geographically external factors that were acting upon the entire Basin area had comparable effects in terms of the major social and economic rearticulations experienced in the Island during the critical Depression years.

Between 1929 and 1939 the contribution of agriculture to the Island's general income suffered a percentage change of -32.2 percent, albeit sugar production rebounded around the mid-thirties. This relative recuperation was mostly due to changes in the federal tariff laws. A subsequent governmental subsidy, together with the mentioned tariff accommodation, provided artificial resuscitation to this sector of the Island's economic sphere. During the Great Depression, though, the general situation of agriculture as a whole was one of arrested development and prolonged decline. This long-term deterioration occurred despite the fact that, even as late as 1938–1939, agriculture was still thirty percent to thirty-one percent of the Island's general income—it was only slightly surpassed by the government sector.[4]

The only other economic sectors to show some expansion at this time were the needle-products home-manufacture interests and the federal/local government's relief and reconstruction activities. Nevertheless, in terms of economic policies, these were not long term solutions. By its very nature, needlework was characteristically organized as an extremely mobile, dispersed, and uncertain fly-by-night type of operation. On the other hand, some of the accretion in the government's economic activity proved to be relatively conjunctural, primarily limited to the 1933–1941 period.[5]

The leading sectors of capitalist production re-adjusted, to a certain degree, to the new situation, and the corresponding shift assumed various forms. Tobacco-products manufacture continued to phase out its factories, while needlework manufacture expanded its domiciliary network. It appears that the substitution of the former by the latter partially reflected capital's adaptation to a more dispersed, mobile, disorderly, and recalcitrant labor force. But this switch also reflected an attempt on the part of capital to, however unevenly, productively recapture this labor force, while at the same time extending further the process of capitalist accumulation. Such a maneuver was only partially successful. The concurrent and growing mechanization of sugar production and the intensification of sugarcane cultivation were two of the historical features of capital's adjustment to the new situation.[6] This allowed the sugar sector to partially relaunch its control over its fraction of the colonized labor force. By attempting to rearticulate the growing irregularity of the "native" laborers, as well as to counteract their trade union activity and broader social unrest, the sugar corporations and the large planters achieved some advantages. As in the preceding three decades, the results in this regard were mixed.

In both the sugar sector and the manufacture of needle-products, capital appeared to be further extending the strategies initiated between 1922 and 1929: amplifying the range and/or intensity of its control over the Island's laborers. The long-term instability of the colonized market was aggravated by the severity of the economic contraction and the subsequent wild fluctuations in the economy during the Depression. Such conditions conferred paramount importance to the general regulation of the "native" working classes, particularly to the reconstitution of some semblance of civil order. As in the pivotal turn-of-the-century juncture, the methods promoted and rearticulated by capital and the State during the Depression years were particularly vicious and harsh. Likewise, the official strategies deployed among the masses of "Porto Ricans" to compensate for the more excruciating consequences of these restructuring methods only ended up extending the radius of bureaucratic and profit-oriented social regulation.

"The Prevalence of Large Inequalities"

Although usurious practices were progressively outlawed and fell into disuse by the late 1930s and early 1940s, they nonetheless persisted in one form or another throughout the entire first half of the twentieth century. At several levels, usury tended to differentially erode the more ancestral elements of the peasant-based sociocultural configuration, particularly in the sugarcane coast.[7] Insofar as usury persisted, it also tended to wear away at the social conditions of the impoverished majorities it leeched on. Despite its decline during the Depression, this was still a major burden precisely because the consumption capacities of the laboring classes were so severely constricted due to the overall economic crisis.

Malnutrition, starvation, and deteriorating health conditions became more prevalent at this time, despite the headway made in the treatment of some of the most widespread contagious diseases. A Preliminary Study issued in 1936 by the Puerto Rico Reconstruction Administration reported that "[i]n depression or prosperity, unemployment, underemployment and irregular employment prevail," wages being "so low that they hardly suffice to allow the rice and beans and codfish which is common among the workers."[8] This same report indicated that "large inequalities" prevailed, while "the lot of the mass of the people ha[d] not been improved," with "[u]ncinaria, tuberculosis, malaria, intestinal diseases, and pneumonia" continuing to "exact a high toll of human lives." Most of the population consumed milk "measured in terms of spoonfuls and the meat they seldom taste[d]" was measured "in terms of ounces" (ibid.).

During the thirties, inflation at times reached very high levels as the income of the "native" majorities dropped considerably, as in the case of wages in the sugar sector. Although, between 1930 and 1939 sugar production employed close to half of the labor force in the Island (see table 2), wages had fallen to 1900–1914 levels.[9] This situation persisted for the better part of the Depression years. U.S. economic historian James Dietz also found recently that "[p]er capita income worsened during the early 1930s and only began to approach the 1930 level again, in nominal value, toward the end of the decade . . . " (p. 139). "By 1933," according to Dietz, "per capita income was nearly 30 per cent below what it had been in 1930," and when "changes in the purchasing power are considered, the decline was even greater." He concludes that while U.S. prices "generally fell, prices in Puerto Rico for many necessities actually increased in some years" (ibid.).

Consequently, general living standards deteriorated with remarkable speed and severity, affecting most of the Island's population.[10]This situation partially contextualizes the explosion of popular unrest and social violence that ensued at this time.

In the 1933 study of living standards, sponsored by the recently created colonial Department of Labor, Artemio Rodríguez found a disparity between the average weekly income that was needed to meet the basic requirements of a laborer household ($11.17) and the average weekly incomes of the principal occupational categories (pp. 5–15). These weekly averages oscillated between $1.27 (field laborers in tobacco farms) and $3.94 (operatives in fruit canning factories). True, prices of foodstuffs did not always climb significantly during this decade. Descartes established that in some of the years during the 1930s food costs had actually dropped.[11] However, these prices still remained well above the buying capacity of the masses of the population. For example, another study, this one commissioned by the Federal Emergency Relief Administration (FERA), calculated that in 1935 the weekly income necessary to meet basic needs was $7.14.[12] A year later, though, the average weekly incomes of agricultural laborers still fluctuated between $3.00 (in the coffee sector) and $4.90 (in the sugarcane sector).[13]

The Great Depression struck the Island particularly hard not just because the conditions of existence of the laboring classes were already deteriorating immediately preceding the 1929 stock market Crash. The effects of the crisis were also compounded by two exceptionally catastrophic hurricanes in 1928 and 1932. The seriousness of the economic contraction that ensued only extended this grim condition to ever broader portions of the impoverished "native" majorities.[14]

The proportion of people officially not reporting any economic activity was very high between 1929 and the Second World War. Despite the fact that there were already almost sixty thousand persons employed in government-based emergency-relief work,[15] in 1936 the Puerto Rico Reconstruction Administration (PRRA) calculated that close to twenty-five percent of the family heads were unemployed. According to Carmen Gautier Mayoral,

> The unemployment situation described by the FERA figure ought not be interpreted . . . as reflecting cyclical unemployment only. It may be estimated with more than reasonable accurateness that not less than 125,000 persons of working age are chronically unemployed in Puerto Rico as a result of social and economic maladjustments. In 1929, a year of prosperity in Puerto Rico, an investigation in the municipality of Ponce showed that 55 percent of the number of men investigated were either partially or totally unemployed. (p. 27)

After federal administrative responsibility for the Island passed in 1934 from the War Department to the Department of the Interior, Interior Secretary Harold Ickes, visited the Island in 1936. Ickes described the situation, saying: "The economic problem in Puerto Rico is a very serious one. There is not enough work to go around, with the result that unemployment is at a high rate."[16] In "La base social de la transformación ideológica del Partido Popular," Quintero Rivera states that in 1938 the FERA estimated that the total number of unemployed persons that year—when added together with their dependents—amounted to 1,121,035 people; this roughly equaled sixty percent of the population of the entire Island (p. 54).

How did the economic conditions created by these changes in what Stuart Hall termed the "social relations of production and the 'hard edge' of productive systems" converge with "the 'insides' of people . . . subjectivity and sexuality"[17] in Puerto Rico at this time?

Repeatedly, the confrontations thus generated would not only be "signaled or marked by a functional change in sign-systems" (to again borrow Spivak's phrase[18]): as never before, such a change would be a violent event.

"Moral Dislocations" and "the Frequency of Fighting"

U.S. capital was experiencing its own savage convulsions and seizures, while the Creole Jünkers continued immersed in their tortuous process of transition and collapse and the State (local and federal) provisionally tried out new forms of social reproduction and economic regulation. Yet, even in the case of the working classes in the towns, coastal plains, and cities (where higher levels of scholarization were clearly present), the degree to which the State determined family life was very reduced. The only plane at which State-related agencies eventually and increasingly regulated the material conditions of part of the Island's poor was with respect to some income supplements.[19]

This type of government involvement was primarily a phenomenon of the mid–1930s and onward and was hardly a regular and organized State mechanism in Puerto Rico until the early 1950s. Such activities were exposed to additional limitations. For example, restrictions existed regarding the available federal, Island-wide, and municipal funds and facilities, as well as in terms of the unfamiliarity and technical incomprehensibility that were part and parcel of this governmental relief and of these new social services.[20] Besides, as Eric Wolf observed, these fledgling agencies tended to be " . . . largely unco-ordinated, located in different places and have the impersonal aura of the bureaucratic organization needed to carry through a large scale program."[21] Therefore they had a limited impact on the social war that was being waged across the entire Island.

One of the indicators of the battle that raged within the colonized social order is the way in which social violence was officially registered. Both the murder and the suicide rates practically tripled between the late 1920s and the mid 1930s (see table 4), and these exceptionally high rates were maintained throughout this decade. The suicide rate alone rose by about fifty percent between the middle and the end of the Depression years. In the bereft, coffee-hacienda bastion of Utuado, for example, Picó determined that the number of successful suicides tripled and the number of suicide attempts increased by a factor of eight between 1925 and 1940.[22]

There was also the rise in the incidence of alcoholism and in the number of popular festivities and everyday episodes that ended in brawls, serious injuries, and even deaths. Again, this is partially and superficially chronicled in the broader construction of such practices as breaches of the peace and disorderly conduct within the criminal-justice system. This type of phenomena increased by fifty percent between 1932 and 1940.[23]

But how did the subaltern subjects read the signs of this violence throughout their daily lives? How did these systems of meaning differ from the ones deployed by the educated and propertied classes ("native" and North American)? Can these different signifying practices and these dissimilar readings be traced within the official record?

Some of the declarations made by members of the impoverished majorities during this decade confirm the social tensions just summarized. However, the Island's laboring classes tended to inscribe such disorder within a different sociocultural map. For instance, in an unusually direct portion of the interviews carried out by Rosario and Carrión among the rural residents of the sugar-cane coast (partially unobstructed by the moral policing which characterized the work of these authors), Rosario and Carrión recorded the following type of statement: "I don't know just what the hell is wrong with the people of this community," because "you see them, in any" card, dice, or domino "game or in any party," where "for the slightest thing, they cut or stab somebody . . . "[24]

Here, such violence appears as something unusual and unexpected: card, dice, and domino games are not supposed to be played in order to beget a knife fight. This scenario would have to be disengaged from that violence which is expected and routine. The other violence is not perceived by the laboring classes as peculiar or abnormal: such as that occurring at a social gathering where members of rival families are present, or during the periods of elections, strikes, and so on.

This contrasts sharply with the results of most of the sociographic studies of the day. These explorations in the social sciences did not simply provide additional authentications of the incidence of such events. Studies of this sort also tended to reinforce the normative and administrative discourses that ideologically framed all such popular practices, regardless of context, as additional evidence of the (endemic) moral depravation of the "native" laboring classes. For example, in his 1935 study of the central-mountain tobacco stronghold of Comerío, the North American social researcher, Charles C. Rogler remarked that the "frequency of fighting [was] apparent from the court records" and that fighting was "surely a most common occurrence among the lower classes" (p. 108). According to Rogler, it was "a local custom to have personal disputes settled with a fist fight 'down by the bridge,'" located in the outskirts of urban Comerío and "out of the beat of the police, but not outside their jurisdiction. Five fights were observed here in two months" (ibid.).

As in the preceding two decades, the gendered nature of much of this social violence is conspicuous. This is specifically true of the display of popularly grounded masculinist texts. Quoting from these local court records, Rogler found the three items corresponding to just one Monday morning (out of a total of six items cited). The first one is fairly straightforward; yet, despite the evident enactment of laboring-poor male-centered discursive practices, there is little or no indication of whether such a quarrel did or did not make sense from the perspective of the participants and their immediate community. Accused of "assault and disturbing the peace," two local men had "quarreled over a fifty cent debt," calling each other "vile names." Both of them were "put in the local jail, in the same cell, where a fight ensued between them" (p. 109).

The second incident reproduces the same mass-based gender codes. While unconsciously referencing the existence of alternative social control mechanisms, there is even less information about the factors which precipitated the fight or about its general circumstances. The charge was described as "carrying a concealed weapon (black jack) and assault." Rogler states that both defendants "had been working for a local carpenter, who appeared as a witness for them." One of them "had a swollen eye, which the policeman on the witness-stand testified had been caused by a blow from the black jack." Having denied this, the "injured party . . . stated in his testimony that the black eye was the result of a fall." The proceedings ended when the "testimony of the carpenter, who wanted both of them to return to work, resulted in their acquittal" (ibid.).

The last episode repeats the textual practices of the other two, but with still less insight into the other meanings and social contexts involved. The police "arrested two men for fighting in the street" charging them with "assault and battery." In his written grievance, initially the "complainant" had declared "that he had been assaulted and that the defendant had smashed his nose badly." However, upon taking the witness stand, "he denied his original complaint and testified that his nose had been smashed in a fall." As a result of this second testimony, he was "sentenced to fifteen days in jail for perjury," while the defendant, "who was the aggressor, was given a ten dollar fine or ten days in jail." Rogler then adds: "Four other cases of a similar nature were disposed of during the morning" (p. 110).

Within Rogler's textual and conceptual universe, the re-telling of such acts serves only to illustrate his general arguments about laboring-class brutality in this Puerto Rican town. Despite whatever Rogler may have intended, such phenomena are—literally and Euro/Americo-centrically—translated into mere effects on a "native" substance which leaves much to be desired: namely, the disorderly and wayward content of "local custom," where the violently chaotic behavior between themselves and against one another "is surely a most common occurrence among the lower classes" in a municipality emblematic of the entire Island. What was the—prevalent—logical conclusion? Such "subject people" needed to be protected from themselves.

Rogler, of course, does not raise questions about why "two men quarrelled over a fifty cent debt." Were they denounced by members of their own family and community networks or by total strangers? Did this event in any way embody contradictions between rural and urban family/community patterns and/or between the multiple "native" racial locations? Did these sociocultural networks intervene or could they have done so? Would two propertied and educated Creoles have been caught "disturbing the peace" and, if they had, would they have been "put in the local jail"? Surely they would not have been fighting over a fifty cent debt! What about two colonizers quarrelling in a Comerío road? For Rogler, these were not pertinent questions. Neither was asking about why one construction worker struck a fellow laborer with a black jack, nor why two other members of the laboring poor fought, ending in the broken nose of one of them. In the end, there is only the mindless and ever-frequent violence ("five fights were observed here in two months") by which "personal disputes [were] settled"—but only "among the lower classes." Respectable and self-controlled gentlemen did not settle their differences in this manner. How could a "native" town—much less the entire Island—possibly do without the enlightened guidance of the colonizers, if the overwhelming majority of these "subject people" were given to such savage "local custom[s]"?

Another example of the ways in which everyday social violence was ideologically represented within similar discourses of race and class—this time, the textual practices of the privileged subject population—may be found in one of the first studies done in the Island on illegitimacy and dependent children. This study further illustrates how the social analysis carried out by the Creole intelligentsia did not differ substantially from research which originated in the colonialist "mother country."

One of the deans of Puerto Rican sociology, José C. Rosario, commented in 1933 that the "parents of this case were both colored," the father being from San Juan and the mother from the sugarcane district of Hatillo located in the northwestern coast of the Island: "He was a baker and she was a laundress."[25] The child "attended school for two years" while the "family lived in Hatillo," but when he "was nine years old his mother died and the father came to San Juan to work at his trade." Although he "attended school for a year longer," the boy had "no home," so he "slept at the bakery with his father." Practically all of the father's income "went for rum and since he became quarrelsome under the influence of liquor, he had several fights for which he served a number of prison terms" (ibid.).

Again, we find that the racialization of the subjects being studied and semiotically fashioned by the gaze of the Creole social philosopher occurs primarily when the persons at hand are understood to be nonwhite. Once more, illegitimacy is positioned within the terrain of degeneration and deficient moral individuation. The broader category maintenance being carried out through this racialization is also evident in the way in which the author contextualizes the occurrence of such illegitimacy among Puerto Rican families. The "large colored population of the island," according to Rosario—"as in the southern States of the Union"—comprised "another factor in the large percentage of consensual marriages with their sequel of illegitimacy." Rosario then categorically maintained that "to this day," if one separates "the colored factor from others that may influence the results, we find a very large correlation between illegitimacy and colored population" (p. 11).

This perspective was often shared by other "native" social scientists of the day, the study carried out by Ada M. González Prieto being a case in point. Although González Prieto observes for this decade that "on the whole, child dependency is no more prevalent among colored children than among white children . . . ," she then goes on to affirm that the "number of dependent children born out of wedlock is very high, being almost one and a half times the number of legitimate children."[26] Since, for González Prieto, "[l]ess than one-fourth of the illegitimate children were legitimated," in cases "where color was known, only one-half as many white children as colored children were classed as being illegitimate, that is born out of wedlock and not legitimated" (ibid.).

In spite of all of this, it is also true that part of the social violence was not focused only inwardly, but was outwardly aimed at the existing symbols and personifications of the social order, such as the police, the propertied classes, and so on. Several events point in this direction. One was the proliferation of riots, protests, and tumultuous labor confrontations during this decade. Another is the growth in crimes against those who owned property. Given the extremely widespread levels of pauperization at this time, the near doubling of the number of burglaries, car thefts, and the buying-and-selling of stolen property between 1932 and 1940 described by Teobaldo Casanova, clearly indicate what social classes were the principal targets of these transgressions (p. 22).

Once more, there is additional evidence of the partially gendered and age-based character of this social violence and of the broader, relatively criminalized reactions to these massive structural dislocations. This is to some degree reflected in the rise of sexual crimes and child neglect as a proportion of the principal causes for arrest during these years and extending to the early 1940s (see table 5). Such gendered violence can also be perceived in the doubling of the number of rapes between 1932 and 1938, according to Casanova (p. 22).

The rise in domestic violence is ostensibly part of this overall picture. It further illustrates some of the salient features of the prevailing social violence of this decade. Incidents such as the ones described by José C. Rosario in his 1933 study, were not uncommon.[27] The first case is quite candid. Rosario begins by identifying a child, Domingo, "born in 1919 in a section of the town of Yabucoa" in the southern coast of Puerto Rico "called the Calvary Mount [in English, in the original]." His parents are then described as "both natives of Yabucoa. The father is a good worker when he is sober, which is seldom the case" (pp. 55–56). From here, Rosario goes on to describe the tragedies of women and the tragic aftermath of Domingo's life. His parents were said to have had "a happy home for a while," but after "liquor interfered . . . things went from bad to worse." When the San Felipe cyclone of 1928 struck the Island, "the mother died, leaving two children in care of the father" who "not long before . . . had married consensually a girl from the same town" (p. 56). When "the new wife . . . decided to abandon her husband," Domingo's father realized her intentions and murdered her, for which "he was given a prison sentence of ten years" (ibid.).

Though the tragedies and violence that visited these women and the suffering that this young boy went through are obviously real, one cannot help but wonder if Rosario chose this particular case as an illustration because it was so overpopulated with the signs of traditional Christian dramas of adversity: the child's name, the section of town he was born in, the repeated incidents of betrayal, the wages of sin, and so on. The anguish of child abuse among the "native" laboring classes turns out to be additionally burdened—and re-placed—by the forms of a morality play. As with Rogler, the underlying circumstances are absent and middle-class cultural maps ("native" or North American) are assumed to have universal validity: the explosive gender and age contradictions that so seriously fragmented the subaltern subjects were merely recycled here as evidence of social cannibalism among the "native" masses.

"Morally Sick Women" and Runaway Children

Power relationships surfaced in other ways within the studies of violence against poor women and children. Using the statistics provided by Casanova (pp. 22, 39), it can be seen that such transgressions were also translated into a 333.3 percentage change in the number of arrests for prostitution between 1932 and 1940 as well as in a 270.3 percentage change in the number of children brought before the courts between 1931 and 1940. During this decade, these women and children were not only (and in increasing numbers) the victims of male-adult violence and/or neglect. They were also participating more and more in the illegalized practices that spread during the Depression. Through contradictory methods, these social subjects made ends meet, despite the shrinking legal sources of income, the rigidly gendered and age-based structures of gainful employment, the rampant domestic violence, the pervasive masculinist/heterosexualized social relations which structured this violence, and the generalization of pauperism.

Regarding prostitution, another local social scientist, Pablo Morales Otero, quoted in 1943 from a study carried out by José C. Rosario during the thirties.

> Among the 61 prostitutes chosen at random, the author found that 26 had been abandoned by their husbands, 7 could not put up with the abuse they received from their relatives, 8 did not have anything to eat or wear, 3 were sold by their mothers, 2 wanted to help out their relatives, 3 wanted to have better clothing, 8 blamed their fall on the fact that they lived surrounded by people engaged in carnal sins, and one because she was an orphan and found herself destitute, without a job, and without a family to speak of.[28]

This report echoed the moral crusade of social reform/science, with all its corollary tropes: broken homes, poverty, immoral upbringing, fallen women. From the group of 115 women "of frenzied life" under scrutiny, "9 had prostitutes among other members of their family, 2 had lived in families where there had been adulterous women, 2 among alcoholic family members, 2 among thieves," while the remainder were said to have come "from virtuous families" (p. 200).

In the study carried out by Rogler, one of the prostitutes he interviewed stated that she "was married in New York when very young," her husband working "as a sailor on the Steamship—." According to Rogler, the woman declared: "I needed a man 'on ground' and not 'on water' . . . so I left my husband." She expressed a preference for making money "and the only way I know is this way," which was why she rhetorically asked: "What's the use of slaving all day long as a servant when money can be earned so easily by this means." The woman ended her interview by saying, "I would recommend this occupation to any poor girl" (p. 79).

This presents a more nuanced situation inasmuch as the "native" woman's voice is given some space. Another woman, in this same study, expressed herself along similar lines. Rogler reports that this woman started by establishing the parameters of her income: "Here they pay three or four dollars a month for servants. We sometimes make that much in a night. If we have bad luck getting clients, we lower the price to as little as fifteen cents." Rogler has her then summarizing her links to the surrounding community: "Sometimes those that own stores give us credit there in payment for visits." Parenthetically, Rogler later places this woman within a family setting: "(The mother of this girl had thirteen children, of whom seven were dead. She said that her daughter was in [a] 'bad business,' but otherwise she was a very good girl. One sister was in the house of correction for robbery; another sister had been a prostitute but had died of gonorrhea.)"[29]

The prevailing codes (Creole and North American) on gender, class, race, and sexuality would immediately position such statements not only as those of a common and brazen trollop. Such intertextual practices tended to inscribe her as the (literal) incarnation of the polymorphous sexuality of the "lesser races" and "evil-disposed classes": she embodied "native" and laboring-class wantonness. The alternative and much more complex meanings of local community suggested in this statement tended to be lost under the fascinated gaze of the colonialist academic.

Yet, once again using Ranajit Guha's terminology, "a closer look at the [official] text can detect chinks which have allowed 'comment,' to worm its way through the plate armour of fact."[30] Both of these "native" women give clear proof of economic resourcefulness and relative social independence in light of the predominant gender structures. The heterosexualized and patriarchical constraints being thus challenged, however, also informed and set limits to the social venue where such survival practices were being enacted. But Rogler, too, was operating under social strictures: those of the researcher who could not appropriately name the very "native" survival practices he was acknowledging, those of the colonizer who could translate the subaltern subjects' words but not their contestatory meaning or context.

Captured within this social research ("Porto Rican" and U.S.-based), these prostitutes were accordingly inscribed as the embodiment of almost every negative social category then imaginable for women—Euro/Americo-centric and "native." A veritable catalog of female vices was displayed. In the words of Rosario, quoted by Morales Otero, "[a]s a rule, these women" were "morally sick people among which" one found the principal characteristics of "versatility, undiscipline, an insatiable character, an ineptitude for any sort of mental concentration," as well as "a permanent infantilism coexisting with generous impulses, a tendency towards gossip, towards lying, superstition" (p. 200). Therefore, these women possessed "temperamental manifestations inherent to unbalanced persons," such as being "poorly fed, materially intoxicated by tobacco and alcohol, carrying on an overexcited life, inundated with all sorts of excess," and finally being "always lacking in the slightest bit of spiritual stimulus" (ibid.).

The manner in which prostitutes and their practices were positioned among the impoverished masses of the Island suggested a different story. As Rogler noted,

> Among the poorer classes from which these girls come there was not found to be a strong social prejudice against them. One prostitute was found to be a most useful and respected girl in her neighborhood. She was the *guiadora de los rosarios* (director of the religious ritual during a rosario). Friends say that they could not conduct these Rosarios without her. (pp. 79–80, in Spanish in the original)

Nevertheless, the social researchers who produced these reports were prone to elide the existence of "native" laboring class, community, and family networks where such women were increasingly tolerated, if not accepted, because the very survival of these networks—particularly in such dire times—depended on the economic and sociocultural solidarity of most of its members. This imperative was often pursued, contradictorily, at the expense of the individual (and unemployed) fathers, husbands, and brothers of these women sex workers. The gendered tensions that erupted in the midst of this protracted and asymmetrical shift within the cultural mapping of the subaltern subjects have already been described above. The social researchers, though, only decried the domestic violence—together with the prostitution—as a contingent element of a social subject who had no history, consciousness, or will of its own.

In a decade of such abrupt economic changes and social displacements, the intelligentsia (colonized and colonizer) did not just re-functionalize the spread of prostitution in order to delineate and police, both ideologically and literally, the boundaries of appropriate female behavior—public and private, social and sexual. Regardless of the intentions of the lone researcher, the official procedure of documenting and analyzing such illicit behavior was also marshalled to authenticate the racial-moral debasement of the subaltern subjects. Respectable men, of course, whether "Porto Rican" or born in the United States, would never be inscribed in such a manner because they could not be imagined within the full breadth of these parameters.

But like the "native" prostitutes, "native" males from the impoverished majorities—particularly those perceived, within Island racial codes, as nonwhite—were another story altogether. Among the latter, infantilism, deception, sexual intemperance, and moral weakness had already been recorded: therein the amalgamation in the signifieds of both social subjects. These dominant knowledges confirmed the dubious morality of most of the colonized population. This representation was scientifically corroborated by the fact that, as a rule, such illegal-gainful activity emerged from within the sociocultural space of the laboring classes, where these practices developed and were more tolerated. Similar to the other forms of criminalized activity during the preceding three decades, the prostitute's blank visage became yet another surface on which to inscribe an always already degenerate populace through the textual practices of the propertied and educated classes (Creole and North American).

In a manner similar to that of the 1910–1929 period, the corrective studies of infant nomadism and delinquency in the 1930s also played out the sordid tale of moral decay, complete with an entire population increasingly in need of supervision. For instance Manuel Cabranes, then "native" Secretary of the Child Welfare

Board in Puerto Rico, observed that the seven "transient" boys under the care of his agency "in some ways presented the most serious community problem." Being homeless and living in the streets these children tended to roam "in groups, depending on begging, earning occasional nickels, watching cars, etc., and sometimes resorting to petty thieving in order to get enough to eat and live." Taken as a whole, they "appeared to be undernourished and underweight but mentally alert."[31]

Regardless of the class bias of such descriptions, domestic abuse obviously boosted the numbers of child itinerants. One of the cases studied by José C. Rosario clearly confirmed an otherwise well known fact: that running away from home was one of the strategies employed by abused children. Rosario in his 1933 study starts by recording the background of this case. Born "in a thatch hut" in the outskirts of a town located in the central-northern hills of the Island, the boy's story is told in the first person: "My father had a small vegetable farden [*sic*] and with its proceeds and the little money that my mother made as a laundress we managed to get along." Corporal punishment became a persistent feature of his life: "My father whipped me frequently to compel me to help him in selling vegetables, as I objected to it for the reason that if I did, I had to be late for school" (pp. 58–59).

The child declared that he continued to juggle his schoolwork with selling vegetables for his father, "but since sales were small my father whipped me frequently because he thought that I was not helping him enough." The aggressions continued and multiplied, and the child ran away for the first time: "For this reason I left him and came to live with my mother, who by that time, was living [with] some other man in Santurce." Living with his mother in this neighborhood adjacent to San Juan, the boy underwent considerable verbal mistreatment: "My mother lost some money and believing that I stole it from her, she frequently insulted me and said that she wished I were dead" (p. 59). Finally, the boy became a permanent urban nomad: "I left home for good and since then I have been selling newspapers." On the date of the interview, he was sleeping "in the entrance to the building of the 'Colmado Badillo' stop 22½" of the Santurce trolley, "and with what little I make I buy my food which usually consists of bread, cheese, and bananas." He admitted that every now and then he begged "for some old clothes from families in the neighborhood of this place" (ibid.).

What were the broader demographic changes that situated this wave of "transient children"? How was this multiply displaced population and its older "native" counterparts repositioned within the New Deal variants of colonialist policy? How did these demographic changes inform the other survival practices and struggles enacted by the colonized laboring classes during the Depression years? These questions are addressed in the remainder of this chapter. As before, attention is paid to the North American and "native" agents of these colonialist policies, and particularly to how said policies produced the subaltern subjects of the popular illegalities, as the focus of both punitive structures/discourses and of economic metamorphosis.

"Increasing the Influence of the Commanding Elements in Our Hills and Valleys"

As the last case cited by Rosario demonstrates, a portion of the rural population of the Island responded to the worsening conditions by migrating to the larger urban areas, where some propertied sectors (local and U.S.-based) were in need of such labor. According to the statistics provided by Descartes, during the 1930–1940 period and in a country whose inhabitants still mainly resided in the countryside, the rural population experienced a percentage change of only 16.6, while the urban population experienced a percentage change of 32.6 (p. 3). The majority of these destitute rural migrants established themselves in the shanty towns that mushroomed around the biggest urban centers. Former colonial Governor Theodore Roosevelt, Jr., had noted in his 1937 text the ubiquitousness of such settlements: "Every city or large town had its slum, where the squalor and filth were almost unbelievable" (p. 108). A significant number of these landless peasants and impoverished sharecroppers were concentrated in the burgeoning squatters communities that bordered San Juan. The significantly poor, capital district of Santurce, for example, experienced a percentage change of 61.4 in the number of peripheral shantytown housing units during this decade.[32]

These were the same shantytowns that Interior Secretary Harold L. Ickes in January of 1936 had described in the following manner, in the first volume of his published diaries. Here was yet another colonizer in this Heart of Darkness of the U.S. Caribbean, echoing the words that Conrad had placed in the mouth of Kurtz: "The horror! The horror!" "We inspected two or three slum areas and they were the worst slums that I have ever seen," the shacks looking "as if a breath would blow them over" and appeared "dirty and unkept" (p. 504). To Ickes, these dwellings were "thoroughly disreputable and disagreeable," surrounded as they were with "[o]pen sewage run[ning] through the streets" and with "no sanitary facilities at all." He found the local children "play[ing] in this sewage, which appears in many cases covered with a thick, green scum" (ibid.).

Although Ickes later had some kind words for the "unbelievable cleanliness" of the shantytown dwellers, particularly the young women, his astonishment is telling. Ickes affirmed the specular character of this panorama of indigence vis-à-vis the colonial enterprise's civilizing mission: "Such slums are a reflection not only upon the Puerto Rican government but upon that of the United States." Like Theodore Roosevelt, Jr., he too found that such a site/sight tested the judgment capacities of the colonizer's gaze: "It is unbelievable that human beings can be permitted to live in such noisome cesspools." Ickes ends this passage by remarking on the bestial/carnal results of such a beastly tableau: "Moreover, the people breed like rabbits" (ibid.).

Though framed in the most benevolent colonialist language of the period, here again are the signifiers of a "native" deficiency and incapability and of ultimate colonialist responsibility—the White Man's Burden. The Island in general and the urban slums in particular were god forsaken spaces, unfit for human habitation. The resulting logic is inescapable: if human existence under such conditions was unbelievable, then in the final analysis the humanity of these inhabitants was suspect. The leitmotif of this narrative by Interior Secretary Ickes is inadequacy. Not only were the urban spaces unfit for human life, the rural spaces were not fit for human habitation either: "Their dwellings are distinctly substandard, . . . pigs, chickens, and burros live in close fellowship with the members of the family." The economy was unfit for human work and the weather was unfit for certain agriculture: "the coffee crop has not recovered from the hurricane of a year or two ago." Not only were the reproductive habits of the population unfit for human progress ("the people breed like rabbits"); so were the skill levels of this population: "The rate of illiteracy is high and there doesn't seem to be a very keen desire on the part of Puerto Ricans to learn English." The roads were also unfit for modern travel, having been deficiently laid out, "with the result that there are steep grades and sharp turns." The road system itself became another metaphor for an entire Island perceived as a perilous obstacle course for modernity: "A drive to Mayagüez was one of the most uncomfortable and most dangerous that I have ever taken" (pp. 504–506).

Even during the New Deal era, the underlying premise of such a colonialist vista is that these problems and deficiencies could only be corrected through what Beveridge thirty years before had called the dynamism of "the virile types of men," and the heroic acts of "the master organizers of the world [who had come] to establish system where chaos reigns" (*Beveridge,* 68, 121). This task had to be accomplished even if it meant risking what Kipling, in "The White Man's Burden," had immortalized as "The blame of those ye better,/The hate of those ye guard." Although, at least in federal circles, the guiding lights of these colonialist perspectives were now Theodore Roosevelt, Jr. and Franklin D. Roosevelt, such viewpoints continued to be informed by Albert J. Beveridge, Josiah Strong, and Theodore Roosevelt, Sr. If sweeping urban slums and uplifting rural brutes were comparable to the twelve labors imposed by Hera, it was because only a civilization/regime such as the North American republic could be compared to that half-god of legendary proportions.

Albeit Ickes was not well versed in the particulars of the new administrative overseas responsibilities of the department he now headed, he had a long-running general concern for "uplifting" colonized peoples under U.S. jurisdiction. In the words of another North American official, Rexford Guy Tugwell, who was also renowned for his benevolent paternalism and colonial-reformist policies, "Mr. Ickes and his first wife had long been interested in Indian affairs; they were indeed persistent agitators for Indian justice. And this may have furnished a forecast of sympathy if the situation of Puerto Rico ever had come to his notice or within his field of influence." According to Tugwell, "Mr. Ickes became the nearest thing we had to a Colonial Secretary."[33]

Ickes was also one of the federal colonialist officials most acutely aware of the need to continue transforming this U.S. Caribbean possession without unnecessarily antagonizing the "native" propertied and educated classes. If the colonial social order was to be preserved, the emergent colonialist author-functions of the privileged Creoles had to be augmented. This is why he fostered the investigation of the Ponce Massacre of 1937, when twenty members of the "Partido Nacionalista" were killed and dozens injured by the colonial police during a peaceful march on Palm Sunday.[34] The Nacionalistas were the most militant expression of the anticolonialism of "native" small-farmers, shopkeepers, and petit-professionals. Their social base and political aspirations partially overlapped with that of the "Partido Liberal," which was the second largest political organization in the Island.[35]

As Ickes noted in the second volume of his published diaries, he and others eventually obtained the resignations of then colonial

Governor Blanton Winship and PRRA Administrator Ernest Gruening, the intellectual authors of such extreme colonialist zeal (pp. 627–629, 641). It is interesting, however, that—as in the federal commission to investigate police atrocities during the 1915–1916 strikes in the Island—what was censured was the exaggerated character of the police response: the need for subordinating "lesser races," even by the legitimate use of force or by the structural brutality of the dispossession process, never had been and never would be in question. Ickes was keenly aware of the broader context that positioned such events, if and when they happened. As he had written in his diary a few months before the massacre, "Gruening, from being a liberal, has apparently decided the mailed fist [was] the proper policy in dealing with subject people" (p. 6).

Ickes, like his British counterparts in India and Africa, never seemed to question that populations understood as "subject people" *had to be subjected*, to again borrow the words of Edward Said (p. 207). Preferably, these "natives" should be fashioned and dominated in the benevolent manner suggested by his contemporary Theodore Roosevelt, Jr.—but subjected nevertheless. As the former, self-styled "'jíbaro' in the Governor's mansion," Roosevelt, Jr., had so bluntly stated in his famous 1937 treatise on the matter,

> During the period of its domination . . . [the more civilized, certainly more virile conquering nation] has brought the subject people into contact with knowledge they did not possess, schooled them or vitalized them. Education, sanitation, public works and science have been widely disseminated. The sentimentalists will urge that old cultures have been destroyed. That may be so, but are not knowledge, health[,] and comfort better for a people than squalor, ignorance, disease[,] and a loincloth?[36]

Despite the overall value it may have had as a cautionary tale, brutalities such as the Ponce Massacre tended to be inscribed outside the cultural mapping and everyday survival practices of most of the "natives," among other things because of the discursive gulf that usually separated the Partido Nacionalista from the on-going, everyday social strife of the laboring poor majorities.

Therefore, the social control and corrective study of "problem populations"[37]in the Island took another route. This was especially true of the regulation of the landless peasants and runaway children that the machineries of capital, together with structural misery, were randomly driving to the shantytowns in the urban sprawl.

Attracting cheap "native" labor to the coast and to the urban areas was one thing. To retain such labor at low cost or even to guarantee that these laborers would mainly—or, much less, exclusively—seek out the capitalist labor market for subsistence purposes was an entire different story. Melossi's conclusion seems particularly appropriate in this case: "And yet the door was still open to the under world, to vagrancy, to crime."[38] These popular practices, taken as a whole, demonstrated not just the limits of the existing forms of economic exploitation—capitalist and pre-capitalist. Once more, they also made evident the structural necessity of deploying and/or expanding other and distinctive disciplinary technologies.

In the case of regulating child nomadism, for example, there was the Child Welfare Board (set up in 1925 and expanded during the 1930s with chapters all across the Island) and of the Social Service Division of the Department of Health (which was formed in 1933 and was also active at this time). There were also broader interventions made by social workers in the Island—indirectly (through the public school system, for example) or directly (within the laboring classes as a whole). Although some of these interventions were already being carried out under the auspices of institutions such as the Island chapter of the American Red Cross at the time of the Great War in Europe (mostly on a voluntary and informal basis), expansion of the professionalization of this sort of activity was primarily a phenomenon of the 1930s and 1940s.[39]

In this context, José C. Rosario and Justina Carrión, in "Rebusca sociológica: una comunidad rural en la región cafetera de Puerto Rico," made some very pertinent observations concerning the rural majorities that lived in isolated mountain communities. "We believe that changing attitudes is of cardinal importance," Rosario and Carrión declared flatly. Both of them found it "imperative that change take place in the attitudes that the peasant ha[d] regarding life" because, as long as "the latter [was] fatally satisfied with his [*sic*] destiny," it was highly doubtful "that changes of any importance [would] take place in his [*sic*] life" (p. 15).

The currency of military and missionary metaphors signaled the emergent social/holy war, as well as defining the stakes.

> The school, social work, and religion have to necessarily play a fundamental role in this crusade. Changes of attitude occur mainly through the *leaders* and these leaders are still, in their great majority, the [school] teachers, the social workers, and the ministers of religion. We have to increase the influence of

> these commanding elements in our hills and valleys so that all of the rural population of Puerto Rico can fall under their influence. (ibid., emphasis in the original)

Increasingly, the armies of Creole social reformers were to occupy and morally police the alleged rural bulwarks of "native" barbarism, in this sense dovetailing with the police occupation of coastal and urban areas imagined as being held hostage by the surge of rabid strikers, rioters, squatters, and criminals of all stripes. Once again using Homi Bhabha's conceptual framework, it appeared that the colonial mimicry of the privileged "natives" tended to reinforce "the strategic function of colonial power, intensify[ing] surveillance."[40]

"A State of Anarchy Exists"

These strategies of moral policing and police occupation surfaced among the propertied and educated classes ("Porto Rican" and U.S.-born) as a partial reaction to the ways in which the colonized laboring classes responded to the crisis. In addition to the other popular illegalities that proliferated during the decade of the thirties, there were waves of melees and demonstrations, mainly in the urban areas, against the rising cost of living between 1933 and 1934. These protests included boycott of utility bills, work stoppages by independent taxi-car owners/drivers, riots, and vandalism against utility-company installations. Such acts prompted a "committee of citizens" to send a telegram in 1933 to the Bureau of Insular Affairs in Washington, D.C. The content of this message summarized the middle-class, "respectable" perspective on these events. The telegram read as follows:

> All towns in Puerto Rico isolated from each other except by telephone or telegraph. Roving mobs composed of worst elements prevent movement of private and public cars on streets and destroying property. Towns state of siege. Citizens unable to leave homes. Some elements threaten to cut off telephone and electric service and with water system of San Juan. Business paralyzed. Police impotent to protect citizens in life, property, and lawful pursuits. A state of anarchy exists. We have requested Acting Governor to call out National Guard and authority for 65th Regiment [of U.S. Army] to give aid.[41]

As in 1898–1899 and 1915–1921, the battle lines were clearly drawn. On the one hand, there were: "citizens," "life," "property and lawful pursuits," and so on. And on the other there were: the "roving mobs," "destruction of property," and "anarchy." Such communications explicitly indicate the severing of the fragile, juridico-ideological linkage (established within the context of the labor struggles of 1915–1921) between the laboring-poor majority that made up most of the "native" population and the (colonized) citizenry, per se.

Although these protests eventually dissipated, their overall effect was compounded because they coincided with one of the two largest general strikes of the decade: the wave of labor stoppages of 1933–1934. As U.S. economic historian James Dietz has recently explained, between July and December of 1933, "there were eighty-five strikes or actions by workers in tobacco, sugar, needlework, baking, and transport, and on the docks, and by *público* drivers"—the "público is a private automobile operated along a regular route by an independent driver-owner" (p. 163). The target of these strikes were not only "the employers but also . . . the government for failing to do anything to alleviate unemployment and suffering" (ibid.).

This was not the first wave of social unrest during that decade, however. Juan José Baldrich has documented the movement of small and medium, Creole tobacco farmers who in 1931 refused to grow the crop in protest for the low prices they were being paid for the leaf. This movement included extensive acts of sabotage against the "strikebreakers" and against the principal tobacco merchants and refiners.[42] On the other hand, Gayer, et al. have indicated that the number of laborers involved in strikes quadrupled between 1932 and 1933, later more than doubling between 1933 and 1934 (p. 223). Picó in *Los gallos peleados* corroborates considerable strike activity involving the tobacco-manufacturing workers of the central-mountain municipality of Utuado during the 1930–1933 period (pp. 116–119). In the latter case, sabotage once again figured prominently among the resistance activities carried out by the workers: torching the high-roofed, open-ended, barnlike structures ("ranchos") used for drying the tobacco leaves, as well as destroying tobacco seedlings with machetes and hoes (ibid.).

Sugar production was the sector most affected by the 1933–1934 strike wave. In September of 1933, there had been attempts to bring to a halt all of the mills in the Eastern coast of the Island in order to protest low wages and company store practices. This initial attempt resulted in fierce confrontations with the police and at least one riot (one dead and three wounded). Despite the high social cost, the work stoppage was thwarted. Another attempt was made in December of that year. The ensuing strike spread to several mill plantations, including the largest mill in the Island. Government arbitration and a sell-out agreement signed by the trade-union federation (the FLT)—whose political wing, the Partido Socialista, was then part of the coalition that presided over the colonial legislature—could not put an end to the strike that year. In late January there was another confrontation between the workers, on the one hand, and the police and strikebreakers, on the other, resulting in a riot and a shooting spree which left eight workers wounded. The general strike materialized, spreading further, at different times involving three fourths of all the mills and plantations in the Island.

In the midst of the struggle, the sugarcane laborers affiliated with the FLT broke ranks with that organization and set up parallel unions. The damage stemming from the torched canefields was compounded by the stoppage itself, resulting in considerable initial losses for the corporations. At the time, the colonial Governor sent a confidential report to the Bureau of Insular Affairs. Through this means, the Governor informed the federal government that, as was usually the case during strikes and election years, he had provisionally hired additional men as to reinforce the local police units. Acknowledging the seriousness of the social crisis, he said he was prepared to mobilize the National Guard and request assistance from U.S. Army troops if the need arose. The principal anti-imperialist political organizations of the day participated with varying degrees of prominence in strike support activities. In addition to the outstanding and vertical stance assumed by the Partido Nacionalista—a real exception to its previous and subsequent political practice—the "Partido Comunista de Puerto Rico," and "Afirmación Socialista Unitaria" also played important roles. Yet, in spite of all the efforts made by the strikers and their partisans, by the first days of February 1934, the last mill-plantation laborers returned to work driven by exhaustion, insufficient income, and confusion.[43]

These confrontations, together with the profound polarizations they embodied and the dire social conditions then prevalent, left a clear imprint on broad sectors of the coastal masses during the Depression. This is the lived experience reflected in the remarks made by sugar-zone laborers, then being recorded by Rosario and Carrión in "Rebusca sociológica: una comunidad rural en la zona cañera." In addition to the second epigraph that opened this chapter, another coastal worker was said to have declared: "Listen, Mister, things are getting so [bad] that we are gonna have t' take on both cop and neighbor," because if "this keeps up, we're gonna have t' turn t' banditry, 'cause I'd rather kill somebody else's cow and eat it before letting myself die of hunger" (p. 9).

As in the previous three decades, existing social strife contributed significantly to a dual yet contradictory process within the popular discourses. There was a tendency to refashion, as well as transgress, the boundaries of the predominant juridical ideologies in terms of what was perceived as legal and illegal, acceptable and unacceptable.

Although the Nacionalistas' undeniably brave struggle did sporadically coincide with large-scale social unrest (as in the sugar-cane general strike of 1934), such concurrence tended to be the exception rather than the rule. The magnitude of this rift can be charted by noting what the Nacionalista high command understood by attaining "the republic." For their supreme leader and principal ideologue, Pedro Albizu Campos, the strategic goal of Puerto Rico's independence would be achieved by following the strict rules and iron command of the Nacionalista organization. Such a task was to be the embodiment of order itself, the Nacionalista party being its consummate reflection.[44]

As I have tried to demonstrate throughout this study, the "native" masses of the Island, rightly or wrongly, understood and lived their unremitting everyday resistances and dramatically explosive confrontations with the existing colonial-capitalist order in very different—mostly disorderly—ways. The second epigraph that opens this chapter suggests the direction of this other (and other-ed) subaltern cultural mapping. The cane laborer interviewed by Rosario and Carrión indicated that "instead of torching the cane-field," he would have burned down the manager's house "with all o' his family inside." According to him this was "the sort o' thing we should be a republic for [i.e., an independent country]," meaning "so that we could turn t' banditry and get even with all o' the wrongs that the workingman is suffering" (p. 9).

But mass-based narratives also bore large amounts of self-deprecating anger and frustration, as expressed by the second laborer interviewed by Rosario and Carrión. Such anger was channeled—in the predominant masculinist terms of the period—against what this person perceived to be insufficient rage in the reactions of the general populace toward the abundant social, economic, and political hardships being faced by most of them. "What we all deserve is t' have our feet tied t' the tails o' two mules and t' then have two [riders] drive them with their spurs up the road" declared the second laborer, because in "no other country in the world do you find men as obedient and as tame as the Puerto Ricans" (ibid.).

There were numerous other work stoppages during the remainder of this decade involving a large number of laborers: Dietz asserts that in 1934–1936 there were between fifty thousand and sixty thousand workers on strike and in 1936–1937 there were 13,119 (p. 164). Interestingly enough, the sectorial composition of the laborers implicated in these strikes was different from what it had been during the first half of the thirties. While eighty-six percent of all the strikers in 1931–1932 were connected to the tobacco and sugar sectors, by 1940 this proportion had dropped to around eighteen percent, as can be seen from the information provided in Quintero Rivera and García's *Desafío y solidaridad* (p. 118). The balance in each case was made up of other sectors of the economy: dockyards, ground transportation, needlework, etc. This partially reflects the effects of the emergent restructuring of the Island's economic sphere.

The other major labor mobilization of the decade was the dockyard strike of 1938. Although the month-long stoppage only directly involved seven thousand laborers, the strategic economic location of this strike unevenly brought to a standstill close to one hundred thousand more laborers indirectly dependent on the docks. This strike is not only important because of the militancy of the laborers, being a prominent example of strikers savagely repressed by the police and causing a large number of wounded strikers. The dockyard strike of 1938 was also important because it mobilized an extremely wide spectrum of laborers: not just the stevedores, but the maintenance workers, security guards, office workers, runners, retailers, and others, as well.[45]

Regardless of the fact that the strike ended in the negotiating table with mixed results, the effort from which it had sprung involved new forms of organized social resistance. This innovative direction in patterns of social opposition continued during the years immediately following 1938. The dockyard strike had itself evolved from the organization of unemployed laborers, expanding it further. As Silén (p. 107) and Galvin[46] have noted, this struggle led directly to the Hunger March on San Juan in 1939 with the participation of thousands of unemployed laborers. One of the other phenomena that was imbricated with both this march and the dockyard strike of 1938 was the spread of organizational efforts among the unskilled laborers. In 1940, this drive eventually resulted in the formation of a new trade union federation (the "Confederación General de Trabajadores" or CGT) which was similar to the militant industrial unionism of the CIO in the United States.[47]

Unfortunately, many of these social mobilizations were going to forfeit whatever autonomy they had as mass-based and formal institutions. This autonomy was eventually lost to the emerging ideological hegemony of the populist political alliance (the "Partido Popular Democrático" or PPD) that was to capture the legislative majority for the next thirty years, riding the wave of economic reconstruction during the Second World War.[48] This is the period examined in the following chapter.

8

"Rage Concentrated Twice Over," 1940–1947

> The *wave* passed. It left in the beaches of our society numerous orphaned families, many individuals deprived of liberty and of their civil rights. And it left the *social restraints* somewhat weak and hurting due to the violent impact of crime.
>
> **—Miguel Meléndez Muñoz, "Apuntes sobre la criminalidad en Puerto Rico" (1948, emphasis in the original)**

> By all ye cry or whisper,
> By all ye leave or do,
> The silent, sullen peoples
> Shall weigh your Gods and you.
>
> **—Rudyard Kipling, "The White Man's Burden" (1899)**

The decade of the forties can, in retrospect, be seen as a transition period between (a) the first half of a century which was overwhelmingly agricultural, rural, and practically monocultural, and (b) the second half of a century which was more industrial, urban, and Welfare-State based. The subsequent industrial and sociopolitical expansion of the fifties and sixties to a large extent was both built on the governmental and economic infrastructure during 1940–1947, and on the official signifying practices and compelling discourses that flourished at this time.[1] Despite ongoing decline, many of the economic features and cultural forms of the previous four decades were still very much in existence, along with some of the accompanying constitutive conflicts and contradictorily textured subjectivities.[2]

Given that this study has advanced an alternative reading of the 1898–1947 period in Puerto Rico—that is, a nonteleological counternarration—how can this closing decade be examined without promoting a vision of historically foreseen closure? One way of doing this is, once again, to recall the analytical axes of this entire research. What did this transition period mean in the case of the subaltern subjects and how did the meanings invoked and lived by the latter subjects affect this transition? Attempting to answer these questions is exceedingly difficult. At one level, the 1940s seemed to reproduce the preceding ways of structuring and positioning the subaltern subjects of the Island. This decade summoned patterns of economic organization which bisected the forms of social control by continually creating the terrain of the popular illegalities: therefore, the subaltern subjects of all these domains continued to overlap.

Yet, in light of the major transformations that were occurring within capitalist production in the Island at this time and due to the emerging ways in which these changes were being confronted by the "native" population, the decade of the forties also personified asymmetrical displacements in the manner in which economic organization and punishment intersected. Such displacements suggest new ways of jointly examining the subaltern subjects of U.S. capitalism in Puerto Rico and the subaltern subjects of colonial labor and criminal-justice structures. What, then, were the elements of continuity and change regarding the various ways of constructing and regulating the subaltern subjects? How was this social construction/regulation challenged, negotiated, endured, and signified?

This chapter delineates the shape of these new transformations and the forces that catalyzed, mediated, and disrupted such changes. It does not recount an unbroken continuity with a past that was either the gestation period of an innovative era,[3] nor the "chronicle of a [political status and/or class] death foretold."[4] As Michel Foucault has argued in "Nietzsche, Genealogy, History,"

> These developments may appear as a culmination, but they are merely the current episodes in a series of subjugations. . . . In placing present needs at the origin, the metaphysician would convince us of an obscure purpose that seeks its realization at the moment it arises . . .
>
> Emergence is always produced through a particular stage of forces. The analysis of the *Entstehung* [beginning] must delineate this interaction, the struggle these forces wage

> against each other or against adverse circumstances, and the attempt to avoid degeneration and regain strength by dividing these forces against themselves.[5]

The present chapter deals with the past that the 1940s "inherited" and with the past that the 1940s seemed to invoke, embody, or substitute (that is, re-present) in terms of what Foucault called "an unstable assemblage of faults and fissures, and heterogeneous layers that threaten the fragile inheritor from within and underneath" (p. 146).

Closing the Cycle of the Old Forms of Property

Several short-term governmental initiatives took place at this time, primarily centered around the local State-capitalist experiments and a limited land reform.[6] Though these particular experiments and reforms were of brief duration, the underlying structural initiatives signaled a more fundamental, Keynesian shift towards a growing involvement of the State in the regulation of the economic sphere. Certain aspects of the new War effort, together with the ascendancy of the populist social alliance (the PPD) and the greatly expanded migratory routes and facilities, all contributed significantly toward counteracting the existing mass/individual discontent during the 1940–1947 period.[7]

At this level, the emergent patterns of economic organization were increasingly being mediated by the overseas extension of the U.S. State which administered Puerto Rico. The expanding field of State economic policing throughout the entire Island apparently had its counterpart in a corresponding accretion of the State's role in literally policing social disorder across all Puerto Rico. If the subaltern subjects of the popular illegalities were still at the crossroads of the economic sphere and the punitive patterns (institutional and discursive), this intersection was defined and patrolled with growing frequency by State mechanisms which reached deeper and wider into the interstices of the "native" majorities' everyday life. But what did these emerging patterns of economic organization look like?

According to Descartes (pp. 50, 53–58) and Perloff (pp. 83–84, 136–137), the amount of the cropland planted in sugarcane virtually remained the same during these years, while the proportional place of sugar among all exports had dropped from 62.1 percent in 1940 to 48.1 percent in 1946. Looking back, it can be said that, for the most part, these figures heralded the end of the Sugar Era in the Island. Admittedly, as Perloff (p. 72) has shown, sugar tonnage levels continued to increase and even reach record levels during the forties and the percentage of the labor force that was employed in this sector also reached record levels at this time (see table 2). However, U.S. corporate investments in this sector were gradually phased out.[8] Tariff protection could no longer compensate for the marketing difficulties and internal organization problems that this sector of capital was experiencing in Puerto Rico. Besides, the labor control and broader social-pacification measures adopted and/or promoted during the previous decade did not generate the full range of expected results. Attempts made to continue such measures during the 1940s were not enough to save sugar from its collapse as a corporate monopoly and as a leading colonial-capitalist venture in the Island.

Tobacco agriculture went through a brief recuperation between 1940 and 1947. The position of the tobacco sector as a proportion of all cropland practically tripled at this time, more than doubling its share in the Island's exports. Nonetheless, this resurgence was relatively shortlived and did not reflect a significant rise in the percentage of the labor force accordingly employed.[9]

The manufacture of needle-products benefited from the changes in the continental market during the World War, shifting growing numbers of its operations from the putting-out-system form to the factory form. This was also true for several other fractions of the proto-industrial manufacturing sector. These shifts were increasingly dependent on female labor. The postwar industrial transformation occurred on the foundations erected by this expansion and thanks to the economic niche being vacated by the previously dominant sugar sector. The inauguration of a different mode of accumulation and social regulation was also concomitant to this embryonic industrialization process.[10]

The capitalist market within the Island also experienced a significant growth during the war years. It is true that relative to what was going to happen in the following decades, the marketing operations of the late 1930s to late 1940s were still rather limited. Nonetheless, during the war there was a notable expansion of these mechanisms regarding U.S.-based and local capital.[11] Radio and newspapers were the primary mechanisms deployed in this regard. Therefore, one of the principal effects of the growth of capitalist marketing was the accretion of the mass media's radius of influence among the general population, particularly within the everyday life of the "native" majorities.

In 1930, for instance, there was only one radio station in the Island (based in San Juan) and an estimated number of five thousand radio sets. Nine years later, there were five additional radio stations (two more in San Juan, two in Ponce, and one in Mayagüez) with an estimated fifteenfold increase in the number of radio sets. By 1949, there were sixteen radio stations (at least one in every district) with an estimated total of 130,000 radio sets. The per capita concentration of this media leverage was certainly impressive. An advertisement issued in 1947 by one of the major radio stations proclaimed: "Puerto Rico has more radios per 1,000 people than any other country in the Caribbean."[12]

"Being Ground Extremely Fine Between . . . Metropolitan Prices and Colonial Preindustrial Wages"

The redistribution of land and "natives" was one of the areas which exemplified the economic activism of the overseas extension of the U.S. colonial State (in North America and in Puerto Rico). To what extent did these measures alter the morphology of the colonized laboring classes? How did the social composition of the rural and urban laborers in Puerto Rico change during an interwar period that seemed to be coming to a definitive close? What were the limitations of these social transformations, both in terms of the social regulation of the laboring population and in terms of the latter's survival strategies? What were the signifying practices which expressed and structured these social transformations and these survival strategies? These are the questions to be addressed in the following sections.

The short-lived, much-touted, and extremely limited land reform implemented by the populist-oriented colonial administrations of 1941–1949 did not substantially transform any of the basic forms of land tenure. Between 1940 and 1950 the number of farmers and farm administrators declined rather than increased, showing a percentage change of -24.2 (see table 1). This is hardly what one would have expected in the wake of an agricultural transformation of such allegedly profound consequences.[13]

The actual outcome, however, was otherwise. The law was mainly aimed at those 500-acre-plus "latifundios" that were explicitly and directly owned *by corporations*. Deliberately or not, this left untouched those corporate-owned "latifundios" that were formally owned and/or registered *by individuals*. Yet, even this formal goal only resulted in the procurement of a little over a third of the openly corporate-owned latifundios by 1947. More significantly, this did not mean that land was going to be broadly distributed among the poor and agriculturally-based laboring classes. The new enterprises were not going to be operated as prosperous, independent, small-to-middle-sized farms, nor as peasant-owned and/or worker-owned production cooperatives. Instead, they were to be restructured as government-owned and management-run large farms, with varying degrees of worker participation. Such was the fate of the most fertile land and of the most efficiently organized properties that were sold to the government. By 1945–1949 funds made available to the Land Authority had been severely reduced and the program was phased out.[14]

One of the partial outcomes of the land reform was the fragmentation of portions of this new government-purchased land, as well as portions of the individually-owned properties whose owners later decided to sell to the government. Perloff asserts that the segments of land resulting from this fragmentation were to be used, but not owned, by landless peasants as microscopic one to three "cuerda" plots or approximately equal to 0.9712 to 2.9136 acres (p. 39). Some of these measures had already been implemented on a smaller scale during the late 1930s, as Descartes has indicated (pp. 187–190). Although the land reform during the forties brought about the partial breakup of the formal land-rent links that many of these sharecroppers had established with the large landowners, it had two other related and contradictory consequences. Since these microscopic land plots were hardly adequate for subsistence purposes, some of these same sharecroppers ended up re-establishing feudal-rent and/or wage-labor contracts with large landowners. Secondly, these poor peasants had to agree to massive relocation in order to receive rent-free use of government land. This meant both a partial dislocation of existing peasant family and community boundaries, in addition to a partial reconstitution of these boundaries in the new villages that were set up. The express purpose of this program was to stem the tide of squatters' settlements into the larger urban areas. The number of government-sponsored villages went from 139 in 1947 to 363 in 1965, a demographic shift which transplanted as much as fifteen percent of the Island's population.[15]

Despite all of these measures, there were two tendencies which emerged in the interwar period and further developed during the first half of the 1940s. This development is related to the question of whether the overall class locations of both the rural and urban "native" majorities experienced any fundamental changes from the mid-1920s to the late 1940s. Again, the available information in this respect is not very precise (it was also replete with demographical and statistical superficialities), but some approximations are nevertheless possible.[16] Although, sugarcane field workers were still by far the most numerically significant and growing fraction among this very unevenly proletarianized mass as a whole, there was a sharp drop in the number of tobacco-products workers as compared to the marked accretion in the number of home-needlework laborers. The number of sugar mill workers also increased considerably though still remaining in last place in this respect. Production-line wage-workers in the utilities, construction, and transportation sectors increased their rate of growth during this decade. With the wartime shift towards government-owned utilities and the expansion of public works, the number of construction workers even surpassed those involved in the utilities and transportation.

However, even when one includes the increase in the non-sugar agricultural workers performing wage labor (partially or totally), the overall proportions of this unevenly dispossessed mass remained basically the same. From the late twenties to the mid forties this mass of laborers still amounted to about two-fifths of all employment in Puerto Rico. Meanwhile, the other two fractions that overlapped with this proletarianized mass (the small farmers, sharecroppers, etc.) shrunk even more. Their numbers fell from about one-fourth to about one-tenth of all employment during this period. The same cannot be said with regard to the urban day laborers and the domestic servants, which as a group remained fundamentally unaltered. The proportion of laborers working in the commercial and service sectors during this period did increase considerably, though. This sector rose from one-twentieth in the mid-twenties to approximately one-sixth by the late forties.

All of this would lead one to conclude that the essential structure of these overlapping class formations did not go through any qualitative, major transformations during these twenty years or so. It seems that despite the ever-extending reach of economic dispossession, the process of locking in these masses within the confines of capitalist production was still haphazard, partial, and episodic. Even though generalized land-rent linkages were unevenly but clearly waning, there were no generalized linkages in the capitalist sense that, strictly speaking, rose to substitute the noncapitalist forms of exploitation. Nothing crystallized to serve as a structural basis for a generational working class. Instead, what tended to predominate were extremely fragmented, erratic, and incomplete linkages of a capitalist character.

Between the mid-1920s and the mid-1940s there was even a retreat with respect to rounding up productive wage-labor under one roof via the factory form. The most typical and widespread representative of this pattern from 1898 to the mid-twenties (the manufacture of tobacco products) experienced a sharp reduction in the number of laborers it employed. This contrasted sharply with the boom in home-needlework employment. Between 1920 and 1947, these two fractions experienced percentage changes of -74.0 and 298.1, respectively (see table 6). Although the number of sugar mill workers practically doubled, even at their peak (1940) they still did not reach 15.0 percent of all corresponding employment. Let us also remember that throughout the first half of this century the average number of laborers in manufacturing establishments—six employees—bore what at that time was a decidedly artisan and noncapitalist imprint.[17]

As Perloff shows, from the late twenties to the mid-forties the largest concentrations of productive wage laborers were in the sugarcane fields (p. 401). This fact, as well as the disappearance of the land plots in the sugarcane plantations, must have been an important element in the promotion of class cohesion and structural delineation. The case of the sugarcane plantations in the southern-coastal municipality of Santa Isabel was not atypical in this respect. U.S. anthropologist Sidney Mintz, in his ethnography of a Puerto Rican canecutter, clearly indicates that "[n]early all perquisites provided to [sugarcane] workers in place of cash had been eliminated" (p. 207). According to Mintz, "[a]ll jobs . . . were now standardized, with stipulated minimum wages, and piece-work survived only in particular jobs—such as cane cutting." The registered rise in these workers' cash incomes was "partly in replacement of the noncash services that had been discontinued" (ibid.). Evidently, this had some bearing on the heights of working class militancy and organization reached by this class fraction.

But there were also strong countertendencies that continually, seasonally, and/or unexpectedly blocked the eventual crystallization and extensive reproduction of such cohesion. The seasonal character of sugarcane employment is a case in point. In conditions of total dispossession, the dreaded "Dead Season" (*tiempo muerto*) could be devastating insofar as it tended to force these laborers and their family members to seek alternate sources of income. This search took them both inside and outside of, not only capitalist production, but inside and outside of the sphere of legal income-gaining activities as well. In the context of the multiple hardships and socioeconomic restrictions brought about by the Depression and the

Second World War itself, it becomes easier to understand the corollary dislocation and centrifugal displacements that tore apart the sugarcane work force. Even this notoriously massive and relatively cohesive fraction of the colonized proletariat was seasonally being dismembered in the midst of its very constitution.

Therefore, this unevenly dispossessed mass of laborers from all sectors still exhibited the basic features of what in other places and historical moments has been understood as transitional capitalism. What tended to solidify or become generalized was the increasing tendency towards the total, episodic, or partial dispersal of the wage laborers within colonial capitalist production. This not only slowed down the general decline of noncapitalist and partially feudal labor relations, it also blurred some of the boundaries between the dying, traditional hacienda system and the emerging, partially wage-based relations in non-sugarcane agriculture. The growing trend towards petty odd-jobbing in the service and commercial sectors was evidently related to this cloaking of the socioeconomic and class boundaries among the Island's laborers. Between 1930 and 1950, such dispersal within the "native" labor force was clearly related to the doubling in the proportion of service-sector workers with respect to all employment (see table 2). This social recomposition was also related to what A. J. Jaffe determined was an almost threefold increase in the number of hucksters and peddlers in the Island during this same period (p. 98).

As before, the transitional capitalism just described (from the 1920s to the 1940s) and the subaltern subjects which embodied this transition were not the sole domain of an unpoliticized economy: the economic physiognomy sketched above should not be perceived as a social technology which produces and profitably assembles the bodies of "native" laborers *first* and then, *later*, is visited by conflicts and sign systems. The accelerated shrinkage of independent direct producers, the general stagnation in the numbers of nonsugar agricultural workers and urban day laborers, and the continued making/remaking of the sugarcane work force (almost on a yearly basis), for instance, were all the intrinsic result of extremely violent clashes whose strands wove together the threadbare fabric of this protracted colonial crisis.

These were the omnipresent conflicts between business needs and physical needs. These were the widespread gendered, age-based, racialized, and otherwise family/community-grounded fractures that tore apart the body/bodies of the subaltern subjects from within and from without. Hastened and partially spawned by the growing misery, these ubiquitous confrontations were written in the bloody ink of sedate colonial offices and secluded country clubs, as well as written in the laughter and defiance of canefield workers who refused to drown in the wake of blood left behind by company thugs and the police. These were the ever-frequent ruptures between the imperatives of particular enterprises—such as the Sugar Trust—and the enterprise of empire—as exemplified by New Deal reformist colonialism. Over the entire colonized space, hundreds of little wars were going on between the two world wars. This was the martial topography which brutally reworked the social composition of the "native" laboring classes. Perhaps such multiple and multiplied wars can begin to make sense—or, at least, an alternate and non-normative sort of sense—if we view these battles through another lens: namely, that of the multiple and multiplied wars that were simultaneously erupting in the fields of meaning. These semiotic explosions, in turn, structured the course and content of transitional capitalism and of the transformation of its subaltern subjects.

The signs of these everpresent confrontations may once again be traced by envisioning their effects on the bodies of the "native" majorities. Here, too, the patterns in the existing cost of living and unemployment levels were emblematic. The living standards of the impoverished majorities did show some improvement during the forties, but these changes were only relative. Although starvation became a much less common occurrence, malnutrition still prevailed.[18] The statistics provided by Descartes (p. 78) and Perloff (p. 177) suggest that the decline in the extent of hunger was counteracted by the rise in the price index for foodstuffs: from 1941 to 1942 this rate manifested a change of thirty-nine percent, maintaining 1942 levels—or surpassing them—for most of that decade. In 1942, the National Resources Planning Board financed a confidential study that corroborated the persistence of grim social conditions in terms of the cost of living for most Island "natives." I will quote in full one of the report's conclusions.

> The total annual cost of providing a minimum decent diet to the 354,417 families in Puerto Rico would be $190,100,000 at the April 1942 price level. This amounts to an average cost per average family of $536 annually. Yet a recent survey indicates that the average annual earnings both in cash and in kind of 1500 families, taken at random from workers in the principal industries of Puerto Rico during the period March to November 1941 was only $ 330 for each family. This is not even sufficient to cover the cost of the minimum diet here indicated, let alone

> cost of housing and clothing. Since November 1941, the index of retail prices has advanced from 136 to 172 (July, 1939 = 100), so that the glaring disparity has become even greater.[19]

According to Hibben and Picó, although average income rose somewhat during these years, the even-greater jump in inflation canceled out much of this advance for many of the Island's laboring-poor sectors (pp. 97–98). During these years, another U.S. liberal social scientist, Raymond Crist, made a no less gloomy retrospective observation. He started out by making explicit the question most of the "native" residents faced on a daily basis: "[h]ow can the worker get a better diet, which would step up efficiency?"[20] Crist answered by indicating that agricultural laborers "must either grow more food or import more" and, because "sugar has preempted most of the good land on which the growing of foodstuffs would have been possible," consequently it appeared "logical and necessary to import more food." This led him to raise a second question: given "their present miserable wages," how could Puerto Rican laborers persist in buying foodstuffs "in the market of continental United States, in competition with workers earning five to ten times as much?" (ibid.).

These questions were similar to those raised by the ex-Governor of Pennsylvania, Robert E. Pattison, during his visit to the Island in 1900 and by the Diffies in the portion of their 1931 study that addressed the price-income differentials among the laboring population in Puerto Rico. And, as in the case of the situation surveyed by these reluctant colonizers and North American anticolonialists, Crist's response was that the root of the problem lay in the inherently conflictive and unequal—therefore, political—content of the economic organization of the Island.

Since the sugar corporations could only continue surviving "behind the U.S. tariff wall," in the same manner the local worker would surely be "forced to pay American prices for consumers' goods, instead of bidding freely on the world market for cheaper produce" (ibid.). These regulations were responsible for adding some five million dollars per year to the cost of rice consumed in the Island—"mainstay of the Puerto Rican diet"—as well as adding between ten to thirty-five percent to "the cost of shoes, which are essential in tropical Puerto Rico to the prevention and control of hookworm." Crist's conclusion was both straightforward and bleak: "Puerto Rican workers have been ground extremely fine between the upper and the nether millstones, that is, between metropolitan industrial prices and colonial preindustrial wages" (ibid.). As Félix

Córdova has correctly argued,what was at issue here was the growing and dangerous gap between the expanding process of capitalist production and the conditions under which the laboring classes were attempting to reproduce their very existence.[21]

Regarding unemployment levels, the decade of the forties exemplified only a difference of degree in terms of much of the situation that had transpired between 1898 and 1939. This problem, however, was hidden by the official figures used to directly document the number of people of employment age expressly searching for (legal) income-gaining activities. There were several factors that must be taken into account in order to understand the ways this structural unemployment was objectively disguised. For one thing, the History Task Force study asserts that a net amount of 46,148 people left the Island for the U.S. between 1940 and 1946 (pp. 186–187). Secondly, 24,100 people in 1940 had jobs in relief work.[22] Hibben and Picó say that this type of emergency employment reached a high point of 49,924 in 1943, subsequently dropping to 5,058 in 1946 (p. 102). Finally, as Descartes showed, 45,000 people from Puerto Rico were employed in the armed forces in 1945 (p. 61). Yet, in spite of all of these safety valves, the number of persons on the unemployment lists virtually remained the same during the first six years of this decade.[23] This would explain Perloff's observation that, for the late 1940s, not only were "a large percentage of the workers unemployed part of the year," it also happened that "when they [did] work they [were] often on a part-time basis" (p. 146). "At certain times of the year," according to Perloff, "as many as a quarter of those employed work[ed] less than thirty hours per week," even as both the unemployed and the underemployed taken together at times added "up to more than a third of the labor force" (ibid.).

The New Trade-Unionism and the Persistence of Informal Social Control Patterns

Despite the extensive neutralization activities carried out under State auspices (local and federal), social resistance during 1940–1947 did not come to a halt. The "native" laboring classes responded to their still dire situation and to the economic changes of these years by adopting strategies that in many ways harked back to those of the Depression Years. Cases in point were the labor movement and the corresponding struggles in and around the centers of production. There were two factors that contributed considerably to the disarticulation of the trade unions at this time: (a) the socioeconomic transformations that were contradictorily intersecting each other and (b) the disjointed ways in which enormous portions of the Island's population were being displaced. Migration was yet another example of the extent to which the different survival mechanisms could be at odds with each other. It illustrates the contradictions that could exist between the various mechanisms which these laboring classes deployed to defend themselves (individually and collectively) from a social change that was being imposed on them.

Besides these socioeconomic changes and the demographic dislocations that materialized at this time, there was also the political opportunism and manipulation brought about by the heads of the populist political alliance (the PPD), once it had obtained the legislative majority and had garnered significant influence within the upper reaches of the colonial executive branch. The PPD leadership began their maneuver by legitimizing the demands of the sugarcane workers who went on strike in January of 1942, led by the new trade union federation (the CGT). Although the ruthless assault launched by the sugar mill's administration resulted in two workers dying at the hands of company supervisors, the strike eventually produced a victory for the union.[24] This was the coup de grace that finished the other trade union federation (the FLT), which had predominated during the first forty years of this century. It also marked the all-too-brief, official recognition of militant industrial-unionism in the Island.

From then on, the captains of the PPD set out to co-opt the leadership of the new federation by absorbing them into the party and into the local government posts commanded by the PPD or where the latter had influence, thereby subordinating the trade union leaders to the directives and priorities of the PPD and of the colonial administration. One of the underlying reasons for this cooption was the prominent role played by the CGT between 1942 and 1944 in two strikes within State-owned factories (cement and glass): the PPD chiefs saw this as detracting from the colonial government's economic policy.[25]

Eventually, in 1945, this resulted in a split within the CGT. According to Galvin, the PPD-led colonial administration now controlled the "official" or "governmental" CGT (pp. 100–102). From the splinter-CGT there emerged in 1947 another and also shortlived attempt at independent industrial unionism in the Island: the "Unidad General de Trabajadores" (UGT). The latter was involved in at least two fiercely contested strikes during the late 1940s with mixed results. Saez Corales maintains that this occurred in the midst of overt governmental-corporate collusion and on the heels of the recently passed, federal antilabor legislation (p. 134). A few years later the UGT became a shell of its former self.

However, the "native" masses conscripted into the budding industrial labor market during the last half of the forties found additional ways of resisting the factory discipline then being extended. The industrialization drive that began at war's end confronted a number of problems: an extremely reduced reservoir of skilled workers, the virtual absence of formal job-training programs, and from the standpoint of capital and the State the still persistent proliferation of what Perloff reports as improper "attitudes towards work" (pp. 246, 248). Again recalling the phrase coined by Clausewitz and recontextualized by Harry Braverman, this last complication partially illustrates the extent to which the movement of colonial-capitalist accumulation was a "*movement [occurring] in a resistant medium* because it involve[d] the control of refractory masses."[26]

There were additional and complementary practices through which the colonized poor reacted to the transformations of the war years, thereby striving to survive despite the large-scale socioeconomic disruption. Some of the official indicators of social violence and illegal income activities reached very high levels in this period, albeit to a lesser degree than during the Depression. During the first half of the 1940s, the rate of arrests for murder remained at twice the level of what it had been during the 1900–1930 period, though not reaching the heights experienced during the Depression; the suicide rate followed a similar pattern (see table 4). This escalation was partially the result of the expansion of the criminal justice system during World War Two.[27] There is complementary evidence of the degree to which mass-based social practices were increasingly being identified as illegal. Such is the case of the fourfold jump in the backlogs reported by the district and municipal courts from the mid-thirties to the mid-forties.[28] Both of these examples illustrate the degree to which the involvement of the postwar State in economic policing overlapped in a vital way with its augmented role in terms of literal policing. Such cases further exemplify the greater degree to which the State was implicated in mapping the subaltern subjects of the popular illegalities; these same instances also epitomize the increased State role in the maintenance of the corresponding social boundaries.

Interpersonal forms of social violence continued to be quite common, as well. Repeatedly, this sort of violence tended to be framed within the masculinist parameters of the preceding decades, both between men themselves and in the ever persistent cases of men attacking women. However, ordinary individuals from the dispossessed majorities were still reluctant to collaborate fully with the expanding authority of the criminal justice system. Such opposition continued to be a mainstay of the structures that culturally mapped this violence among the colonized majorities. At this time, for example, a court clerk in a central-mountain municipality reported the following sarcastic use of community-grounded informal social control mechanisms to obstruct the functioning of the formal regulatory technologies—as quoted by U.S. anthropologist Eric Wolf.

> The policeman asks the wounded man who struck him, and the policeman will say: so and so did. But when the case comes before court, they don't give evidence against each other. The judge then asks who the assailant was. The wounded man then points to an individual who up to this point was not involved in the case. The newly designated aggressor then names someone else as the man whom he hit, and there will be witnesses to confirm this. By the time they are half-way through, no one knows who did the assaulting and who was assaulted. Only the other day the judge roared, "Why don't you kill him next time, so we'll know who died!" (pp. 252–253)

In the rural areas, this ideological inscription still occasionally bridged the gaps between the peasantry and the large landowners. In this same vein, Wolf provides another vignette which epitomizes the primacy of patriarchical-family devices over State-based institutions in the municipality he studied. When a man was brought before the judge for having "struck his wife's uncle with an axe," "the uncle refused to testify against the nephew." The former told the court "that he suffered from epileptic fits, had fallen to the ground, . . . hurt himself with an axe," and that the nephew had only "picked up the axe and come under suspicion because he had been seen holding it" (p. 253).

"As for My Crimes, I Find Them Justified . . . "

The right to individually enact coercive reprisals directly, without official institutional mediation, continued to be recognized and affirmed among the "native" laboring classes. In this manner, the State monopoly of legitimate violence continued to be persistently challenged, ignored, and/or circumvented. Nevertheless, the gendered character of these forms of social violence was repeatedly evident. This reality is confirmed by the interviews performed during the 1940s by José C. Rosario with several "native" men found guilty of murder. The first convict declared, "[a]s for my crimes, I find them justified, because in one case I was defending my brother and I committed the second crime in self defense."[29]

Rosario quoted the second felon as admitting that his "third crime arose out of a discussion with a lady that accused me of having stolen a piece of meat from her home." The woman's lover had hit him "in the face twice" and, becoming "extremely angry," the felon "ran home, took a machete, and with it . . . attacked the woman who had accused" him. According to the convict cited by Rosario, the woman died the following day "[a]s a result of the wounds" he gave her, but he then added immediately: "With her insults toward my family and toward me, this woman drove me crazy, and I didn't think of punching her twice instead of using the machete" (p. 172).

Here again was the figure of the male laborer who enacted his rightful rage against those that had wronged him. But these acts appeared again (to the reading public) as a—literally—isolated and isolating account of social sickness. One more time, there was little context established by the social scientist. The culprit's actions and words were assumed to be self-evident: literally, speaking for themselves and pronouncing the truth of the convict's culpability. It was a 1940s version of the Juan B. Soto narrative in which the artisan Artemio Martínez in 1919 killed a woman that had treated him unjustly.[30] In Rosario's account, the woman who died twenty years later was killed because she had lashed out with insults and false accusations: she is minimalized to a shrill provocation. As in the 1920s case (retold by Córdova Chirino) of Pascual Ramos killing a fellow laborer who had sullied his honor, so too and a couple of decades later this other man had taken his first two lives.[31] Curiously enough, these first two victims remain unidentified in terms of gender, the universal/generic implication then being that they were both male. As in the 1919 and 1926 accounts, the signs of butchery abounded, as bodies were reduced and sectioned: animal bodies, blood, gashes, human bodies, long blades, etc.

Nonetheless, although the first two acts were inscribed as acts of defense that were comparable to each other (brother, self), in the third event the nearest figure to which the victim was textually compared was the allegedly stolen piece of meat. These two objects (the woman and the meat) were the links joining two men who were fighting each other: their bodies come together over a woman/piece-of-meat. The homosocial implications of all these crimes/events should in this sense be noted.[32] And while the (male) physical aggressor is spared the blade, the (female) verbal aggressor was physically assaulted with a machete. At all three levels—the insults/accusations, the butchery text, and the metonymical relations—the woman's body was reduced.

The statements of three more felons provided additional evidence of the masculinism that shaped such social violence and of the ways in which the corrective studies of colonial "pathology" textured these events. The next convicted murderer covered much of the same ground as the previous case. Here was Artemio Martínez once more, resurrected within Rosario's narrative, this time with very little mediations or displacements: "In the second case, I killed my [extramarital] lover because she was unfaithful and I also killed the person with whom she was being unfaithful to me with" (p. 174).

The next felon described a much more complicated scene, introducing new elements. The prisoner started by attempting to distinguish his first killing from his second. The former was "against the husband of a woman who I fell in love with. Her husband and I had an argument and I dealt him several machete blows, as a result of which he died" (p. 175). The change of murder venue seems to be the principal difference between the two killings, insofar as the second one "was also related to a married woman." The incident transpired "while another convict and I were working in the insular tuberculosis reclusion center." There the felon quoted by Rosario "spoke on several occasions with the wife" of his fellow inmate, "who came to see him frequently." On one of the occasions in which the interviewed narrator was talking to this married woman, the woman's husband became "very jealous and assaulted" his perceived rival. Therefore, "I struck him with the machete I was working with and killed him" (ibid.).

In this instance the victims were both male. However, the two male antagonists continued to meet violently over the body of a woman. This time the setting was marked by the explicit signs of disease (social, physical, moral), reinforcing the general narrative of pathology being formulated with such dispassionate objectivity. As in the case of one of the previous felons, the other two women in question were exchangeable commodities: they were the bodies in a bloody text of possession among men who were dispossessed.

The last account is very similar to the initial killings of the first convict because it too was a case of self-defense. "The crime that brought me to this prison consisted of having killed two armed men who attacked me violently" (p. 197). Having just come back from the U.S. mainland—"to see my mother, who was sick"—this interviewed felon discovered that his father and brother "had been threatened with death by the two men who attacked me." The latter concludes: "undoubtedly, they confused me with my brother. In resisting the aggression, I killed both of them" (ibid.).

Here, anew, the markers of the laboring-poor's informal regulatory mechanisms were reduced to the meaningless blood feuds of primitives. There was no context given, or transcribed, because presumably no context was requested or required. As in most of the other descriptions, even this last narration—the most plausible and warranted incident among all these cases—was made to appear again as haphazard and unconnected. As in the second account, the signs of sickness were present, once again suggesting the proximity of contagion and social pestilence. Mistaken identities were thus transformed into the identification of mistakes. Through the masterly gaze of the Creole social philosopher, the failures and shortcomings of these laboring poor "natives" ended up confirming the scholarly order of the Creole social scientist and his mastery over the colonial-capitalist dominating frameworks. The already and finally contained "native" was being definitively represented by his, also "native," but educated, superior.

Here, too, the predominant gender categories were being preserved at a juncture during which the foundations of the mass-based gender order were being shaken by the effects of a war, by massive demographic dislocations, and by economic transformations that tended to rely more on female factory labor. Once again, the existing State monopoly over the use of violence was being disrupted at a juncture during which the legitimacy of the U.S. metropolitan State as a whole was being questioned overseas (in Europe and in the Pacific) and from within (through the dispersed and multiple disorders of the colonized majorities). And once again, the transgressions of the "native" laboring classes were being individuated by the ever broadening colonial-capitalist "author-functions" of the Creole intelligentsia.

Many of the increasingly important income-gaining activities of the laboring poor continued to be persecuted during this decade. The home manufacture of rum was once more a case in point. Eric Wolf was keenly aware of this when he observed: "Brewing rum [was a] recognized source of income which aids many a father of a family who could not otherwise make ends meet." One peasant he interviewed addressed the issue in a very direct manner:

> I make *caña* [illegal rum]. I have eight children and this small farm. I do it for my family. Look, here is a bottle. If they catch me with it, they throw me in jail right away. But then the rum disappears. No one knows where. . . . They will never put an end to this in Puerto Rico. A poor man takes care of himself by making rum. (p. 251)

As had occurred during the decades of the twenties and thirties, the driving force behind these practices was both the search for socioeconomic autonomy and the need to transcend the still pervasive poverty. One storekeeper asked Wolf "[h]ow do you think the stores make a living? Do you think they do it by selling a couple of biscuits per day?" He added that if stores "didn't have the wild rum to sell, they would be without their pigs" (p. 252). Wolf then commented that such earnings were made possible "by the market for the product. Store-bought rum costs one dollar for four-fifths of a quart, whereas illegally made rum costs one dollar per liter." He found that the local residents identified it as "'our rum,' the rum of the rural neighborhood": *ron caña* was perceived "as the 'rum of the country' (*ron del país*)," whereas "store-bought rum [was] considered 'rum from over there' (*ron de allá*), from the United States, despite the fact that it [was] manufactured on the island by Puerto Rican firms" (ibid.).

The persistence of the underground lottery should be viewed in this same light. Such illegal sources of income were not just supplementary: occasionally, they became the basis of a household's entire livelihood. Mintz documents the illegal activities of a worker's wife who sold tickets in the underground lottery or "bolita": "There were times when for four or five weeks in a row she made the money in the house, sometimes because she sold the prize-winning tickets (on commission), other times because we won ourselves." In the woman's own words: "And our house—I can say that more than half of the money invested in it we got out of bolita. I made the most of it—I used it in buying wood and I repaired the house" (pp. 179–180).

Together with staging cockfights in unlicensed pits, slaughtering and selling uninspected pork, and so on, all of these unauthorized ways of making a living were very difficult to police and suppress. In this respect, they were similar to the popular, masculinist narratives on social violence in general and on informal justice in particular. As we saw in the passages just quoted, these popular illegalities comprised a fundamental ingredient of the socioeconomic and semiotic reproduction of the family/community networks. These mechanisms were not just occasional forms of subsistence: they constituted basic components in the fashioning of social subjects, both individually and collectively. Routinely, the popular illegalities unfolded as lines of demarcation, verifying or cancelling one's membership within the networks of family and community and one's access to the paths of information thus defined among the "native" majorities in the Island.

Again, there were unmistakable distinctions between, on the one hand, these subsistence forms and their broader sociocultural context and, on the other hand, the official legal ideology of the colonial social order. The manufacture of illegal rum once again illustrates this split. Wolf commented in his study that the existing laws created contradictions even among some of the "law-enforcing agents, who, as private individuals, understand the appeal of the forbidden activities, even though they are called on officially to stamp them out." On the other hand, "most poor people in the town and country do not regard these activities as illegal" (p. 251).

It was not just a question of being reluctant to cooperate with the established authorities. As during the preceding decades, it was still a matter of—literally—positioning oneself within a social topography dichotomized by the law, with all the textual and economic contradictions this generated. At this level, the underground lottery further exemplifies the difficulty of fashioning the subaltern subjects of the popular illegalities.

According to the Mintz ethnography, one of the members of the cane-cutter's family indicated that people preferred "to play bolita (rather than the government-sponsored lottery)" because "it was easier for them, and they felt they won more easily playing this game" (p. 181). This family member acknowledged that when the clients of the bolita-numbers seller "used to want to buy a favorite number, they could get it more easily than if it were in the legal lottery . . . " The customers would remark, "'I want to play such and such a particular number,' and they could buy it easily. In the legal lottery this is difficult to do." But these were not the only reasons for the bolita's popularity: "in a bolita series composed of a thousand numbers, those thousand numbers are almost entirely sold here in the barrio." The advantages became obvious since it was "a rarity when the winner doesn't turn up here in the barrio" (ibid.).

The Golden Age of Crime Journalism

The proliferation of these illegalized activities was dutifully reported in copious press stories. This brand of journalism was partly due to the continuing rise in the urban manifestations of such phenomena. Based in the big cities, the tabloids were therefore increasingly exposed to the popular illegalities, particularly to social violence. The manufacture of the news in this regard was extended to the recasting of historical memory. The "famous executed murderers" series carried by *El Imparcial* and written by Córdova Chirino during 1948–1949 was one of the more notorious examples of such popular historicist narration. Newspaper coverage of this sort had a considerable, but perhaps disproportionate, impact on public perceptions of the phenomenon.

The distortion effects of this sensationalism were noted at the time by one of the first statisticians of recorded crime in the Island. In the opening paragraph of his famous 1948 tract on this topic, Teobaldo Casanova affirmed:

> Often in the daily press of Puerto Rico there appear reports and opinions on crime in this country. Most of these articles describe, display, or sound the alarm on the rise of crime, and in all of them one observes the absence of evidence to substantiate the conclusions that have been reached. Rarely a couple of months go by without somebody writing on the subject, be it a mere opinion, a report, or a feature or editorial in the newspaper that is publishing the piece. (p. 1)

In this manner Casanova was laying the groundwork for invalidating what he perceived to be the lay, nonacademic, and nonscientific perspectives on the crime question. In contrast to these crude viewpoints, Casanova counterposed his statistical models regarding criminal patterns in the Island. This was the direct descendant of the legal-anthropological, social work, and psychiatric paradigms that had been describing and explaining such behavior since the early twentieth century in the Island: for example, the previously cited writings of de Diego, Samalea Iglesias, Fleagle, Soto, Bary, Mixer, Berga y Ponce de León, and Rogler, among others. In all of these instances, the aim was to reconstitute the epistemic community of academia and its hegemony over discourses on crime.

As in the years of 1898–1906, 1915–1921, and the 1930s, crime was made-to-appear-again (literally: re-presented) within the newspapers of the 1940s as an uncontrollable and terror-laden roller in the midst of a defenseless, partially apathetic, and confused citizenry. For instance, one 1943 news story in *El Imparcial* sounded the alarm against "the wave of crimes, of robberies and of banditry in broad daylight, that advances brazenly through the towns and the countryside." Once again, this terror was being unleashed in the face of governmental incompetence and tolerance of illegal activity: "The newspapers report daily on the new and numerous blood deeds, murders, robberies, seductions, etc., without the Public Authorities demonstrating concern for such a state of affairs." The result was, of course, the complete collapse of civility and order: "These bullies, satyrs, and bandits, once having perpetrated their vandalism, continue through the streets and town squares, beaming haughtily their smiles of satisfaction."[33]

Clearly, the collective memories being invoked here were the activities of: the peasant insurgency of 1898–1899; the so-called Republican Mobs of 1900–1904; the strike waves and social unrest of 1915–1921; and the Depression years—the rabble in arms acting with impunity, the widespread disorder, the wanton disregard for life and property, the ineffective colonial administration, and so on.

Another example of this same genre of journalism covers much of the same textual and social territory. In a 1945 article which appeared in this same newspaper, another "native" petit-intellectual begins by flatly stating that "[i]f the number of crimes that are being committed in Puerto Rico on a daily basis is alarming, the indifference with which we contemplate this tragic problem is even more alarming." As in preceding decades, one of the resounding leitmotifs was the interminable ubiquity of these shameful acts:

> Rarely a day goes by without banner headlines and macabre photographs appearing in our press regarding the carrying out of a crime. The problem is so tragic, now, that the following phrase is heard with frequency: "Who have they killed today?"[34]

Here the burden of responsibility was shifted to an anonymous and disembodied citizenry which was, nevertheless, expected to rise to action in order to put an end to this relentless onslaught. The problems posed by this narrative were even greater when one remembers that the faceless and generic public could not act on its own volition because it never convened: its only material, legitimate, and everyday expression was the State (the "public" in "public administration"). Yet this was the very institution which had been decried by others as being incompetent. Within this context, the paralysis and inadequacy thus suggested could only point to the colonized condition of the society in which these events were occurring.

> This serious social problem requires study, calm meditation, and above all a solution. We cannot, we must not gaze passively at those banner headlines that leave such a profound impression on everybody in general and on youth in particular. We must prevent this state of affairs from being accepted as a measure of our culture. We must put an end to this painful spectacle that humiliates us. (ibid.)

The call to action was a call to reflection because these disorderly acts, in turn, reflected negatively on the character of Puerto Rican society. The specular coupling was in this case counterproductive for the Creole propertied and educated classes: here, the transgressions of unrestrained "subject people" re-presented, in particular, the ineptitude of privileged "subject people" in terms of successfully identifying and regulating such unruliness. In general, these unchecked "native" violations re-present the deficiencies of the cultural-national/racial community whose site/sight these propertied and educated Creoles saw themselves as possessing and embodying (in a second sense, literally: re-presenting). The alternative proposed by the "native" professional in this case was further corrective study. In this manner, the crime question continued to mark the outer edge of that behavior which was being perceived as acceptable: morally, culturally, and politically.

Because of this signifier function, the Island's intelligentsia increasingly read the subaltern subjects of the popular illegalities in a distinctive way: the subjects of this disorder were now transmuted into one of the problems that accompanied the birth of the new economic order, a situation that in turn was translated as a problem of guaranteeing social order. The modernity and progress heralded by emergent large-scale industrialization seemed to also multiply the spaces where the social chaos of urban primitives could thrive.

However, portions of this cultural mapping were not only pertinent to the propertied and educated classes. In the case of some of the more spectacular expressions of social violence, this normative inscription of criminal practices also became increasingly relevant—though for different reasons—to the expanding numbers of the laboring poor. The latter unevenly began fashioning as criminal those extremely undesirable practices carried out by individuals who belonged to different reticulations of kinship and neighborhood.

This shift in popular perceptions was partly due to the monumental social rupture and large-scale demographic displacements that were taking place then, particularly in the case of the masses of people flocking to the urban areas. But it could also be ascribed to the rise in advertising-based communications, as electronic and print news extended the radius of their information processing capacity. Potentially grotesque and alarming incidents occurring in other distant communities were as common as before, but simply less known. With the greater leverage of the mass media, such events started becoming household words and the topics of everyday conversation. This was unfolding regardless of the fact that members of a person's own webs of socioeconomic support and cultural meaning might be carrying out the same types of activities. As the quotes of the "native" convicted murderers suggest, it was mainly within the confines of one's family and community network that the motives and rationales of such social violence could become familiar, comprehensible, meaningful, recognizable.

These laboring-poor masses were an important part of the growing audience of the tabloids and of the radio stations. Likewise, they were part of the expanding political base of the new, populist forms of State and party mobilization. Therefore, the Island's poor majorities rapidly became one of the principal battlegrounds in the struggle to enlarge or reduce the social base of the budding populist and State-directed project in its attempt to safeguard the integrity of the Island's social fabric. These were attempts to interpellate the impoverished majorities through the prevailing civic discourses that circulated, rather prominently, as a result of mass media activities.

The Road to Modernity: "The General Alteration of People's Moods"

Insofar as crime was one of the foremost signifiers of everything that was profane, antigovernmental, and barbarous, it was the indispensable antipode of the narratives of civility. Although growing segments of the "native" majorities were being recruited by such sign systems, the fragmented, contradictory, peripheral, and discontinuous character of this incorporation was not immediately evident at the time. On the surface, what seemed to prevail was the burgeoning social consensus that was allegedly materializing against this assault of criminal violence, depravation, and pillage. Once more, the culprit was depicted as an amorphous, faceless enemy which always came from the external perimeter of Puerto Rican society.

These were the textual boundaries being delineated, even as they shifted, in the 1948 observations of the liberal essayist Miguel Meléndez Muñoz: "The savage crimes that have occurred lately have caused indignation and have had a profound effect on all of Puerto Rican society. This attitude shows that the social mechanism that has tempered our people and that rules the way it expresses its sensibilities, is still susceptible to reacting to events of great magnitude . . . "[35]

The image of a "society under siege" rapidly became one of the hallmarks of this decade and of the following forty years. The increasingly urbanized landscape was to serve as the topographical con-text for this terror. Nevertheless, the official consensus ideology had a contradictory underside: the urban spaces being positioned in this grisly setting were simultaneously the places inhabited by a sizeable portion of the mass base of this alleged consensus. Many of the landless peasants and urban/poor laborers that constituted this "tempered people" also happened to be converging on the urban shantytowns and slums. Meléndez Muñoz's writings in this regard were once again extremely emblematic.

> And then in the other part, a fatal and sinister *part,* we have the Capital City of the Island, surrounded tightly by a circle or belt of shantytowns, on all of its sides and boundaries, even by sea—the marshy shantytown of the Martín Peña Channel [Caño de Martín Peña]—, as if it was a ring of delinquent misery, of unceasing pain, of rage concentrated twice over, ready to expand, against the society whose margins it is destined to inhabit. (p. 815, emphasis in the original)

Here the San Juan of the mid-1940s was conceived as a beleaguered citadel of morality, a virtuous fortress being choked by an iron collar of iniquity: the putrid encampments of the urban barbarians. This image very selectively fed on the historical memories of past raids ("even by sea"). The latter was a direct reference to the invasions carried out by the British and Dutch buccaneers of the sixteenth through eighteenth centuries against the old walls of the capital city. However, this textual maneuver conveniently sidestepped the more recent shelling of San Juan by U.S. battleships in 1898. Through such historical coupling and cautious allusions, visions of plundering villains, looting sprees, and diabolic illegality were conjured to inform the turbulent present of "delinquent misery": hence, the emergent displacement of the local incarnation of Caliban—from rural beast to urban monstrosity.

Some of the other, concrete intertextual strategies being summoned here are equally portentous. This was distinctively the case of the geographic site of the shantytown being mentioned. The making of the shantytown at the Caño de Martín Peña ensued during the migratory waves of the 1930s. The physical construction of this settlement, and of the community that emerged within it, was no small feat. As another U.S. anthropologist would write thirty years later,

> Around 1935, the first families arriving at the shanty town found only mangrove growing in the swampy land destined to become their home. They cleared and filled in a few plots to construct their houses and built plank sidewalks connecting different parts of the shanty town. Today [1973] street names such as O'Higgins, Colón, Pablo Nuñez commemorate the struggle of these first families in the places where they established their homes.[36]

Originally squatters, these landless peasants and urban laborers had to literally reclaim this land from the sea and from the governmental authorities that resisted their settling there. In such a way, they attempted to carve out an existence—legally and illegally—within the socioeconomic constraints of the Depression and the war years. These were the historical battles and conditions that get erased, mis-recognized, and/or uprooted in the Meléndez Muñoz narrative.

In its place looms the Caño de Martín Peña itself. It seemed, for Meléndez Muñoz, that this was a space where topography overdetermined the specific social and moral fabric of the residents.

> We have in this very same Capital City, which is where crime is increasing the most, nearly *six thousand* school-age children . . . without schools. We have a floating population, made up of individuals without a trade or profession, without known legal means of income that live and dress and stroll and do not work and . . . play. Yet the play does not alternate with study or with work, as is suggested by modern pedagogy. (p. 815, emphasis in the original)

In this sense, it must be borne in mind that a *caño* is not only a synonym for "channel." It is also the final destination of excrement and waste (a sewer, a gutter), as well as being the subterranean lair of vermin and of tunnelling rodents (a burrow). This was the canvas on which these shantytown dwellers were rendered as roving underground parasites, shifting from one wretched hole to another, but forever wallowing in bodily and moral filth.

> We have, according to a census carried out during the War almost *five* thousand prostitutes in the metropolitan area. This amounts to *two* percent of the population of San Juan . . . Cabarets, night clubs, whorehouses, houses where Jorge's ear is summoned . . . , who knows how many there are and where they are? (ibid., emphasis in the original)

These lay discourses on physical and mental pathology suture the religious narratives of sin—carnal and otherwise. The impoverished residents of the greater metropolitan area were thus reinscribed as the embodiment of menacing vices, their subjectivities being constituted through pathologization, even as these "native" laborers were simultaneously becoming the object of much official social control.

Such textual practices clearly coincide with the narrative of Secretary of the Interior, Harold Ickes, in his January 1936 visit to San Juan and its slums. In this case, the similarities between a prominent Creole intellectual like Meléndez Muñoz and a high-ranking colonial officer such as Ickes are even more striking when compared to the sensationalist portrayal of this same sociophysical space made by another U.S. writer in the mid-1940s. Wenzell Brown spent two years in the Island teaching school to young "natives" from the slum areas. Author of the melodramatic *Puerto Rico: Dynamite on Our Doorstep,* he returned in 1945 and spent several months in Puerto Rico, the result of which was a chapter of *Angry Men—Laughing Men: The Caribbean Caldron.* The expressed purpose of this last trip to the Island was, in his words, that of "checking on the changes which had taken place and tracing the development of my students to see if the leaven of democracy had affected them advantageously."[37]

On this second journalistic safari across the Caribbean, Brown repeatedly asserted that Puerto Rico was a place he knew very well. In the outskirts of the San Juan metropolitan area he returned to what he understood to be "the worst slums in the world" (p. 183). It was the very embodiment of architectural absurdity, a place where "[w]ithin a few blocks of splendid residential sections are slums that surpass any I have ever seen. The worst of these is El Fanguito—The Little Mud" (p. 187). These were the same shantytowns that a decade before Interior Secretary Harold Ickes, in the first volume of his published diaries, had also described as " . . . the worst slums that I have ever seen."[38] Like Meléndez Muñoz, Brown too beheld the clustered netherworld of the teeming rodents: "[h]ere live thousands on thousands of people, [where] from six to fifteen people sleep on the broken flooring of a single room or in hammocks made of burlap bags slung across the room" (p. 187). Once more, these textual practices were not too distant from the descriptions made by Ickes of both urban and rural poverty: "The dwellings . . . [were] thoroughly disreputable and disagreeable. . . . Moreover, the people breed like rabbits . . . " (p. 504).

For Brown, as with Meléndez Muñoz, these were the filthy warrens of the "native" primitives, basking in a fetid quagmire and calling it a dwelling: the pigsties where no human being could possibly live. Brown found "little shacks . . . made of tin and corrugated cardboard" that stood "on stilts in the black, malodorous mud," even as the "backwash of the bay beat against them" carrying "the accumulated waste of the city beneath the houses." These houses could only be reached "by rickety board walks, and if the rotten planking breaks under one, it mean[t] a plunge knee-deep into black mire" (p. 187). Compare this to Ickes' descriptions of much of the Island a decade before:

> Open sewage runs through the streets and around the buildings and there are no sanitary facilities at all. The children play in this sewage, which in many cases is covered with thick green scum. The houses appear to be dirty and unkept. . . . It is unbelievable that human beings can be permitted to live in such noisome cesspools. . . . Pigs, chickens, and burros live in close relationship with the members of the family. (pp. 504, 505)

Finally, like Meléndez Muñoz, Brown emphasized the depravity, fury, and passion that thrived in this ungodly milieu. "Such slums as these, though on a smaller scale, dot the entire Island," wrote Brown. And supposedly these were the slums that begot "a tangled skein of bastardy, violent crime, incest, hate, and a wild surging rage that seeks an object against which it may vent itself" (p. 187). Although Ickes was much more subtle, there was still his admonition that these were "thoroughly disreputable and disagreeable" surroundings, where people such as himself found human life—quite literally—unimaginable.

Once again and regardless of the causes each privileged observer understands were at work, a significant part of the "native" space was found wanting. And once again, most of these "subject people" were inscribed as unfit. Although the form of these normative discourses has changed substantially and the author-functions now included Creole intellectuals, such signifying practices clearly harked back to Reverend Josiah Strong's "races, which like the African and the Malay, are many centuries behind the Anglo-Saxon,"[39] as well as to Brigadier General George Davis' "evil-disposed classes."[40]

Yet there was another way of interpreting Island social reality and this second perspective surfaced concurrently with the texts just mentioned. This other mainstream trend was exemplified by the much less impressionistic research carried out by a group of cultural anthropologists under the direction of the eminent U.S. scholar Julian Steward.[41] This line of inquiry was not as overburdened with the desire to signal "native" deficiencies which need to be corrected, as in the case of the writings of Ickes, Rosario, Carrión, Rogler, Meléndez Muñoz, and Brown. In this sense, the Steward study and the research that sprang from it (such as the Mintz ethnography cited above) continue to be some of the most valuable sources of empirical information about Island society and culture in the 1940s.

However, the Steward study is still also the intellectual heir of U.S. rural sociologist Fred Fleagle, whose 1917 examination of Island conditions was not intended to be "a criticism of Porto Rico or of Porto Ricans [*sic*] . . . ," but rather "an exposition of the social situation as it exists, and do not differ greatly, either in quality or in character, from similar facts which could be gathered relating any country."[42] In a colonial situation, the underlying positivism which grounds such interpretations ultimately tend to re-present as given and as natural the social reality being described. At this level, the reinscription of the facticity—but not of the factitiousness and historicity—of the prevalent social order in Puerto Rico became one of the effects of these studies. The reproduction of this problem materialized totally independent of the best intentions of these researchers (some of whom were even politically progressive).

This is what makes the Steward study similar to the nineteenth-century British travel accounts in Africa analyzed by Mary Louise Pratt. Referring to the gaze of one of these European adventurers, Pratt notes: " . . . this eye seems powerless to act or interact with this landscape. Unheroic, unparticularized, without ego, interest, or desire of its own, it seems to do nothing but gaze from the periphery of its own creation, like the self-effaced, non-interventionist eye that scans the Other's body."[43] This is the same objectivist detachment found in the Steward study. As Pratt has remarked, though, within a colonial context this self-effaced gaze/exploration still generates Euro-centric, naturalizing effects.

> To the extent that it strives to efface itself, the invisible eye/I strives to make those informational orders natural, to find them there uncommanded, rather than to assert them as products/producers of European knowledges or disciplines. . . . In the body of the text European enterprise is seldom mentioned, but the sight/site as textualized consistently presupposes a global transformation that, whether the I/eye likes it or not, is already understood to be underway. (p. 144)

This genre of academic disengagement seemed to be more appropriate for a period in which growing numbers of educated "natives" were being absorbed into the colonialist bureaucracy and into the corresponding author-functions. It was as if the transformative narratives and social practices that advanced the colonialist enterprise were now best left to the privileged "subject people," while the colonizer-intellectual cadre receded into an "unheroic, unparticularized . . . self-effaced, non-interventionist" background. Nevertheless, the colonizers in this seemingly invisible backdrop still "presuppose[d] a global transformation that, whether the [colonizer's] I/eye like[d] it or not, [was] already understood to be underway."

The first type of ideological representation—that is, the one exemplified by the Ickes, Brown, and Meléndez Muñoz texts—was canonized as social science in the Island when one of the leading Puerto Rican sociologists of the day went so far as to say that the migration of landless peasants to towns and cities, together with the subsequent urban sprawl, were *the* principal causes of this crime wave. According to José C. Rosario's study *El problema de la criminalidad en Puerto Rico,* the "changes in the economic situation of the country" together with "any situation that created a general alteration of people's moods" were all responsible for "influenc[ing] criminal activity." Rosario saw "certain social patterns of the people" as being "additional causes of crime." However, topping all of these other motives was "immigration as the principal determinant behind the increase in crime" (p. 60).

For Rosario, these social disorders were also the inevitable birth pangs of social and moral advancement: a sort of rite of passage that would eventually usher Puerto Rico into the modernity already being experienced in the continental United States. In the emblematic and blunt evolutionism of the Euro/Americo-centric social sciences and humanities, this distinguished member of the Creole intelligentsia reinforced the erasure of Puerto Rico's historical specificity by recasting all of "native" society as what Visvanathan called the "contemporary ancestors" of the West[44]—again, in this case, the United States. Here was an educated "native" positioning the entire Island, particularly its dispossessed majorities, as "a Euro-American past so long gone that we can find no traces of it in Western spaces."[45] In Rosario's own words:

> The growth of crime is one of the labor pains; of the birth of urban expansion, which is the delivery of progress. More stable times will surely come in the future. For now, we must expect even more criminal activity. We will have to pass through ten years, perhaps through twenty years, of the stage that the United States is going through at this time. (p. 60)

That it was a "native" intellectual who casually performed this maneuver, rather than a colonialist agent from North America, exemplifies the degree to which such discursive chains (racist, colonialist) had already shackled prominent members of the Creole educated strata, not only in terms of favoring the "civilizing mission," but also in terms of sponsoring and expediting it themselves.[46]

Descriptions akin to the ones made by Meléndez Muñoz, Brown, Ickes, and Rosario partially distort the complexity of the migration process itself, both within Puerto Rico and between the Island and the United States. It was true that the migration to the towns and cities was dramatic during the Second World War and the immediate postwar years. It was also true that the enlargement of the capital city was not as dramatic as during the height of the Depression. However, while the rural population in Puerto Rico only rose by one percent during 1940–1950, the urban population in the Island as a whole jumped by fifty-eight percent. This displacement process now tended to reinforce the degradation of work skills within the relocated labor force that came from the mountains and hills of the Island. Migration overseas soared even more dramatically: the change of the external migratory balance between 1939 and 1949 was 1,041.7 percent.[47]

Rural-to-urban migration in Puerto Rico took place from the mountains and rural valleys to the Island's urban coast and/or to the northeastern seaboard of the United States. As in the previous decade, this was a response to the—now final—collapse of the principal forms of surplus extraction that had predominated until then.

Yet, even more so than during the Depression years, such responses took several routes that were contradictorily imbricated. It was both a flight from the stranglehold of a non/protocapitalist land rent system in its death throes and a flight from the home-needlework archipelago predicated on absolute surplus value and dismally low wages. Some migration to the United States and to the large cities in the Island was also expressed as a partial flight from the increasingly intensified production in the sugar mills-plantations.

Finally, it was a flight from the budding and still sparse industrial enterprises being set up by the local government and by the new generation of incoming U.S. corporations. In this last case, it was also a flight *to* the new opportunities that were burgeoning in terms of *urban* forms of economic survival. To some extent, this included the jobs that were opening as a result of the very recent industrialization process, the expansion of service employment, and the accretion of government jobs and the institutionalized social wage payments. Yet, simultaneously, it also overlapped with the growing urban underground economy.

The dispossessed "natives" who migrated came looking for a better life and for an improvement in their social conditions. The fact that some of these efforts were declared illegal or became criminalized in the midst of a more reduced wage market than what was expected was no design of their own—moral or otherwise. Neither could they ultimately share the blame for the at times violently self-destructive ways in which some of these elements reacted to the brutality of the structural conditions under which the old transformations were running their course or under which the new ones were being born. In this sense, the situation in urban Puerto Rico was comparable to, though not the "contemporary ancestor" of, what Gareth Stedman Jones has pointed out for late nineteenth-century London:

> It can now be seen that the theory of urban degeneration bore little relation to the real situation of the . . . poor. . . . What it provided, was not in fact an adequate explanation of [urban] . . . poverty, but rather a mental landscape within which the middle class could recognize and articulate their own anxieties about urban existence.[48]

CONCLUSION

9

The Subjects in Question

As we have seen, "dealing with . . . subject people"[1] and with the rise of "the evil-disposed classes"[2] between 1898 and 1947 was not an easy task in Puerto Rico. This is because the subjects in question were neither the inert products of an expected birth nor of a given nature. Rather as I have argued throughout, they were the disputed constructs of unstable, social, and historical forces.

Some of these subjects/texts were triumphantly staged by their own authors: literally the acts of self-made men. This was the hegemonic subject of colonialism: what Theodore Roosevelt had designated as the mostly white, North American, "finer set of young fellows,"[3] what Beveridge had baptized as the "nobler and more virile types of men,"[4] and what Tugwell in 1946 still saw as the "truer friend[s] among outsiders."[5] This was the colonizer subject which enacted the Euro/Americo-centric epic (from the United States and in Puerto Rico), an enterprise that institutionally and textually coupled the fashioning of the subaltern subjects of U.S. capitalism, colonial labor, and law and order in the Island.

A second group of subjects in question—the privileged "subject people"—alternately attempted to seize or negotiate the mechanisms of exploitation and progress and of containment and representation. These were the ones who saw themselves as the legitimate heirs of the Island and its struggles: for U.S. citizenship, for "home rule," for joining the North American federation, or for joining the Latin American community of nations, but always for being able to rule their propertied homes and spaces. They did so for national-cultural freedom and the right to live off the wage-slavery or noncapitalist servitude of others; and for acceptance as equals among the colonizers (in Puerto Rico and in the United States) by carrying out the intellectual surveillance and paternal preservation of the colonized majorities. Despite this odd combination of noble and self-serving gestures, the Western[ized] parameters of these forms of subjectivity and these educated social practices continued to be trapped within colonial mimicry. To paraphrase Homi Bhabha again,[6] the sociocultural and political differences invoked by the "native" intelligentsia persisted in reproducing the dominant strategic function of colonial power. For instance, even the politically anticolonialist elements within the Unionista, Liberal, Nacionalista, and PPD high commands remained within the colonial paradigms of Euro/Americo-centric perspectives. The economic programs, political alternatives, and cultural efforts of these party leaders proceeded to fall under the shadow of the West.

Still others, the many, were the other[ed] subjects. They had to be fashioned as questionable even as the subjectivities thus created, in turn, generated still greater questions and proposed new forms of contradictory subjectivity. Such were the queries expressed by the "native" popular illegalities regarding the conditions that constituted the colonized laboring classes as a cheap, accessible, and pliable labor force. And yet the socioeconomic transformations announced by the War of 1898 took place, albeit not in their original form, extent, or orientation; not for the colonizers; not for the colonized; not for the propertied and educated classes ("native" and North American); and not for the laboring majorities.

These were the subjects who came into being as a result of redrawn boundaries. Such subjects shifted positions within and across these various boundaries, sometimes negating these boundaries, sometimes reinforcing them, and sometimes doing both at the same time. Such boundaries existed between different and differing national-political jurisdictions; between the limits of property and the proprieties of limitation; between the frontiers of physical and cultural survival; between morally and literally policed perimeters; between the centered colonizers and the peripheral colonized and within the peripheral colonized themselves; between the margins of nationality, race, class, gender, sexuality, age, and the law; and between the confines of colonial capitalism and of capitalist colonialism.

These were the social subjects that had to be anticipated and imagined before the representatives of the new colonialism even encountered their new Caribbean wards. It was a process of imagination and of corrective study whose insignia was the invention of a place and a people that had not existed before—"Porto Rico" and "Porto Ricans"—and whose imaginary existence has persisted, even after the Island's "natives" and "their" descendants were officially baptized in 1932 with the name "they" had always thought was "theirs."

This book has argued and illustrated the need to combine an analysis of what Stuart Hall called the "social relations, production, and the 'hard edge' of productive systems" with an examination of "the 'insides' of people, . . . subjectivity and sexuality."[7] The terrain in which this argument has been made corresponds to the intersection of capitalism, colonialism, and punitive structures and discourses in Puerto Rico and their corresponding subjects during the first half of this century. The first chapter established the general theoretical framework for this study. In the second and third chapters I demonstrated the structural logic and immediate effects of the colonial capitalist project during its formative period, focusing on the needs of the new social order in terms of defining, fabricating, and intercepting the disorderly and chaotic "natives." The remainder of the book explored the various ways in which most of the Island's population responded to the process of colonial, capitalist, and punitive inscription; in chapters four through eight, I also explained the changes that developed in the texture and consequences of the dispossession process and the resistances to it up to and including the 1940s. In the sections that follow, I deal with the implications of the entire investigation and advance some tentative conclusions.

Linking the "Insides" and the "Outsides" of People

Understood in its broader sense, the structurally brutal manner in which most of the colonized population was dispossessed was one of the principal intersections of the "insides" and the "outsides" of people. Paradoxically, it was also one of the most invisible instances of such convergence. On the one hand, colonial-capitalist dispossession was a process that unfolded in the most general and "external" fashion imaginable. Its logic was so outwardly abstract that it literally seemed to descend from the skies, out of nowhere, with no tangible connections to what was transpiring in the daily lives of the "native" majorities. This was the narrative of Fate, of fatality, of forces beyond human comprehension, and of the absence of any accountability. Like the hurricanes, the droughts, and the earthquakes, it seemed that famine, disease, and generalized poverty were natural calamities that could be neither foreseen nor prevented.

Yet some of the effects of dispossession were simultaneously inscribed in the most "internal" manner possible. Within such sign systems, the results of the dispossession process were attributed to the individual rapacity of the usurer, to the insatiability and selfishness of the U.S. corporations and of the large Creole landowners and merchants, to the avarice of corrupt politicians ("native" and North American), to the ruthlessness of a specific policeman, to the arbitrariness of a certain judge, to the particular greed of the strikebreaker, and so on. From this viewpoint, the victims of hunger had identifiable victimizers, and the unemployed knew the names of their aggressors. These misfortunes were therefore the deliberate design of some sinister person or persons.

As this study has shown, both discourses were taken up by the propertied and by the dispossessed, by the "native" and by the North American, in varying degrees and at different moments.[8] These explanations present some problems, though. The terribly detached and impersonal machinations of generalized hunger and malnutrition killed real, live individuals, with names and faces. But these were subjects who had been individuated as expendable because they were collectively constructed as potentially exploitable under the socioeconomic and politico-cultural conditions of colonial difference.

The conditions of existence of these "native" laborers were so precarious and harsh because that is the way in which wild beasts are domesticated: in the words of Dario Melossi, "[t]o train a horse you must first capture and tame it."[9] To carry this out (as if by design or unknowingly), to try to modify it from above through benevolent guidance, and/or to accept what Fred Fleagle described as "the social situation as it exists"[10] were all social practices grounded on the premise that, ultimately, the "natives"—all or most of them—were beastly, bestial, beast-like or, just simply, beasts. This was why "they" could not be treated as "ordinary men." And this was why such inhumanity and/or unmanliness had to be continually imagined, identified, codified, cultivated, and disciplined: in a word, colonized.

Within this context, the quandaries faced by the colonial-capitalist enterprise endlessly materialized at multiple levels. On the one hand, the "natives" had to be invented yet, on the other hand, they had to have been always already there. "Porto Ricans" had to be rescued from the centuries of Spanish/tropical medievalism, yet "Porto Ricans" did not exist before 1898. The "natives" had to be changed (civilized) but they had to stay the same (not-equal to the civilizers): like their British counterparts, U.S. colonizers had what

Bhabha termed a "desire for a reformed, recognizable Other, as *a subject that is almost the same, but not quite*" (p. 126, emphasis in the original).

Most of "Porto Rico" was a very down-to-earth, basic place, whose materiality was unmistakable. Yet for colonial officials such as Ickes it was "unbelievable that human beings . . . [could] be permitted to live in such noisome cesspools," a fact which in turn made their occasional cleanliness equally "unbelievable" (p. 504). Likewise, Theodore Roosevelt, Jr. discovered there "squalor and filth [that] were almost unbelievable."[11] On the one hand, the place and its people were undoubtedly real but, on the other hand, the existence of "these" people was still hard to believe. In this last case, it could very well be said that "Porto Ricans," like the other colonized and the colonized Others of Africa, Asia, and the rest of Latin America, belonged to what Albert Memmi critically designated as "the realms of the imagination."[12] "Porto Rico," like Crusoe's island and similar to what Octave Mannoni classified as the other "desert islands of the imagination," was indeed "peopled with imaginary beings, but that is after all their *raison d'être*": for if the world of "Porto Rico" was "emptied of human beings as they really are, it can be filled with creatures of our [that is, the colonizer's] imagination: Calypso, Ariel, Friday."[13]

Nonetheless, there were additional aporias within this colonialist universe. If the "natives" were so passive and torpid, how could "they" also be "evil-disposed" criminals and raging vandals? According to Kipling's "The White Man's Burden," this was all for "their" own good ("To veil the threat of terror / And check the show of pride") and, yet, "they" were all a bunch of ingrates ("The blame of those ye better / the hate of those ye guard"). Theodore Roosevelt, Jr. understood "them" to be "highly civilized, culturally sensitive" people.[14] And yet, if that was true, what was the point of the North American "civilizing mission" in the Island? On the one hand, the colony was enormously profitable and a prime asset (for the corporations), yet, on the other hand, it was "the poorhouse of the Caribbean" and a terrible burden (for the Island's population and parts of the federal bureaucracy). Not all "natives" were alike because some of "them" made good assistants, performing colonialist author-functions and other forms of surrogacy yet, ultimately, the "good native" was an oxymoron because "they" could not be trusted, having to be supervised at some level or other.

These are some of the tensions which express the ways in which the "insides" of the colonial subjects (colonizers and colonized) were connected to the "outside" of these same subjects. Such contradictions also suture the "inside" and the "outside" of additional and corollary processes that unfolded at this time. The "inside" of a particular event, such as the murder of Otilia Rivera by Artemio Martínez in 1919, and the ways in which this event were inscribed and regulated were, in turn, linked to the "outside" processes of the labor strife and other transgressions of the second decade of U.S. colonization. The "inside" of the convicted-murderer narratives of the 1940s was correlated to the "outside" of the growing instability in the predominant gender codes within the impoverished majorities. The "inside" of specific cases of child nomadism between 1910 and 1921 or in the Depression years was socioeconomically and textually spliced to the "outside" of the misery, scarcity, and high costs of living during those periods, as well as to the "outside" of the moral policing by Creole and North American reformers.

The "inside" of rural-laborer penury and "artifice" during the 1920s was linked to the "outside" of the socioeconomic counterattack launched by the U.S. corporations and to the "outside" of declining world prices of some agricultural products. The "inside" of the concrete cases of rural theft, urban revolts, and their corresponding representations during the 1898–1909 period were coupled to the "outside" of the economic shock due to the War of 1898 and to the regime of accumulation then inaugurated. The "inside" of the shifts executed by tobacco manufacture and sugar refining in the second and third decades is associated with the "outside" of the popular illegalities taken as a whole, and so on.

In almost every case, the role of these illegalized "native" responses is paramount. This is why the overall morphology, the general results, and the measure of such transgressions need to be evaluated in a more detailed manner.

The Popular Illegalities and the Structures and Strictures of Colonial-Capitalist Dispossession

In Puerto Rico what Braverman has called the "resistant medium"[15] turned out to be a population that structured their defiance and survival through an entire range of unlawful practices. What were the main features of the popular illegalities during the entire period? How were they recorded and codified? And what was the relationship between the principal traits of the subaltern subjects of such practices and the subaltern subjects of labor exploitation? Seen as a whole, between 1898 and 1947, to what extent did the former constitute a mediation between the latter and the subaltern subjects of official punitive patterns?

Taking the first half of this century as a whole, disorderly conduct and assault (all types) figured among the first five specific causes of arrest, disorderly conduct usually topping the list (see table 5). Even in years that purportedly indicated a stable pattern of arrests—for example, 1913, 1927, 1929, and 1932—there were nevertheless unusually high rates of murder, homicide, and/or suicide. This seems to confirm the elevated levels of social violence that were being officially registered and criminalized.

Nevertheless, the prominent place occupied by gambling and violations of sanitary laws during the selected years also reflects the interdiction of some of the more important economic subsistence activities of the "native" majorities. Among them were: illicit card and dice games, buying and selling numbers in the underground lottery, preparing and selling noninspected pork, selling watered milk, manufacturing clandestine rum, staging cockfights in unlicensed pits, and so on. Much the same could be said during this first half-century about the place occupied by such crimes as theft (all types), burglary, and smuggling, albeit to a lesser degree.

Using the arrest figures available (with the exception of the numbers for 1899), it seems that the rates of arrest for disorderly conduct, fighting, assault (all types), arms violations, murder, etc., are higher than the rates for gambling, theft, burglary, robbery, smuggling, and so on (see table 4). Even though this runs counter to some of the observations of the day,[16] there is one notable exception in this regard, namely, Miguel Meléndez Muñoz. In 1948, Meléndez Muñoz underscored this very point: "Crime occurs, then as now, more against [*individual*] *persons* than against *property*. Its rising development started after the First World War and right in the midst of the Prohibition."[17]

This proportional distribution between the two general categories of illegalized popular behavior should not be all that odd given that one of the definitive features of the entire period was the uneven collapse of the noncapitalist forms of labor exploitation intertwined with the large-scale and irregular implantation of capitalist relations within a colonial context. The contradictory articulation of both forms of surplus extraction still relied mostly on the productive capacities (extensive or intensive) of the laboring classes rather than on their consumption capabilities and potential. Neither of these forms of surplus extraction fully controlled at this time what Spitzer calls "the social context which surrounds and conditions all economic activity."[18]

Consequently, the official methods of social control and the conditions of existence of the laboring classes that had characterized the nineteenth century intermingled with the ascendant methods of the early half of the twentieth century. Land rent combined with starvation and peasant-squatter's labor contracts combined with absolute surplus-value extraction. Personalized and localized police coercion in the haciendas combined with police repression in the dockyards, in the company towns of the sugar plantations and in the tobacco-trust strongholds. The rural-patriarchical and centuries-old sign systems that reticulated everyday meanings and material culture combined with Church-based and urban-professional but noncapitalist traditions of monitoring and social custody. Both forms and traditions, in turn, combined with the newer, "softer," capitalist regulatory systems: public schools, government health campaigns, social work, and so on.

The proportional distribution of the categories of transgressive behavior would seem to be associated with the hybrid character of the entire first half of this century. In this sense, the first half of the twentieth century appeared to be only *a direct continuation* of the nineteenth century. Yet, in longer historical perspective, these first forty-nine years appear to have constituted *a decisive break* with the preceding ninety-eight years. In the end, the twentieth century did not inherit the nineteenth any more than the nineteenth century was the prefiguration of the twentieth. The entire 1898–1947 period seems to correspond to what Foucault identified as "an unstable assemblage of faults, fissures, and heterogeneous layers that threaten the fragile inheritor from within and from underneath."[19] In these "faults, fissures, and heterogenous layers" one may find the traces of continuity and rupture that materialized at this time, even as their inherent instability defeats any totalizing and definitive explanation that would completely encompass the phenomenon being made-to-appear-again (that is, re-presented) through historical analysis. What we are left with, therefore, is an approximation . . . and a contested one, at that: the disputed representation of disputed representations.

The subaltern subjects that were produced under such conditions also embodied similar hybridities. The subaltern subjects of the implantation and development of U.S. capitalism in Puerto Rico were both a structural premise and an effect of this economic transformation. The subaltern subjects of the North American "civilizing mission" could someday be "educated . . . to the full stature of American manhood, and then crown[ed] . . . with the glory of American citizenship."[20] And yet, synchronously, the same subaltern subjects would still be seen forty years later by Theodore Roosevelt, Jr. as "fundamentally different" from "their" fellow U.S. citizens (p. 115). The subaltern subjects of law and order, whose "unchained masses . . . [of a] mob turned loose on society" could create a rural "Saturnalia of crime . . . [and] reign of terror," according to General Davis, were read as a response to the hideous past of "Spanish rule."[21] But the same subjects were scientifically diagnosed fifty years later in terms of the future: namely, as what José C. Rosario had called "one of the labor pains; of the birth of urban expansion, which is the delivery of progress."[22]

Between 1898 and 1947, then, what seems to have emerged was a very complex and conflictive intersection of mechanisms and subject formations that were supposed to be substituting each other but never completely did so. What did this have to do with whether the popular illegalities tended more toward the disruption of civil order, including social violence, or toward violations of property laws? For much of this period what ensued was a contradictory conflation of regulatory technologies, marking the demarcation between two distinct historical eras. These eras are analogous to what Foucault has examined in a different setting and period (without suggesting to have seen in eighteenth-century France the future of the Caribbean). One of the fundamental requirements of these emergent forms was "the growth in the apparatus of production, which was becoming more and more extended and complex," and since this apparatus was also "becoming more costly . . . its profitability had to be increased."[23] According to Foucault, the formation of the "disciplinary methods corresponded to these two processes, or rather, no doubt, to the new need to adjust their correlation" (ibid.)

Seen in totality, the noncapitalist forms of domination, public administration, and social instruction in the Island could not meet this need, being impeded from performing such systemic regulatory functions "by the irregular and inadequate extension of their network, by their often conflicting functioning, but above all by the 'costly' nature of the power that was exercised in them" (ibid.).

The limitations of the older regimes of accumulation of wealth and of the accumulation of "men" were translated as a question of cost and efficiency. The similarity here is with those phenomena that in the colonized context were registered as corruption, excessive force, insufficiently focused force, and so on. This type of social control in Puerto Rico proved too costly for a number of reasons. On the one hand, "the resistance it encountered forced it into a cycle of perpetual reinforcement." On the other hand, "it proceeded essentially by levying (levying on money or products by royal, seigniorial, ecclesiastical taxation)." Such levying was deployed against persons or time "by *corvées* of press-ganging, by locking up or banishing vagabonds" (p. 219). The structural tension lay in the fact that the new regimes of accumulation operated under different structural principles.

> The development of the disciplines marks the appearance of elementary techniques belonging to a quite different economy: mechanisms of power which, instead of proceeding by deduction, are integrated into the productive efficiency and into the use of what it produces. For the old principle of "levying-violence," which governed the economy of power, the disciplines substitute the principle of "mildness-production-profit." (ibid.)

Puerto Rico's situation during the first half of this century is sufficiently analogous to what Foucault describes so as to be able to draw some comparisons. Chief among these were the eminently colonized circumstances that combined both noncapitalist and capitalist mechanisms of social discipline and labor regulation: the Island's social space and its "native" majorities expressed elements of both "eras" without being either. As Jean-Paul de Gaudemar[24] argues in a broader context, these were technologies of power and social relations that still depended mostly on physical coercion, on physical extortion, and on some use of force during this transition period. It would appear that the "native" laboring classes responded in kind.

This is what would explain, to some extent, the apparent preponderance of practices related in general to the disruption of civil order, and in particular to social violence, rather than to alternate, but illegalized, income activities among the colonized population. This would also partially explain the corresponding criminalization patterns. The primary contradiction seemed to materialize at the point in which the laboring classes and both forms of exploitation converged: "levying violence" and "a relationship of direct domination, including physical domination," and the social space in which both were being reproduced, legitimized, and represented.

The subaltern subjects of the popular illegalities constituted the focus of the multiple and imbricated economies of exploitation: capitalist and noncapitalist, manufacture-based and partially industrial, factory organized and putting-out system. Yet the same subjects became the simultaneous focus of diverse and overlapping punishment structures and discourses: regular and irregular, disciplinary and "levying violence," moral policing and physical extortion. Within the terms of each particular "era," none of these hybrid sets of economic patterns and punitive patterns made sense without the survival practices and resistances embodied by these subaltern subjects. The principal target of both these arrays of patterns was still the containment and representation of these subaltern subjects. All of these colonial[ist] forms of subjection summoned one another across the "native" bridge that connected them: namely, the subaltern subjects of the popular illegalities.

The "Porto Rican" of the "Porto Ricans"

As we have seen, the containment and representation of these "native" popular illegalities was increasingly being executed by some of the "natives" themselves. This not only refers to the role of various sectors of the Island's population as being, literally, the foot soldiers of this punitive crusade. I am mainly describing the rising prominence of the privileged Creoles in designing, elaborating on, and expanding the colonialist manichean allegories that patterned most Puerto Ricans as "Porto Ricans": as the codification critically examined by Said in terms of objects "in need of corrective study by the West."[25]

The invention of "Porto Rico," like the creation of the "Orient," meant that the Island became an object of North American colonialist knowledge. This, of course, could not be limited to ineffectual and—literally—unproductive intellectual speculation because the possession of such knowledge could not be separated from the ability to obtain it. For "Porto Rico" to emerge from the historical and geographical vacuum, it had to be constructed at the intersection of U.S. capitalist-colonial knowledge and power: it had to be physically and spatially accessible to the power relations and surveillance mechanisms of the new colonizers. In a manner similar to that of European Orientalism, the new and hegemonic colonial discourses in the Caribbean determined that

> The object of such knowledge is inherently vulnerable to scrutiny; this object is a "fact" which, if it develops, changes, or otherwise transforms itself . . . , nevertheless is fundamentally and ontologically stable. To have such knowledge of such a thing is to dominate it, to have authority over it. And authority here means for "us" to deny autonomy to "it" . . . since we know it and it exists, in a sense, as we know it. (p. 32)

North American knowledge of "Porto Rico" *was* "Porto Rico" for the U.S. colonizers. This meant being able to control its population for the purpose of advancing the colonial-capitalist project, which included anticipating, producing, and regulating any disorders that promoted instability within the new regime. "Porto Rico," like the "Orient," was "viewed as if framed by the classroom, the criminal court, the prison, the illustrated manual" (p. 41).

The author-functions of this process of "framing" were more frequently being assumed by other "Porto Ricans," the ones who aspired to be not Other but Self with respect to the colonizer, either as juridical equals under U.S. jurisdiction or as juridical equals in the international arena. The purpose of such colonial mimicry was not being the hirelings or minions of the colonialists in the construction, preservation, and policing of the colonial social order. Any mere "native" could and did do that. Rather, the crowning achievement of this would be the recognition (by the colonialists, by the "native" majorities, and by themselves) of propertied and educated "native" subjects as having colonialist or para-colonialist agency. The road to such accomplishments, again borrowing from JanMohammed's text, meant having the privileged Creoles "be inducted . . . to fulfill the author-function of the colonialist writer."[26]

Such induction into colonialist author-functions does not mainly refer to the much discussed process of assimilation on the part of colonized intelligentsia.[27] Instead, it alludes to the propensity among most colonized propertied and educated classes to structure their juridico-political and signifying practices by recognizing themselves within the West and operating on the basis of such an acknowledgment. This interpellation operated even in the case of those "native" intellectuals who were anticolonialist. This is one of the most overlooked legacies of the first half-century of U.S. colonialism: the celerity with which even the anticolonialist intellectuals were textually and culturally recruited into these author-functions.

Colonialism reproduces a cultural consensus whereby broad sectors of the colonized population, particularly the literate and property-owning "native" classes of the colony, actively participate in the sign systems that constitute the various oppressed groups as subordinate: class exploitation (individual or collective), racism, paternalism, machismo, heterosexism, and so on. These are the structural trenches where colonial-capitalist relations are perpetually dug in, this being the site from which all possible expressions of reform, "home rule," neocolonial independence, and even anti-imperialism can be negotiated. As Ashis Nandy has observed in the case of colonial and neocolonial India,

> When such a cultural consensus grows, the main threat to the colonizers is bound to become the latent fear that the colonized will reject the consensus and, instead, of trying to redeem their "masculinity" by becoming counterplayers of the rulers according to the established rules, will discover an alternative frame of reference within which the oppressed do not seem weak, degraded and distorted men trying to break the monopoly of the rulers on a fixed quantity of machismo.[28]

Such is the insidiousness of Westernization and of colonialism.

The propertied and educated Creoles of the early twentieth century, of course, were not aware of this, nor could they have been.[29] They took a different road by trying to confirm that in fact they did have a history of their own and that, like the North American colonizers, their "contemporary ancestors" were also the laboring poor of the Island. To again use Said's (p. 207) terminology, by textually producing the "backward, degenerate, uncivilized, . . . delinquent" inferiority of the "native" impoverished majorities, the colonized upper stratum attempted to show that, while they had a specular reference point, a history, they presently shared absolutely nothing with most "Porto Ricans." The Creole Jünkers, intelligentsia, bureaucrats, bourgeoisie, and others, tried to demonstrate that they had nothing "in common . . . [with a contemporary] identity best described as lamentably alien" (ibid.), even as they "turned to [this laboring-poor identity] as they did to their children."[30] By being able to "see through, analyze"[31] their own kind in terms of their role in the reproduction of these colonialist discourses on crime and disorder, the "Porto Rican" propertied/educated classes became juridically and chronologically alien unto their kind in an effort to re-locate and imaginatively locate themselves inside the definitive boundaries of the law and (Western) History.

Accordingly, they could perhaps demonstrate (to the colonized laboring poor, to the U.S. colonialists, and to themselves) that they belonged to an-other kind. They could perhaps show that they belonged to a breed which *almost* possessed, what Torgovnick has called, "a Euro-American past."[32] Unfortunately for these Creoles, the only claim some of them could make to a past "so long gone that one could find no trace of it in Western spaces" (ibid.) was an Iberian past, not an Anglo-Saxon one. In spite of this, the "Porto Rican" upper stratum persisted in their efforts to establish that they belonged to a breed which, if not quite the adult/manly colonialist, was at least not as subjected, not as feminized, not as infantilized as most of the Island's transgressive and allegedly backward inhabitants.

True, the subaltern subjects were eventually constituted as being in need of subjection, with the privileged "natives" playing an increasingly greater role in this process of containment and representation. With the expanding author-functions and regulatory practices of the educated and propertied Creoles, the subaltern subjects of difference did in fact materialize. The social dichotomization mobilized by U.S. colonial-capitalism, with the aid of more and more Creole lieutenants, did fabricate these dispossessed subjects. But the majorities that made up these "subject people" were perennially not-quite constructed, and never with certainty, never quietly. In this sense (borrowing once more from Bhabha), the subaltern subjects in Puerto Rico both "intensifie[d] surveillance, and pose[d] an immanent threat to . . . 'normalized' knowledges and disciplinary powers" (p. 126).

NOTES

Chapter 1

1. Stuart Hall, "Signification, Representation, Ideology: Althusser and the Post-Structuralist Debates," *Critical Studies in Mass Communication,* 2: 2 (June, 1985): 102–103.

2. Michel Foucault, *Discipline and Punish: The Birth of the Prison* (New York: Vintage Books, 1977), 170, 194, 217.

3. Michel Foucault, "The Subject of Power," in *Michel Foucault: Beyond Structuralism and Hermeneutics,* edited by Hubert Dreyfus and Paul Rabinow (Chicago: The University of Chicago Press, 1983), 212.

4. I agree with this aspect of Spivak's critique of Foucault and Deleuze. See Gayatri Chakravorty Spivak, "Can the Subaltern Speak?" in *Marxism and the Interpretation of Culture,* edited by Cary Nelson and Lawrence Grossberg (Urbana: University of Illinois Press, 1988), 271–272, 280.

5. See Frantz Fanon, *Black Skin, White Masks* (New York: Grove Press, 1967), 109–140; Albert Memmi, *The Colonizer and the Colonized* (Boston: Beacon Press, 1970), 89, 91; Octave Mannoni, *Prospero and Caliban: The Psychology of Colonization* (Ann Arbor: The University of Michigan Press, 1990), 17.

6. Edward Said, *Orientalism* (New York: Vintage Books, 1979), 207.

7. My own previous work is reduced, oftentimes, to such "great narrative of the modes of production" and its corollary "narrative of the transition from feudalism to capitalism." See, for example, Kelvin Santiago, "Algunos aspectos de la integración de Puerto Rico al interior del Estado metropolitano," *Revista de Ciencias Sociales,* XXIII: 3–4 (July–December, 1981): 297–347; Kelvin Santiago, "El Puerto Rico del siglo XIX: apuntes para su análisis," *Revista de Ciencias Sociales: Hómines,* VI: 1–2 (January–December, 1981): 7–23.

8. Gayatri Chakravorty Spivak, "Subaltern Studies: Deconstructing Historiography," in *In Other Worlds: Essays in Cultural Politics,* edited by Gayatri Chakravorty Spivak (New York: Routledge, 1988), 197.

9. Joan Scott, "Gender: A Useful Category for Historical Analysis," in *Coming to Terms: Feminism, Theory, Politics* edited by Elizabeth Weed (New York: Routledge, 1989), 83.

10. See Samir Amin, *Eurocentrism* (New York: Monthly Review Press, 1989).

11. Ashis Nandy, *The Intimate Enemy: Loss and Recovery of Self Under Colonialism* (Delhi: Oxford University Press, 1989), xii.

12. Bill Ashcroft, Gareth Griffiths, and Helen Tiffin, *The Empire Writes Back: Theory and Practice in Post-colonial Literatures* (New York: Routledge, 1989), 2.

13. Amin, *Eurocentrism,* 98–99.

14. Trinh T. Minh-ha, *Woman, Native, Other: Writing Postcoloniality and Feminism* (Bloomington: Indiana University Press, 1989), 54.

15. The dispute over the legitimacy of this or that European lineage has marked what Roberto Fernández Retamar—following José Martí—has called the European Americans. See Roberto Fernández Retamar, *Caliban and Other Essays* (Minneapolis: University of Minnesota Press, 1989), 21–36. In Latin America and the Spanish-speaking Caribbean, such conflicts hark back to the social differences between Europeans born in Spain and Spaniards born in the overseas colonies. Subsequent shifts in hemispheric hegemony further complicated such claims to a "civilized" heritage: from Spain to Great Britain and from both to the United States of America. During the 1898–1947 period, prominent Latin American writers—such as the Uruguayan José Francisco Rodó (in *Ariel*) and the Puerto Rican Antonio Pedreira (in *Insularismo*)—denounced as major irony the ways in which European North Americans called into question the Western birthright of Europeans from Central, Southern, and Caribbean America.

16. I realize that referring, for example, to a "colonial intellectual" is *grammatically* less awkward for many readers than using the term "colonized intellectual." However, for me the difference is *conceptual*: in this book, the white/North-American social scientist and his/her Puerto Rican counterpart are both colonial intellectuals, while only the latter is a colonized intellectual.

17. Jean-Paul Sartre, "Preface," in Frantz Fanon, *The Wretched of the Earth* (New York: Grove Press, 1968), 7.

18. In addition to the already cited essays by Gayatri Chakravorty Spivak, see Arcadio Díaz Quiñones, "Recordando el futuro imaginario: la

escritura histórica en la década del treinta," *Sin Nombre,* XIV (April–June, 1984): 19; Derek Attridge, Geoff Bennington, and Robert Young (eds.), *Post-Structuralism and the Question of History* (New York: Cambridge University Press, 1990).

19. Denise Reiley, *"Am I That Name?" Feminism and the Category of "Women" in History* (Minneapolis: Minnesota University Press, 1988), 2–5.

20. Michel Foucault, "Truth and Power," in *Power/Knowledge,* edited by Colin Gordon (New York: Pantheon, 1980), 133.

21. Carroll Smith-Rosenberg, "The Body Politic," in *Coming to Terms,* 101.

22. Louis Althusser, "Ideology and Ideological State Apparatuses," in *Lenin and Philosophy and Other Essays* (London: New Left Books, 1971), 163.

23. Diane Macdonell, *Theories of Discourse: An Introduction* (London: Basil Blackwell, 1986), 66.

24. Janet Abu-Lughod, "On the Remaking of History: How to Reinvent the Past," in *Remaking History,* edited by Barbara Kruger and Phil Mariani (Seattle: Bay Press, 1989), 112, emphasis in the original.

25. A number of critical sociologists and social historians have recently reached similar conclusions. See, for example, Drew Humphries and Martin Greenberg, "Social Control and Social Formation: A Marxian Analysis," in *Toward a General Theory of Social Control: Vol. 2, Selected Problems,* edited by Donald Black (Orlando: Academic Press, 1984), 171–208; Stanley Cohen, *Visions of Social Control* (Oxford: Polity Press, 1985); Michael Ignatieff, "State, Civil Society, and Total Institutions: A Critique of Recent Social Histories of Punishment," in *Social Control and the State,* edited by Stanley Cohen and Andrew Scull (London: Basil Blackwell, 1985), 75–105.

26. Steven Spitzer, "Notes Toward a Theory of Punishment and Social Change," in *Research in Law and Sociology,* II (1979): 224–225. Over the course of the past two and a half decades, the available literature produced on the relationship between criminalization, capitalist transition, and/or economic development has been remarkably extensive, covering an exceptionally broad range of historical cases. Unfortunately, the overwhelming majority of these studies have dealt only with Europe or North America. In addition to the sources mentioned in the previous endnote, see, for example, John Tobias, *Crime and Industrial Society in the Nineteenth Century* (New York: Shocken Books, 1968); Louis Chevalier, *Laboring Classes and Dangerous Classes in Paris During the First Half of the Nineteenth Century* (Princeton: Princeton University Press, 1973); Eric Monkkonen, *The Dangerous Class: Crime and Poverty in Columbus, Ohio,*

1860–1885 (Cambridge, Mass.: Harvard University Press, 1975); Douglass Hay, Peter Linebaugh, and E.P. Thompson, (eds.), *Albion's Fatal Tree: Crime and Society in Eighteenth-Century England* (New York: Pantheon Books, 1975); E.P. Thompson, *Whigs and Hunters: Origins of the Black Act* (New York: Pantheon Books, 1975); Charles Tilly, Louise Tilly, and Richard Tilly, *The Rebellious Century, 1830–1930* (Cambridge, Mass.: Harvard University Press, 1975); Howard Zehr, *Crime and the Development of Modern Society: Patterns of Criminality in Nineteenth-Century Germany and France* (London: Crown Helen/Rowan and Littlefield, 1976); Jan Smith, "Violence, Property Rights, and Economic Growth in Pre-Industrial Europe," *Research in Law and Sociology*, III (1980): 87–106; V.A.C. Gatrell, Bruce Lenman, and Geofrey Parker (eds.), *Crime and the Law: The Social History of Crime in Western Europe since 1500* (London: Europa Publishers, 1980); Dario Melossi and Massimo Pavarini, *The Prison and the Factory: The Origins of the Penitentiary System* (Totowa, New Jersey: Barnes and Noble Books, 1980). The most important precursor of much of this research was, of course, Georg Rusche's and Otto Kirchheimer's *Punishment and Social Structure*, published in 1939.

27. The term "popular illegalities" is used here in the Foucaultian sense. See Foucault, *Discipline and Punish*, 257–292.

28. Consequently, there was an obvious discontinuity between the structural requirement that capital had regarding these specific "methods for administering the accumulation of men" and the types of criminal-justice mechanisms/discourses that were in fact developed. As Foucault correctly observed in the case of eighteenth- and nineteenth-century France, these are two phenomenons that historically cannot be separated. However enormous the contradictions and complexities involved, these two phenomenons were two aspects of one and the same process. It must be kept in mind that the corresponding distinction is purely a methodological abstraction.

29. Deborah P. Britzman, *Practice Makes Practice: A Critical Study of Learning to Teach* (Albany: State University of New York Press, 1991), 13.

30. Ranajit Guha, *Elementary Aspects of Peasant Insurgency in Colonial India* (Delhi: Oxford University Press, 1983), 15.

31. Ranajit Guha, "The Prose of Counter-Insurgency," in *Selected Subaltern Studies*, edited by Ranajit Guha and Gayatri Chakravorty Spivak (New York: Oxford University Press, 1988), 57.

32. Martha Knisey Huggins, *From Slavery to Vagrancy in Brazil: Crime and Social Control in the Third World* (New Brunswick, New Jersey: Rutgers University Press, 1985), 55.

33. The category of *social violence* is used here as synonymous with

those individual or group expressions of physical force, or the implied threats of such force, that emanate from or arise within the dispossessed masses that make up the majority of the population. This is to distinguish such violence from the use/threat of physical coercion or harm that emanates from the State apparatuses and/or from the institutional mechanisms of large property in general and from capital in particular.

Chapter 2

1. Carroll Smith-Rosenberg, "The Body Politic," in *Coming to Terms: Feminism, Theory, Politics*, edited by Elizabeth Weed (New York: Routledge, 1989), 101.

2. I tend to agree with the argument Foner provides to demonstrate why this war has historically been misnamed: the existing nomenclature erroneously centers the U.S. and Spain as the principal and original antagonists. See Philip Foner, *La guerra hispano/cubana/americana y el nacimiento del imperialismo norteamericano, 2 Vols.* (Madrid: Akal Editores, 1975).

3. However, the first such restructuring took place between 1788 and 1898 when the overwhelmingly non-capitalist exploitation of most of the Island's inhabitants started being partially and very contradictorily promoted by the Spanish Crown in order to transform the Island into a self-sustaining exporter of agricultural products, primarily sugar and coffee. See History Task Force, *Labor Migration Under Capitalism: The Puerto Rican Experience* (New York: Monthly Review Press, 1979), 67–92; Angel Quintero Rivera, "La clase obrera y el proceso político en Puerto Rico–I," *Revista de Ciencias Sociales*, 18: 1–2 (March–June, 1974): 145–200; Francisco Scarano, *Sugar and Slavery in Puerto Rico: The Plantation Economy of Ponce, 1800–1850* (Madison, Wisconsin: The University of Wisconsin Press, 1984). The mostly capitalist, dispossession process did not crystallize until immediately after the U.S. invasion; albeit, in retrospect, it could be said that the road for this process had been unwittingly paved during the previous quarter-century.

4. Frank Bonilla and Ricardo Campos, "Imperialist Initiatives and the Puerto Rican Worker: From Foraker to Reagan," *Contemporary Marxism*, 5 (Summer, 1982): 4–5.

5. See Jordi Maluquer de Motes, "El mercado colonial antillano en el siglo XIX," in *Agricultura, comercio nacional y crecimiento económico en la España contemporánea*, edited by Jordi Nadal and Tortella (Barcelona: Editorial Ariel, 1974), 342–344; Jordi Nadal, *El fracaso de la revolución industrial en España, 1814–1913* (Barcelona: Editorial Ariel, 1975); Manuel Tuñón de Lara, *La España del siglo XIX, vol. 2* (Barcelona: Editorial Laia, 1977), 56–66.

6. See Rudolf Hilferding, *El capital financiero* (Madrid: Editorial Tecnos, 1973), 263–264, 354–355, 370; Nikolai Bukharin, *La economía mundial y el imperialismo* (Córdoba: Cuadernos de Pasado y Presente no. 21, 1973), 99–100, 107–108, 133–134.

7. Quoted in Claude G. Bowers, *Beveridge and the Progressive Era* (New York: Praeger Publishers, 1932), 76.

8. See Félix Córdova, "Algunos aspectos de la penetración capitalista en Puerto Rico," *Punto Inicial*, 2 (December, 1976): 21; History Task Force, *Labor Migration*, 93; Rick Seltzer, "An Analysis of the Empirical Evidence on the Origins of American Imperialism," *Review of Radical Political Economy*, 11: 4 (Winter, 1979): 102–111.

9. See Harold Faulkner, *Economic History of the United States* (New York: MacMillan Company, 1928), 251; Bukharin, *La economía mundial*, 127. For a brief but fairly accurate description of the differences between this form of expansionism and the character of previous U.S. territorial expansion, see, Oscar Pino Santos, *La oligarquía yanqui en Cuba* (México: Editorial Nueva Imagen, 1975), 15–18.

10. Harry H. Powers, "The War as a Suggestion of Manifest Destiny," *Annals of the American Academy of Political and Social Sciences*, 12 (September, 1898): 183–184.

11. Albert Memmi, *The Colonizer and the Colonized* (Boston: Beacon Press, 1970), 54.

12. See Thomas McCormick, "Insular Imperialism and the Open Door: The China Market and the Spanish-American War," *Pacific Historical Review*, 32 (May, 1963): 155; Ramiro Guerra, *La expansión territorial de los Estados Unidos* (La Habana: Instituto Cubano del Libro, 1973), 305–309, 337; Foner, *La guerra, vol.1*, 376; Tulio Halperin Donghi, *Historia contemporánea de América Latina* (Madrid: Alianza Editorial, 1977), 282–283.

13. In Puerto Rico there were a few pockets of very localized and marginal armed resistance to the first contingents of U.S. troops that landed there in the summer of 1898. See Carmelo Rosario Natal, *Puerto Rico y la crisis de la Guerra Hispanoamericana* (Hato Rey: Ramallo Brothers Printing Company, 1975), 239; Fernando Picó, *1898: la guerra después de la guerra* (Río Piedras: Ediciones Huracán, 1987), 62–64. The threat to the arrival of U.S. troops in Cuba was potentially much more serious but extremely confusing. See Guerra, *La expansión territorial*, 380–389; Foner, *La guerra, vol.2*, 7–47.

14. See, for example, Robert T. Hill, "Porto Rico or Puerto Rico?" *The National Geographic Magazine*, 10: 12 (December, 1899): 516–517.

15. "Puerto Rico" literally means "rich port." This was the name

eventually adopted by the Spanish Crown to identify what the aboriginal Tainos had called "Borikén," literally: the Land of the Proud Lord.

16. Edward Said, *Orientalism* (New York: Vintage Books, 1979), 40, 42, 54.

17. V. Y. Mudimbe, *The Invention of Africa: Gnosis, Philosophy, and the Order of Knowledge* (Bloomington: Indiana University Press, 1988), 1–2.

18. Alfred T. Mahan, *Lessons of the War with Spain and other Articles* (Boston: Little, Brown, and Co., 1918), 28–29.

19. Mahan, *Lessons of the War with Spain,* 231–232.

20. Josiah Strong, *Expansion Under New World Conditions* (New York: n.p., 1900), 36.

21. W.A. Peffer, "A Republic in the Philippines," *North American Review,* 168 (1899): 319.

22. The general notion behind this is that the embryonic development of superior animals progresses up a sequence of phases embodied by the adult forms of inferior animals. In the case of human beings, this amounted to assuming that white children were physically and ontologically similar to adult "savages" who, in turn, were physically and ontologically similar to the Stone-Age ancestors of Western men. The biology and being of Western children implied that these infants had to repeat—literally: climb up—the lower rungs of the developmental ladder where the adult members of the "lesser races" were still irremediably stuck and where the primeval forbearers of Europe had once been. See Stephen Jay Gould, *Ontogeny and Phylogeny* (Cambridge, Mass.: Belknap Press of Harvard University Press, 1977). The gender analog of this gelled in the anatomical literature of the eighteenth century, concluding that white women were physically similar to the men of the "lesser races" and to white children in general. See Londa Schiebinger, "Skeletons in the Closet: The First Illustrations of the Female Skeleton in Eighteenth-Century Anatomy," in *The Making of the Modern Body,* edited by Catherine Gallagher and Thomas Laqueur (Berkeley: University of California Press, 1987), 63–72; Nancy Leys Stepan, "Race and Gender: The Role of Analogy in Science," in *Anatomy of Racism,* edited by David T. Goldberg (Minneapolis: University of Minnesota Press, 1990).

23. Quoted in Morrison Swift, *Imperialism and Liberty* (Los Angeles: n.p., 1899), 71.

24. Franklin H. Giddins, *Democracy and Empire, with Studies of their Psychological, Economic, and Moral Foundation* (New York: n.p., 1900), 243.

25. Quoted in Elting Morrison, ed. *The Letters of Theodore Roosevelt, Vol. V* (Cambridge, Mass.: Harvard University Press, 1952), 499.

26. Shiv Visvanathan, "From the Annals of the Laboratory State," *Alternatives*, 12: 1 (January, 1987): 41.

27. The Filipino insurgency was eventually brought to its knees primarily by the large-scale carnage carried out by the U.S. occupation forces: more than a quarter of a million dead "natives." See James H. Blount, *The American Occupation of the Philippines, 1898–1912* (Quezón-P.I.: Malaya Books, 1968); Renato Constantino, *A History of the Philippines* (New York: Monthly Review Press, 1975), 198–280.

28. See Faulkner, *Economic History*, 252, 253; Gavan Daws, *Shoals of Time: A History of the Hawaiian Islands* (Honolulu: The University of Hawaii, 1974), 289–293; Noel Kent, *Hawaii: Islands Under the Influence* (New York: Monthly Review Press, 1983), 65–68; Foner, *La guerra, vol.1*, 368, 371, 375, 377, 384; Halperin Donghi, *Historia contemporánea*, 290.

29. Alfred T. Mahan, *The Influence of Sea Power Upon History* (New York: Hill and Wong, 1968), 25.

30. See José Herrero, *La mitología del azucar: un ensayo de historia económica de Puerto Rico, 1900–1970* (Río Piedras: Centro de Estudios de la Realidad Puertorriqueña, Cuadernos de CEREP no. 5, 1971), 4–6; Halperin Donghi, *Historia contemporánea*, 308; Constantino, *History of the Philippines*, 290–307; Pino Santos, *La oligarquía yanqui*, 21–22; María D. Luque de Sánchez, *La ocupación norteamericana y la Ley Fóraker: la opinión pública puertorriqueña* (Río Piedras: Editorial Universitaria, 1980), 33–34; Ronald Takaki, *Pau Hana: Plantation Life and Labor in Hawaii* (Honolulu: University of Hawaii Press, 1983), 16–29; Kent, *Hawaii*, 56–72; Kelvin Santiago, "Concentración y centralización de la propiedad en Puerto Rico, 1898–1929," *Revista de Ciencias Sociales: Hómines*, 6: 2 (January–July, 1983): 5–14.

31. See Suzy Castor, *La ocupación norteamericana de Haití y sus consecuencias* (México: Siglo XXI Editores, 1971), 17–19, 22–27, 53–68; Guerra, *La expansión territorial*, 422–427, 429–431, 435–436; Pino Santos, *La oligarquía yanqui*, 30–32; Halperin Donghi, *Historia contemporánea*, 284, 290–294, 321–323, 345–346; William Paul Adams, ed. *Los Estados Unidos de América* (México: Siglo XXI, 1979), 247–248, 254–255; Lester Langley, *The Banana Wars: An Inner History of the American Empire, 1900–1934* (Lexington, Kentucky: University Press of Kentucky, 1983); Bruce J. Calder, *The Impact of Intervention: The Dominican Republic During the U.S. Occupation of 1916–1924* (Austin: University of Texas Press, 1988).

32. See Castor, *La ocupación norteamericana*, 28–35, 75–109; Carlos Vilas, "La política de la dominación en la República Dominicana," in *Impe-*

rialismo y clases sociales en el Caribe, edited by Carlos Vilas, Andre Corten, Mercedes Acosta, and Isis Duarte (Buenos Aires: Cuenca Ediciones, 1973), 163–165; Pino Santos, *La oligarquía yanqui,* 33–112; Halperin Donghi, *Historia contemporanea,* 293, 332, 342–343, 348; Jaime Wheelock Román, *Imperialismo y dictadura: crisis de una formación social* (México: Siglo XXI Editores, 1978), 124–140; Calder, *The Impact of Intervention,* 72–86.

33. One of the exceptions in this respect was the Virgin Islands, which the U.S. government obtained from Denmark in 1917.

34. See Justine and Bailey Diffie, *Porto Rico: A Broken Pledge* (New York: Vanguard Press, 1931), 45–62, 89–95, 107–119; Sol Luis Descartes, *Basic Statistics on Puerto Rico* (Washington, D.C.: Office of Puerto Rico, 1946), 50, 53–58; Harvey Perloff, *Puerto Rico's Economic Future: A Study in Planned Development* (Chicago: University of Chicago Press, 1950), 83–84, 136–137; Herrero, *La mitología;* Angel G. Quintero Rivera, "Background to the Emergence of Imperialist Capitalism in Puerto Rico," *Caribbean Studies,* 13:3 (October, 1973): 56–63; Andrés Ramos Mattei, "Riqueza azucarera: una fuente olvidada para nuestra historia," *Caribbean Studies,* 13: 3 (October, 1973): 103–109; Andrés Ramos Mattei, "Las inversiones norteamericanas en Puerto Rico y la Ley Fóraker, 1898–1900," *Caribbean Studies,* 14:3 (October, 1974): 53–69; Myriam Muñiz Varela, "Análisis del capital monopólico azucarero y el papel del estado en el proceso de transición al capitalismo: 1898–1920," *Revista de Ciencias Sociales,* 23: 3–4 (July–December, 1981): 443–496; Muriel McAvoy, "Early United States Investors in Puerto Rican Sugar," paper presented at the 14th Conference of Caribbean Historians, San Juan, Puerto Rico, April 16–21, 1982; James Dietz, *Economic History of Puerto Rico* (Princeton: Princeton University Press, 1986), 106–113; Angel Quintero Rivera, *Patricios y plebeyos: burgueses, hacendados, artesanos y obreros—las relaciones de clase en el Puerto Rico de cambio de siglo* (Río Piedras: Ediciones Huracán, 1988), 150–179.

35. E. Fernández García, ed. *El Libro de Puerto Rico* (San Juan: "El Libro Azul" Publishing Company, 1923), 580; Diffie, *Broken Pledge,* 112–116; Ramos Mattei, "Las inversiones norteamericanas": 57; Ramos Mattei, "Putting the Steam on Sugar," *Sunday San Juan Star Magazine* (October 4, 1979): 2–4; Santiago, "Concentración y centralización": 29–33.

36. Robert T. Hill, *Cuba and Porto Rico with the Other Islands of the West Indies* (New York: Century Co., 1898), 418–419.

37. Mary Louise Pratt, "Scratches On the Face of the Country; Or What Mr. Barrow Saw in the Land of the Bushmen," in *"Race," Writing, and Difference,* edited by Henry Louis Gates, Jr. (Chicago: The University of Chicago Press, 1986), 144, 146.

38. See Joseph L. Marcus, *Labor Conditions in Porto Rico* (Washington, D.C.: Department of Labor, Government Printing Office, 1919); Diffie, *Broken Pledge,* 180–184; Félix Mejías, *Condiciones de vida de las clases jor-*

naleras de Puerto Rico (San Juan: Universidad de Puerto Rico, 1946), 29–30.

39. See Walter E. Weyl, "Labor Conditions in Porto Rico," *Bulletin of the Bureau of Labor,* 61 (November, 1905): 729; Negociado del Trabajo, *Cuarto informe del Negociado del Trabajo* (San Juan: Bureau of Supplies, Printing, and Transportation, 1916), 7; Fred K. Fleagle, *Social Problems in Porto Rico* (Boston: D.C. Heath Co., 1917), 62–67; José E. Cuesta, *Puerto Rico, Past and Present: The Island After Thirty Years of American Rule* (New York: Eureka Print Co., 1929), 115–116; Victor Clark, ed., *Porto Rico and its Problems* (Washington, D.C.: Brookings Institution, 1930), 424–425; Garver and Fincher, *Unsolved*: 23; Perloff, *Puerto Rico's Economic Future,* 53; Eric R. Wolf, "San José: Subcultures of a 'Traditional' Coffee Municipality," in *The People of Puerto Rico,* edited by Julian H. Steward (Urbana: University of Illinois Press, 1956), 227, 234.

40. See, for example, Henry K. Wells, *The Modernization of Puerto Rico* (New Haven: Yale University Press, 1969), 92.

41. United States Bureau of the Census, *Thirteenth Census of the United States: Statistics for Porto Rico* (Washington, D.C.: Government Printing Office, 1913), 88.

42. Perloff, *Puerto Rico's Economic Future,* 102.

43. The empirical evidence in this regard is rather scarce. However, a cursory comparison of the names and locations of the main commercial agents and enterprises, both immediately before 1898 and in the following two decades, gives some idea of the modifications in this respect. See José Blanch, *Directorio comercial e industrial* (San Juan: Tipografía La Correspondencia, 1894); Cayetano Coll y Toste, *Reseña: el estado social, económico e industrial de la isla de Puerto Rico al tomar posesión de ella los Estados Unidos* (San Juan: Imprenta La Correspondencia, 1899), 372–375; Andrés Blanco Fernández, *España y Puerto Rico de 1820 a 1930* (San Juan: Tipografía Cantero Fernández,1930), 126–266.

44. See Clark, *Porto Rico,* 437–438; Diffie, *Broken Pledge,* 128–129.

45. For general descriptions and analyses of the measures traditionally studied within this context, see Edward J. Berbusse, *The United States and Puerto Rico, 1898–1900* (Chapel Hill: University of North Carolina Press, 1966); Herrero, *La mitología;* Angel Quintero Rivera, "La clase obrera y el proceso político de Puerto Rico–II: capitalismo y proletariado," *Revista de Ciencias Sociales,* 18: 3–4 (September–December, 1974): 61–110; Ramos Mattei, *Apuntes sobre la transición hacia el sistema de centrales en la industria azucarera: contabilidad de la Central Mercedita* (Río Piedras: Cuadernos de CEREP no. 4, 1974); Truman Clark, *Puerto Rico and the United States, 1917–1933* (Pittsburgh: University of Pittsburgh Press, 1975); Angel Quintero Rivera, *Conflictos de clase y política en Puerto Rico* (Río Piedras: Ediciones Huracán, 1976); Luque de Sánchez, *La Ley*

Fóraker; Kelvin Santiago, "Algunos aspectos de la integración de Puerto Rico al interior del Estado metropolitano," *Revista de Ciencias Sociales*, 23: 3–4 (July–December, 1981): 297–347.

46. Dario Melossi, "Strategies of Social Control in Capitalism: A Comment on Recent Work," *Contemporary Crises*, 4:4 (October, 1980): 382–383.

47. See Carlos Vilas, "La política de la dominación": 158–165; Agustín Cueva, *El desarrollo del capitalismo en América Latina* (México: Siglo XXI Editores, 1977), 79–164; James Dietz, "Imperialism and Underdevelopment: A Theoretical Perspective and Case Study of Puerto Rico," *The Review of Radical Political Economy*, 11: 4 (Winter, 1979): 23.

48. See, for example, H.A. Landsberger, ed. *Rural Protest: Peasant Movements and Social Change* (London: Macmillan, 1974); Stanley Diamond, "The Rule of Law Versus the Order of Custom," in *In Search of the Primitive: A Critique of Civilization* (New Brunswick: Transaction Books, 1974); Charles Van Onselen, *Chivaro: African Mine Labour in Southern Rhodesia, 1900–1933* (London: Pluto Press, 1976); Francis Snyder, *Capitalism and Legal Change: Transformation of an African Social Formation* (London: Academic Press, 1981); P. Underwood, *Disorder and Progress: Bandits, Police, and Mexican Development* (Lincoln, Nebraska: n.p., 1981); Walter Rodney, *The History of the Guyanese Working People, 1881–1905* (Kingston: Heinemann Educational Books, 1981); Eric R. Wolf, *Las luchas campesinas del siglo XX* (México: Siglo XXI Editores, 1982); Issa G. Shivji, "Semi-proletarian Labour and the Use of Penal Sanction in the Labour Law of Colonial Tanganyika, 1920–1938," in *Crime, Justice, and Underdevelopment*, edited Colin Sumner (London: Heinemann Publishers, 1982); Louise C. Sweet, "Inventing Crime: British Colonial Land Policy in Tanganyika," in ibid., 61–89; Martha Knisey Huggins, *From Slavery to Vagrancy in Brazil: Crime and Social Control in the Third World* (New Brunswick, New Jersey: Rutgers University Press, 1985); David Trotman, *Crime in Trinidad: Conflict and Control in a Plantation Society, 1838–1900* (Knoxville: The University of Tennessee Press, 1986); Donald Crummey, ed. *Banditry, Rebellion, and Social Protest in Africa* (London: James Currey Publishers, 1986); Richard W. Slatta, ed., *Bandidos: The Varieties of Latin American Banditry* (New York: Greenwodd Press, 1987).

49. See Eugenio Fernández Méndez, *Historia cultural de Puerto Rico, 1493–1968* (San Juan: Ediciones "El Cemí," 1970), 149–178, 214–223; Robert A. Manners and Julian H. Steward, "The Cutural Study of Contemporary Societies: Puerto Rico," in *Portrait of a Society: Readings in Puerto Rican Sociology*, edited by Eugenio Fernández Méndez (Río Piedras: University of Puerto Rico Press, 1972), 30; Angel Quintero Rivera, "La clase obrera y el proceso político en Puerto Rico–I," *Revista de Ciencias Sociales*, 18: 1–2 (March–June, 1974): 160–161; Rosa Marazzi, "El impacto de la inmigración a Puerto Rico, 1800–1830: análisis estadístico," ibid.: 8, 10, 39.

50. Much of the general information on this socio-cultural configuration came from the following sources: A. Hyatt Verrill, *Porto Rico Past and Present and San Domingo of Today* (New York: Dodd, Mead, and Company, 1919); Marcus, *Labor Conditions*; Francisco M. Zeno, *El obrero agrícola o de los campos* (San Juan: Tipografía La Correspondencia de Puerto Rico, 1922); Fernández García, *El Libro de Puerto Rico*; Helen V. Bary, *Child Welfare in the Insular Possessions of the United States, Part I: Porto Rico* (Washington, D.C.: U.S. Child Welfare Bureau, Government Printing Office, 1923); Knowlton Mixer, *Porto Rico and its Conditions* (New York: Macmillan Company, 1926); Antonio Rodríguez Vera, *Agrarismo por dentro y trabajo a domicilio* (San Juan: Tipografía La Democracia, 1929); Cuesta, *Puerto Rico Past and Present*; Clark, ed., *Porto Rico and its Problems*; José C. Rosario, *The Development of the Puerto Rican Jíbaro and His Present Attitude Toward Society* (Río Piedras: University of Puerto Rico, 1935); José C. Rosario and Justina Carrión, "Rebusca sociológica: una comunidad rural en la región cafetera de Puerto Rico," *University of Puerto Rico Summer School Review*, 15: 1 (1937): 8–15; José C. Rosario and Justina Carrión, "Rebusca sociológica: una comunidad rural en la zona cañera," *University of Puerto Rico Summer School Review*, 15: 5 (1937): 4–14; Turnbull White, *Puerto Rico and its People* (New York: Stokes Publishers, 1938); Charles C. Rogler, *Comerío: A Study of a Puerto Rican Town* (Lawrence: University of Kansas, 1940); Pablo Morales Otero and Manuel A. Pérez, *Health and Socio-Economic Studies in Puerto Rico* (San Juan: School of Tropical Medicine, 1941); Donald F. Griffin, *Minimum Decent Living Standards for Puerto Rico* (San Juan: National Resources Planning Board, Field Office, Region XI, July, 1942); Mejías, *Las clases jornaleras*; Lydia Roberts and Rosa L. Stefani, *Patterns of Living in Puerto Rican Families* (Río Piedras: University of Puerto Rico, 1949); Perloff, *Puerto Rico's Economic Future*; Robert A. Manners, "Tabara: Subcultures of a Tobacco and Mixed Crops Municipality," in *The People of Puerto Rico*, 93–170; Wolf, "San José"; Miguel Meléndez Muñoz, "Estado social del campesino puertorriqueño," in *Obras completas, vol. 1* (San Juan: Instituto de Cultura Puertorriqueña, 1963); Fernández Méndez, *Historia cultural*; Mayonne J. Stycos, "Family and Fertility in Puerto Rico," in *Portrait of a Society*, 81–92; Fernando Picó, *Los gallos peleados* (Río Piedras: Ediciones Huracán, 1983); Quintero Rivera, *Patricios y plebeyos*; Picó, *1898*; Andino Acevedo González, *¡Que tiempos aquellos!* (Río Piedras: Editorial Universitaria, 1989).

51. These observations do not place any value judgements on such a socio-cultural configuration. I am not counterpoising an allegedly indomitable and intrepid peasant majority to a supposedly confused and brittle proletarian minority. Neither am I advancing Enlightenment-based or nineteenth-century propagated romanticisms concerning the imagined virtues or inherent nobility of rural life and customs—as once again became popular within certain sectors of the Creole propertied and educated classes after 1898, particularly following the 1920s. Instead, my purpose is the critique of such idealizations—among other things—by

illustrating the constructed character, contradictions, limitations, and gains of *all* the colonized subjects, while simultaneously demonstrating the extensive degree to which the Island's laboring classes flowed into one another.

52. See Azel Ames, "Labor Conditions in Porto Rico," *Bulletin of Department of Labor,* 34 (May, 1901): 413–414; Diffie, *Broken Pledge,* 104; Manners, "Tabara," 110–111.

53. Of course, there was also a reduced number of small landowning peasants which, in varying degrees, merged with the sharecroppers and even with the rural wage laborers. Oftentimes, these were subsistence farmers or small farmers involved in some petty-commercial agriculture. This last pattern of labor was usually not enough to keep such farmers—and their families—above having to periodically/seasonally enter into land-rent and/or wage-labor contracts with the large landowners or any other employer. See Manners, "Tabara," 141–142; Wolf, "San José," 224–225. Even when grouped together with the middle and rich farmers and farm administrators, they were scarcely above ten percent of the population gainfully involved in agriculture during the 1898–1947 period. (See table 2) Here we must assume that the data on land tenure has been accurately measured. Additionally, we must remember that most of the "latifundios" were absentee-owned and therefore manager-run. In this context, then, we can extrapolate that at the time more than three fourths of this very heterogeneous statistical ensemble was composed of small to middle land-holding farmers whose rural property averaged, in size, about the same as those of tenant farmers (sharecroppers, etc.) (see table 6).

54. Fleagle, *Social Problems,* 61; Marcus, *Labor Conditions,* 32–33, 41; Clark, *Porto Rico and its Problems,* 14, 27–29, 504; Diffie, *Broken Pledge,* 181–182; Mejías, *Las clases jornaleras,* 27–28; Perloff, *Puerto Rico's Economic Future,* 146; Wolf, "San José," 227, 234; A.J. Jaffe and Lydia Fort de Ortiz, "The Human Resource: Puerto Rico's Working Force" in *Portrait of a Society,* 111–112; Quintero Rivera, "La clase obrera–II": 96.

55. See, for example, Carmen Diana Deere, "Rural Women's Subsistence Production in the Capitalist Periphery" in *Peasants and Proletarians,* edited by Robin Cohen, et al. (New York: Monthly Review Press, 1979), 133–148.

56. In this second case, see for example, Shivji, "Penal Sanctions in the Labour Law"; Huggins, *From Slavery to Vagrancy.*

57. See, for example, Quintero Rivera, *Conflictos de clase.*

58. Henry K. Carroll, *Report on the Island of Porto Rico; Its Population, Civil Government, Commerce, Industries, Productions, Roads, Tariff, and Currency, With Recommendations* (Washington, D.C.: U.S. Government Printing Office, 1899), 51.

59. See José C. Rosario and Justina Carrión, "Problemas sociales: el negro: Haití-Estados Unidos-Puerto Rico," *Boletín de la Universidad de Puerto Rico,* 10: 2 (December, 1939): 120–143; Mintz, "The Culture History of a Puerto Rican Sugar Cane Plantation: 1876–1949," in *Portrait of a Society,* 148, 150; Quintero Rivera, "La clase obrera–I"; Gervasio Garcia, *Primeros fermentos de organización obrera en Puerto Rico, 1873–1898* (Río Piedras: Cuadernos de CEREP no. 1, 1974); César Andreu Iglesias, *Memorias de Bernardo Vega* (Río Piedras: Ediciones Huracán, 1977); José Luis González, *El país de cuatro pisos y otros ensayos* (Río Piedras: Ediciones Huracán, 1980), 22–35; Quintero Rivera, *Patricios y plebeyos,* 69–80.

60. Determining their numbers depends a great deal on the racial taxonomy being used. In terms of the official/federal racial distribution, see: U.S. Bureau of the Census, *Fifteenth Census of the United States; Agriculture: Porto Rico* (Washington, D.C.: Government Printing Office, 1932), 170; U.S. Bureau of the Census, *Sixteenth Census of the United States; Puerto Rico; Bulletin no. 2: Characteristics of the Population* (Washington, D.C.: Government Printing Office, 1941), 8; U.S. Bureau of the Census, *Seventeenth Census of the United States; Printed Report no. 53: Puerto Rico* (Washington, D.C.: Government Printing Office, 1951), 107. It must be borne in mind that in Puerto Rico, as in most of the remainder of the Caribbean, the racial codification is much more complex and varied than in the U.S. mainland (where one is *either* white *or* non-white). Contrary to the North American case, in Puerto Rico there is a broad spectrum of gradations and of corresponding value judgements. This spectrum is delineated by the two poles represented by those who are perceived as "black" and those who are perceived as "white." This process relies more on immediate, physical appearance than on lineage; at the same time, all of these gradations are variously overdetermined by class identifications as well as by levels of education. See, for example, Eduardo Seda Bonilla, "Social Structure and Race Relations," *Social Forces,* 40: 2 (December, 1961): 141–148; Charles Rogler, "The Role of Semantics in the Study of Race Distance in Puerto Rico," in *Portrait of a Society,* 49–55; Charles Rogler, "The Morality of Race Mixing in Puerto Rico," ibid., 57–64. None of this is meant to imply—as it is often mythologized—that traditional racial codes in the Island are supposedly more benign or any less problematic than those in the United States. They are simply different. Unfortunately, the corresponding analysis falls outside the reach of the present inquiry.

61. See Clark, *Porto Rico and its Problems,* 43–50; Wolf, "San José," 240, 257–258; Angel G. Quintero Rivera, "Clases sociales e identidad nacional: notas sobre el desarrollo nacional puertorriqueño," in *Puerto Rico: identidad nacional y clases sociales (coloquio de Princeton)* (Río Piedras: Ediciones Huracán, 1979), 42–43.

62. See Bary, *Child Welfare*; Mixer, *Porto Rico and its Conditions,* 184–185; Samuel J. Crumbine, et al., *An Inquiry Into the Health, Nutritional, and Social Conditions in Porto Rico As They May Affect the Children*

(New York: American Child Health Association, 1930), 156–159; Clark, *Porto Rico and its Problems,* 39–50; José C. Rosario, *A Study of Illegitimacy and Dependent Children in Puerto Rico* (San Juan: Imprenta Venezuela, 1933); Rogler, *Comerío;* Jacob Crane, "La vivienda obrera en Puerto Rico," *Revista Internacional del Trabajo,* 29: 6 (June, 1944): 1–26; Manners, "Tabara," 126–140; Wolf, "San José," 257–259; Elena Padilla Seda, "Nocorá: The Subculture of Workers on a Government Owned Sugar Plantation," in *The People of Puerto Rico,* 265–313; Sidney Mintz, "Cañamelar: The Subculture of a Rural Plantation Proletariat," in ibid., 314–417; Kathleen Wolf, "Growing Up and its Price in Three Puerto Rican Subcultures," in *Portrait of a Society,* 250–259; Sidney Mintz, "The Folk-Urban Continuum and the Rural Proletarian," ibid., 155–166; Quintero Rivera, *Patricios y plebeyos,* 125–126.

63. See Clark, *Porto Rico and its Problems,* 45–46; Manners, "Tabara," 102, 132–133; Wolf, "San José," 244, 247, 258–259.

64. Mintz, "Folk-Urban Continuum."

65. Luis M. Díaz Soler, *Historia de la esclavitud negra en Puerto Rico* (Río Piedras: Editorial Universitaria, 1970), 152–163; Laird Bergard, *Coffee and the Growth of Agrarian Capitalism in Nineteenth-Century Puerto Rico* (Princeton: Princeton University Press, 1983), 54–59; Francisco Scarano, *Sugar and Slavery in Puerto Rico: The Plantation Economy of Ponce, 1800–1850* (Madison, Wisconsin: The University of Wisconsin Press, 1984), 28–34.

66. See Fray Iñigo Abbad y Lasierra, *Historia geográfica, civil y natural de la isla de San Juan Bautista de Puerto Rico: nueva edición anotada en la parte histórica y continuada en la estadística y económica por José Julián Acosta y Calbo* (San Juan: Imprenta y Librería de Acosta, 1866), 74; Cayetano Coll y Toste, ed. *Boletín Histórico de Puerto Rico, tomo 11* (San Juan: Tipografía Cantero Fernández, 1924), 127–161, 255–262; Alejandro Tapia y Rivera, *Mis memorias o Puerto Rico cómo lo encontré y cómo lo dejo* (New York: D. E. Laisne and Rossboro, Inc. 1928), 77–78, 95, 110–111; Rosario and Carrión, "El negro": 88–128; Díaz Soler, *Historia de la esclavitud,* 225–261.

67. See, for example, Scarano, *Sugar and Slavery,* 137–143.

68. Andrés Ramos Mattei, "La importación de trabajadores contratados para la industria azucarera puertorriqueña, 1860–1880," in *Imigración y clases sociales en el Puerto Rico del siglo XIX,* edited by Francisco Scarano (Río Piedras: Ediciones Huracán, 1981), 134–141.

69. For a thorough critique of this paradigm, see Isabelo Zenón Cruz, *Narciso descubre su trasero: el negro en la cultura puertorriqueña, vol. 1* (Humacao, Puerto Rico: Editorial Furidi, 1974).

70. Antonio Gramsci, *Selections from the Prison Notebooks* (New York: International Publishers, 1980), 324.

71. Leo S. Rowe, *The United States and Porto Rico* (New York: Longmans, Green, and Co. 1904), 103.

72. George W. Davis, *Report of Brigadier General George W. Davis U. S. V., On Civil Affairs of Porto Rico* (Washington, D.C.: Government Printing Office, 1900), 18.

73. See, for example, Clark, *Puerto Rico and the United States*, 13–14, 63; Juan Flores, *Insularismo e ideología burguesa en Antonio Pedreira* (La Habana: Casa de Las Americas, 1979), 49–57.

74. See Manners, "Tabara," 129; Wolf, "San José," 227, 238; Sidney Mintz, *Worker in the Cane: A Puerto Rican Life History* (New York: W.W. Norton and Company, 1974), 144–145; Picó, *Los gallos peleados*, 73–74.

75. Stan Steiner, *The Islands: The Worlds of Puerto Ricans* (New York: Harper and Row, 1974), 93.

76. See Fernández García, *El Libro de Puerto Rico*, 381–418; Cuesta, *Puerto Rico Past and Present*, 128–130; Clark, *Porto Rico and its Problems*, 72–89; Mejías, *Las clases jornaleras*, 183–188; Perloff, *Puerto Rico's Economic Future*, 214–216; Wolf, "San José," 258.

77. My maternal grandmother, for example, firmly placed the mountain peasant within an aphoristic bestiary whose members she had been warned against as a young girl growing up in an artisan and poor fishing community in the southeastern coast of the Island during the 1890s. This perspective crystallized in one of her often repeated sayings, which would roughly translate as "jíbaro, pigeon, and cat: three [very] ungrateful animals." As a child, I also remember listening to various adult relatives (who had grown up in poor-artisan urban settings) use the term "ara[d]o"—a noun, literally designating a "plough"—as an adjective meaning "stupid" and "dull-witted."

Chapter 3

1. All translations from Spanish to English and from Italian to English are mine unless otherwise indicated.

2. See Albert Memmi, *The Colonizer and the Colonized* (Boston: Beacon Press, 1970), 45–117; Karl Marx, *Capital, vol. 1* (New York: Vintage Books/Random House, 1977), 830–932; Ashis Nandy, *The Intimate Enemy: Loss and Recovery of Self Under Colonialism* (Delhi: Oxford University Press, 1989), 1–48.

3. Andrew Ure as quoted in Marx, *Capital*, 549.

4. Dario Melossi, "Strategies of Social Control in Capitalism: A Comment on Recent Work," *Contemporary Crises*, 4: 4 (October, 1980): 382–383.

5. Stuart Hall, "Signification, Representation, Ideology: Althusser and the Post-Structuralist Debates," *Critical Studies in Mass Communication*, 2: 2 (June, 1985): 102.

6. Jean-Paul de Gaudemar, "Preliminari per una genealogia delle forme di disciplina nel proceso di lavoro capitalistico," *Aut-Aut*, 167–168 (September–December, 1978): 226.

7. Steven Spitzer, "The Rationalization of Crime Control in Capitalist Society," in *Social Control and the State*, edited by Stanley Cohen and Andrew Scull (London: Basil Blackwell, 1985), 322–323, 324, emphasis in the original.

8. I am not partial to conspiracy theories, nor have I found anything that might warrant this sort of analytical contrivance.

9. Michel Foucault, *Discipline and Punish* (New York: Vintage Books, 1977), 30.

10. This was related, of course, to the fact that even by the late nineteenth century most of the Island's population still had direct access, not only to the fruits of overseas commerce—legal and, oftentimes, illegal—and other mostly prohibited sources of sustenance, but also to small plots of land. See Francisco del Valle Atiles, *El campesino puertorriqueño* (Tipografía J. González Font, 1887), 131; Salvador Brau, *Ensayos (disquisiciones sociológicas)* (Río Piedras: Editorial Edil, 1972), 33–38; Gervasio García, *Primeros fermentos de organización obrera en Puerto Rico, 1873–1898* (Río Piedras: Cuadernos de CEREP no. 1, 1974), 9; Fernando Picó, *Libertad y servidumbre en el Puerto Rico del siglo XIX* (Río Piedras: Ediciones Huracán, 1979), 104–105, 119; Fernando Picó, *Vivir en Caimito* (Río Piedras: Ediciones Huracán, 1988), 31–32, 155.

11. Albert G. Robinson, *The Porto Rico of Today* (New York: Charles Scribner's Sons, 1899), 161.

12. Robert T. Hill, *Cuba and Porto Rico With Other Islands of the West Indies* (New York: Century Co., 1898), 167.

13. C. Michelson and R. E. Pattison, "Robert E. Pattison Describes How Imperialism Has Made of Porto Rico a Land of Horror," *New York Journal*, 6: 534 (October 7, 1900): 49.

14. Just a year before (in March of 1899) though, the U.S. Insular Commission denounced as false all the reports circulating in the Island

about the incidence of starvation and about people dying of hunger. See U.S. Insular Commission, *Report of the U.S. Insular Commission to the Secretary of War Upon Investigations Made into the Civil Affairs of the Island of Porto Rico With Recommendations* (Washington, D.C.: U.S. War Department, Division of Customs and Insular Affairs, Government Printing Office, 1899), 7. However, in April of 1899 General Roy Stone publicly declared in one of the local newspapers that hunger was unequivocally quite widespread, particularly among the laborers in the coffee-growing zones of the Island's mountains. Cited in, Edward Berbusse, *The United States and Puerto Rico, 1898–1900* (Chapel Hill: University of North Carolina Press, 1966), 103. In August of 1899 the Island was pummeled by an exceptionally strong hurricane and the military authorities confirmed the difficulties involved in ascertaining the precise volume of the damage because significant portions of the poor majority of the populace had already been in a condition of borderline starvation during the first half of that year. See George W. Davis, *Report of Brigadier General George W. Davis on Civil Affairs of Porto Rico* (Washington, D.C.: Government Printing Office, 1900), 67–69, 133–136; George W. Davis, *Annual Report of the War Department for the Fiscal Year Ended June 30, 1900—Part 13: Report of the Military Governor of Porto Rico* (Washington, D.C.: Government Printing Office, 1902), 210–219, 455–466, 671–694; Berbusse, *The United States in Puerto Rico*, 104–105.

15. Both quotes are from Blanca Silvestrini, *Violencia y criminalidad en Puerto Rico (1898–1973): apuntes para un estudio de historia social* (Río Piedras: Editorial Universitaria, 1980), 37.

16. Azel Ames, "Labor Conditions in Porto Rico," *Bulletin of Department of Labor*, 34 (May, 1901): 385. Ames, however, misrecognizes the preceding circumstances when providing his own perception of social conditions in "Porto Rico" before 1898:

> . . . though the island is one of great resources and has a good record for thrift, there is reason to believe that from the earliest days of the Spanish occupation this condition of things as to the laboring classes has been only too prevalent—and at times worse, in some respects, than at present. (ibid.)

17. Fred K. Fleagle, *Social Problems in Porto Rico* (Boston: D.C. Heath, Co., 1917), 74.

18. Andino Acevedo González, *¡Que tiempos aquellos!* (Río Piedras: Editorial Universitaria, 1989), 141.

19. Arthur Yager, *Nineteenth Annual Report of the Governor of Porto Rico* (Washington, D.C.: Government Printing Office, 1919), 501.

20. Helen V. Bary, *Child Welfare in the Insular Possessions of the United States, Part I: Porto Rico* (Washington, D.C.: U.S. Child Welfare Bureau, Government Printing Office, 1923), 26.

21. Both of these circumstances were, in turn, tied to an entire spectrum of corollary health problems. For information on the dismal health conditions of the laboring classes during the first few decades of this century, see Vergne Castelo, *El paludismo en Puerto Rico* (San Juan: Tipografía Mercantil, 1914); Francisco M. Zeno, *El obrero agrícola o de los campos* (San Juan: Correspondencia de Puerto Rico, 1922); Bary, *Child Welfare*; Carmelo Honoré, *Problemas sociales* (San Juan: Negociado de Materiales, Imprenta y Transporte, 1925); Samuel J. Crumbine, et al., *An Inquiry Into the Health, Nutritional, and Social Conditions in Porto Rico As They May Affect Children* (New York: American Child Health Association, 1930); Antonio Fernós Isern and José Rodríguez Pastor, *Estudio de la mortalidad infantil en Puerto Rico* (San Juan: Departamento de Sanidad, Bureau of Supplies, Printing, and Transportation, 1930); W.C. Earl, "Malaria in Puerto Rico," *American Journal of Tropical Medicine*, 10 (1930): 207–230; W.C. Earl, "Malaria in Puerto Rico and its Relation to the Cultivation of Sugar Cane," *Southern Medical Journal*, 23 (1930): 449–453; Manuel A. Pérez, "Factors Contributing to a High Death Rate in Puerto Rico," *The Puerto Rican Journal of Public Health and Tropical Medicine*, 6: 4 (June, 1933): 421–462; E.B. Phelps and J. V. Dávila, "Diarrhea and Enteritis in Puerto Rico: Relation to Water Supplies," *Puerto Rico Review of Public Health and Tropical Medicine*, 5: 3 (April, 1933): 468–487; Bailey K. Ashford, *Soldier In Science* (New York: W. Morrow and Company, 1934); José Rodríguez Pastor, Pablo Morales Otero, and G.C. Payne, "Tuberculosis Surveys in Puerto Rico: A Study of a Coast and a Mountain Municipality," *Puerto Rico Journal of Public Health and Tropical Medicine*, 10: 4 (June, 1935): 451–479; Joseph W. Mountin, et al., "Illness and Medical Care in Puerto Rico," *Public Health Bulletin*, 257 (Washington, D.C., 1937): 19–29; Blanca Silvestrini, "The Impact of the U.S. Public Health Policy on Puerto Rico, 1898–1913," paper presented at the 14th Conference of Caribbean Historians, San Juan, Puerto Rico, April 16–21, 1982; Acevedo González, *¡Que tiempos aquellos!*, 148–155.

22. See Berbusse, *United States in Puerto Rico*, 189; Ramos Mattei, "Las inversiones norteamericanas en Puerto Rico y la Ley Fóraker, 1898–1900," *Caribbean Studies*, 14: 3 (October, 1974): 59–60; José G. del Valle, "Situación económica de Puerto Rico en 1899," in *Crónicas de Puerto Rico*, edited by Eugenio Fernández Méndez (Río Piedras: Editorial Universitaria, 1967), 565.

23. María Dolores Luque de Sánchez, *La ocupación norteamericana y la Ley Fóraker: la opinión pública puertorriqueña* (Río Piedras: Editorial Universitaria, 1980), 147–148, 151.

24. Raymond Crist, "Sugar Cane and Coffee in Puerto Rico: The Pauperization of the Jibaro, Land Monopoly, and Monoculture," *The American Journal of Sociology and Economics*, 7 (January–April–July, 1948): 181–182.

25. Negociado del Trabajo, *Segundo informe del Negociado del Trabajo* (San Juan: Bureau of Supplies, Printing, and Transportation, 1914), 25.

26. See Negociado del Trabajo, *Cuarto informe del Negociado del Trabajo* (San Juan: Bureau of Supplies, Printing, and Transportation, 1916), 7, 9; Joseph Marcus, *Labor Conditions in Porto Rico* (Washington, D.C.: Department of Labor, Government Printing Office, 1919), 19; Truman Clark, *Puerto Rico and the United States, 1917–1933* (Pittsburgh: University of Pittsburgh Press, 1975), 37–38, 106, 109–110, 118–119.

27. La Democracia, "Editorial," *La Democracia* (January 13, 1917): 4.

28. See, James Dietz, *Economic History of Puerto Rico* (Princeton: Princeton University Press, 1986), 130.

29. See U.S. Bureau of the Census, *Fifteenth Census of the United States; Agriculture: Porto Rico* (Washington, D.C.: Government Printing Office, 1932), 181–183; History Task Force, *Labor Migration Under Capitalism: The Puerto Rican Experience* (New York: Monthly Review Press, 1979), 107.

30. Knowlton Mixer, *Porto Rico and its Conditions* (New York: Macmillan Company, 1926), 172–173.

31. Asamblea Legislativa de Puerto Rico, *Primer informe de la comisión legislativa para investigar el malestar y desasosiego industrial y agrícola y que origina el desempleo en Puerto Rico* (San Juan: n.p., February 3, 1930), 61.

32. Nelson A. Miles, "The War With Spain," *North American Review*, 168: 510 (May–July, 1899): 133.

33. Some scholars of Puerto Rican history have in fact made such propositions regarding the unfulfilled promises of liberal political institutions. See, for example, Manuel Maldonado Denis, *Puerto Rico: una interpretación histórico-social* (México: Siglo XXI Editores, 1969), 57–59; Kal Wagenheim, *Puerto Rico: A Profile* (New York: Praeger, 1970), 63–64. I have not found the scrutiny of intentions very useful when carrying out social-historical/historical-sociological analyses primarily because intentions are apparently more germane to the study of isolated individuals. This is not to say that the examination of the social effects of particular practices (individual or institutional) is a no less contested enterprise, but it does seem to be more materially grounded—thus lending itself more readily to historicization.

34. Pratt, "Scratches On the Face of the Country; Or What Mr. Barrow Saw in the Land of the Bushmen," in *"Race," Writing, and Difference*, edited by Henry Louis Gates, Jr. (Chicago: The University of Chicago Press, 1986), 139–140.

35. Edward Said, *Orientalism* (New York: Vintage Books, 1979), 40, emphasis in the original.

36. Quoted in Claude G. Bowers, *Beveridge and the Progressive Era* (New York: Praeger Publishers, 1932), 68.

37. Theodore Roosevelt, *The Works of Theodore Roosevelt: The Strenuous Life* (n.p.: P.F. Collier & Son, Publishers, 1903 [?]), 11.

38. See George Fredrickson, *The Black Image in the White Mind: The Debate on Afro-American Character and Destiny, 1817–1914* (Middletown, Connecticut: Wesleyan University Press, 1971), 165–319; Herbert Shapiro, *White Violence, Black Response: From Reconstruction to Montgomery* (Amherst: The University of Massachusetts Press, 1987), 64–92; Nell Irvin Painter, *Standing at Armageddon: The United States, 1877–1919* (New York: W. W. Norton, 1987), 110–230; Ronald Takaki, *Iron Cages: Race and Culture in 19th-Century America* (New York: Oxford University Press, 1990), 148–279; Alexander Saxton, *The Rise and Fall of the White Republic: Class Politics and Mass Culture in Nineteenth-Century America* (London: Verso, 1990), 247–377. This phenomenon is, of course, not the exclusive province of white-U.S. nationalism. See Benedict Anderson, *Imagined Communities* (London: New Left Books, 1983), 137–139; Nandy, *The Intimate Enemy*, 11, 32–33; Etienne Balibar, "Paradoxes of Universality," in *Anatomy of Racism*, edited by David T. Goldberg (Minneapolis: University of Minnesota Press, 1990), 283–294.

39. See Gladys Jiménez-Muñoz, "Wanting Identities: Citizenship and Women's Rights in Puerto Rico, 1898–1929," paper presented at the XVI International Congress of the Latin American Studies Association, Washington, D.C., April 4–6, 1991.

40. *Congressional Record*, 56th Congress, 1st Session, vol. 33, (1900), 1946.

41. *Congressional Record*, 56th Congress, 1st Session, vol. 33, (1900), 3637.

42. Quoted by Frederic Coudert, "The Evolution of the Doctrine of Territorial Incorporation," *The American Law Review*, 60 (November–December, 1926): 824.

43. José A. Cabranes, *Citizenship and the Empire* (New Haven: Yale University Press, 1979), 96.

44. *Congressional Record*, 64th Congress, 2nd Session, (1917), 3008.

45. Quoted in Elting Morison, ed., *The Letters of Theodore Roosevelt, vol. 5* (Cambridge, Mass.: Harvard University Press, 1952), 501.

46. Gladys Jiménez-Muñoz, "Deconstructing Colonialist Discourses:

The Links Between the Women's Suffrage Movements in the United States and in Puerto Rico," paper presented at the Second Southern Conference on Women's History, Chapel Hill, North Carolina, June 7–8, 1991.

47. This was one of the common images within the internal normalizing discourses that centered white, male, middle-class respectability at this time. See, for example, Sander Gilman, *Difference and Pathology: Stereotypes of Sexuality, Race, and Madness* (Ithaca: Cornell University Press, 1985), 39–58; Georg Mosse, *Nationalism and Sexuality: Middle-Class Morality and Sexual Norms in Modern Europe* (Madison: Wisconsin University Press, 1985), 23–113; Takaki, *Iron Cages*, 148–154, 253–279.

48. Shiv Visvanathan, "From the Annals of the Laboratory State," *Alternatives,* 12: 1 (January, 1987): 41.

49. Christopher Miller, *Blank Darkness: Africanist Discourses in French* (Chicago: The University of Chicago Press, 1985), 44.

50. Josiah Strong, *Expansion Under New World Conditions* (New York: n.p., 1900), 289.

51. Elihu Root, *The Military and Colonial Policy of the United States: Addresses and Reports,* collected and edited by Robert Bacon and James Brown Scott (Cambridge, Mass.: Harvard University Press, 1916), 164–165.

52. It must be remembered that since at least the late eighteenth century, the Western propertied and educated classes held as common knowledge that "inferior" climates (such as the tropics) were detrimental to the emergence of "superior races," this being a major contributing factor to the backwardness of the "lesser races" and/or to the degeneration of Europeans who stayed there too long. See Thomas Gossett, *Race: The History of an Idea in America* (Dallas: Southern Methodist University Press, 1964), 330–332.

53. Milton G. Fowles, *Down in Porto Rico* (New York: n.p., 1906), 146.

54. See Kelvin Santiago, "Algunos aspectos de la integración de Puerto Rico al interior del Estado metropolitano," *Revista de Ciencias Sociales*, 23: 3–4 (July–December, 1981): 297–347.

55. In the case of the popular illegalities during the nineteenth century in Puerto Rico, see, for example, Cayetano Coll y Toste, ed., *Boletín Histórico de Puerto Rico, tomo 5* (San Juan: Tipografía Cantero Fernández, 1918), 22–23, 146–147; Cayetano Coll y Toste, ed., *Boletín Histórico de Puerto Rico, tomo 6* (1919), 242–248; Cayetano Coll y Toste, ed. *Boletín Histórico de Puerto Rico, tomo 11* (1924), 152, 272–273; Cayetano Coll y Toste, ed., *Boletín Histórico de Puerto Rico, tomo 12* (1925), 87–93; Luis M. Díaz Soler, *Historia de la esclavitud negra en Puerto Rico* (Río Piedras: Edi-

torial Universitaria, 1979), 207–224; Brau, *Ensayos,* 46–47, 56; Andrés Ramos Mattei, "La importación de trabajadores contratados para la industria azucarera puertorriqueña, 1860–1880," in *Inmigración y clases sociales en el Puerto Rico del siglo XIX* (Río Piedras: Ediciones Huracán, 1981), 135–139; Jesús Lalinde Abadía, *La administración española en el siglo XIX puertorriqueño* (Sevilla: Escuela de Estudios Hispanoamericanos, Universidad de Sevilla, 1980), 47–49; Guillermo Baralt, *Esclavos y rebeldes* (Río Piedras: Ediciones Huracán, 1981).

56. Fleagle, *Porto Rico and its Problems,* 66. Unfortunately, Fleagle could not resist blaming the victim for getting used too rapidly to part-time employment. Seeing part-time employment as less honorable, the North American rural sociologist and resident colonizer immediately added:

> Part time employment tends to low standards of living, because during the period of reduced financial income the standards of living are lowered, and when it is found that the family can exist on the reduced income there is little inducement for seeking work . . . (Ibid., 66–67)

This was how the "native" peasant family allegedly contributed to its own moral and economic debasement.

57. See Thomas Mathews, *Puerto Rican Politics and the New Deal* (Gainesville: University of Florida Press, 1969), 14, 301–303; Henry K. Wells, *The Modernization of Puerto Rico* (New Haven: Yale University Press, 1969), 96–111; Angel G. Quintero Rivera, "El Partido Socialista y la lucha política triangular de las primeras décadas bajo la dominación norteamericana," *Revista de Ciencias Sociales,* 19: 1 (March, 1975): 47–100.

58. Eric Wolf, "San José: Subcultures of a 'Traditional' Coffee Municipality," in *The People of Puerto Rico,* edited by Julian H. Steward (Urbana: The University of Illinois Press, 1956), 226, 235–238; Sidney Mintz, *Worker in the Cane: A Puerto Rican Life History* (New York: W.W. Norton and Company, 1974), 150–153.

59. Pedro Vales, Astrid A. Ortiz, and Noel M. Mattei, *Patrones de criminalidad en Puerto Rico: apreciación socio-histórica: 1898–1980* (Río Piedras: n.p., 1982), 19–20.

60. This sort of administrative accounting category tends to ignore the following issues: the variations in the effectiveness of police campaigns; the fluctuations in the ways in which such effectiveness was defined at various historical junctures; the widely differing ways in which the crimes to be interdicted were defined in each period and in each particular moment; the oscillations in the infractions of the penal code that got overlooked by the police for multiple reasons; and the vicissitudes regarding the number of members in the police force who were available for such duties.

61. The intellectual and political ancestry of the racism and sexism embedded in such narratives is traceable, of course, from the Western paradigm of "the Great Chain of Being" up to the latter's Social-Darwinist offspring of the late-nineteenth and twentieth centuries. See Arthur O. Lovejoy, *The Great Chain of Being: A Study of the History of an Idea* (Cambridge, Mass.: Harvard University Press, 1936); Stephen Jay Gould, *The Mismeasure of Man* (New York: W.W. Norton & Company, 1981), 31–143; Page DuBois, *Centaurs and Amazons: Women and the Pre-history of the Great Chain of Being* (Ann Arbor: The University of Michigan Press, 1984), 1–18; Gilman, *Difference and Pathology*, 231, 235, 237; V. Y. Mudimbe, *The Invention of Africa: Gnosis, Philosophy, and the Order of Knowledge* (Bloomington: Indiana University Press, 1988), 10–20; Patrick Brantlinger, *Rule of Darkness: British Literature and Imperialism, 1830–1914* (Ithaca: Cornell University Press, 1989), 21–27, 33, 39, 173–198, 218–220.

62. *Congressional Record*, 56th Congress, 1st Session, vol. 33, (1900), 2105.

63. *Congressional Record*, 56th Congress, 1st Session, vol. 33, (1900), 2043.

64. Davis, *Report on Civil Affairs*, 102.

65. Quoted in Morrison Swift, *Imperialism and Liberty* (Los Angeles: n.p., 1899), 71.

66. Josiah Strong, *The New Era or the Coming Kingdom* (New York: n.p., 1893), 69.

67. Roosevelt, *The Strenuous Life*, 9.

Chapter 4

1. Stuart Hall, "Signification, Representation, Ideology: Althusser and the Post-Structuralist Debates," *Critical Studies in Mass Communication*, 2: 2 (June, 1985): 102.

2. See Angel Rivero, *Crónica de la Guerra Hispanoamericana en Puerto Rico* (San Juan: Instituto de Cultura Puertorriqueña, 1972), 548–549; Mariano Negrón Portillo, *Cuadrillas anexionistas y revueltas campesinas en Puerto Rico, 1898–1899* (Río Piedras: Centro de Investigaciones Sociales, Universidad de Puerto Rico, 1987), 32, 40–41, 42. These armed detachments of civilians occasionally overlapped with the small number of roving bands of deserters from the Spanish army who were also involved in the looting and pillage of the large haciendas. See Henry K. Carroll, *Report on the Island of Porto Rico; Population, Civil Government, Commerce, Industries, Productions, Roads, Tariffs, and Currency With Recommendations by Henry K. Carroll* (Washington, D.C.: Government Print-

ing Office, 1899), 602–603. The two phenomenons should not be mistakenly equated, however, with a very different expression of civilian armed force: the local, pro-U.S. volunteers who also took up arms. This third group tried to facilitate and hasten the dismantling of the Spanish colonial regime, but did so in order to turn over the government to the U.S. troops. Such activity occurred under the leadership of the local—and minority—fractions of the propertied and educated classes who favored the transformation of Puerto Rico into a province of the North American federal union. Negrón Portillo, *Cuadrillas anexionistas,* 15–28.

3. Gayatri Chakravorty Spivak, "Subaltern Studies: Deconstructing Historiography," in *In Other Worlds: Essays in Cultural Politics* (New York: Routledge, 1988), 203.

4. See George W. Davis, *Annual Report of the War Department for the Fiscal Year Ended June 30, 1900—Part 13: Report of the Military Governor of Porto Rico* (Washington, D.C.: Government Printing Office, 1902), 97; Carmelo Rosario Natal, *Puerto Rico y la crisis de la Guerra Hispanoamericana* (Hato Rey: Ramallo Brothers Printing Company, 1975), 260–263; Juan M. Delgado, "Las partidas sediciosas del '98," *Suplemento En Rojo, Claridad* (March 17–23, 1978): 6; Blanca Silvestrini, *Violencia y criminalidad en Puerto Rico, 1898–1973: apuntes de un estudio de historia social* (Río Piedras: Editorial Universitaria, 1980), 25; Fernando Picó, *1898: la guerra después de la guerra* (Río Piedras: Ediciones Huracán, 1987), 149–154.

5. Fernando Picó has taken note of these similarities within the textual practices of the new colonizers. See Picó, *1898,* 204–205.

6. George W. Davis, *Report of Brigadier General George W. Davis, U.S.V., On Civil Affairs of Puerto Rico, 1899* (Washington, D.C.: Government Printing Office, 1900), 19.

7. Nelson A. Miles, *Serving the Republic* (New York: Harper and Brothers Publishers, 1911), 107–180; Robert M. Utley, *The Indian Frontier of the American West, 1846–1890* (Albuquerque: University of New Mexico Press, 1984), 141, 178–179, 184–188, 191–193, 198, 201.

8. Davis, *Report of the Military Governor,* 102. This Davis report is also partially mistaken as to the extent of starvation among the general population during the last decades of the nineteenth century.

9. Quoted in Claude G. Bowers, *Beveridge and the Progressive Era* (New York: Praeger Publishers, 1932), 68.

10. Shiv Visvanathan, "From the Annals of the Laboratory State," *Alternatives,* 12: 1 (January, 1987): 41.

11. Albert Memmi, *The Colonizer and the Colonized* (Boston: Beacon Press, 1970), 83.

12. Edward Said, *Orientalism* (New York: Vintage Books, 1979), 41.

13. Ibid., 207.

14. Theodore Roosevelt, *The Works of Theodore Roosevelt: the Strenuous Life* (n.p.: P.F. Collier & Son, Publishers, 1903 [?]), 9.

15. Quoted in Silvestrini, *Violencia y criminalidad,* 21.

16. Quoted in Lidio Cruz Monclova, *Historia de Puerto Rico (siglo XIX), tomo III, tercera parte (1885–1898)* (Río Piedras: Editorial Universitaria, 1964), 355.

17. Cayetano Coll y Toste, ed., *Boletín Histórico de Puerto Rico, tomo XI* (San Juan: Tipografía Cantero Fernández, 1924), 161, emphasis in the original.

18. Angel G. Quintero Rivera, *Conflictos de clase y política en Puerto Rico* (Río Piedras: Ediciones Huracán, 1976).

19. See Davis, *Report of the Military Governor,* 104.

20. Carroll, *Report on the Island of Porto Rico,* 597–599; Silvestrini, *Violencia y criminalidad,* 26; Picó, *1898,* 171–180. There is a considerable amount of political mythology to the contrary within the traditional socio-historical critiques of U.S. colonialism. See, for example, Juan Antonio Corretjer, *La lucha por la independencia de Puerto Rico* (San Juan: n.p., 1949), 37–38; Loida Figueroa, *Breve historia de Puerto Rico, vol. 2* (Río Piedras: Editorial Edil, 1970), 220. Unfortunately, there does not appear to be much historical evidence to substantiate these claims. See Picó, *1898,* 158; Negrón Portillo, *Cuadrillas anexionistas*; Ramón López, "Aguila Blanca: notas sobre la imaginación histórica," *Suplemento En Rojo, Claridad* (July 27–August 2, 1990): 19–22. The initial, popular reaction to the North American troops was overwhelmingly positive and friendly insofar as the U.S. military presence was primarily understood as a vehicle for the eradication of Spanish rule in the Island. See Rosario Natal, *Puerto Rico y la crisis,* 221–257; María D. Luque de Sánchez, *La ocupación norteamericana y la Ley Fóraker: la opinión pública puertorriqueña* (Río Piedras: Editorial Universitaria, 1980), 51–81.

21. Josiah Strong, *Expansion Under New World Conditions* (New York: n.p., 1900), 36.

22. Homi Bhabha, "Of Mimicry and Man: The Ambivalence of Colonial Discourse," *October,* 28 (Spring, 1984): 126.

23. See Picó, *1898,* 157; López, "Aguila Blanca."

24. See William F. Willoughby, *Territories and Dependencies of the United States: Their Government and Administration* (New York: The Century Company, 1905), 131–143, 163–170; E. Fernández García, *El libro de*

Puerto Rico (San Juan: "El Libro Azul" Publishing Company, 1923), 273–277.

25. See Leo S. Rowe, *The United States and Porto Rico* (New York: Longman, Green, and Co., 1904), 206–207; Manuel Rodríguez Ramos, "Nuestro código penal vigente y el anteproyecto de reforma de 1926," *Revista Jurídica de la Universidad de Puerto Rico,* 1: 1 (March, 1932): 49–59; Edward J. Berbusse, *The United States in Puerto Rico, 1898–1900* (Chapel Hill: University of North Carolina Press, 1966), 83–84; José Trías Monge, *El sistema judicial de Puerto Rico* (Río Piedras: Editorial Universitaria, 1978), 48–49, 50, 52–53, 59–63, 67.

26. See Fernández García, *El libro de Puerto Rico,* 278–281; Lydia Peña Beltrán, *Treinta años en las cárceles de Puerto Rico* (San Juan: Librotex, Inc., 1986), 27.

27. Ranajit Guha, "The Prose of Counter-Insurgency," *Selected Subaltern Studies,* edited by Ranajit Guha and Gayatri Chakravorty Spivak (New York: Oxford University Press, 1988), 57.

28. Said, *Orientalism,* 40.

29. Michel Foucault, *Discipline and Punish: The Birth of the Prison* (New York: Vintage Books, 1977), 220–221.

30. David Trotman, *Crime in Trinidad: Conflict and Control in a Plantation Society, 1838–1900* (Knoxville: The University of Tennessee Press, 1986), 103–104.

31. See William H. Hunt, *Second Annual Report of the Governor of Porto Rico* (Washington, D.C.: Government Printing Office, 1902), 237; William H. Hunt, *Third Annual Report of the Governor of Porto Rico* (Washington, D.C.: Government Printing Office, 1903), 308; Beekman Winthrop, *Fifth Annual Report of the Governor of Porto Rico* (Washington, D.C.: Government Printing Office, 1905), 144–145; Beekman Winthrop, *Sixth Annual Report of the Governor of Porto Rico* (Washington, D.C.: Government Printing Office, 1906), 200; George R. Colton, *Tenth Annual Report of the Governor of Porto Rico* (Washington, D.C.: Government Printing Office, 1910), 57; George R. Colton, *Eleventh Annual Report of the Governor of Porto Rico* (Washington, D.C.: Government Printing Office, 1911), 68–69; George R. Colton, *Twelfth Annual Report of the Governor of Porto Rico* (Washington, D.C.: Government Printing Office, 1912), 62–63; Fred K. Fleagle, *Social Problems in Porto Rico* (Boston: D.C., Heath Co., 1917), 84–85; A. Hyatt Verrill, *Porto Rico Past and Present and San Domingo of Today* (New York: Dodd, Mead, and Company, 1919), 152–153.

32. José de Diego, *Apuntes sobre la delincuencia y la penalidad* (San Juan: Tipografía La Correspondencia, 1901), 33, emphasis in the original.

33. See José C. Barbosa, *El problema de razas* (San Juan: Imprenta

Venezuela, 1937), 51–52; Isabelo Zenón Cruz, *Narciso descubre su trasero: el negro en la cultura puertorriqueña, vol. I* (Humacao, Puerto Rico: Editorial Furidi, 1974), 118–119.

34. La Democracia, "Editorial," *La Democracia* (August 29, 1900): 3.

35. See, for example, Nestor A. Rigual, *Reseña de los mensajes de los gobernadores de Puerto Rico, 1900–1930* (Río Piedras: Editorial Universitaria, 1967), 29–30; Angel G. Quintero Rivera, "El Partido Socialista y la lucha política triangular de las primeras décadas bajo la dominación norteamericana," *Revista de Ciencias Sociales,* 19: 1 (March, 1975): 55–56; Silvestrini, *Violencia y criminalidad,* 42–50; Mariano Negrón Portillo, *Las turbas republicanas, 1900–1904* (Río Piedras: Ediciones Huracán, 1990), 70–213.

36. Negrón Portillo has made similar observations. See *Las turbas republicanas,* 167.

37. La Democracia, "Editorial," *La Democracia* (November 9, 1900): 4.

38. See Cruz Monclova, *Historia de Puerto Rico,* 271.

39. Negrón Portillo, *Las turbas republicanas,* 178–179, 181–182.

40. La Democracia, "Editorial," *La Democracia* (December 11, 1900): 2.

41. La Democracia, "Editorial," *La Democracia* (November 10, 1900): 1.

42. See Gervasio García, *Primeros fermentos de organización obrera en Puerto Rico, 1873–1898* (Río Piedras: Cuadernos de CEREP no. 1, 1974); Igualdad Iglesias de Pagán, *El obrerismo en Puerto Rico, época de Santiago Iglesias (1895–1905)* (Palencia de Castilla: Ediciones Juan Ponce de León, 1973), 105, 184–185, 195, 205–207, 212–213, 222–226, 243–247, 293, 299, 304, 333–335; Angel G. Quintero Rivera, "Socialista y tabaquero: la proletarización de los artesanos," *Revista Sin Nombre,* 8: 4 (January–March, 1978): 100–138; Negrón Portillo, *Las turbas republicanas,* 105–109. Negrón Portillo provides an alternative explanation for this political pact. See, *Las turbas republicanas,* 82, 137–149.

43. On electoral violence in general during the 1898–1947 period, see Truman Clark, *Puerto Rico and the United States, 1917–1933* (Pittsburgh: University of Pittsburgh Press, 1975), 17; Silvestrini, *Violencia y criminalidad,* 70, 72. On the augmentation of police ranks during elections see, for example, Winthrop, *Fifth Annual Report,* 144. As late as 1940 colonialist personnel, this time a high-ranking federal official such as Secretary of the Interior Harold L. Ickes, would comment: "Hell is certainly popping up in Puerto Rico, with the usual gunplay that accompanies elections there." Harold L. Ickes, *The Secret Diary of Harold L. Ickes: The Lowering Clouds, 1939–1941, Vol. 3* (New York: Simon and Schuster, 1954), 348.

44. This is one of the fundamental contributions of Negrón Portillo's study on the 1900–1904 urban political violence.

45. G. Milton Fowles, *Down in Porto Rico* (New York: n.p., 1906), 146.

46. Quoted in Elting Morison, ed. *The Letters of Theodore Roosevelt, vol. 5* (Cambridge, Mass.: Harvard University Press, 1952), 501.

47. See Negociado del Trabajo, *Primer informe del Negociado del Trabajo* (San Juan: Bureau of Supplies, Printing, and Transportation, 1912), 88–89; Meyer Bloomfield, *A Study of Certain Social, Educational, and Industrial Problems in Porto Rico* (Washington, D.C.: n.p., 1912), 23, 24–25; Iglesias de Pagán, *El obrerismo en Puerto Rico,* 119–122, 124, 126, 128–131, 171–175, 183–185, 195–198, 208, 243–244.

48. Winthrop, *Fifth Annual Report,* 144.

49. See Winthrop, *Fifth Annual Report,* 144–145; Winthrop, *Sixth Annual Report,* 200; Juan Angel Silén, *Apuntes: para una historia del movimiento obrero puertorriqueño* (Río Piedras: Editorial Cultural, 1978), 66–67.

50. See Quintero Rivera, "La lucha política triangular": 61.

51. Just the same, this raises questions regarding how exactly such investments were brought about, and to what extent they were actually successful. The brief and relative rise in living standards would only account for part of this situation. For one thing, these standards were not rising so rapidly. On the other hand, the relative improvement in living standards was distributed extremely unevenly within the breadth and depth of the social terrain which inscribed the laboring poor majorities.

Chapter 5

1. Fred K. Fleagle, *Social Problems in Porto Rico* (Boston: D.C. Heath, Co., 1917), 86.

2. A. Hyatt Verrill, *Porto Rico Past and Present and San Domingo of Today* (New York: Dodd, Mead, and Company, 1919), 147.

3. Meyer Bloomfield, *A Study of Certain Social, Educational, and Industrial Problems in Porto Rico* (Washington, D.C.: n.p., 1912), 24.

4. See George R. Colton, *Tenth Annual Report of the Governor of Porto Rico* (Washington, D.C.: Government Printing Office, 1910), 57; George R. Colton, *Eleventh Annual Report of the Governor of Porto Rico* (Washington, D.C.: Government Printing Office, 1911), 68–69; George R. Colton, *Twelfth Annual Report of the Governor of Porto Rico* (Washington, D.C.: Government Printing Office, 1912), 62–63; Fleagle, *Social Problems in Porto Rico,* 84–85; Verrill, *Porto Rico Past and Present,* 152–153.

5. Truman Clark, *Puerto Rico and the United States, 1917–1933* (Pittsburgh: University of Pittsburgh Press, 1975), 17.

6. See Negociado del Trabajo, *Cuarto informe del Negociado del Trabajo* (San Juan: Bureau of Supplies, Printing, and Transportation, 1916), 11–12; Arthur Yager, *Fifteenth Annual Report of the Governor of Porto Rico* (Washington, D.C.: Government Printing Office, 1915), 446; U.S. Bureau of the Census, *Fifteenth Census of the United States; Agriculture: Porto Rico* (Washington, D.C.: Government Printing Office, 1932), 183.

7. Victor Clark, ed. *Porto Rico and its Problems* (Washington, D.C.: Brookings Institution, 1930), 637.

8. Negociado del Trabajo, *Cuarto informe*, 11.

9. Negociado del Trabajo, *Segundo informe del Negociado del Trabajo* (San Juan: Bureau of Supplies, Printing, and Transportation, 1914), 25.

10. David Trotman, *Crime in Trinidad: Conflict and Control in a Plantation Society, 1838–1900* (Knoxville: The University of Tennessee, 1986), 64.

11. See Arthur Yager, *Seventeenth Annual Report of the Governor of Porto Rico* (Washington, D.C.: Government Printing Office, 1917), 552–553; Arthur Yager, *Eighteenth Annual Report of the Governor of Porto Rico* (Washington, D.C.: Government Printing Office, 1918), 632–633; Joseph L. Marcus, *Labor Conditions in Porto Rico* (Washington, D.C.: Department of Labor, Government Printing Office, 1919), 19; Silvestrini, *Violencia y criminalidad en Puerto Rico, 1898–1973: apuntes de un estudio de historia social* (Río Piedras: Editorial Universitaria, 1980), 60.

12. See Arthur Yager, *Twentieth Annual Report of the Governor of Porto Rico* (Washington, D.C.: Government Printing Office, 1920), 557–559; E. Mont Reily, *Twenty-Second Report of the Governor of Porto Rico* (Washington, D.C.: Government Printing Office, 1922), 35; Silvestrini, *Violencia y criminalidad*, 63, 69–70.

13. Ranajit Guha, "The Prose of Counter-Insurgency," *Selected Subaltern Studies*, edited by Ranajit Guha and Gayatri Chakravorty Spivak (New York: Oxford University Press, 1988), 71.

14. See Clark, *Porto Rico and its Problems*, 637, 639; Arthur D. Gayer, et al., *The Sugar Economy of Puerto Rico* (New York: Columbia University Press, 1938), 194, 205.

15. See Verrill, *Porto Rico Past and Present*, 152–153; Fleagle, *Social Problems in Porto Rico*, 84–85; Silvestrini, *Violencia y criminalidad*, 62, 67–68; Fernando Picó, *Los gallos peleados* (Río Piedras: Ediciones Huracán, 1983), 37, 45–46.

16. Juan B. Soto, "El delincuente desde el punto de vista de la psicología y la sociología criminológicas," *Puerto Rico,* 1: 1 (May, 1919): 73.

17. Knowlton Mixer, *Porto Rico and its Conditions* (New York: Macmillan Company, 1926), 179.

18. Awilda Palau de López, *Esbozo de la historia legal de las instituciones de menores de Puerto Rico* (Río Piedras: Editorial Universitaria, 1970), 29–39.

19. Luis Samalea Iglesias, *La delincuencia infantil en Puerto Rico: notas para una conferencia* (San Juan: Real Hermanos, 1916), 3.

20. Quoted in Samalea Iglesias, *La delincuencia infantil en Puerto Rico,* 10.

21. The reports of the colonialist social reformers contain abundant examples of such discourses. See, for example, Fleagle, *Social Problems in Porto Rico,* 102–104; Helen V. Bary, *Child Welfare in the Insular Possessions of the United States, Part 1: Porto Rico* (Washington, D.C.: U.S. Child Welfare Bureau, Government Printing Office, 1923), 25–29, 54–65; Mixer, *Porto Rico and its Conditions,* 179.

22. Michel Foucault, "What Is an Author?" in *Language, Counter-Memory, Practice: Selected Essays and Interviews by Michel Foucault,* edited by Donald F. Bouchard (Ithaca: Cornell University Press, 1977), 130–131.

23. Abdul JanMohamed, "The Economy of Manichean Allegory: The Function of Racial Differences in Colonialist Literature," in *"Race," Writing, and Difference,* edited by Henry Louis Gates, Jr. (Chicago: The University of Chicago Press, 1986), 82.

Chapter 6

1. See Sol Luis Descartes, *Basic Statistics on Puerto Rico* (Washington, D.C.: Office of Puerto Rico, 1946), 50, 53–58; Harvey Perloff, *Puerto Rico's Economic Future: A Study in Planned Development* (Chicago: University of Chicago Press, 1950), 136–137.

2. See José G. del Valle, "Situación económica de Puerto Rico en 1899," in *Crónicas de Puerto Rico,* edited by Eugenio Fernández Méndez (Río Piedras: Editorial Universitaria, 1967), 565, 567; María D. Luque de Sánchez, *La ocupación norteamericana y la Ley Fóraker: la opinión pública puertorriqueña* (Río Piedras: Editorial Universitaria, 1980), 113.

3. Angel G. Quintero Rivera, "La clase obrera y el proceso político en Puerto Rico–I" *Revista de Ciencias Sociales,* 18: 1–2 (March–June, 1974): 180–182.

4. See Rafael de J. Cordero, *La economía de Puerto Rico y sus problemas* (Río Piedras: Universidad de Puerto Rico, 1949), 12; Jorge J. Serrallés, "Farm Prices and Price Relationships of Sugar and Sugar Cane in Puerto Rico from 1910 to 1945," *Agricultural Experimental Station Bulletin,* 87 (1949): 8–9, 53–54.

5. Victor Clark, ed. *Porto Rico and its Problems* (Washington, D.C.: Brookings Institution, 1930), 646.

6. Such a process is evidently associated with the distinction made by Spitzer between extensive-extractive regimes of social exploitation and discipline vs. intensive regimes. See Steven Spitzer, "The Rationalization of Crime Control in Capitalist Society" in *Social Control and the State,* edited by Stanley Cohen and Andrew Scull (London: Basil Blackwell, 1985), 322–323, 324.

7. Examples of such oversight, particularly in terms of the second factor, may be found in Félix Córdova, "Algunos aspectos de la penetración capitalista en Puerto Rico," *Punto Inicial,* 2 (December, 1976): 19–54; Angel G. Quintero Rivera, *Conflictos de clase y lucha política en Puerto Rico* (Río Piedras: Ediciones Huracán, 1976), 63–76; History Task Force, *Labor Migration Under Capitalism: The Puerto Rican Experience* (New York: Monthly Review Press, 1979), 96–103; Wilfredo Mattos Cintrón, *La política y lo político en Puerto Rico* (México: Ediciones Era, 1980), 66–78; Kelvin Santiago, "La concentración y centralización de la propiedad en Puerto Rico, 1898–1929," *Revista de Ciencias Sociales—Hómines,* 6: 2 (January–July, 1983): 5–14; James Dietz, *Economic History of Puerto Rico* (Princeton: Princeton University Press, 1986), 104–118, 124–134; Angel G. Quintero Rivera, *Patricios y plebeyos: burgueses, hacendados, artesanos y obreros—las relaciones de clase en el Puerto Rico de cambio de siglo* (Río Piedras: Ediciones Huracán, 1988), 158–179.

8. Karl Polanyi, *The Great Transformation* (New York: Rinehart, 1944), 186–187.

9. Arthur D. Gayer, et al., *The Sugar Economy of Puerto Rico* (New York: Columbia University Press, 1938), 181–204.

10. Beyond the obvious use of police force, this again leaves pending the question of the measures taken by the State to address the persistence of public disorder. It also leaves for further analysis the question of just how successful these penal deployments were or were not.

11. See Arcadio Díaz Quiñonez, "Recordando el futuro imaginario: la escritura histórica en la década del treinta," *Revista Sin Nombre,* 14 (April–June, 1984): 16–35; María Elena Rodríguez, "Tradición y modernidad: el intelectual puertorriqueño ante la década del treinta," *Op. Cit.* 3 (1987–88): 45–65; Arcadio Díaz Quiñonez, "Tomás Blanco: la reinvención de la tradición," *Op. Cit.* 4 (1988–89): 147–182.

12. See Charles E. Gage, "The Tobacco Industry in Puerto Rico," *United States Department of Agriculture, Circular no. 519* (Washington, D.C.: Government Printing Office, 1939), 45–46; Erich W. Zimmerman, *Staff Report to the Interdepartmental Committee on Puerto Rico* (Washington, D.C.: n.p., September 9, 1940), 226–227.

13. Luisa Hernández Angueira, "Auge y decadencia de la industria de la aguja en Puerto Rico, 1914–1940" (Ph.D. diss., Universidad Nacional Autónoma de México, 1983), 29–30.

14. See John K. Winkler, *Tobacco Tycoon: The Story of James Buchanan Duke* (New York: Random House, 1942), 74–87; Victor Perlo, *The Empire of High Finance* (New York: International Publishers, 1957), 182–183; Alfred Eichner, *The Emergence of Oligopoly: Sugar Refining as a Case Study* (Baltimore: Johns Hopkins University Press, 1969), 70–92; Hernández Angueira, "Industria de la aguja," 37–40.

15. Joseph Marcus, *Labor Conditions in Porto Rico* (Washington, D.C.: Department of Labor, Government Printing Office, 1919), 41.

16. Quoted in E. Fernández García, *El libro de Puerto Rico* (San Juan: "El Libro Azul" Publishing Company, 1923), 672.

17. U.S. House of Representatives Subcommittee of the Committee on Insular Affairs, *Investigation of Political, Economic, and Social Conditions of Puerto Rico* (78th Cong., 2nd Sess., H. Res. 159, 1943), 894–895.

18. Perloff, *Puerto Rico's Economic Future,* 138–141; Thomas C. Cochran, *The Puerto Rican Businessman: A Study of Cultural Change* (Philadelphia: University of Pennsylvania Press, 1959), 22–24. Within this context, it must be remembered that the United States dominated such a commercial exchange since the second half of the nineteenth century. After 1898, the leading role of the United States persisted. It began absorbing sixty-five percent of all exports from Puerto Rico and being responsible for seventy-eight percent of all imports to the Island in 1901, reaching ninety-eight percent of all exports from Puerto Rico and ninety-two percent of all imports to the Island by 1942. See Descartes, *Basic Statistics,* 49.

19. See Clark, *Porto Rico and its Problems,* 48–49, 467; U.S. Bureau of the Census, *Fifteenth Census of the United States; Agriculture: Porto Rico* (Washington, D.C.: Government Printing Office, 1932), 170, 181; José L. Vázquez Calzada, *La población de Puerto Rico y su trayectoria histórica* (Río Piedras: Centro Multidisciplinario de Estudios Poblacionales, 1978), 374–375.

20. This interpretation borrows extensively from previously cited data, incorporating additional statistical material from the following sources: U.S. Bureau of the Census, *Thirteenth Census of the United States: Statistics for Porto Rico* (Washington, D.C.: Government Printing Office,

1913), 58; U.S. Bureau of the Census, *Fifteenth Census,* 48; F.P. Barlett and Associates, *A Development Plan for Puerto Rico* (San Juan: Technical Paper no. 1, Puerto Rico Planning, Urbanizing, and Zoning Board, January, 1944), 16, 24; Tomás Hibben and Rafael Picó, *Industrial Development of Puerto Rico and the Virgin Islands of the United States* (n.p.: Report of the United States Section, Caribbean Commission, July, 1948), 247; Perloff, *Puerto Rico's Economic Future,* 64; U.S. Bureau of the Census, *Seventeenth Census of the United States; Printed Report no. 53: Puerto Rico* (Washington, D.C.: Government Printing Office, 1951), 145, 150; A. J. Jaffe, *People, Jobs, and Economic Development* (New York: The Free Press of Glencoe, 1959), 98; U.S. Bureau of the Census, *U.S. Census of Agriculture; 1959; Final Report, Vol. 1–Part 53: Puerto Rico* (Washington, D.C.: Government Printing Office, 1961), 3; Vázquez Calzada, *La población de Puerto Rico,* 374–377.

21. Land plots and feudal rents were still in existence among the laborers that seasonally migrated to the coast as sugar cane workers. See Azel Ames, "Labor Conditions in Porto Rico," *Bulletin of the Department of Labor,* 34 (May, 1901): 413–414; Quintero Rivera, *Conflictos de clase,* 93. These subsistence, control, and obstructive mechanisms lingered even among some of the sugar cane workers that settled within the plantations themselves. See Clark, *Porto Rico and its Problems,* 560; Sidney Mintz, "The Culture History of a Puerto Rican Sugar Cane Plantation: 1876–1949," in *Portrait of a Society: Readings in Puerto Rican Sociology,* edited by Eugenio Fernández Méndez (Río Piedras: University of Puerto Rico Press, 1972), 149–150.

22. See Negociado del Trabajo, *Segundo informe del Negociado del Trabajo* (San Juan: Bureau of Supplies, Printing, and Transportation, 1914), 27; Clark, *Porto Rico and its Problems,* 461–462; Justine and Bailey Diffie, *Porto Rico: A Broken Pledge* (New York: Vanguard Press, 1931), 171–173.

23. See Marcus, *Labor Conditions,* 40–41; Antonio Rodríguez Vera, *Agrarismo por dentro y trabajo a domicilio* (San Juan: Tipografía La Democracia, 1929), 120–132; Clark, *Porto Rico and its Problems,* 27, 48–49, 468–472; Diffie, *Broken Pledge,* 181–182; Zimmerman, *Staff Report,* 259–262; Félix Mejías, *Condiciones de vida de las clases jornaleras de Puerto Rico* (San Juan: Universidad de Puerto Rico, 1946), 29–31; Hernández Angueira, "La industria de la aguja"; María del Carmen Baerga, "La articulación del trabajo asalariado y no-asalariado: hacia una re-evaluación de la contribución femenina a la sociedad puertorriqueña (el caso de la industria de la aguja)," in *La mujer en Puerto Rico,* edited by Yamila Azize (Río Piedras: Ediciones Huracán, 1984): 89–111.

24. Examples of this may be found in Angel Quintero Rivera, "La clase obrera y el proceso político en Puerto Rico–II: capitalismo y proletariado," *Revista de Ciencias Sociales,* 18: 3–4 (September–December, 1984):

61–110; Mattos Cintrón, *La política y lo político,* 55–56, 66; Angel G. Quintero Rivera and Gervasio García, *Desafío y solidaridad* (Río Piedras: Ediciones Huracán, 1982), 93–98; Taller de Formación Política, *La cuestión nacional: el Partido Nacionalista y el movimiento obrero puertorriqueño (aspectos de las luchas económicas y políticas de la década de 1930–40)* (Río Piedras: Ediciones Huracán, 1982), 69.

25. See, for example, Juan Angel Silén, *Apuntes: para una historia del movimiento obrero puertorriqueño* (Río Piedras: Editorial cultural, 1978), 58–59; Mattos Cintrón, *La política y lo político,* 54–56; Santiago, "Concentración y centralización"; Alice Colón, Margarita Mergal, and Nilsa Torres, *La participación de la mujer en la historia de Puerto Rico (Las primeras décadas del siglo veinte)* (Río Piedras: Centro de Investigaciones Sociales, Universidad de Puerto Rico, and New Brunswick: Rutgers University, 1986), 21–24; Dietz, *Economic History,* 98–112.

26. Additional instances of this perspective may be found in Córdova, "La penetración capitalista"; Mattos Cintrón, *La política y lo político,* 56–60, 64–65, 67–69, 74–84; Marcia Rivera Quintero, "Incorporación de la mujer al mercado de trabajo en el desarrollo del capitalismo," in *La mujer en la sociedad puertorriqueña,* edited by Edna Acosta Belén (Río Piedras: Ediciones Huracán, 1980), 49–51, 60–61; Kelvin Santiago, "Algunos aspectos de la integración de Puerto Rico al interior del Estado metropolitano," *Revista de Ciencias Sociales,* 23: 3–4 (July–December, 1981): 297–347; Taller de Formación Política, *La cuestión nacional,* 69–79; Quintero Rivera, *Patricios y plebeyos,* 111–113.

27. See, for example, César Andreu Iglesias, *Memorias de Bernardo Vega* (Río Piedras: Ediciones Huracán, 1977); Angel Quintero Rivera, "Socialista y tabaquero: la proletarización de los artesanos," *Revista Sin Nombre,* 8: 4 (January–March, 1978): 100–138; Ricardo Campos and Juan Flores, "Migración y cultura nacional puertorriqueñas: perspectivas proletarias," in *Puerto Rico: identidad nacional y clases sociales (coloquio de Princeton),* edited by Angel G. Quintero Rivera, et al. (Río Piedras: Ediciones Huracán, 1979): 81–146; Amilcar Tirado Aviles, "Ramón Romero Rosa, su participación en las luchas obreras, 1896–1906," *Revista Caribe,* 2: 2–3 (1980–1981): 3–26; Yamila Azize, *La mujer en la lucha: historia del feminismo en Puerto Rico, 1898–1930* (Río Piedras: Editorial Cultural, 1985), 61–88; Rubén Dávila Santiago, *El derribo de las murallas (orígenes intelectuales del socialismo en Puerto Rico)* (Río Piedras: Editorial Cultural, 1988); Norma Valle Ferrer, *Luisa Capetillo: historia de una mujer proscrita* (Río Piedras: Editorial Cultural, 1990).

28. An exceptionally transparent example of this is Quintero Rivera's summary—in *Patricios y plebeyos*—of early twentieth-century arguments concerning the results of the U.S. invasion:

> In the face of the "four-hundred years of ignorance and servitude" of the Spanish era, . . . the North American presence was

> the closest thing to a bourgeois revolution given the existing class configuration. It represented the modernization of the economy: oppressive and alienating due to its capitalist wage relations, but positive with respect to the development of the productive forces, especially free wage labor, *the element that made possible the socialist agenda.* (pp. 110–111, my emphasis)

29. In this sense, proletarian agency is still locked into the general and teleological parameters of mainstream Marxist viewpoints. The new historical scholarship on Puerto Rico did not invent this evolutionist teleology. Although framed within the investigation of a different time period, one of the most extreme examples of this same evolutionism may be found in some of my own previous work, where I provide a conceptual defense of the implantation of pre-capitalist relations of exploitation in Puerto Rico during the nineteenth century on the basis that, "objectively speaking" and "in historical perspective," this "unfortunately painful and brutal" process nevertheless "represented as necessary a step forward . . . as did slavery in Classical Antiquity." See Kelvin Santiago, "El Puerto Rico del siglo XIX: apuntes para su análisis," *Revista de Ciencias Sociales—Hómines,* 5: 1–2 (January–December, 1981): 13–14. The latter statement, of course, was theoretically grounded in Engels' *Anti-Dühring.* No, they/we only inherited and further elaborated on this outlook from the broader and antecedent philosophies of history and "Sciences of Man" that emerged in the West from the late eighteenth to the early twentieth centuries—Marxism, included. The common logic underlying these otherwise dissimilar epistemologies is that history and humanity ("Mankind") move through ascending stages, each one more advanced than its predecessor, each one the forerunner of the subsequent stage.

30. One of the works of Juan Flores tends to avoid this epistemological trap. See Juan Flores, *Insularismo e ideología burguesa en Antonio Pedreira* (La Habana: Casa de Las Americas, 1979), 25–26, 46–47. However, Flores does not completely escape this evolutionism. For instance, in this same study he recuperates a partially acritical usage of the narratives of "primitivism" when describing indigenous resistances and slave rebellions within the context of popular insurgencies—already (ontologically?) classified as "primitive"—as being the "socio-historical legacy" of the "modern popular culture" of workers and peasants. See ibid., 46.

31. Fernando Picó, *Los gallos peleados* (Río Piedras: Ediciones Huracán, 1983), 174.

32. Gayatri Chakravorty Spivak, "Subaltern Studies: Deconstructing Historiography," in *In Other Worlds: Essays in Cultural Politics* (New York: Routledge, 1988), 197.

33. Helen V. Bary, *Child Welfare in the Insular Possessions of the United States, Part I: Porto Rico* (Washington, D.C.: U.S. Child Welfare Bureau, Government Printing Office, 1923), 26.

34. Franklin H. Giddings, *Democracy and Empire, with Studies of their Psychological, Economic, and Moral Foundation* (New York: n.p., 1900), 305, emphasis in the original.

35. Elihu Root, *The Military and Colonial Policy of the United States: Addresses and Reports,* collected and edited by Robert Bacon and James Brown Scott (Cambridge, Mass.: Harvard University Press, 1916), 164–165.

36. Asamblea Legislativa de Puerto Rico, *Primer informe de la Comisión Legislativa para investigar el malestar y desasosiego industrial y agrícola y que origina el desempleo en Puerto Rico* (San Juan: February 3, 1930), 68.

37. Theodore Roosevelt, Jr., "Children of Famine," *The Review of Reviews,* 81: 1 (January, 1930): 73.

38. See, for example, Carmelo Honoré, *Problemas sociales* (San Juan: Negociado de Materiales, Imprenta y Transporte, 1925), 14.

39. See Horace M. Towner, *Twenty-third Annual Report of the Governor of Porto Rico* (Washington, D.C.: Government Printing Office, 1923), 78.

40. Theodore Roosevelt, Jr., *Report of the Governor of Porto Rico* (Washington, D.C.: Government Printing Office, 1930), 2.

41. See Angel Quintero Rivera, "El Partido Socialista y la lucha política triangular de las primeras décadas bajo la dominación norteamericana," *Revista de Ciencias Sociales,* 19: 1 (March, 1975): 62–89; Truman Clark, *Puerto Rico and the United States, 1917–1933* (Pittsburgh: University of Pittsburgh Press, 1975), 79–84, 91–105.

42. Quoted in Horace M. Towner, *Twenty-seventh Annual Report of the Governor of Porto Rico* (Washington, D.C.: Government Printing Office, 1928), 32.

43. Teobaldo Casanova, *Estudios estadísticos del crimen con especial referencia a Puerto Rico* (San Juan: Casanova, Inc., 1967), 39.

44. See, for example, Francisco R. de Goenaga, *Antropología médica y jurídica* (San Juan: Imprenta Venezuela, 1934), 39–74; José Córdova Chirino, *Los que murieron en la horca* (San Juan: Editorial Cordillera, 1975), 88–125; Fernando Picó, *Gallos peleados,* 149, 159.

45. Until the U.S. Congress passed the Jones Act of 1917, "Porto Rican" men could only elect the lower house of the colonial legislature, the upper house doubling simultaneously as the Governor's cabinet whose members (like the Governor himself) had been directly appointed by the President of the United States. Women's suffrage in Puerto Rico was par-

tially obtained in 1929 but only for literate women. The expansion of this right to all women had to wait until 1935. All "native" men had formally obtained this right (free of property qualifications) in 1904. Starting with the Jones Act, both the Supreme Court in the Island and the "U.S. District Court for Porto Rico" (Federal Court) could no longer appeal directly to the U.S. Supreme Court. Instead, they had to go through the federal circuit court system. The Jones Act also gave the "Attorney General of Porto Rico" constitutionally invested authority over the Island's court system. See José Trías Monge, *El sistema judicial de Puerto Rico* (Río Piedras: Editorial Universitaria, 1978), 77–79.

46. Quoted in Thomas Mathews, *Puerto Rican Politics and the New Deal* (Gainesville: University of Florida Press, 1960), 23.

47. Michel Foucault, "What Is an Author?" in *Language, Counter-Memory, Practice: Selected Essays and Interviews by Michel Foucault,* edited with an introduction by Donald F. Bouchard (Ithaca: Cornell Unversity Press, 1977), 130–131.

48. Abdul JanMohamed, "The Economy of Manichean Allegory: The Function of Racial Difference in Colonialist Literature," in *"Race," Writing, and Difference,* edited by Henry Louis Gates, Jr. (Chicago: The University of Chicago Press, 1986), 82.

49. Edward Said, *Orientalism* (New York: Vintage Books, 1979), 207.

50. Homi Bhabha, "Of Mimicry and Man: The Ambivalence of Colonial Discourse," *October,* 28 (Spring, 1984): 126.

51. This changed slightly in 1948 when the first "native" colonial Governor was chosen by direct popular election. To this day (1992), however, the "native" residents cannot elect the members of the U.S. Congress nor the U.S. President who are constitutionally "entrusted" with setting the juridico-political guidelines for whatever [legally] transpires in the Island.

52. *Congressional Record,* 64th Congress, 1st Session, Appdx. (1916), 1036.

53. *Congressional Record,* 64th Congress, 2nd Session, (1917), 3008.

54. This geopolitical phrase was popularized after the War of 1898. Stephen Bonsal even wrote a book on the Caribbean that bore this same title: *The American Mediterranean* (1912).

55. José A. Cabranes, *Citizenship and the American Empire* (New Haven: Yale University Press, 1979), 6.

56. In all fairness, this "proficiency" had been emerging much earlier. See, for example, Francisco Del Valle Atiles, *El campesino puertor-*

riqueño (n.p.: Tipografía J. González Font, 1887); José de Diego, *Apuntes sobre la delincuencia y la penalidad* (San Juan: Tipografía La Correspondencia, 1901); Salvador Brau, *Ensayos (disquisiciones sociológicas)* (Río Piedras: Editorial Edil, 1972). The only new element was more quantitative than qualitative: more "Porto Rican" professionals were receiving instruction in the United States and more North American colonialist officials were becoming aware of "native" skills in the area of middle-class social philosophy and moral policing. See, María M. Lizardi, "Origins and Development of Social Work Education in Puerto Rico" (Ph.D. diss., University of Tulane, 1983).

57. See James D. Richardson, ed. *A Compilation of the Messages and Papers of the Presidents, Vol. XV* (New York: Bureau of National Literature, 1910), 7386–7387; Gordon K. Lewis, *Puerto Rico: libertad y poder en el Caribe* (Río Piedras: Editorial Edil, 1969), 152.

58. See Theodore Roosevelt, Jr., *Colonial Policies of the United States* (Garden City, New Jersey: Doubleday, Doran, and Company, Inc., 1937), 119–120; Clark, *Puerto Rico and the United States*, 135–136, 138–141.

59. See Lester Langley, *The Banana Wars: An Inner History of American Empire, 1900–1934* (Lexington: The University of Kentucky Press, 1983), 181–216; George Black, *The Good Neighbor: How the United States Wrote the History of Central America and the Caribbean* (New York: Pantheon, 1988), 34–57.

60. Roosevelt, *Colonial Policies*, 118–119. In this manner, the colonial administration of Theodore Roosevelt, Jr. prefigured some of the policies jointly championed by the Creole colonial administrations of the 1950s and 1960s and by the U.S. State Department regarding the Island as "the bridge between two cultures."

61. The defenders of the present juridico-political status of Puerto Rico did not deliberately produce this deception. Regardless of the individual intentions involved, I am primarily referring to the structural and blind artifices behind this process. By "misleading" I mean that the current constitutional condition of the Island produces an inverted, distorted, and displaced understanding of its actual social effects. Juridico-politically, the perceived history and contemporary reality of Puerto Ricans in the Island is different from the history and contemporary reality actually constituting the "native" residents of the Island as social subjects. This is a history and a reality that continues to mark those of us who are Puerto Rican "natives" in the U.S. mainland. This difference does not only stem from the effects of all juridical ideology. See Louis Althusser, *Lenin and Philosophy and Other Essays* (London: New Left Books, 1971), 202–205. In particular, it is a difference that stems from a *colonial* juridical ideology. Unfortunately, the extent to which the current constitutional status of the Island is criticized

by those who favor different political formulas—advocates of Puerto Rico joining the U.S. federal union, as well as independence supporters—is also the extent to which even these "alternative" camps have been interpellated by the very ideology that produces the "Commonwealth of Puerto Rico" and its members. One of the signs of this interpellation is the commonplace reduction of colonialism, per se, to the existent juridical status of the Island. Such reductionism counterposes "U.S. statehood" and "national independence" to the "Commonwealth." Meanwhile, we continue to forget that, borrowing again from Ashis Nandy, "[n]one of them is true but all of them are realities." Ashis Nandy, *The Intimate Enemy: Loss and Recovery of Self Under Colonialism* (Delhi: Oxford University Press, 1989), xiv.

62. Shiv Visvanathan, "From the Annals of the Laboratory State," *Alternatives,* 12: 1 (January, 1987): 41.

63. Frantz Fanon, *Black Skin, White Masks* (New York: Grove Press, 1967), 24.

64. Trinh T. Minh-ha, *Woman, Native, Other: Writing Postcoloniality and Feminism* (Bloomington: Indiana University Press, 1989), 56.

65. Knowlton Mixer, *Porto Rico and its Conditions* (New York: Macmillan Company, 1926), 195.

66. Pablo Berga y Ponce de León, *De la delincuencia juvenil y de los tribunales de niños* (San Juan: n.p., August 14, 1930), 11.

67. José E. Cuesta, *Porto Rico, Past and Present: The Island After Thirty Years of American Rule* (New York: Eureka Print Co., 1929), 75–76.

Chapter 7

1. Edward Said, *Orientalism* (New York: Vintage Books, 1979), 205.

2. Miguel Meléndez Muñoz, "Apuntes sobre la criminalidad en Puerto Rico," *Obras Completas, Vol. 2* (San Juan: Instituto de Cultura Puertorriqueña, 1963), 814. The original article was published in March-April of 1948.

3. See Ernest Mandel, *Tratado de economía marxista, vol.2* (México: Ediciones Era, 1974): 112–134; Agustín Cueva, *El desarrollo del capitalismo en América Latina* (México: Siglo XXI Editores, 1977), 166–167, 170–172, 193–196; Tulio Halperin Donghi, *Historia contemporánea de América Latina* (Madrid: Alianza Editorial, 1977), 357–358, 367–368.

4. See U.S. Tariff Commission, *Preliminary Report: Puerto Rico's Economy With Special Reference to United States—Puerto Rican Trade* (Washington, D.C.: U.S. Tariff Commission, 1943); Esteban Bird, *Report on*

the Sugar Industry in Relation to the Social and Economic System of Puerto Rico (San Juan: Bureau of Supplies, Printing, and Transportation, 1941), 39–41; Dudley Smith, *Puerto Rico's Income* (Washington, D.C.: Association of Sugar Producers of Puerto Rico, 1943), 18; Association of Sugar Producers of Puerto Rico, *Some Considerations On Sugar for Trade Agreement Negotiations* (Washington, D.C.: n.p., December, 1946), 10–12; Harvey Perloff, *Puerto Rico's Economic Future: A Study of Planned Development* (Chicago: University of Chicago Press, 1950), 80–95, 398–399; Robert A. Manners, "Tabara: Subcultures of a Tobacco and Mixed Crops Municipality," in *The People of Puerto Rico,* edited by Julian H. Steward (Urbana: The University of Illinois Press, 1956), 106.

5. See Victor Clark, ed., *Porto Rico and its Problems* (Washington, D.C.: The Brookings Institution, 1930), 466–474; Puerto Rico Department of Agriculture and Commerce, *Annual Book of Statistics—1934–1935* (San Juan: n.p., 1935), 99; Perloff, *Puerto Rico's Economic Future,* 31–37; Thomas Mathews, *Puerto Rican Politics and the New Deal* (Gainesville: University of Florida Press, 1960), 243, 282–283, 323–324.

6. See José Herrero, *La mitología del azucar: un ensayo en historia económica de Puerto Rico, 1900–1970* (Río Piedras: Cuadernos de CEREP no. 5, 1971), 41–46; Angel G. Quintero Rivera, "La base social de la transformación ideológica del Partido Popular en la década del cuarenta," in *Cambio y desarrollo en Puerto Rico,* edited by Gerardo Navas Dávila (Río Piedras: Editorial Universitaria, 1980), 55–56.

7. See Manners, "Tabara," 117; Elena Padilla Seda, "Nocorá: The Subculture of Workers On a Government Owned Sugar Plantation," in *The People of Puerto Rico,* 265–313; Sidney Mintz, *Worker in the Cane: A Puerto Rican Life History* (New York: W.W. Norton and Company, 1974). Nonetheless, usurious practices also had to, simultaneously and conflictively, absorb various aspects of this socio-cultural configuration, as well as concede some of the social space occupied by these peasant family/community forms. See Sidney Mintz, "The Folk-Urban Continuum and the Rural Proletarian," in *Portrait of a Society: Readings in Puerto Rican Sociology,* edited by Eugenio Fernández Méndez (Río Piedras: University of Puerto Rico Press, 1972), 160–163.

8. Quoted in Carmen Gautier Mayoral, "Interrelation of U.S. Poor Relief, Massive Unemployment, and Weakening of 'Legitimacy' in 20th Century Puerto Rico," *Caribbean Studies,* 19: 3–4 (November–December, 1980): 26.

9. See Arthur D. Gayer, et al., *The Sugar Economy of Puerto Rico* (New York: Columbia University Press, 1938), 181–204; James Dietz, *Economic History of Puerto Rico* (Princeton: Princeton University Press, 1986), 139–142.

10. See Artemio P. Rodríguez, *A Report on Wages and Working Hours*

in Various Industries and On the Cost of Living in the Island of Puerto Rico During the Year 1933 (San Juan: Bureau of Supplies, Printing, and Transportation, 1934); José C. Rosario and Justina Carrión, "Rebusca sociológica: una comunidad rural en la región cafetera de Puerto Rico," *University of Puerto Rico Summer School Review,* 15: 1 (1937): 8–15; José Rosario and Carrión, "Rebusca sociológica: una comunidad rural en la zona cañera," *University of Puerto Rico Summer School Review,* 15: 5 (1937): 4–14; Donald Griffin, *Minimum Decent Living Standards for Puerto Rico* (San Juan: National Resource Planning Board, Field Office, Region 11, July, 1942); Earl S. Garver and Ernest B. Fincher, *Puerto Rico: Unsolved Problem* (Elgin, Illinois: Brethren Publishing House, 1945), 22–26; Mathews, *Puerto Rican Politics,* 137, 149–188, 201.

11. Sol Luis Descartes, *Basic Statistics on Puerto Rico* (Washington, D.C.: Office of Puerto Rico, 1946), 78.

12. Rita R. Lang, *Recopilación de datos sobre nutrición adaptada a Puerto Rico y recomendación para la preparación de alimentos que reparten las comisarías y jardines comunales* (San Juan: Administración Federal de Auxilio de Emergencia de Puerto Rico, 1935), 3, 21, 31.

13. See Pablo Morales Otero and Manuel A. Pérez, "Health and Socio-Economic Conditions On a Sugar Cane Plantation," in *Health and Socio-Economic Studies in Puerto Rico* (San Juan: School of Tropical Medicine, 1941), 61–70; Pablo Morales Otero and Manuel A. Pérez, "Health and Socio-Economic Conditions in the Tobacco, Coffee, and Fruit Regions," in ibid., 260–270.

14. See Samuel L. Rodríguez, "The Economic Progress of Puerto Rico" (M.A. thesis, School of Business, University of Chicago, 1930), 60–62; Theodore Roosevelt, Jr., "Children of Famine," *The Review of Reviews,* 81: 1 (January, 1930): 72–73.

15. Quintero Rivera, "La base social," 50.

16. Harold L. Ickes, *The Secret Diary of Harold L. Ickes: The First Thousand Days, 1933–1936, vol. 1* (New York: Simon and Schuster, 1953), 504.

17. Stuart Hall, "Signification, Representation, Ideology: Althusser and the Post-Structuralist Debates," *Critical Studies in Mass Communication,* 2: 2 (June, 1985): 102.

18. Gayatri Chakravorty Spivak, "Subaltern Studies: Deconstructing Historiography," in *In Other Worlds: Essays in Cultural Politics* (New York: Routledge, 1988), 197.

19. See Charles C. Rogler, *Comerío: A Study of a Puerto Rican Town* (Lawrence: University of Kansas, 1940), 68–98; Garver and Fincher, *Unsolved Problem,* 90–100.

20. See Mathews, *Puerto Rican Politics*, 243–286, 323–324; Gordon K. Lewis, *Puerto Rico: libertad y poder en el Caribe* (Río Piedras: Editorial Edil, 1969), 167–220.

21. Eric Wolf, "San José: Subcultures of a 'Traditional' Coffee municipality," in *The People of Puerto Rico*, edited by Julian Steward (Urbana: University of Illinois Press, 1956), 251.

22. Fernando Picó, *Los gallos peleados* (Río Piedras: Ediciones Huracán, 1983), 82.

23. See Teobaldo Casanova, *Estudios estadísticos del crimen con especial referencia a Puerto Rico* (San Juan: Casanova, Inc., 1967), 22.

24. Rosario and Carrión, "Zona cañera," 9.

25. José C. Rosario, *A Study of Illegitimacy and Dependent Children in Puerto Rico* (San Juan: Imprenta Venezuela, 1933), 54–55.

26. Ada María González Prieto, "A Study of One-hundred Twenty-four Dependent Children in Puerto Rico (1935–1938)" (M.A. thesis, Catholic University of America, 1939), 60.

27. What is, obviously, missing from such accounts is the extent to which the physical abuse of children was also found within the households of the propertied and educated classes in the Island. Insofar as the latter children were—by definition—not dependent or indigent, the domestic violence perpetrated against them remained absent from such studies. A corollary effect of this class-based occlusion is that domestic violence continued to be represented as metonymic to the laboring classes.

28. Pablo Morales Otero, *Nuestros Problemas* (San Juan: Biblioteca de Autores Puertorriqueños, 1958), 199–200.

29. The fact that even in this remote municipality these women were conversant in the urban, commercial pharmacology of the day is significant. According to Rogler, one prostitute declared: "We use permaganate, lysol, 'sublimate,' and foam powder to wash ourselves after sex relations," while adding later on: "[a]ll of us are taking salvarsan" (*Comerío*, 79). These statements show the extent to which such technology was mediating sex work among the poor majorities in the Island during the Depression years.

30. Ranajit Guha, "The Prose of Counter-Insurgency," in *Selected Subaltern Studies*, edited by Ranajit Guha and Gayatri Chakravorty Spivak (New York: Oxford University Press, 1988), 15.

31. Manuel Cabranes, "A Study of One-hundred and One Dependent Children in Arecibo, Puerto Rico," *Department of Health Bulletins*, 1: 9 (November, 1937): 204.

32. See Manuel A. Pérez, *Estudio preliminar de las condiciones de*

vida en los arrabales de San Juan (San Juan: Puerto Rico Reconstruction Administration, 1939); Robert W. Stevens, "Los arrabales de San Juan: una perspectiva histórica," *Revista de Ciencias Sociales*, 24: 1–2 (January–June, 1985): 171.

33. See Rexford G. Tugwell, *The Stricken Land: The Story of Puerto Rico* (Garden City, New Jersey: Doubleday & Company, Inc., 1947), 2, 3.

34. Harold L. Ickes, *The Secret Diary of Harold L. Ickes: The Inside Struggle, 1936–1939, vol. 2* (New York: Simon and Schuster, Inc., 1954), 47, 148–149, 329, 627–628. This massacre was eventually investigated (at a local and federal levels) without any justice for the wronged martyrs and their supporters. See Mathews, *Puerto Rican Politics*, 309–315.

35. See, for instance, Wilfredo Mattos Cintrón, *La política y lo político en Puerto Rico* (México: Ediciones Era, 1980), 83–91; Juan J. Baldrich, "Class and the State: The Origins of Populism in Puerto Rico, 1934–1952" (Ph. D. dissertation, Yale University, 1981), 70–150; Luis Ferrao, *Pedro Albizu Campos y el nacionalismo puertorriqueño* (Río Piedras: Editorial Cultural, 1990).

36. Theodore Roosevelt, Jr., *Colonial Policies of the United States* (Garden City, New York: Doubleday, Doran, & Company, Inc., 1937), 198–199.

37. The term "problem population" is used here according to Steven Spitzer, "Towards a Marxian Theory of Deviance," in *Theories of Deviance*, edited by S.H. Traub and C.S. Little (Itasca, Illinois: F.E. Peacock Publishers, 1985), 412, 416–417.

38. Dario Melossi, "Strategies of Social Control in Capitalism: A Comment of Recent Work," *Contemporary Crises,* 4: 4 (October, 1980): 383.

39. See Manuel Cabranes, "The Child Welfare Board," *Department of Health Bulletins*, 1: 6 (August, 1937): 105–137; González Prieto, "A Study of Dependent Children": 6–8; María M. Lizardi, "Origins and Development of Social Work Education in Puerto Rico" (Ph.D. dissertation, University of Tulane, 1983), 60–130.

40. Homi Bhabha, "Of Mimicry and Man: The Ambivalence of Colonial Discourse," *October*, 28 (Spring, 1984): 126.

41. Quoted in Blanca Silvestrini, *Violencia y criminalidad en Puerto Rico, 1898–1973: apuntes de un estudio de historia social* (Río Piedras: Editorial Universitaria, 1980), 75.

42. Juan J. Baldrich, *Sembraron la no siembra: los cosecheros de tabaco puertorriqueños frente a las corporaciones tabacaleras, 1920–1934* (Río Piedras: Ediciones Huracán, 1988), 79–110.

43. See Quintero Rivera, "La clase obrera y el proceso político de Puerto Rico–IV: la desintegración de la política de clases," *Revista de Ciencias Sociales*, 20: 1 (March, 1976): 3–48; Juan A. Silén, *Apuntes: para una historia del movimiento obrero puertorriqueño* (Río Piedras: Editorial Cultural, 1978), 91–101; Blanca Silvestrini, *Los trabajadores puertorriqueños y el Partido Socialista, 1932–1940* (Río Piedras: Editorial Universitaria, 1979), 55–72; Silvestrini, *Violencia y criminalidad,* 76–80; Angel G. Quintero Rivera and Gervasio García, *Desafío y solidaridad* (Río Piedras: Ediciones Huracán, 1982), 106–111; James Dietz, *Economic History of Puerto Rico* (Princeton: Princeton University Press, 1986), 163–170; Georg Fromm, "El Nacionalismo y el movimiento obrero en la década del treinta," *Op.Cit.* 5 (1990): 37–103. The most detailed description of these events is Taller de Formación Política, *¡Huelga en la caña!* (Río Piedras: Ediciones Huracán, 1982).

44. See, for example, Ferrao, *Pedro Albizu Campos,* 125–148. For a very different interpretation of the Nacionalistas and their leadership, see Taller de Formación Política, *La cuestión nacional* (Rio Piedras: Ediciones Huracán, 1982).

45. See Silvestrini, *Violencia y criminalidad,* 79–80; Quintero Rivera and García, *Desafío y solidaridad,* 112–113, 118–120. To date the most thorough description of this event is Taller de Formación Política, *No estamos pidiendo el cielo: huelga portuaria de 1938* (Río Piedras: Ediciones Huracán, 1988).

46. Miles Galvin, *The Organized Labor Movement in Puerto Rico* (Cambridge, Mass.: Harvard University Press, 1979), 94.

47. See Juan Sáez Corales, "25 años de lucha: mi respuesta a la persecución," in *Lucha obrera en Puerto Rico,* edited by Angel G. Quintero Rivera (Río Piedras: Centro de Estudios de la Realidad Puertorriqueña, 1971), 131; Quintero Rivera, "La desintegración de la política de clases": 30–34; Quintero Rivera and García, *Desafío y solidaridad,* 120–121.

48. See Silén, *Apuntes,* 108–118; Galvin, *Organized Labor Movement,* 94–101; Quintero Rivera, "La base social," 82–102.

Chapter 8

1. See Emilio González Díaz, "El populismo en Puerto Rico, 1939–1952" (Ph. D. dissertation, Facultad de Ciencias Políticas y Sociales, Universidad Autónoma de México, 1977); Leonardo Santana Rabell, *Planificación y política durante la administración de Luis Muñoz Marín: un análisis crítico* (Santurce: Editorial Análisis, 1984); Arcadio Díaz Quiñones, "Recordando el futuro imaginario: la escritura histórica en la década del treinta," *Revista Sin Nombre,* 14 (April–June, 1984): 27–32.

2. See Félix Mejías, *Condiciones de vida de las clases jornaleras de Puerto Rico* (San Juan: Universidad de Puerto Rico, 1946); Rafael de J. Cordero, *La economía de Puerto Rico y sus problemas* (Río Piedras: Universidad de Puerto Rico, 1949); Eric Wolf, "San José: Subcultures of a 'Traditional' Coffee Municipality," in *The People of Puerto Rico,* edited by Julian H. Steward (Urbana: University of Illinois Press, 1956), 171–264; Robert Manners, "Tabara: Subcultures of a Tobacco and Mixed Crops Municipality," in ibid., 93–170; Sidney Mintz, *Worker in the Cane: A Puerto Rican Life History* (New York: W.W. Norton and Company, 1974).

3. Many of the socio-economic and political studies that were written during the fifties and sixties reflect a proclivity toward such interpretations. See, for example, E. P. Hanson, *Transformation: The Story of Modern Puerto Rico* (New York: Simon and Schuster, 1955); Charles T. Goodsell, *The Administration of a Revolution: Executive Reform in Puerto Rico Under Governor Tugwell, 1941–1946* (Cambridge, Mass.: Harvard University Press, 1965); Henry K. Wells, *The Modernization of Puerto Rico* (New Haven: Yale University Press, 1969).

4. The paraphrase, of course, comes from the title of the novel by Gabriel García Marquez, *Crónica de una muerte anunciada.* Much of the new historiography on Puerto Rico follows this teleological lead. See, for example, History Task Force, *Labor Migration Under Capitalism: The Puerto Rican Experience* (New York: Monthly Review Press, 1979); Angel G. Quintero Rivera, "La base social de la transformación ideológica del Partido Popular en la década del cuarenta," in *Cambio y desarrollo en Puerto Rico,* edited by Gerardo Navas Dávila (Río Piedras: Editorial Universitaria, 1980), 35–119; Wilfredo Mattos Cintrón, *La política y lo político en Puerto Rico* (México: Editorial Era, 1980); James Dietz, *Economic History of Puerto Rico* (Princeton: Princeton University Press, 1986). The same seems to be true for the older anti-colonialist scholars of Puerto Rican history during the fifties and sixties. See, for example, Manuel Maldonado Denis, *Puerto Rico: una interpretación histórico-social* (México: Siglo XXI Editores, 1969); Gordon K. Lewis, *Puerto Rico: libertad y poder en el Caribe* (Río Piedras: Editorial Edil, 1969).

5. Michel Foucault, "Nietzsche, Genealogy, History," in *Language, Counter-Memory, Practice: Selected Essays and Interviews by Michel Foucault,* edited with an introduction by Donald F. Bouchard (Ithaca: Cornell University Press, 1977), 148–149.

6. See Harvey Perloff, *Puerto Rico's Economic Future: A Study of Planned Development* (Chicago: Chicago University Press, 1950), 37–40, 56–57, 260–266, 334; Wolf, "San José," 204; Elena Padilla Seda, "Nocorá: The Subculture of Workers On a Government Owned Sugar Plantation," in *The People of Puerto Rico,* 278–279; Matthew D. Edel, "Land Reform in Puerto Rico-Part I," *Caribbean Studies* (October, 1962): 26–60; Matthew Edel, "Land Reform in Puerto Rico-Part II," *Caribbean Studies* (January,

1963): 28–50; Miguel Guerra Mondragón, "The Legal Background of Agrarian Reform in Puerto Rico," in *Portrait of a Society: Readings in Puerto Rican Sociology,* edited by Eugenio Fernández Méndez (Río Piedras: University of Puerto Rico Press, 1972), 167–182; Sol Luis Descartes, *Basic Statistics on Puerto Rico* (Washington, D.C.: Office of Puerto Rico, 1972); David F. Ross, *The Long Uphill Path: A Historical Study of Puerto Rico's Program of Economic Development* (Río Piedras: Editorial Edil, 1976), 61–75; Emilio Pantojas García, "Estrategias de desarrollo y contradicciones ideológicas en Puerto Rico, 1940–1978," *Revista de Ciencias Sociales,* 21: 1–2 (March–June, 1979): 89–99; Dietz, *Economic History,* 182–201.

7. See Wells, *Modernization,* 135–219; Lewis, *Libertad y poder,* 192–250; Mattos Cintrón, *La política y lo político,* 112–133; Juan J. Baldrich, "Class and the State: The Origins of Populism in Puerto Rico, 1934–1952" (Ph.D. dissertation, Yale University, 1981), 137–255.

8. See Perloff, *Puerto Rico's Economic Future,* 74–76; Wells, *Modernization,* 162–163; José Herrero, *La mitología del azucar: un ensayo en historia económica de Puerto Rico, 1900–1970* (Río Piedras: Cuadernos de CEREP no. 5, 1971), 77–79, 90–92.

9. See Descartes, *Basic Statistics,* 50, 53–58; Perloff, *Puerto Rico's Economic Future,* 83–84, 136–137; Manners, "Tabara."

10. See Perloff, *Puerto Rico's Economic Future,* 60; History Task Force, *Labor Migration Under Capitalism,* 123; Miriam Muñiz Varela, *Crisis económica y transformaciones sociales en Puerto Rico, 1973–1983* (Río Piedras: Centro de Investigaciones Sociales, 1986).

11. John K. Galbraith and Richard Holton, *Marketing Efficiency in Puerto Rico* (Cambridge, Mass.: Harvard University Press, 1955).

12. Luis Hernández, "The Genesis of the Consumer Culture in Puerto Rico: Notes Towards a Critical and Historical Perspective" (unpublished typewritten document, 1984), 11, 13–14, 20, 21.

13. The PPD publicity for this land reform was initially framed in a populist discourse that, at times, bordered on anti-imperialist and anti-large-property posturing. For example, one of the PPD campaign slogans that caught on at the time was "Down With the Fanged Ones!" ("¡Abajo los colmillús!"), which was a direct reference to North American large propertied interests. The preamble of the law institutionalizing this reform (the "Ley de Tierras" of 1941) even incorporated a local version of the internationally renown, radical-agrarian slogan: "Land to the Tiller!" See Andrés Sánchez Tarniella, *La economía de Puerto Rico* (Madrid: Afrodisio Aguado S.A. Editores, 1971), 105. In the context of Puerto Rico between the Wars, this sort of language would mainly have been directed against the U.S. Sugar Trust. See Mattos Cintrón, *La política y lo político,* 73–123. To a lesser degree, it would have mobilized peasant opposition to the remnants of the Creole Jünkers.

14. See W.L. Packard, "The Land Authority and Democratic Process in Puerto Rico," *Journal of Inter American Economic Affairs* (Río Piedras: reprint by Editorial Universitaria, 1948), 73–74; Perloff, *Puerto Rico's Economic Future,* 37–38; Seda Padilla, "Nocorá," 278–283; Edel, "Land Reform–I": 38, 52–53, 56–57; Mario Villar Roses, *Puerto Rico y su reforma agraria* (Río Piedras: Editorial Edil, 1967).

15. See Packard, "Land Authority," 94; Perloff, *Puerto Rico's Economic Future,* 39; Manners, "Tabara," 108–113, 115–117; Wolf, "San José," 204–206; Wells, *Modernization,* 173–174; Dietz, *Economic History,* 200–201.

16. See U.S. Bureau of the Census, *Thirteenth Census of the United States: Statistics for Porto Rico* (Washington, D.C.: Government Printing Office, 1913), 58; U.S. Bureau of the Census, *Fifteenth Census of the United States; Agriculture: Porto Rico* (Washington, D.C.: Government Printing Office, 1932), 48; F.P. Barlett and Associates, *A Development Plan for Puerto Rico* (San Juan: Technical Paper no. 1, Puerto Rico Planning, Urbanizing, and Zoning Board, January, 1944), 16, 24; Thomas Hibben and Rafael Picó, *Industrial Development of Puerto Rico and the Virgin Islands of the United States* (n.p.: Report of the United States Section, Caribbean Commission, July, 1948), 247; Perloff, *Puerto Rico's Economic Future,* 64; U.S. Bureau of the Census, *Seventeenth Census of the United States; Printed Report no. 53: Puerto Rico* (Washington, D.C.: Government Printing Office, 1951), 145, 150; A.J. Jaffe, *People, Jobs, and Economic Development* (New York: The Free Press of Glencoe, 1959), 98; U.S. Bureau of the Census, *U.S. Census of Agriculture; 1959; Final Report, vol. 1–Part 53: Puerto Rico* (Washington, D.C.: Government Printing Office, 1961), 3; José Vázquez Calzada, *La población de Puerto Rico y su trayectoria histórica* (Río Piedras: Centro Multidisciplinario de Estudios Poblacionales, 1978), 374–377.

17. See U.S. Bureau of the Census, *Thirteenth Census,* 88; Perloff, *Puerto Rico's Economic Future,* 101.

18. See S. Díaz Pacheco, "Consumo de alimentos en la zona rural de Puerto Rico," *Boletín,* 57 (Río Piedras: Estación Experimental Agrícola, March, 1941): 13; Perloff, *Puerto Rico's Economic Future,* 321, 387; Pablo Morales Otero, *Nuestros problemas* (San Juan: Biblioteca de Autores Puertorriqueños, 1958), 104–115.

19. Donald F. Griffin, *Minimum Decent Living Standards for Puerto Rico* (San Juan: National Resources Planning Board, Field Office, Region 11, July, 1942), 8, 14.

20. Raymond Crist, "Sugar Cane and Coffee in Puerto Rico: The Pauperization of the Jibaro, Land Monopoly, and Monoculture," *The American Journal of Sociology and Economics,* 7 (January–April–July, 1948): 472.

21. Félix Córdova, "Algunos aspectos de la penetración capitalista en Puerto Rico," *Punto Inicial,* 2 (December, 1976): 47–48.

22. U.S. Bureau of the Census, *Sixteenth Census of the United States; Puerto Rico; Bulletin no. 2: Characteristics of the Population* (Washington, D.C.: Government Printing Office, 1941), 48.

23. See U.S. Bureau of the Census, *Sixteenth Census*, 48; Perloff, *Puerto Rico's Economic Future*, 147.

24. Juan A. Silén, *Apuntes: para una historia del movimiento obrero puertorriqueño* (Río Piedras: Editorial Cultural, 1978), 108; Miles Galvin, *The Organized Labor Movement in Puerto Rico* (Cambridge, Mass.: Harvard University Press, 1979), 96.

25. See Juan Sáez Corales, "25 años de lucha: mi respuesta a la persecución," in *Lucha obrera en Puerto Rico*, edited by Angel G. Quintero Rivera (Río Piedras: Centro de Estudios de la Realidad Puertorriqueña, 1971), 131–132; Silén, *Apuntes*, 114.

26. Harry Braverman, *Labor and Monopoly Capital: The Degradation of Work in the Twentieth Century* (New York: Monthly Review Press, 1974), 67.

27. See Alberto Yordán, *Crime in Puerto Rico* (Mayagüez: Research Project in Social Problems of Puerto Rico, vol. 3, University of Puerto Rico, College of Agriculture and Mechanical Arts, 1947), 15–18.

28. Teobaldo Casanova, *Estudios estadísticos del crimen con especial referencia a Puerto Rico* (San Juan: Casanova, Inc., 1967), 3.

29. José C. Rosario, *El problema de la criminalidad en Puerto Rico* (Río Piedras: Colegio de Pedagogía, Universidad de Puerto Rico, 1952), 169.

30. Juan B. Soto, "El delincuente desde el punto de vista de la psicología y la sociología criminológicas," *Puerto Rico*, 1: 1 (May, 1919): 73–75.

31. José Córdova Chirino, *Los que murieron en la horca* (San Juan: Editorial Cordillera, 1975), 233–236.

32. The theoretical framework for this observation comes from the work of Eve Kosofsky Sedgwick, *Between Men: English Literature and Male Homosocial Desire* (New York: Columbia University Press, 1985).

33. Juan Carreras, "Carreras achaca la ola de crímenes al Partido Popular de Puerto Rico," *El Imparcial* (December 15, 1943): 8.

34. Francisco Gaztambide Vega, "El problema del crimen en Puerto Rico," *El Imparcial* (July 8, 1945): 4.

35. Miguel Meléndez Muñoz, "Apuntes sobre la criminalidad en Puerto Rico," in *Obras Completas, Vol. 2* (San Juan: Instituto de Cultura Puertorriqueña, 1963), 822.

36. Helen I. Safa, *The Urban Poor in Puerto Rico: A Study in Development and Inequality* (New York: Holt, Rinehart, and Winston, 1974), 9.

37. Wenzell Brown, *Angry Men—Laughing Men: The Caribbean Caldron* (New York: Greenberg Publishers, 1947), 183.

38. Harold L. Ickes, *The Secret Diary of Harold L. Ickes: The First Thousand Days, 1933–1936, vol. I* (New York: Simon and Schuster, 1953), 504.

39. Josiah Strong, *Expansion Under New World Conditions* (New York: n.p., 1900), 319.

40. George W. Davis, *Report of Brigadier General George W. Davis, U.S.V., On Civil Affairs of Puerto Rico, 1899* (Washington, D.C.: Government Printing Office, 1900), 19.

41. Besides Steward, the principal authors featured in this study are: Robert Manners, Sidney Mintz, Elena Padilla, Raymond Scheele, and Eric Wolf. See Steward, ed., *The People of Puerto Rico.*

42. Fred K. Fleagle, *Social Problems in Porto Rico* (Boston: D.C. Heath, Co., 1917), iii–iv. For a remarkably similar perspective, see the introduction to *The People of Puerto Rico.*

43. Mary Louise Pratt, "Scratches in the Face of the Country; or, What Mr. Barrow Saw in the Land of the Bushmen," in *"Race," Writing, and Difference,* edited by Henry Louis Gates, Jr. (Chicago: The University of Chicago Press, 1986), 143.

44. Shiv Visvanathan, "From the Annals of the Laboratory State," *Alternatives,* 12: 1 (January, 1987): 41.

45. Marianna Torgovnick, *Gone Primitive: Savage Intellects, Modern Lives* (Chicago: University of Chicago Press, 1990), 186–187.

46. This was, of course, the eve of the postwar development theories that remodeled former and present colonial conditions within the parameters of a new manichean allegory. From then on colonized peoples and countries would increasingly be reconstituted, by the sources of foreign capital and by the privileged "natives," not as "savages" but as "traditional," "underdeveloped," or "developing" societies and peoples who had to be assisted along the way toward a "modernity" epitomized by North America and Western Europe. See, for example, Arturo Escobar, "Discourse and Power in Development: Michel Foucault and the Relevance of His Work to the Third World," *Alternatives,* 10: 3 (Winter, 1984–1985): 384–390. Puerto Rico would shortly afterwards (1950–1965) become one of the showcases of such uplift.

47. See Crist, "Sugar Cane and Coffee": 333–334; Perloff, *Puerto Rico's Economic Future,* 201; Mintz, *Worker in the Cane,* 207; History Task Force, *Labor Migration Under Capitalism,* 186–187; U.S. Bureau of the Census, *1980-Census of Population; vol. 1, General Population Characteris-*

tics; Part no. 53: Puerto Rico (Preliminary Report) (Washington, D.C.: Government Printing Office, 1980), 9; Robert W. Stevens, "Los arrabales de San Juan: una perspectiva histórica," *Revista de Ciencias Sociales*, 24: 1–2 (January–June, 1985): 171–172.

48. Gareth Stedman Jones, *Outcast London* (New York: Pantheon Books, 1984), 151.

Chapter 9

1. Harold L. Ickes, *The Secret Diary of Harold L. Ickes: The First Thousand Days, 1933–1936, vol. 1* (New York: Simon and Schuster, 1953), 6.

2. George W. Davis, *Report of Brigadier General George W. Davis, U.S.V., On Civil Affairs of Puerto Rico, 1899* (Washington, D.C.: Government Printing Office, 1900), 19.

3. Theodore Roosevelt, *The Works of Theodore Roosevelt: The Strenuous Life* (n.p.: P.F. Collier & Son, Publishers, 1903 [?]), 501.

4. Quoted in Claude G. Bowers, *Beveridge and the Progressive Era* (Cambridge, Mass.: Houghton Mifflin Company, 1932), 68.

5. Rexford Guy Tugwell, *The Stricken Land: The Story of Puerto Rico* (Garden City, New York: Doubleday & Company, Inc., 1946), 3.

6. Homi Bhabha, "Of Mimicry and Man: The Ambivalence of Colonial Discourse," *October*, 28 (Spring, 1984): 126.

7. Stuart Hall, "Signification, Representation, Ideology: Althusser and the Post-Structuralist Debates," *Critical Studies in Mass Communication*, 2: 2 (June 1985): 102.

8. Both perspectives may also be found in the older historical studies of the Island and in the new historiographies of Puerto Rico.

9. Dario Melossi, "Strategies of Social Control in Capitalism: A Comment on Recent Work," *Contemporary Crises*, 4: 4 (October, 1980): 182.

10. Fred K. Fleagle, *Social Problems in Porto Rico* (Boston: D.C. Heath, Co., 1917), iii.

11. Theodore Roosevelt, Jr., *Colonial Policies of the United States* (Garden City, New York: Doubleday, Doran, & Company, Inc., 1937), 108.

12. Albert Memmi, *The Colonizer and the Colonized* (Boston: Beacon Press, 1970), 7.

13. Octave Mannoni, *Prospero and Caliban: The Psychology of Colonization* (Ann Arbor: The University of Michigan Press, 1990), 101.

14. Quoted in Truman Clark, *Puerto Rico and the United States, 1917–1933* (Pittsburgh: University of Pittsburgh Press, 1975), 141.

15. Harry Braverman, *Labor and Monopoly Capital: The Degradation of Work in the Twentieth Century* (New York: Monthly Review Press, 1974), 67.

16. See, for example, A. Hyatt Verrill, *Porto Rico Past and Present and San Domingo of Today* (New York: Dodd, Mead, and Company, 1914), 146–150; Fleagle, *Social Problems*, 85; Knowlton Mixer, *Porto Rico and its Conditions* (New York: Macmillan Company, 1926), 93.

17. Miguel Meléndez Muñoz, "Apuntes sobre la criminalidad en Puerto Rico," *Obras Completas, Vol. 2* (San Juan: Instituto de Cultura Puertorriqueña, 1963), 814, emphasis in the original.

18. Steven Spitzer, "The Rationalization of Crime Control in Capitalist Society," in *Social Control and the State,* edited by Stanley Cohen and Andrew Scull (London: Basil Blackwell, 1985), 324.

19. Michel Foucault, "Nietzsche, Genealogy, History," in *Language, Counter-Memory, Practice: Selected Essays and Interviews by Michel Foucault,* edited with an introduction by Donald F. Bouchard (Ithaca: Cornell University Press, 1977), 146.

20. Senator Sereno Payne, quoted in *Congressional Record,* 56th Congress, 1st Session, vol. 33 (1900), 1946.

21. George W. Davis, *Annual Reports of the War Department for the Fiscal Year Ended June 30, 1900: Part 13: Report of the Military Governor of Porto Rico on Civil Affairs* (Washington, D.C.: Government Printing Office, 1902), 97.

22. José C. Rosario, *El problema de la criminalidad en Puerto Rico* (Río Piedras: Colegio de Pedagogía, Universidad de Puerto Rico, 1952), 60.

23. Michel Foucault, *Discipline and Punish: The Birth of the Prison* (New York: Vintage Books, 1977), 218.

24. Jean-Paul de Gaudemar, "Preliminari per una genealogia delle forme di disciplina nel proceso di lavoro capitalistico," *Aut-Aut,* 167–168 (September–December, 1978): 226.

25. Edward Said, *Orientalism* (New York: Vintage Books, 1979), 41.

26. Abdul JanMohamed, "The Economy of Manichean Allegory: The Function of Racial Difference in Colonialist Literature," in *"Race," Writing, and Difference,* edited by Henry Louis Gates, Jr. (Chicago: The Chicago University Press, 1986), 82.

27. See Frantz Fanon, *Black Skin, White Masks* (New York: Grove Press, 1967), 17–40; Memmi, *Colonizer and the Colonized,* 121–129.

28. Ashis Nandy, *The Intimate Enemy: Loss and Recovery of Self Under Colonialism* (Delhi: Oxford University Press, 1989), 11.

29. Many of their counterparts today are not aware of this either. The complexity of this problem for the most part still tends to elude the majority of Puerto Rican intellectuals—myself included.

30. Fanon, *Black Skin, White Masks,* 132.

31. Said, *Orientalism,* 207.

32. Marianna Torgovnick, *Gone Primitive: Savage Intellects, Modern Lives* (Chicago: The University of Chicago Press, 1990), 186.

INDEX

Abbott, Lyman, 26, 74
Africa as signifier, 23, 25–26, 64, 74, 87, 223. *See also* Racial codes
Althusser, Louis, 15, 10, 281n. 61
Ames, Azel, 54, 56, 59, 61, 62, 124, 260n. 16
Artisans. *See* Urban/coastal laborers

Bary, Helen V., 58, 147–148, 161, 215
Banking and credit, 29, 32, 58, 137
Berga y Ponce de León, Pablo, 162, 215
Beveridge, Senator Albert J.: and North American racial codes, 63, 66, 73, 74, 82, 185, 229; and U.S. expansionism, 22, 23, 25, 26. *See also* Infantilization; Feminization
Bhabha, Homi K.: and desire for reformed Other, 88, 156, 160, 233; and postcolonial theories, 7; and slippage, excess, and difference, 98, 242; and surveillance, 121, 188, 230, 242. *See also* Colonial mimicry; Racial codes
Brown, Wenzell, 221–223, 224, 225

Carroll, Commissioner Henry K., 41, 79–80
Casanova, Teobaldo, 177, 178, 215, 279n. 43
Children: and domestic violence, 123–124, 130–131, 177, 182, 285n. 27; and hunger, 56–57, 148–149; and justice system, 125, 126, 161–162, 178; and narratives of deficient upbringing, 124–125, 128–129, 162–163, 175–176, 273n. 21; and popular illegalities, 124–131, 161–162, 178; and child care, 39, 43; runaway, 123–131, 161, 176, 181–183, 186, 187, 220, 234
Citizenship and Creole rights: the Insular Cases, 64–65; and the laboring classes, 115, 119, 188–189, 236–237; and local administration, 89, 154–160, 216, 229, 279–280n. 45, 280n. 51; and propertied and educated “natives,” 86, 154–160, 188–189, 229. *See also* Infantilization; Racial codes
Coffee: general regional conditions, 42–43, 44, 56, 171, 172, 184; production, 29, 40, 42, 136, 137, 139, 142; and rural social contradictions, 59, 79–80, 99, 124;

Coffee *(continued)*
stagnation and decline, 29, 139–140, 154, 184, 187. *See also* Peasantry; Picó, Fernando; Wolf, Eric
Colonial administration in Puerto Rico: and economic conditions, 168, 187, 195, 197, 200–201; and Island politics, 106, 155–156, 207–208, 218–220; organization of, 88–91; and social contradictions, 151, 164, 190, 197, 207–208, 214, 220. *See also* Citizenship and Creole rights; Colonial governors
Colonialist author–functions (educated/propertied Creoles), 129–130, 155–156, 185, 212, 223–225, 239–242, 280–281n. 56
Colonial governors (in general), 60, 88–89, 96–97, 156, 188, 190. *See also* Davis, George W.; Reily, E. Mont; Roosevelt, Theodore, Jr.; Towner, Horace M.; Winthrop, Beekman; Yager, Arthur
Colonial mimicry: and educated Creoles, 95–98, 156, 160, 188, 230, 240; and "native" laboring classes, 121–122, 188; and U.S. colonizers, 88, 156, 160, 240, 292n. 46. *See also* Bhabha, Homi K.
Commerce and marketing, 29, 32, 143, 198–199, 252n. 43, 275n. 18
Confederación General de Trabajadores (CGT), 192, 207
Cost of living: and hunger, 56–58, 147–150; and poverty, 58–60, 137, 170–171, 203–206, 262n. 21; and social disorder, 94, 188, 203–204, 213, 234. *See also* Peasantry; Urban/coastal laborers
Crime and social disorder, theories of, 12–15, 245n. 25, 245–246n. 26, 246–247n. 33, 253n. 48. *See also* Foucault, Michel; Melossi, Dario; Spitzer, Steven
Crime journalism: from 1898 to 1909, 84–85, 95, 99, 103; from 1910 to 1921, 119–120, 127–130; from 1922 to 1929, 152–154; during 1940s, 214–218
Criminal justice system: organization of, 88–89; specific instances, 114, 152, 173–174, 265n. 60, 274n. 10; versus subaltern social control practices, 164, 208–209. *See also* Juvenile justice; Police
Crist, Raymond, 59, 205
Cuba: politics and society, 47, 158; and Spanish-Cuban-North American War, 21, 24, 27, 30, 64, 248n. 13

Davis, Brig. Gen. George W.: and new colonial regime, 89, 90–91; and North American racial codes, 45, 67, 124; and social conditions in Puerto Rico, 56, 77, 81–84, 237. *See also* Colonial governors; Peasant insurgency
de Diego, José, 95–98, 215
de Gaudemar, Jean-Paul, 51, 238

Educated and propertied Creoles: and destitute children, 127, 162, 163; and indigent women, 122–123, 181, 212; and Island racial codes, 42, 44–46, 95–97, 103–105, 244n. 15; and laboring classes, 79–80, 84–87, 94–99, 103–105, 122–123, 187–188; and political practice, 70–71, 86, 99, 103–105, 185, 229–230; and U.S. colonizers, 83–84, 86–88, 154–160, 185, 295n. 29
Electoral violence, 99, 103–107, 116, 270n. 43. *See also* "Republican Mobs"; Riots; Social violence
England and the English: as compared to U.S., 23, 28, 59, 63–64, 83, 186; and U.S. expansionism, 25, 83

Fall, Senator Robert B., 65, 156
Fanon, Frantz, 5, 7, 160
Federación Libre de Trabajadores (FLT), 105, 116, 190, 207
Federal government: and Island social conditions, 57–58, 168, 171–172, 184, 190; and Puerto Rican politics, 89, 155–159, 166, 184–186; and colonial discourses, 24, 64–67, 87, 156–160, 184–186. *See also* U.S. Congress
Feminization, discourses of: by propertied and educated Creoles, 94–97, 103–105, 127, 241; by U.S. colonialists, 63–66, 82–83, 155–156, 249n. 22, 263n. 39, 263–264n. 46, 264n. 47, 266n. 61. *See also* Gender; Infantilization
Fleagle, Fred K.: and colonial discourses, 57, 62–63, 74, 116–117, 223, 232, 265n. 56; and social conditions, 61, 112, 116, 124
Foraker Act, 64–65, 89, 113, 137
Foucault, Michel: and eurocentrism, 5, 243n. 4; and the fashioning of the social subject, 5, 53, 129, 155; and technologies of domination, 3, 13, 90–91, 236–238, 246n. 27; and theorizing history, 10, 196–197, 246n. 28
Fowles, Milton G., 67, 106

Gender and sexuality, social production of: among educated Creoles, 94–97, 103–105, 127, 177–180; among the laboring classes, 119–123, 130–131, 151–152, 180–181, 210–212, 291n. 32; Island patriarchical formations in general, 38–39, 43, 234; and U.S. colonialist discourses, 63–66, 82–83. *See also* Feminization; Infantilization; Social violence
Germany, 21, 23, 28, 66, 122
Giddins, Franklin H., 26, 148
Great Britain. *See* England
Guha, Ranajit, 7, 14, 90, 108, 119, 179–180. *See also* Spivak, Gayatri Chakravorty; Subaltern Studies

Hall, Stuart: and differences within social fields, 4, 51, 62, 78, 136, 171, 231; and theories of history, 7, 9
Hawaii, 22, 27, 30, 64
Hill, Robert T., 30–31, 54, 67
History, conceptualizing: in contemporary Puerto Rico, 145–147, 259n. 8, 262n. 33, 268n. 20; among educated Creoles, 219, 224–225, 241; general aspects, 4, 6, 8–12, 53, 196–197, 237, 244–245n. 18; and U.S. colonial discourses, 26–27, 66–67, 82–86, 108, 118–119, 159–160, 181. *See also* Feminization; Infantilization; New Historiography; Racial time
Homicide and murder: and labor unrest, 112, 120; among laboring classes, 152–153, 177, 209–212; and narratives of educated Creoles, 96, 98, 177, 209–212, 215–216; official record of, 89, 172, 208, 215–216, 235; and peasant insurgency, 79, 80. *See also* Social violence
Hunger and malnutrition: from 1898 to 1921, 53–58, 259–260n. 14; from 1922 to 1929, 147–149; during 1930s, 169–170, 182, 191, 192; during 1940s, 203–205; and social unrest, 78, 90–91, 94, 108, 124, 128, 232

Ickes, Interior Secretary Harold L., 171, 183–186, 221–225, 233, 270n. 43

Incorporation of Puerto Rico into world economy, 21, 27–33, 136–139, 142–144, 167–169, 197–199, 247n. 3. *See also* Coffee; Needle–products; Sugar; Tobacco
Indians (Native Americans), 23, 46–47, 64, 81, 185, 267n. 5
Infantilization, narratives of: among educated Creoles, 95–97, 105, 155–156, 180–181, 224–225, 241, 249n. 22; and U.S. discourses of racial time, 52, 62–67, 74, 118, 155, 158, 266n. 61. *See also* Citizenship and Creole rights; Feminization

JanMohamed, Abdul, 130, 156, 240
Jones Act, 89, 156–157, 279–280n. 45
Juvenile justice, 125–129, 161–162, 178. *See also* Criminal justice system; Police

Kipling, Rudyard, 77, 111, 118–119, 135, 165, 185, 195, 233

Labor Bureau. *See* Negociado del Trabajo

Mahan, Alfred T., 24–25, 29, 74, 75
Mannoni, Octave, 5, 7, 233
Meléndez Muñoz, Miguel, 166–167, 219–223, 224–225, 235
Melossi, Dario, 33, 50, 187, 232
Memmi, Albert: and colonial situations, 23, 82, 85, 87–88, 95, 233; and postcolonial theories, 5, 7
Miles, Major General Nelson A., 49, 61, 74, 81, 118
Mintz, Sidney, 202, 213, 214, 223, 276n. 21, 292n. 4
Mixer, Knowlton, 124–125, 161, 163, 215
Mudimbe, V.Y., 7, 24, 249n. 17, 266n. 61

Nandy, Ashis, 7, 11, 240–241, 263n. 38, 281–282n. 61
Nationalists. *See* Partido Nacionalista
Needle–products manufacture: and Island economy, 21, 144, 145, 148, 189, 192, 201–202; and U.S. corporations, 142–143, 168–169, 198. *See also* Women and extra–domestic labor
Negociado del Trabajo, 59–60, 114, 117, 148, 149, 170
Negrón Portillo, Mariano, 104, 266–267n. 2, 268n. 20, 270n. 36, 270n. 42, 271n. 44. *See also* Peasant insurgency; "Republican Mobs"
New Historiography of Puerto Rico: and economic determinism, 274n. 7, 277n. 26, 278n. 29; and evolutionist perspectives, 145–147, 276–277n. 24, 277n. 25, 277–278n. 28, 278n. 29, 288n. 4, 293n. 8; and working–class culture, 277n. 27, 278n. 30. *See also* History

Orient, the, and Orientals: as similar to "Porto Rico," 24, 64, 119, 129, 166, 239; as similar to "Porto Ricans," 24, 63–65, 82–83, 156, 186, 241
Orientalism, relevant critiques of, 6–7

Panama Canal, 27, 64
Partidas sediciosas. *See* Peasant insurgency
Partido Federal Americano, 99
Partido Nacionalista, 185–186, 190, 191, 286n. 34, 286n. 35, 287n. 44
Partido Popular Democrático (PPD), 193, 197, 207–208, 289n. 13
Partido Republicano, 96, 103, 104, 190

Partido Socialista, 70, 116, 150, 190
Partido Unionista, 99, 164
Pattison, Robert E., 54, 55, 56, 58, 205
Philippines, 21, 27, 30, 64, 73, 250n. 27
Peasant insurgency (1898–1899), 78–84, 266–267n. 2. *See also* Social violence
Peasantry: and class composition, 39–41, 142–145, 202–206, 255n. 53, 275–276n. 20, 276n. 21; colonial discourses on, 81–86, 183–188, 254–255n. 51; and dispossession process, 39–41, 50–54, 283n. 7; general social conditions, 38–41, 142–143, 169, 199–201, 259n. 10, 289n. 13; and hunger, 54–61, 148; and popular illegalities in general, 32–33, 67–71, 94–98, 163–164, 212–214; and racial identification, 43–47, 94–99; and rural unrest, 78–86, 103, 117, 118, 119, 172; and migration to urban/coastal regions, 41–43, 99, 103, 219, 225–226
Picó, Fernando: and conceptualizing history, 146–147, 267n. 5, 268n. 20; and cultural configuration of laboring classes, 254n. 50; and general social contradictions, 87, 172, 259n. 10; and popular illegalities, 151–152, 160, 163, 189, 248n. 13; and wayward children, 124, 125. *See also* History; New Historiography; Peasantry
Police: and anti–labor repression, 105–109, 112–119, 151, 189–190, 192; organization of, 88–89, 270n. 43; and repression of "common crime," 94, 124–125, 127–130, 161, 163, 174, 209, 213; and repression of Partido Nacionalista, 185–186, 286n. 34; on riot duty, 103, 106–109, 114, 117–118, 188. *See also* Criminal justice system; Juvenile justice
Popular illegalities: conceptual aspects, 13, 15, 234–239, 246n. 27; and dispossession process, 68–71, 90–91; making bootleg rum, 160, 163–164, 212–214; and normative practices of educated Creoles, 84–87, 94–99, 103–105, 119–131, 209–212; and peasant insurgency, 78–84; theft and/or burglary, 124–130, 160–162, 177, 179, 182, 210, 234–235; underground lottery (bolita), 213–214; and urban unrest, 103–109, 112–131, 142, 151–152, 172–282; other instances, 160, 213, 264–265n. 55. *See also* Children; Prostitution; Social violence; Strikes; Women
"Porto Rico," colonialist invention of: and "common crime," 129, 175, 179–181; and Island social conditions, 147–148, 183–184, 221–224, 230–234, 281n. 60, 281–282n. 61; and labor unrest, 107–108, 118–119; and peasant insurgency, 80–87; and Spanish–Cuban–North American War, 23–28, 30–31, 248–249n. 15; and U.S. racial codes, 45–46, 61–67, 73–74, 106, 156–160, 185–186. *See also* Feminization; Infantilization
Postcolonial theories, 6–8, 12, 244n. 16, 281–282n. 61. *See also* Subaltern Studies
Pratt, Mary Louise, 30, 62, 223–224
Prohibition, 163–164. *See also* Popular illegalities
Prostitution, 178–181, 221, 285n. 29

Quintero Rivera, Angel G.: and cultural configuration of laboring classes, 254n. 50, 277n. 27; and economic determinism, 274n. 7, 277n. 26; and evolutionist perspectives, 276–277n. 24, 277n. 25, 277–278n. 28, 288n. 4; with Gervasio García, 150, 192, 276–277n. 24, 287n. 43, 287n. 45, 287n. 47; and Island economy, 137, 247n. 3, 252–253n. 45, 276n. 21; and limitations of labor market, 150, 171; and urban unrest, 192, 270n. 35, 287n. 43, 287n. 45. *See also* History; New Historiography

Racial codes, Puerto Rican: and laboring classes, 103–105, 120; origins and articulation, 43–45, 46–47, 256n. 60, 257n. 69, 258n. 73; and propertied Creoles on social unrest, 87–88, 103–105; and propertied Creoles on social degeneration, 94–97, 120, 122–123, 129–130, 175–176

Racial codes, U.S.: its broader cultural context, 249n. 22, 264n. 47, 264n. 52, 266n. 61, 292n. 46; and "common crime," 129, 179–181; and invention of "Porto Rico," 45–46, 61–67, 73–75, 156–160, 229–234; and Island social conditions, 147–148, 183–184, 221–223, 256n. 60; and labor unrest, 107–108, 118; and peasant insurgency, 80–87; and Spanish-Cuban-North American War, 23–28. *See also* Feminization; Infantilization

Racial time ("lesser races" as past West already lived out): its broader cultural context, 249n. 22, 266n. 61, 292n. 46; and Island social conditions, 183–186, 224–225; and local politics, 159, 241; and social unrest, 108, 118; and Spanish-Cuban-North American War, 66–67, 83. *See also* Infantilization; Racial codes, U.S.; Visvanathan, Shiv

Reily, Governor E. Mont, 118–119, 157–159

"Republican Mobs," 99, 103–106, 270n. 39. *See also* Electoral violence; Riots; Social violence

Riots: and urban unrest, 103–109, 118, 188, 189–190; and "Republican Mobs," 99; and Spanish-Cuban-North American War, 87. *See also* Social violence

Robinson, Alfred G., 19, 30, 31, 54, 67

Rogler, Charles C., 173–175, 178, 179–180, 215, 223, 285n. 29

Roosevelt, President Theodore: and gendered racial codes, 63–64, 229; and invention of "Porto Rico," 65, 74; and U.S. expansionism in general, 26, 75, 83, 118, 185. *See also* Infantilization

Roosevelt, Governor Theodore, Jr.: and Island social conditions, 149, 150, 183, 184, 233; and role of educated Creoles, 158–160, 237; and U.S. civilizing mission, 185–186

Root, Secretary of War Elihu, 67, 74, 148

Rosario, José C.: on crime, 179, 210–212, 224–225, 237; with Justina Carrión, 165, 173, 187–188, 190–192; on dependent children, 165, 176–178, 182–183

Said, Edward: on colonialist invention of subject populations, 24, 63, 74, 156, 166, 241; on corrective study by the West, 3, 16, 129, 239; on European colonial administration, 64, 65, 82–83, 186; and postcolonial theories, 7. *See also* Oriental; Orientalism

Samalea Iglesias, Luis, 125–127, 129, 215
Service sector: employment, 31–32, 145, 201, 203; and rest of society, 168, 172, 187, 226
Shanty towns, 41, 99, 142, 183–186, 219–222, 225–226. *See also* Urban/coastal laborers
Silvestrini, Blanca: on labor conflicts, 119, 286n. 41, 287n. 43, 287n. 45; on peasant insurgency, 268n. 15, 268n. 20; on rampant poverty, 55, 58, 260n. 15; on theft, 94; on urban unrest in general, 270n. 35, 270n. 43; on violence against children, 125
Slavery and slaves, 39, 41, 44–46, 96, 97
Smith–Rosenberg, Carroll, 10, 20
Social support practices (among laboring classes): cultural configuration of, 38–39, 42–43, 254n. 50; and popular illegalities, 163–164, 180–181, 208–209, 217–218
Social violence: defined, 15, 246–247n. 33; and children, 123–124, 130–131, 177, 182, 285n. 27; in general, 68, 70, 94, 138, 167, 170, 215–218; and interpersonal conflicts, 103, 172–178, 208–212; and labor unrest, 107–109, 112–119, 142, 150–154, 188–193, 207–208; and peasant insurgency, 78–84; and "Republican Mobs," 99, 103–104; and Spanish-Cuban-North American War, 87–88; conceptual conclusions, 235–239
Soto, Juan B., 120–123, 125, 127, 129, 210, 215
Spanish-Cuban-North American War, 21–28, 63, 74–75, 167, 247n. 2
Spain and Spanish colonization: and cultural formation, 46–47; and Island social conditions, 54, 58, 78, 79, 80, 232, 237; and Spanish–Cuban–North American War, 21–23, 26–27, 63, 78–83, 88–90
Spitzer, Steven: on forms of labor exploitation, 51–53; on problem populations, 15, 286n. 37; on punishment and economic organization, 12, 235, 245n. 26, 274n. 6
Spivak, Gayatri Chakravorty: on conceptions of history, 12, 14–15, 147, 172; and postcolonial theories, 5–6, 7, 243n. 4; on reading counterinsurgency texts, 79, 97
Strikes: from 1898 to 1909, 107–109, 112; from 1910 to 1921, 112, 113–119, 142, 216; from 1922 to 1929, 138, 150–152; during 1930s, 189–193, 287n. 43, 287n. 45; during 1940s, 207–208
Strong, Reverend Josiah, 25, 30, 66, 74, 87, 185, 223
Subaltern Studies: Guha, Ranajit, 7, 14, 90, 108, 119, 179–180; Spivak, Gayatri Chakravorty, 5–7, 12, 14, 79, 97, 147, 172, 243n. 4. *See also* Postcolonial theories
Sugar agriculture: and Island economy, 28, 40, 44, 197–199, 205; jobs and wages, 60, 144, 169–171, 202; and the labor process, 33, 41, 42, 154, 201, 202–203; and local politics, 96, 103; and social unrest, 107, 108, 113–119, 151, 189–191, 207; and world market, 21, 137–138, 167–168. *See also* Urban/coastal laborers; Peasantry; Strikes
Sugar refining: and Island economy, 136–138; and labor force, 144–145, 168–169; and strike activity, 189–191, 204, 207
Sugar and U.S. corporations: and geopolitical context, 27–28; and

Sugar and U.S. corporations (*continued*)
Island economy, 29, 142, 168–169, 197–200, 289n. 13; and labor force, 139, 190, 204–205, 207
Suicide, 112, 120, 152, 172, 208

Tobacco agriculture: and Island economy, 28–29, 44, 136–137, 139, 198; and labor force, 40, 189
Tobacco manufacture: and Island economy, 21, 29, 136, 137, 167–168; and labor force, 144, 145, 154, 170, 198, 201–202; and social unrest, 107, 112–113, 117–118, 151–152, 192; and U.S. corporations, 29, 42, 136, 137, 142–143, 151
Trade-union activity, 105–109, 116–119, 150–152, 169, 189–193, 206–208. *See also* Strikes
Trinh T. Minh-ha, 7, 8, 19, 160

Unemployment: and class formation, 42, 206–207; and Island poverty, 60, 147, 169–170, 181, 204; official record of, 61, 150, 171; and social unrest, 167, 189, 192
Underemployment: and class formation, 42, 145, 150, 202–203, 206; and Island poverty, 169–170, 177, 182; and popular illegalities, 71
Urban/coastal laborers: and class composition, 41–42, 144–145, 275–276n. 20; cultural configuration of, 41–42, 43–46, 258n. 77; general social conditions, 61, 150, 186–188, 199, 200–203; and hunger, 55, 59; and popular illegalities in general, 68–71, 123–124, 152, 161, 182–184, 217–220, 225–226; and racial identification, 41–42, 43–46, 104–105, 120, 122–123, 152–154, 256n. 59; and "Republican Mobs," 99, 103–104; and strike activity, 107–109, 112–113, 117, 188–192, 207; and other forms of social unrest, 86–87, 88, 94, 106. *See also* Peasantry
U.S. Congress: and Island conditions, 113–114, 168, 170, 208; and colonial administration, 89, 155–156, 279–280n. 45, 280n. 51; and colonial discourses, 26, 64–65, 73–74, 166
Usury, 31, 60, 71, 169, 232, 283n. 7

Visvanathan, Shiv, 7, 27, 66, 77, 82–83, 159, 225. *See also* History; Infantilization; Racial codes, U.S.; Racial time

War with Spain. *See* Spanish-Cuban-North American War
Winthrop, Governor Beekman, 107–109
Wolf, Eric: and colonial discourses, 223–224, 292n. 41; and local government institutions, 172, 209; and rural cultural configuration, 42–43, 47, 209, 212–214, 254n. 50; and social conditions, 71, 213–214, 255n. 53
Women and extra-domestic labor, 143, 144, 198, 212. *See also* Needle–products; Prostitution
Women, violence towards: from 1898 to 1909, 81; from 1910 to 1921, 119–123, 129–130; from 1922 to 1929, 152, 279n. 44; during 1930s, 174, 177; during 1940s, 209, 210–211. *See also* Gender; Social violence

Yager, Governor Arthur, 113, 116